IN SEARCH OF
THE HOLY GRAIL

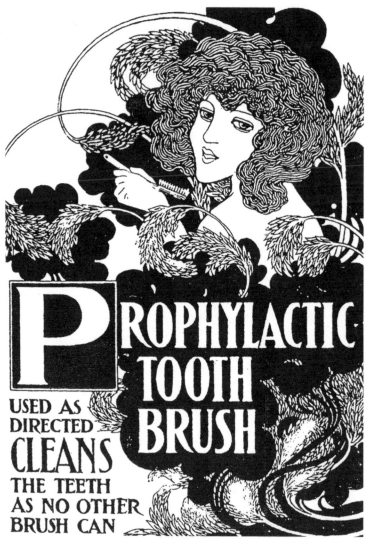

The Prophylactic Tooth Brush, poster by Will H. Bradley, late 1890s, influenced by D. G. Rossetti's *The Blessed Damozel*. Pre-Raphaelite medievalism for popular consumption.

In Search of the Holy Grail

The Quest for the Middle Ages

Veronica Ortenberg

hambledon
continuum

Hambledon Continuum
A Continuum imprint

The Tower Building
11 York Road
London, SE1 7NX
UK

80 Maiden Lane
Suite 704
New York, NY 10038
USA

First published 2006 in hardback
This edition published 2007 in paperback

ISBN 1 85285 383 2 (hardback)
ISBN 1 85285 532 0 (paperback)

A description of this book is available from the
British Library and from the Library of Congress.

Typeset by Carnegie Publishing, Lancaster,
and printed in the United Kingdom by MPG Books Ltd, Cornwall.

Contents

Illustrations

Illustration Acknowledgements

The author and publishers are grateful to the following for permission to reproduce illustrations: Château de Versailles et de Trianon, pl. 1; English Heritage, pl. 7; Madame Tussaud's, pl. 6; Past Times, pl. 8.

Introduction

To search for the Holy Grail is to search for an impossible dream. It is also to reuse a medieval myth. This book is concerned with the dream of rewriting, reinterpreting, reconstructing, reshaping, indeed finding again, the golden age of the medieval period – as people seem to have done constantly since the sixteenth century. It illustrates, sometimes discursively but in a forthright way, my own understanding of this subject, which is emphatically **not** the legacy of the Middle Ages itself, but the way in which the medieval world has been known, perceived, understood, used and indeed misused by its successors.

The idea of the 'Middle Ages' was itself born in the later seventeenth century, well into what are thought of as 'Modern' times. It has ever since been the fate of the 'Medieval' to be whatever the 'Modern' is not – for better or for worse. When medieval is not used as an insult, as it is when people talk about medieval 'superstition', 'oppression', 'intolerance' or 'torture chamber', it has historically been either the resort of those determined to repudiate the present or an attempt to reinforce current values by way of contrast. The Middle Ages could be defined as a time of social and natural harmony and of spiritual insight by contrast with a ruthlessly competitive, materialistic modern era; or as an age of religious persecution and barbarity by those for whom tolerance, reason and progress began after the eighteenth-century Enlightenment and Industrial Revolution.

Western culture, writes Umberto Eco,[1] one of the foremost commentators on the subject of the perception of the Middle Ages today, has relatively little to do with the Greek and Roman worlds, from which it acquired, at a higher intellectual level, some of its ideals about philosophy, including ethics, politics and aesthetics, and some legal principles. Our contemporary world, both on an ideological and a practical level, goes back essentially to the Middle Ages and to the Judaeo-Christian view of life which dominated them. If one were to parody the famous question from the Monty Python film *The Life of Brian*, 'What did the Romans ever do for us?', and adapt it to the Middle Ages, the list of answers would be exceptionally long. It would include, for example, the framework of national states and the urban and rural topography of Europe (churches, castles, public buildings, as well as the villages and parishes, the farms and field systems).

Our way of counting time since the year of the Incarnation and of divid-
ing the weekdays and Sundays, major feasts and holidays and our
administrative divisions at regional and county level are medieval in origin. So are many European institutions (monarchy, parliaments, courts and
legal systems, aristocracy, town councils, banks, insurance, universities with
their exams, degrees and colleges) and the surviving, often still considerable, landed property belonging to some of these institutions. Our still
predominant intellectual framework of scholasticism, transformed in the
nineteenth century and beyond into dialectics, harks back to medieval universities. Medieval art and architecture is seen everywhere in Europe. And
an exceptionally influential literature and mythology, as well as rites of
passage, customs and traditions of medieval origins, have become part
of our western unconscious.

Whatever overall view of the period they take, nobody, at the beginning
of the twenty-first century, can deny the overwhelming impact on our
lives of our medieval inheritance – nobody really does. Many people look
back with fascination at the medieval period, either studying it or just enjoying looking at its traces and myths. Yet in traditional orthodoxy the
so-called 'Renaissance' of the sixteenth century in effect got rid of the 'back-
ward' medieval past and, until the nineteenth-century Romantic revival of
interest in the Middle Ages, the period was then completely ignored. The
term 'Renaissance' is in itself significant. It came into use late in the eighteenth century, denoting the 'rebirth of culture', by which was meant
'classical' culture, after the 'barbaric' interlude of uncultured centuries,
sitting in the 'middle' between the glorious classical epoch of the Greco-
Roman world and the 'Renaissance'. Many, even among the relatively
cultured elite today, have grown up with this image, while at the same time
happily assuming that anything 'dark' and esoteric can only belong to the
Middle Ages, not the 'Renaissance'.[2] The aim of this book is to show
the vitality and continuing influence of the medieval period: from the late
fifteenth century onwards, the traditionally-reckoned 'end' of the Middle
Ages, only a very few actually regarded the period as the Dark Age of a
barbaric past.

Historians have long understood that there can never be such a thing as
a perfect image of what the past was like, even with the most rigorous study
of written sources and archaeological documentation. In the context of
medievalism the issue of accuracy is irrelevant. In this book, nothing,
whether book, image, film, reproduction or re-enactment, is criticised on
the basis of 'historical inaccuracy', because inaccuracy is taken for granted.
It is not this distortion which is my study, it is how and by whom the
Middle Ages were understood and used. The use of the medieval in political,

cultural, aesthetic and other ways has come from different ways of seeing the past. It is these ways, and what lay behind them, that are of interest to me.

Many contemporary perceptions, although some may like to think them new, are not. Why were people interested in the Middle Ages in the past (that is from the sixteenth to the early twentieth centuries)? Are they interested in the Middle Ages today for the same reasons? One needs to return to the sixteenth century and do a brief survey of the nature of this interest in the four centuries before ours to identify both similarities and differences.[3] From the start, escapism has been one of the major elements of the fascination with the medieval, with the desire to escape away from the harsh realities of the present and be allowed to take refuge into a world where reason gives way to emotion, reality to imagination. For a long time the English have set this trend. Several reasons have been traditionally invoked for this.

While I was writing this book, I went round asking anyone who did not manage to get away fast enough what they saw as the reasons for the current taste for the Middle Ages – and here are some of the responses. Nostalgia for country roots in a country of early industrialisation and urbanisation has already been mentioned. The Reformation signified a cut-off point, when the colourful and socially-binding traditions of the past preserved in the social and religious life of Catholic countries, like saints' festivals or pilgrimages, disappeared. Thus a void and a break-up of the continuity found in some other European countries was created. While the Church of England has succeeded in continuing or replacing some of these, with Harvest Festivals, Maypoles and the like, the more radical Protestant movements, interested in introspection and reason, did not offer such alternatives in terms of either spectacle or fantasy world. This thirst for a fantasy world as remote as possible from the pragmatic everyday one may thus have become even more powerful, and allowed for a suspension of disbelief that Mediterranean people, more cynical in many ways, find more difficult. It has even been suggested to me that the frequently grey English weather itself leads to a more introspective, brooding, temperament, which translates into a taste for the Romantic and the supernatural. There is also a very specific English association of nostalgia with an end-of-era feeling, leading people to take refuge in a more brilliant past.

Interesting as many of these arguments are, some at least if not all could conceivably be applied to history in a more general way, and not necessarily to the Middle Ages. Whole books could, and have, been written about the contemporary interest in history in general, and in Heritage in particular, about the sociological implications and the possible reasons for this renewed popularity in the late twentieth century. This is not my direct concern here. What is, however, is why, of all the available periods of history on offer 'on the shelf', the Middle Ages have been so specially favoured. What is it that makes them so attractive in the popular imagination? The purpose of this book is to provide some answers to these questions.

Acknowledgements

When, as a medievalist, I began investigating the post-medieval impact and image of the Middle Ages, I rapidly discovered that medievalism had become an acknowledged academic subject with a well-charted history of its own in the last thirty years, especially in the United States. Even when one leaves out studies on, for example, the Gothic Revival, the Gothic novel, Victorian art or the Oxford Movement, there is by now a well-established group of scholars working on medievalism. Research is today vigorously pursued especially through the major journal *Studies in Medievalism*, of which I have made considerable use. The founders of this approach about the impact of the medieval were Leslie Workman, an English scholar working in America, and his wife Kathleen Verduin. Two important early contributors in the English-speaking world were the literary critic Alice Chandler[1] and art historian Mark Girouard.[2] Others have emerged in the last twenty years, including literary scholars such as Heather Arden, Stephanie Barczewski, Jane Chance, Elizabeth Emerson, Frank Gentry, Michael Glencross, Norris Lacy, A. C. Lupack, Debra Mancoff, Tom Shippey, Clare Simmons, John Simons, Roger Simpson, Paul Szarmach and Andrew Wawn. Other scholars include specialists of art and architecture, such as Megan Aldrich, Christopher Brooks and Laura Morowitz, of historiography and antiquarianism, such as William Calin, Valerie Brand, Barbara Keller, Rosamund Sweet and D. R. Woolf, and the increasingly numerous specialists of film, notably Kevin Harty and Jeffrey Richards. While several of these scholars began life as medievalists themselves, the discipline appears to have now developed to the point where it is possible to specialise in medievalism from quite early on. One good example of this is Tom Shippey who, after himself first working on Old English and Middle English literature, moved on to write about Tolkien, and has since moved on again to the study of medievalism, being now the driving force behind *Studies in Medievalism.*

Although at its most elaborate and vital in England and the American academic Establishment, the interest in the subject has also increased in Continental Europe, especially in Germany, France and Italy, with works on literature, art and architecture, historiography, and film. In Italy[3] the foremost contribution has been Umberto Eco, who was the first to discuss in the 1980s the impact of medievalism on contemporary society, and the uses and abuses of the Middle Ages today in Europe and America. He brought the subject within the orbit of the average reading public interested in the workings of contemporary culture, in his two essays published in English in 1986 in *Travels in Hyperreality*, 'Dreaming the Middle Ages' and 'Living in the New Middle Ages'.

To all these scholars, and numerous others whose works I have used, my debt is enormous. The aim of this book is to bring together a synthesis of current research and thinking in these fields, from both the English-speaking world and that of scholars working in other countries and languages. To make this available to students and general readers has been the aim of the first chapters. When dealing with more contemporary issues on the other hand, I have pursued my own research on the basis of books on anything from politics, sociology, cultural studies, media studies and others, and of general observation, newspapers, magazines, popular literature, television, film, debates, conversations and just about everything which I felt was relevant and significant. The second part of the book therefore is clearly expressive of my own interpretation and views as a medievalist studying the perception of the Middle Ages among my contemporaries, and as a participating member of contemporary society reflecting on its roots and directions.

This book began life as part of my university teaching at the University of Wales, Lampeter, within the framework of an interdisciplinary degree in Medieval Studies. The purpose of that teaching was to try and make students interested in the Middle Ages willing and able to think about the current use of the medieval period in the world around them. It therefore owes a debt of gratitude to these students, who contributed ideas and views on various subjects, including those who, at first, rather resented having to 'waste' time on this rather than on studying things medieval. Most eventually relented, and agreed to 'play the game', to my great advantage. They were prepared not only to reflect on the subject they were studying, but to bring to it a variety of sometimes critical but always constructive views. Some have been directly acknowledged here. To them, and to my colleagues there, this book is dedicated.

My more direct thanks go to those colleagues who have read specific chapters, Dr Clare Brant, Professor Malcolm Higgs, Professor Jeffrey Richards, Professor Malcolm Smith, and the late Patrick Wormald. I am especially grateful to Professor Tom Shippey, who read the whole book, and provided valuable comments throughout. I am also grateful to friends and acquaintances who have patiently answered my questions and fed me occasional information on an informal basis. They are too numerous to mention individually, but I should like to single out Dr Janet Burton, Dr C. W. Marx and Dr Elisabeth Lorans. My father, with his wide-ranging knowledge and keen editorial eye, has been of great help both through informal discussions and through his reading of the first draft; so have some imaginary conversations with my mother. The technical assistance for the bibliography, as well as the support given in a more general way by J. D. West-Harling, have been invaluable. My thanks for their help and forbearance goes to the staff of the various libraries where I have worked, including the Bodleian, Sackler and Taylorian libraries in Oxford, the British Library in London, and others both in the UK and abroad. My thanks go also to Hambledon and London, and Tony Morris who commissioned the book for them. Above all, it is a duty but, first and foremost, a very great pleasure to acknowledge how much the constant support, the patient and repeated editing, and the fruitful discussions I have had over the last couple of years with my editor Martin Sheppard, have contributed to shaping the book, allowing me to experience the writing of it as a great joy.

Survival and Revival

Was Shakespeare the first medievalist? Contrary to many people's impression, most of Shakespeare's plays are not set in the ancient world but in the Middle Ages. Even if one leaves aside the eight history plays covering the reigns between King John and Henry VII, there are at least eleven plays set specifically in the Middle Ages. These are, in no particular order, the tragedies *Hamlet*, *King Lear*, *Macbeth*, *Othello*, *Romeo and Juliet*, the comedies *As You Like It*, *The Merry Wives of Windsor*, *The Taming of the Shrew*, and also *Cymbeline*, *The Two Gentlemen of Verona* and *The Merchant of Venice*. Several other plays, either without a specific time setting (*All's Well that Ends Well*, *Measure for Measure*, *The Tempest*, *The Winter's Tale*) or set in the classical world (*Antony and Cleopatra*, *Coriolanus*, *Julius Caesar*, *Lucrece*, *Midsummer Night's Dream* and *Timon of Athens*) have been nevertheless shown to contain various elements inspired from medieval traditions. In the last fifty years, literary and theatre criticism have extensively shown the influence of a variety of medieval sources of inspiration on Shakespeare's plays.[1] Some of these influences are direct ones, obviously in the form of chronicles for the history plays but also for *Hamlet* (the thirteenth-century Danish chronicler Saxo Grammaticus), *Macbeth*, or in the form of romances like King Leir, the Otuel stories for Othello, *Rosalynde* for *As You Like It*, and the occasional individual characters such as Oberon, modelled on Huon of Bordeaux.[2]

Beyond such clear and direct sources, it has become clear how great the impact of several medieval genres had been. The first such genre was the tradition of moralities, miracle plays and homilies, with their pastoral and didactic aim.[3] Moralities and miracle plays, notably the Coventry cycle, were still performed in Shakespeare's day, as were popular mummers' plays. In 1597 the Admiral's Men were still putting on the story of Uther Pendragon. The second genre to provide inspiration to Shakespeare was popular theatre and poetry regularly performed by actors or amateurs as local entertainment, for example the St George, Robin Hood, mummers' plays, and ballads.[4] Romances, the Arthurian cycle with the *Brut*, pastoral and troubadour poetry belonged to a more aristocratic tradition, which had moved down the social scale to the middle class and yeomanry with great success.[5] Lastly, specific medieval authors and texts, of which the best known are

Lydgate, Gower, Chaucer, Dante, Boccaccio, the *Romance of the Rose* and the *Parliament of Fools*, added the inspiration of complex written material, both English and foreign, to the mix.[6]

From the moralities and miracle plays such as *Pride of Life, The Castle of Perseverance, Wisdom, Mankind, Everyman* and *Thomas à Becket* came both content and form. These plays were essentially didactic, moralistic, even propagandistic, blending tragedy and comedy for entertainment, but thematically focusing on the issues of forgiveness of sin, redemption and reconciliation. They incorporated several specific devices. Among these were the use of allegories and other background figures illustrating Vices and Virtues; a subplot centred around a fool or clown; traditional characters such as the braggart soldier, the comic yokel, the witty servant and the shrewish wife; and staple debates between body and soul, youth and age, fortune and nature, love and riches, pride and humility. Other traditional themes often used in the moralities and miracle plays were those of life as a pilgrimage, old age as a decaying fruit, the mutability of life in the decay of beauty and the transience of worldly things, and virtue surviving after death.

The plays also addressed the issues of citizenship, political responsibility and the nature of government, as well as conscience and the nature of man. Such issues could be made clear through the use of the theme of the Wheel of Fortune, which exemplifies the rise and fall in the fate of kings and powerful rulers, their downfall in particular bringing with it personal and social misery. Both *All's Well That Ends Well* and *Troilus and Cressida* have been regarded as perfect examples of moralities; but most other Shakespeare plays incorporate some of these themes and elements in some form or another. The theme of redemption to expiate guilt and find peace is paramount in *King Lear,* including the sacrifice of the innocent (Cordelia) on the way; it is associated with repentance, demanded by Hamlet of Gertrude for example. The issue of individual conscience is essential for both Macbeth and his Queen, and for Hamlet, while Macbeth, like Richard III and Iago, are partly embodiments of the figure of Vice in both popular theatre and the moralities. The imagery of life as a pilgrimage is found repeatedly in *Coriolanus, Measure for Measure* and *Henry V,* while the traditional description of the ages of man appears, for example, in *As You Like It.* Also part of the medieval allegorical repertoire is the analogy (though originally found in Livy as well as in St Paul) between the body politic and the physical body, so aptly illustrated in *Coriolanus.* The fool figure, found in so many history plays, as well as, for example, in *Hamlet* and *King Lear,* is another device inherited by the moralities from popular theatre, while the chorus talking to the audience was also an indispensable feature of the morality plays, indeed the key to their understanding by the audience. In addition conventions such as the vow, the bribe, the love token, substitution and disguise, as well as dramatic units and patterns, and staging devices and artifices, and even aspects of the Christian liturgy which were an intrinsic part of such dramas, were adopted by Shakespeare in many of his plays, regardless of their topic and setting, *Timon* and *Julius Caesar* as much as *Lear, Hamlet, Macbeth, The Merry Wives* or *Henry V* and *Richard III*. It has been claimed that Shakespeare adapted the morality play for a secular purpose instead of a religious one, with the secular salvation of England through health and wealth being the ultimate aim at stake.

A similar wealth of devices came from the folk plays and ballads. National feeling was strong in the traditional St George and Robin Hood plays, and *Henry V* is an example of its use. *The Merry Wives of Windsor* and *A Midsummer Night's Dream* reflect the triumph of life over death associated with the revival of the year. The latter, but also *Macbeth*, include supernatural elements, the devil, Hell, magicians, witches, spells and other traits of popular plays. Similar sources also saw the use of specific devices like riddles, games, proverbs and characters such as the Lord of Misrule (Lear) and devil-like figures like Caliban. More particularly, it has been pointed out that Shakespeare deliberately chose to follow an English national tradition rather than the classical one in his choice of not excluding comedy from tragedy but combining them together. Thus, for example, it has been claimed that the lack of unity and the multiplicity of the places of action in *Cymbeline* is precisely a reflection of this traditional English theatre, rather than being, as used to be said, due to the weakness of the play itself.

Another set of themes (as well as the whole plot in some cases) were borrowed from the genre of romances and courtly love tradition. Chivalry (Hotspur, Hal), knight service, fealty and homage are present in most history plays but also in *Troilus and Cressida* and *Timon of Athens*. Courtly love and its stages of courtship and devices such as families divided and reunited, tribulations and wanderings of the lovers, faith and patience in their ordeal are part of both the tragic scene of *Romeo and Juliet* and of *The Winter's Tale, Twelfth Night* and *The Tempest*. Specific formal conventions such as the lyrical forms of the pastorelle or the death lament occur, as does the cliché of the curative power of music, put to such effective use in *Twelfth Night*. The garden settings for love scenes and the Rose of Love were also popular medieval devices, used in romances like the *Romance of the Rose*, as well as by Dante and Boccaccio; we find them repeatedly throughout the plays, for example in *Romeo and Juliet* and *Cymbeline*. Last but by no means least, praising of the simple, rural life in order to criticise the decadence of court life, as in the *Winter's Tale*, was a standard component of medieval pastoral poetry.

Many of the above, whether allegories with a moral and religious meaning such as the Wheel of Fortune or the Rose of Love, also belong to the literary tradition of the Middle Ages in Chaucer, Lydgate, Gower, the *Romance of the Rose* and Dante, all known to Shakespeare. The kingly plays, *Timon* or *King Lear*, are only some of the ten which include the Wheel of Fortune theme, also known as the Fall of Princes, used by Dante, Lydgate or the authors of the *Romance of the Rose*. Dante's use of Christian allegorical examples, like that of Ugolino, was adapted in *Macbeth*, while the dangers of excessive love, a point made several times by Lydgate and Gower, is reprised in *Anthony and Cleopatra* and, of course, *Lear*. Chaucer's work, romances and stories were naturally borrowed and adapted in terms of plots and ideas, in *Troilus* and *The Two Gentlemen of Verona*. The second was based on the Knight's Tale, and the former on the Troy story from Caxton.

Finally, various Shakespearean themes belonged to the general intellectual background of the period. These were shared conventions and ways of understanding and explaining the world and man's perception of it. One such major tradition was that of matching the four elements: fire, water, earth and air, with the four chief fluids of the body: blood, phlegm, choler and melancholy. Each of these defined a corresponding 'humour' of the body, and explained each person's dominant character traits. The convention was based on the principles of ancient medicine, which had continued to dominate medieval thinking. An interest in astrology, going back to the first world civilisations, was also a component part of medieval thinking. It became even more obsessive during the fifteenth and sixteenth centuries in the West, which was, after all, the age of famous practitioners of the art: Louis XI, John Dee and Nostradamus, though that period saw some equally famous detractors of astrology, including Pico della Mirandola.[7] A few other themes came more directly from the medieval tradition, for example the importance of the blood feud and revenge for lost honour, associated with the old Germanic traditions long before the 'feudal' world. The use of fools and folly as a means of showing up supposedly sane people, and even more as a device allowing free speech and criticism of kings and powerful men, was another frequent medieval topos. Such also was the theme of the Dance of Death, whose metaphysical meaning, especially common after the fourteenth century and its traumatic succession of plagues and wars, was to underline the equality of all before death and the frivolity of trying to outwit an opponent who always had the last laugh. The metaphor of the world as a stage, reflecting the cosmos and society in the way a play does, became a cliché of sixteenth-century thinking. Most of Shakespeare's plays include references to some of these themes. The background iconography and visual world of the Middle Ages as represented through pageantry, processions, civic, court and religious ceremonies, and symbols like the throne room, funeral, death-bed scene, banquets, trials, music, battles and weapons was equally important for Shakespeare. Such an inventory of Shakespeare's medieval heritage may seem superfluous: he was of course largely a product of his time and education. Shakespeare's genius nevertheless resided in part in being able to borrow all this from his predecessors, who had used it in more conventional ways, and turn it into something exceptional. There is, however, no doubt that he had inherited, technically and intellectually, much from medieval forms and traditions.

Shakespeare's use and interpretation of the Middle Ages may be seen within a broader context too. Why are so many of his plays set in the Middle Ages, rather than at any other periods in the past? The answer may seem obvious and hardly worthy of comment, since the 'Middle Ages' were, to all intents and purposes, the age preceding Shakespeare's own, and therefore clearly where he was most likely to get his stories from. But this explanation is not quite sufficient. Shakespeare, educated in a good grammar school where he was fed on Ovid and the classics, was in the habit of using Roman writers, philosophers and playwrights, such as Livy and Seneca, for his inspiration. When he did not do so, one must assume he made a deliberate choice of taking his stories from recent chronicles for his kings plays, or from less commonly known medieval chroniclers. The use of political material relating to fourteenth- and fifteenth-century events and recounting the histories of recent kings of England is self-explanatory, since Shakespeare was, by choice or prudence, a strong exponent of Tudor propaganda, especially in his vilification of the defeated York side and the glorification of the Lancastrian kings, the ancestors of the Tudors.[8] But what about the other plays, *King Lear, Macbeth, Hamlet, Romeo and Juliet*? Perhaps Shakespeare used the Middle Ages as a framework for themes, ideas and feelings, such as ambition, remorse, fear of old age, revenge, death and love, which had to be more general and abstract, which could be placed outside a time frame because they were felt to belong to 'human nature'. It is almost as though Shakespeare perceived these 'Dark Ages' to be more appropriate for 'human themes', while his classically set plays are more apt to run as narratives around the core of political debate about power and the exercising of it, as witnessed by *Julius Caesar, Coriolanus* and *Timon of Athens*.

While this is only a very broad view, to which exceptions can be found as soon as examples are given, the general point stands, exemplifying very early on a certain way of using the medieval period, as a peg for general ideas. These can be set in it because it is both still familiar in very general terms, while nevertheless suitably distant and obscure for things to be taken out of context and interpreted as best suits the writer. This way of dealing with the

Middle Ages was used by almost every historian, political thinker, philosopher, art historian and dramatist, from the moment the medieval period came to be identified as such, and has not ceased today.

Most people today still regard the 'Renaissance' (meaning the sixteenth-century 'Renaissance', especially in Italy) as the age of rediscovery of, and thus return to, the 'classical world' (meaning Greek and Roman), which was finally 'reborn' after the cultural decadence of the Middle Ages. We are told that the Middle Ages were regarded as the 'twilight between two civilisations',[9] both by humanists like Erasmus, and by nineteenth- and early twentieth-century critics of the Renaissance specialising in Italian art, such as Jacob Burckhardt and Bernard Berenson, for whom they epitomised an age of unreason and blind faith based on ignorance, under the yoke of a powerful and oppressive church.[10] The very invention of the word 'middle' to define the period between the civilisation of the Ancients and the rebirth of that civilisation during the sixteenth century expressed the contempt felt by those who regarded that period as no more than an aberration between the proper, real past of the classical ages, and the revival of the glories of these Greek and Roman times during the sixteenth century. The creator of the term 'Middle Ages' and the first to define that period was the German scholar Johannes Keller (better known as Cellarius) writing in the 1650s.[11]

As a result of this attitude, the medieval period, it is argued, fell into a well of neglect and lack of interest. Doubtless some Renaissance scholars and artists were supporters of a *tabula rasa*, as witness the destruction by popes and architects of the stupendous fourth-century basilica of Old St Peter's in Rome in the late sixteenth century, to make room for Bernini's church. Even then, however, the destruction of Old St Peter's to satisfy the popes and the Counter Reformation's programme did not go unrecorded. Marten van Heemskerck, when in Rome, made a set of drawings of what he could see, even as the demolition went on, with the avowed purpose of keeping a record of the early Christian and medieval church.[12] Nevertheless, for well over a century now, it has become increasingly clear that such unilateral views of the sixteenth-century Renaissance, though well expressed by skilful writers like Voltaire and other Enlightenment figures, may have belonged to some parts of the European elite, but were rarely held in other circles. In actual fact, even that elite was very far from being free of 'medievalism', consciously or not, willingly or not.

Two things are clear. First, the Middle Ages did not *stop* in the sixteenth century but continued to live on in various forms, whether that of popular romances and theatre, of architecture, and generally of unconscious influences on writers and artists brought up on medieval forms. Shakespeare is only one example of the surviving influence of medieval liturgy and popular theatre. Botticelli is another, through his use of the imagery of courtly love in his paintings. This was medieval *survival*. Secondly, the sixteenth and even more so the seventeenth and eighteenth centuries saw continuous manifestations of interest in the medieval period. English seventeenth-century Gothic architecture, the appeal made to the medieval past for the purposes of arguing 'modern' constitutional issues and political ideas about the origins of the nation, philology and ethnic kinship of the Germanic peoples, and religious polemics, were part of the way in which the seventeenth and eighteenth centuries used medieval history to discuss, argue, defend and resolve contemporary issues of major importance. England and France during the Elizabethan period, the Commonwealth, the Glorious Revolution and the French Revolution were the more immediately obvious settings for such an approach. This was medieval *revival*. At the same time as these themes were running through the intellectual elite's perceptions, an attraction for the strangeness and mystery of the medieval period remained a strand throughout European culture from the sixteenth century onwards, especially in England and Germany.

In a conscious way, literature, poets and composers were constantly reviving the Middle Ages. Ariosto's and Tasso's great epic poems, *Orlando Furioso* and *Gerusalemme Liberata* are sixteenth-century rewritings of medieval romance themes, on the background of the crusades and the *Chanson de Roland*, while imitations of medieval romances of chivalry, the most famous being *Amadis des Gaules*, vied in their success with the dozens of late medieval chivalric romances such as *Huon of Bordeaux* and *Guy of Warwick*, the Alexander and Charlemagne romances and the *Romance of the Rose*. These romances, equivalent to our novels of love and adventures, were printed repeatedly and translated throughout Europe.[13] Cervantes's *Don Quixote* ridicules the courtly and chivalric ethos of the Don, who is fighting imaginary enemies perceived as threatening his values, and opposes to this the pragmatic 'modern' realism of the hard-headed Sancho, who belongs to a socially rising class. Nevertheless, the idealistic old-fashioned knight is seen as an object of nostalgia for a lost world, not unlike Malory's knights. In addition, even while subverting the genre of medieval romance, the narrative style and types of *Quixote* are themselves very much part and parcel of it. Botticelli illustrated Dante's *Divine Comedy*, and Dürer used medieval 'dress' for his allegorical paintings and woodcuts. Spenser's *Faerie Queene* is a good example of the way in which medieval themes were constantly thought about and rephrased at the height of the so-called 'classical age', through the reuse of moral allegories of the quest, courtesy and chivalric symbolism.[14] Sir Philip Sidney's medievalist taste, based on reworked medieval romances and pastoral mode, is evidently at work in the *Arcadia* and in poems like 'Asphodil and Stella'.[15] Significantly, it went beyond his work and was implemented in his own life and career, which reflected his perception of himself as a knight, fighting the enemies of his religion as defender of his faith, in this instance as a Protestant hero, and dying a chivalric death in the process.

Corneille's *Le Cid* in seventeenth-century France, Grillparzer's *Ottokar* and Lessing's *Nathan the Wise* in the eighteenth-century German-speaking world respectively, are all based on medieval heroes, and set in a medieval context, eleventh-century moorish Spain, medieval Bohemia and the Crusades. Like Shakespeare, these playwrights also used the Middle Ages as a framework for contemporary ideals. Corneille wanted to illustrate the concept of honour, the French gentleman's dearest possession, on account, it is claimed, of its descent from the medieval chivalric ideal; hence, what better way to highlight its origins than by choosing a medieval background for the play? A century later, Lessing used the Crusades as the background for his characteristically Enlightenment plea for religious tolerance. Christopher Marlowe and John Ford also set plays in the Middle Ages. Less famous but equally significant were Middleton's play *Hengist, King of Kent* (c. 1615–22), Milton's plan to write his great epic poem on King Arthur (before he decided to switch to the Book of Genesis and produce *Paradise Lost*), and Dryden's intention to write a play about Arthur (later altered to become Purcell's libretto).[16] Even that greatest of 'Augustans', Alexander Pope, rewrote both Chaucer's Wife of Bath and the story of Abelard and Heloïse, the latter being uncommonly popular throughout the seventeenth and eighteenth centuries.[17] The story was so much part of European consciousness that its use in his novel *Julie: ou la Nouvelle Héloïse* needed no explanation by Rousseau, in most ways one of the most unmedievalising of writers and philosophers of the Enlightenment.

Classical composers also used the Middle Ages. Purcell set King Arthur to music. Handel in his operas *Attila* and *Rodelinda* dealt respectively with the eponymous leader of the Huns in the fifth century and the fate of a Lombard queen. As for many contemporary operas, especially the Italian style known as *opera seria* (serious as opposed to comic), the plots were largely fictitious and meant to provide an exotic canvas for the musical bravura. They traditionally used, however, Greek or Roman historical themes or mythology. The choice of the Middle Ages as an alternative background for such libretti is therefore significant. It obviously reflected a presumed familiarity with the period (even if it was a largely imaginary view). Above all, it shows that such topics were regarded as suitable for royal and aristocratic audiences, and could be expected to provide such audiences with models of noble and heroic behaviour. The sheer number of operas with medieval themes, and their popularity with audiences, may be taken as proof that they must have been to the taste of their aristocratic patrons. On a par with these, and aimed at the same audience, were the numerous operatic versions of *Armida*, based on Tasso's poem (including ones by Handel and Gluck), and equally numerous versions of *Amadis*, three of which were by Lully (1684), Handel (1715), and Johann Christian Bach (1799).

Needless to say, whether in literature, theatre, poetry or art, the examples given above are but the tip of an iceberg which includes literally hundreds of minor and now illegible, unwatchable or unlistenable to novels, plays and operas. These include, to quote entirely at random, Le Moyne's seventeenth-century epic *Saint-Louis: ou la sainte couronne reconquise*, de Belloy's *Siège de Calais* (1765) and even Voltaire's mock epic poem *Jeanne la Pucelle*,[18] as well as eighteenth-century epic poems about King Alfred in England and academic history paintings of national heroes. Theatre, with its ideal-ised medieval chivalric themes to be understood as a model for the contemporary aristocracy, continued to produce long heroic plays until the end of the eighteenth century, with a strong Anglo-Saxon bias in England in particular.[19]

Another form which appealed to the world of the aristocracy in the early sixteenth century in England remained the pseudo-medieval, or rather adapted and shortened medieval versions of such Middle English or French romances as *Guy of Warwick* or *The Seven Champions of Christendom*, and derivative material such as *The Famous Historie of Chinon of England*, with their mix of chivalric and courtly elements.[20] It has been claimed that, in addition to the appeal of the chivalric ethos, medieval romances were also associated with a desire to uphold Catholicism, and that this kind of medievalism may have been a way of preserving the traditional religion within the confines of the Tudor state.[21] Increasingly, the popularity of the romances descended the social scale. First they reached the urban wealthy middle classes of the sixteenth and seventeenth centuries, who enjoyed escapist fantasy, but also gradually came to appropriate and convert their content, which they transformed so that the virtues of the heroic English knight would be replaced by those of the English merchant and artisan.[22] After these affluent middle classes moved on to reading novels or to satis-fying antiquarian interests by reading history and collecting, the success of the romances did not die out but reached the rural communities of agri-cultural labourers, the urban poor and the children of the gentry. Such romances and ballads, providing cheap adventure stories with a moralising tone, remained the core of popular literature, often circulating in the form of popular chapbooks through chapmen or *colporteurs*, notably between

1700 and the 1840s.[23] Successful markets for these precursors of the Readers' Digest were to be found in America in the eighteenth and early
nineteenth centuries, and amongst the poorer categories among women,
servant girls and other workers, some of whom made up part of the readership of the Gothic novels, and for the same reasons. In France too this
kind of literature was published, by the *Bibliothèque bleue* then under the
imprint of the *Bibliothèque universelle des romans, Nouvelle bibliothèque universelle des romans* and the *Bibliothèque universelle des dames* in the
eighteenth century.[24]

Apart from literature and theatre, between the sixteenth and eighteenth centuries the interest in the medieval period manifested itself in two ways:
through collecting, and through reinterpreting. First to be collected as relics
of the past were medieval manuscripts. At the papal court the great collectors were humanists like Tommaso Parentucelli (the first proper collector
and librarian of the Vatican Library and later Pope Nicholas V between 1447
and 1455),[25] and Enea Silvio Piccolomini (pope under the name of Pius II
from 1455 and also a collector of medieval manuscripts),[26] followed later by
Cardinal Baronius (1538–1607), one of the first editors of medieval church
material in his *Annales Ecclesiastici* (1588).[27] Baronius was also a famous
historian in his time, and a great supporter of church reform. He saw the
purpose of his work as being to celebrate the unity of the church one and
universal across the ages. He therefore deliberately wrote in the style of a
medieval chronicler rather than as a rhetorical humanist. In 1584 he published, under the aegis of the papacy, the standard calendar and martyrology
of the church, still in use after hundreds of years in the 1960s.

Other fifteenth- and sixteenth-century princely courts of Italy, like the
Florentine court of the Medici, as well as independent humanists such as
Pico della Mirandola, Angelo Poliziano, Marsilius Ficino and Flavio Biondo,
were also collectors.[28] One of the best-known Italian humanists and historians was Polydore Vergil, who spent most of his life in England as a papal
collector and then archdeacon of Wells, under the patronage of Henry VII
and Henry VIII. During his time in England between 1502 and 1555, he wrote
the first real post-medieval English history, the *Anglicae historiae* (1534–55).
Despite some English opposition to him on account of his 'debunking' the
popular version by Geoffrey of Monmouth, notably from John Leland,
Vergil's European reputation was such that he exerted great influence on his
English contemporaries.[29] Another humanist who also travelled to England
was Pico della Mirandola, whose influence led to his having a biography
written of him by Sir Thomas More.[30] Numerous aristocratic families like
the Barberini amassed large collections of medieval manuscripts during the

seventeenth century, though the best-known collector in Italy was the refugee and Catholic convert Queen Christina of Sweden.[31] Her own father, Gustavus Adolphus, king of Sweden, had collected manuscripts such as the Gothic *Codex Argenteus* to highlight the early medieval history of Sweden.

Germany too had its collectors, for example Urich von Hütten, while in France such collectors were often the same people as the first historians and philologists, the latter studying either history or the French language for the sake of identifying national origins.[32] Prominent among the first such historians in the sixteenth century were Etienne Pasquier (*Recherches de la France*, 1560), Claude Fauchet (*Antiquitez gauloises et françoises*, 1579) and Henri Estienne. Another collector was Jean de Nostredame, author of *Les vies des plus célèbres et anciens poètes provençaux* (1575), better known under the name of Nostradamus for his controversial 'prophecies'. All of them had considerable influence on the greatest of seventeenth-century medievalists, the lawyer Du Fresne Du Cange, the founder of medieval Latin studies in France, and author of the still widely used glossary of medieval Latin words, published in 1678, and editor of the two most famous French medieval chroniclers, Villehardouin and Joinville. Du Cange had had some illustrious predecessors in his interest in language, in particular in the origins of French, in Geoffroy Tory, author of *Champfleury* (1529), a defender of the national idiom on the grounds of its ancient roots. This was the line taken also by Clément Marot, Guillaume Budé and the most authoritative of humanists, Joachim Du Bellay, in his often reprinted *Deffence*, first published in 1549.

This first wave of medieval scholarly interest, closely linked to the development of a national feeling based on the glories of the national past and language, receded after the 1580s.[33] By the seventeenth century what took its place, temporarily, was an interest in the Middle Ages as a result of the insistence on the antiquity of the Catholic Church, its language, liturgy, rights and observances. Apart from Du Cange, the great historians of the seventeenth century who promoted the collecting and editing of medieval documents were the Benedictine Jean Mabillon and the monks of the Benedictine congregation of St-Maur.

England, however, was by far the earliest and most advanced country in terms of collecting and saving its past, even the most distant. The best known saviour was Matthew Parker (1504–1575).[34] The son of a manufacturer from Norwich, an undergraduate then fellow of Corpus Christi College in Cambridge, then its master, he was appointed archbishop of Canterbury in 1558. He sponsored the English translation of the Bible, was one of the signatories of the draft of the Thirty-Nine Articles, and one of the men who established Anglicanism as the state religion of the kingdom. His purpose was to show the antiquity of the Church of England and to demonstrate that, before papal power took over during the later Middle Ages, there had been an older and purer practice of Christianity in England.[35] In this, he was supported by another antiquary and book collector, John Bale (1495–1563), originally a Carmelite monk then a fervent Protestant convert, who became a bishop in Ireland and ended his life as a canon at Canterbury under Parker. Bale was a friend of the great antiquary John Leland (1503–1552), who himself had been authorised by Henry VIII to search the libraries of monastic houses and colleges for medieval manuscripts in 1533. Bale also accumulated a huge library, which he took with him to Ireland, but it was subsequently lost during his later peregrinations.

Parker was granted licence by the Queen in 1558 to seek 'auncient recordes or monumentes' from the libraries of monasteries suppressed by Henry VIII. He thus created the earliest remaining major antiquarian collection in England, rescuing dozens of manuscripts from the libraries of Christ Church and St Augustine's abbey in Canterbury, and from Durham. Since a point needed to be made about the existence of a historical precedent for the translation of the text of the Bible and the celebration of services in the vernacular, Parker's collection included every kind of Anglo-Saxon text: King Alfred's translation of the Bible, homilies in Old English, lives of English saints, Old English verse, music from the Anglo-Saxon cathedrals of Winchester and Worcester, the earliest copy of the Anglo-Saxon Chronicle (now known as the Parker Chronicle), and manuscripts of great symbolic significance such as the St Augustine Gospels. Parker also collected Anglo-Saxon manuscripts of major early medieval authors, such as Sedulius Scotus and Prudentius's *Psychomachia*, written between the eighth and the eleventh centuries in England and Wales, and later medieval texts too, for example Matthew Paris's *Chronicle*. All in all, he gathered over six hundred medieval manuscripts, mostly Anglo-Saxon, which he bequeathed to his Cambridge college, on the strict condition that they would be checked every year and that, should any be found missing, the collection would go to Caius College. Needless to say, most are still in possession of Corpus Christi College today. Occasionally the need arises for some manuscripts to leave the college. A notable example is the St Augustine Gospels, on which every archbishop of Canterbury since 1942, when the tradition was either revived or possibly set up in what was itself a medievalist gesture, has had to swear his oath when enthroned: at such times police are highly visible guarding the manuscript with far more zeal than they need to guard the new archbishop.

Parker not only collected and saved dozens of Anglo-Saxon manuscripts that would have otherwise been lost, he also generously passed them round to his friends, such as Laurence Nowell, the first genuine Anglo-Saxon scholar in sixteenth-century England, and William Lambarde, the Elizabethan jurist, who was himself a collector and discoverer of medieval manuscripts.[36] Private collections of medieval manuscripts began at that stage. Humphrey, duke of Gloucester put together such a collection, subsequently lost, but his idea of a private library was implemented by Thomas Bodley (1545–1613), the real founder of the Bodleian Library in Oxford. Francis Junius (1589–1677), who had been the first promoter of the study of Old English at the university of Leiden and the editor of Old English and Gothic Gospel books and of the Caedmon poem, and Sir Robert Cotton (1571–1631) were among such collectors. Their array of books formed the nuclei of the Bodleian or the Royal (later to become the British) Library, and of Oxford and Cambridge colleges.[37] Private collectors such as the Herbert family as earls of Pembroke and Henry Savile also accumulated manuscripts.[38] In the eighteenth century Sir Hans Sloane and Sir Robert Harley left their collections to the Royal Library.[39] These were followed by Francis Douce (1757–1834), who bequeathed his collection of books and prints to the Bodleian. These collections were not restricted to illuminated manuscripts, purchased for their aesthetic value alone, but comprised large numbers of books whose contents – liturgical texts, sermons, theological commentaries, collections of laws, charters and others – were deemed both useful to historically-minded patrons and interesting for the collector.

Collecting was not enough. It was compounded by the subsequent editing of the texts. From the first, printers like Caxton, Wynkyn de Worde, Alder Manutius and Plantin Moretus produced editions of major medieval texts, notably Dante, Boccacio and Chaucer. Numerous medieval texts continued to be reprinted at regular intervals, even though they were often bowdlerised, to make them more palatable and less 'indecent' to contemporary audiences, as was the case for example with Dryden's edition of Chaucer.[40] Sometimes editing was done for specific polemical purposes, the best known case being that of the so-called Donation of Constantine, a text which purported to be the grant to the pope, by the Emperor Constantine in 327, of Italy, Rome and supreme political power over the whole of the Western Roman Empire, and on which the attempts by later medieval popes to establish their political authority in Europe was based. Close scrutiny of the text by the Italian scholar Lorenzo Valla around 1440 showed it to have been an eighth-century fabrication. (The manufacturing of manuscripts, an important medieval device, did not cease after 1500: in 1938 a German Catholic monk produced a fake medieval manuscript incorporating a map of Vinland, which showed that America had in fact been 'discovered' by a member of the medieval clergy.)

In 1565 Thomas Stapleton, student of divinity, an English Recusant who had taken refuge in Louvain like many of his contemporaries, published in Antwerp the first English translation of Bede's *Ecclesiastical History*.[41] Its purpose was to reclaim England's Roman Catholic heritage, through the first national writer to have highlighted the debt owed by the English church to Rome and to the popes for having initiated the conversion, and thus the 'salvation', of the English people. The translation was pointedly dedicated to Queen Elizabeth, in an attempt to make her return to her Catholic roots; while it failed in its ambitions, the book was repeatedly reprinted throughout the seventeenth century by the Jesuits who had taken refuge in St-Omer. The polemical value of Bede had begun: he was reclaimed at once by the Catholics and the Puritans, both on the grounds of the antiquity of the English church, for or against, Rome.

Medieval texts were edited out of antiquarian interest, of the kind that prompted Dugdale's *Monasticon* (in three volumes published in 1655, 1661 and 1673), Tanner's *Notitia Monastica* in the eighteenth century, and Wilkins's *Leges* and *Concilia Magnae Britanniae* (1737), or as a reflection of a more general interest in the history of the church. On the Continent this was often a part of the general Counter Reformation Catholic revival. It gave birth to such major seventeenth- and eighteenth-century projects as Mabillon's collection of liturgical documents, his *Museum Italicum*, comprising medieval Italian documents in context (1687), and above all the work which made him the founder of the science of diplomatic, *De re diplomatica* (1681). The *Acta Sanctorum* was a vastly ambitious project to provide a complete edition of all hagiographical material by the Society of Bollandists; and there were other attempts at complete histories, diocese by diocese, in the *Gallia Christiana* and the *Italia Sacra*.

In England, editors and historians used medieval sources to highlight the fact that the Anglo-Saxon church, once 'pure and uncorrupted' to use the contemporary cliché, had been contaminated by the papacy in the later Middle Ages, hence justifying the Reformation, which brought back that original purity. Such is the gist of Bale's work and of John Foxe's *Book of the Martyrs*. Interest in the medieval in England was, however, not exclusively ecclesiastical: in 1568 Lambarde translated collections of Anglo-Saxon laws (*Archaionomia*), which he valued as the first manifestations of common law, and in the seventeenth century Thomas Rymer edited medieval treaties in his *Foedera*. Most famously, the great Elizabethan lawyer Sir Edward Coke was particularly interested in Anglo-Saxon constitutional history and legislation.[42]

In Italy too Ludovico Antonio Muratori (1672–1750) published a collection of secular as well as ecclesiastical sources, including medieval Italian chronicles and other documents, in his *Rerum Italicarum scriptores* and *Antiquitate Italicae Medii Aevi*, while his near contemporary Angelo Fumagalli (1728–1804), abbot of Sant' Ambrogio in Milan, taught palaeography and diplomatic, and published the first major collection of Lombard charters.

In order to understand these documents, the first editors had to teach themselves what were to become the basic skills of later scholars: old languages, palaeography and numismatics.[43] Between 1550 and 1730 attempts were made to produce treatises in these fields, to help the increasing number of antiquarians and scholars interested in such documents. Inspired by the Cottonian library, Humfrey Wanley became the main authority on medieval palaeography, while Lawrence Nowell and William Lambarde had already taught themselves Old English. Archbishop Ussher convinced Sir Henry Spelman to create the first lectureship in Old English studies at Cambridge. Its first holder in the 1640s, Abraham Wheloc, who was also professor of Arabic, provided editions of Bede and the *Anglo-Saxon Chronicle* in Old English, while the second incumbent produced the first Old English dictionary. The first, Elizabethan, Society of Antiquaries, was founded in 1586, and comprised aristocratic collectors, heralds, archivists, lawyers, academics, local historians, MPs and clergy, and included men such as Parker, Spelman, Cotton, Camden and Stow.[44] Its interests were British and Anglo-Saxon antiquities, etymology and general philology, and some literature. The society was dissolved by James I, who felt it was a hotbed of potential opposition, but it was later refounded as the Royal Society, and again as the Society of Antiquaries after 1718.

While antiquaries like John Leland or Sir Henry Selden were still uncommon in the late sixteenth century, from the seventeenth and especially in the eighteenth century their number was steadily rising. The first were interested in, and wrote about, the 'antiquities of' a county or an area. Lambarde's *Perambulation of Kent* was published in the 1570s, topographers such as Hooker or Carew collected material for Exeter and Cornwall, and William Dugdale (1605–1686) produced the *Antiquities of Warwickshire*. Subsequently, major antiquaries like William Camden (1551–1623) in his *Britannia* (published edition in Latin in 1586; in English in 1610) wrote about the whole of Britain, though local antiquarians such as Anthony à Wood (1632–1695) and Thomas Hearne (1678–1735) in Oxfordshire also continued to work into the eighteenth century. Generally, England from the mid seventeenth century saw the rise of antiquarianism as part of the well-to-do gentleman's main leisure activity. It began as a staple diet of the gentry and aristocracy with a taste for culture and the past, and the time and money to indulge it, whether this past was medieval in England or represented by the

Grand Tour through France and Italy.[45] The taste then reached further down into society to simple gentlemen, well-off merchants and tradesmen and very specifically to clergymen.

Collecting manuscripts was only one of the interests of this elite. Another form of collecting, increasingly represented in the newly-opened museums of the eighteenth century, focused on objects and artefacts.[46] It is a mistake to think of museums as repositories simply of the Greek and Roman arte-facts found thanks to the renewed interest in excavations carried out in Rome or the rediscovered Pompeii. Medieval sites were also excavated and their finds catalogued and exhibited: British and Anglo-Saxon ones in Eng-land; Frankish ones like the Childeric treasure from Tournai in Belgium. The latter was published in 1655 by J. J. Chifflet,[47] a great achievement since it was subsequently destroyed during the French Revolution and the draw-ings are now almost our only remaining record. Antiquarians were interested in more general antiquities, coins, artefacts, even relics (though in England they took good care to make the point that they saw these merely as 'curiosities' and not as 'popish worship'). A whole new network of exchanges developed between these collectors, who kept each other abreast of discoveries and helped each other interpret and value their new-found treasures. Local antiquarian societies emerged, contrasting with the great national and royal societies across western Europe.

Similar interests influences the writing of history. After the topographical accounts of England, with their histories of areas, towns, castles and churches, in works such as Camden's *Britannia*, Leland's collected papers (published in 1715 by Hearne under the title *Collectanea*) and Parker's *De antiquitate Britannicae Ecclesiae* (1570), narrative histories were attempted, first going back to the Norman Conquest, then further back to Anglo-Saxon and even British times. Among the earliest examples were Samuel Daniel's history down to Edward III, the histories of England by John Stow in 1580, and the collective work known under the name of Hollinshed.[48] Outside Britain historians, such as Francesco Guicciardini in Florence and Flavio Biondo in Rome, also began writing 'medieval history' from the sixteenth century.

The writing of history, other than purely descriptive, belongs, however, to the realms of interpretation. Collecting, cataloguing, editing, translating and other forms of recording were only the first steps and the most obvious. But from the start interpretation ran parallel to them, a clear sign that the inter-est in the Middle Ages was not due to simple antiquarian curiosity. The opportunity to use the Middle Ages as a frame of reference on which to hang views, criticisms and positions was perceived and used. One such example is the adaptation of the medieval past by Shakespeare. Another is the use made of allegedly medieval political and social institutions to 'prove' contemporary viewpoints right. In particular lawyers and political figures chose specific aspects of the Middle Ages to reinforce their theory of religious or constitutional superiority. Such an interpretative method was applied to political ideas from the sixteenth century onwards.

Medieval institutions (or those perceived as such) were used as a way of proposing solutions to current debates about constitutional, political, legal and social problems through a search for the roots and assumed truths of their nature in the past. One such issue was the God-given right of kings to rule while being answerable to God alone, without consulting their 'natural' advisers, the nobility in France and parliament in England. An issue of great importance within the framework of French royal absolutism in the seventeenth and eighteenth centuries, it was set out during the eighteenth-century debate between the 'Germanists' and the 'Romanists'.[49] The Germanists claimed that the French nobility had arisen out of the Frankish conquest of the early Middle Ages, and that it was a 'blood aristocracy' that had originally chosen the king from amongst themselves. Consequently it had the right and the duty to provide a check on royal absolutism, which was in effect an usurpation of their rights. The Romanists, who did not accept the idea of a Frankish conquest but saw the Franks as a group which had gradually settled in Roman Gaul and thus on a par with the local inhabitants, subjects of the Roman emperor, claimed that the nobility had no historic role as such – they supported the monarchy as the oldest and most venerable institution and, by extension, also supported *ancien régime* absolutism. The controversy began in the 1730s, and retained a high profile until the French Revolution, especially after major figures among Enlightenment philosophers, such as Montesquieu, joined the ranks of the Romanists. Montesquieu was also one of the most enthusiastic of eighteenth-century medievalists, praising what he called the *gouvernement gothique* as a model of balance between the civil liberties of the people, the prerogatives of the nobility and clergy, and the power of kings.

Much of the knowledge of eighteenth-century French writers, philosophers and the general public about the Middle Ages (and about what they regarded as one and the same thing, feudal society and chivalry), came from two key texts, whose influence cannot be overestimated either in France or in England. They were the work of a man from the *petite noblesse* of recent origin, Jean-Baptiste de La Curne de Sainte-Palaye.[50] At first interested in philology and in antiquities, he wrote his *Histoire littéraire des troubadours* and then in 1750–52 the *Mémoires sur l'ancienne chevalerie*. This tried to make sense of the medieval period on the basis of every source de Sainte-Palaye could find to use, historical and literary. He presented a (sentimentalised) version of the age of chivalry as the 'good old days', and contributed greatly to shaping the eighteenth-century interest in the 'primitive', the imagined simplicity of life, closeness to nature and values of the 'natural', the mystical, the *merveilleux chrétien* of purity and simplicity of the medieval church before the Council of Trent. But his message was also a political one, a rebuff to the nobility of his day, which had lost the values that had defined chivalry, to defend the poor and the weak, and to provide justice. The subtext to this was that, once the nobility had ceased to fulfil its function, they could no longer expect to be the political and social leaders that they had been in the past. The success of the book with both nobility and bourgeois audiences was colossal. Its influence on, for example, Richard Hurd's *Letters on Chivalry and Romance* (1762) and Bishop Percy's *Reliques of Ancient English Poetry* (1765) was considerable. Edward Gibbon's account of chivalry relies almost exclusively on the *Mémoires*, as does much of Scott's and Southey's work, historical writing well into the nineteenth century (for example, Hallam's *View of the State of Europe in the Middle Ages* of 1819), and German poetry and philosophy, notably Herder.

The issue of the balance of power between a king who claimed to be responsible to God alone, and the desire for representation through parliament, as exemplified in Magna Carta, was first debated in England in the first half of the seventeenth century in relation to James I's treatise for his son, the *Basilikon Doron*. This prompted a larger debate on the nature of royal power.[51] The question was first raised under James I by Sir Robert Filmer, then by William Prynne and Thomas Hobbes in the 1640s, after the Restoration by Sir Matthew Hale and William Dugdale, and finally in the wake of the 1688 Revolution in the controversy between Sir Robert Brady and William Petyt, arguing for and against the theory that it was the king who originally created all institutions, including parliament, and that the monarchy must therefore be of greater antiquity.

In the seventeenth century the issue of royal power became embodied in the later made-famous concept of the Norman Yoke. There had been already in the sixteenth century a trend to use the historic concepts of both *Saxonism* or *Teutonism* and *Immemorialism*, in both England and France, mostly by lawyers and legal historians. They saw the legal system of English common law as having its origins in some immemorial Germanic past, going back 'longer than one could remember', to King Arthur, Lucius and the British kings, and to Brutus of Troy, the mythic founders of England. The main proponent of this theory had been Sir Edward Coke, lord chief justice under James I and the first serious scholar to work on the history of the common law, in his *Reports*, published after 1600. For Coke the common law was made by 'antiquity, its character as the immemorial custom of England';[52] England had always been ruled by common law, which he also called the *laga Edwardi*, the law of Edward the Confessor, later reiterated by Henry I and other kings, and culminating in Magna Carta. The Norman Conquest, to that extent, had hardly existed. Coke was not a Saxonist or Teutonist. He did not acknowledge the view, held by some, that this immemorial custom had its roots in the Germanic past which represented primitive Teutonic freedom in terms of the assembly of the nation and the origins of law and of parliament. This would have meant for Coke the acceptance of a 'foreign' conquest, that by the Saxons.

English legal historians were not alone in promoting the Saxonist or Teutonist model: it had in fact first been propounded by French lawyers and professors from the 1560s onwards. These included Jean Bodin, François Hotman (in his *Anti-Tribonian* and the *Francogallia* of 1567 and 1573) and the professors of the Bourges and Toulouse universities, notably François Cujas, first editor of the medieval Lombard laws under the name of *Liber feudorum*.[53] French humanists and lawyers began to study the legal systems of the past in order to help restore justice and peace on the basis of historical precedent after the French sixteenth-century Wars of Religion. This is how they came to create a constitutional history based on antiquarian studies, being led to regard the Germanic past as the root of the assembly of the nation, parlements and the law and, ultimately, feudalism.

The roots of feudalism were thought by Hotman, Pietro de Gregorio in Sicily and Sir Henry Spelman in England to have originated in Germanic family law. Spelman, another lawyer and amateur historian, and the author of the *Archaeologus*, placed the origins of feudal law in a Germanic past, but he was, above all, the first to attribute its development to the Norman introduction of feudal tenure in England.[54] Gradually 'Immemorialism' as a political theory faded, and the concept of 'Saxonism' evolved into that of a 'free' Anglo-Saxon peasantry, who were the original model for both the constitution and the laws of England, as established and practised within the framework of the Anglo-Saxon witan or royal council or assembly of the people, and through the jury system within the localities. On this 'primitive' model, it was claimed, had been superimposed the Norman Yoke of the French feudal system, with its pernicious innovations in the form of serfdom and increasingly arbitrary royal power. In England at least, the main interest shifted away from the history of law to that of the constitution and of the antiquity of parliament, which was foremost in people's minds during the debates of the Jacobean and Stuart eras. The

Norman Yoke theory was first articulated during the seventeenth-century Commonwealth:

> Before 1066 the Anglo-Saxon inhabitants of this country lived as free and equal
> citizens, governing themselves through representative institutions. The Nor-
> man Conquest deprived them of this liberty, and established the tyranny of an
> alien King and landlords. But the people did not forget the rights they had lost.
> They fought continuously to recover them, with varying success. Concessions
> (Magna Carta, for instance) were from time to time extorted from their rulers,
> and always the tradition of lost Anglo-Saxon freedom was a stimulus to ever
> more insistent demands upon the successors of the Norman usurpers .[55]

This theory was set out in moderate and scholarly terms at first by James
Harrington in his *Oceana* (1656),[56] then increasingly in revolutionary terms
by John Hare, by the Levellers John Lilburne, John Walwyn and Hugh Peter,
and finally, in its most extreme form of 'primitive communism', which
regarded parliament, law and property as Norman inventions, and
demanded their abolition, by the Diggers. They contrasted the Norman
Yoke with the primitive liberty of the Saxons, regarding feudalism, and the
Norman Conquest which had brought it to England, as the French root of
all evil and of the tyrannical rule of 'foreign kings' from whom Charles I was
deemed to descend. In December 1649 the Diggers declared to Fairfax:

> Seeing the common people of England by joynt consent ... have cast out
> Charles our Norman oppressour, wee have by this victory recovered ourselves
> from under his Norman yoake, and the land now is to returne into the joynt
> hands of those who have conquered – that is, the commonours – and the land
> is to bee held noe longer from the use of them [the commoners] by the hand
> of anye [who] will uphold the Norman and kingly power still.[57]

Discredited as a result of its Leveller and Digger connections, the Norman
Yoke theory only returned to favour in the second half of the eighteenth
century as a component of Whiggism, being described to various degrees by
William Blackstone, Catherine Macaulay and Lord Bolingbroke.[58] Thomas
Jefferson and Tom Paine exported it to the American colonies and it came
to play a considerable part in the American Revolution.[59] In England, too,
defending the Glorious Revolution of 1688, even as he was strongly condemning the French one, Edmund Burke summarised his position thus: the
English one 'was made to preserve our ancient and indisputable liberties,
and that ancient constitution of government which is our only security for
law and liberty'.[60] The debate lasted well into the nineteenth century with
the controversy between the two Victorian historians Freeman and Round.[61]
It lingered on even as late as Thoreau's *Speech of a Saxon Ealdorman*

within the American consciousness. In England the understanding of Magna Carta as the bedrock of English liberties of the people represented in parliament (though of course Magna Carta was Norman and did not claim, at any time, to give representation to anyone but the barons), led to the incorporation of the term 'Charter' in their political manifesto, giving its name to the nineteenth-century socialist reformers known as Chartists.[62]

All these debates, over two centuries, reflect the importance of medieval history on English political culture. Until the later eighteenth century history was regarded as a mirror through which one could assess contemporary events and draw lessons from the past, since it was all about 'human nature', which was the same everywhere at all times. This explains the constant attempts to find roots in the past for present institutions (the law, parliament, the constitution) and to return to that imaginary past (Anglo-Saxon), even by revolutionaries whose line of reasoning was in effect *anti-historical* (wanting the return to *before*). They too could only express their theories in historical terms: in order to reject the past, they needed first to examine it and then interpret it in a suitable way. Similarly, it explains the extent to which the writing of history could be regarded as a dangerous pastime, just as the editions of certain texts, such as Bede, could be turned into polemic. Sir John Hayward clearly touched a nerve with Queen Elizabeth when writing about the deposition of Richard II, and was executed for his pains, and Sir Robert Cotton was closely questioned after the publication of his work on Henry III, perceived as a criticism of Charles I.[63]

Earlier James I had refused to allow the refounding of the Society of Antiquaries, previously dispersed because of its members' perceived political activities. These members included Camden, Daniel and Selden, many of them lawyers and sons of rich merchant or artisan families, and frequently supporters of the rights of parliament. All this provides a clear example of the use of the past, and of academic debate, in order to discuss safely, as well as to find solutions to, contemporary problems, within the framework of a society for which no revolution was possible through the creation of new systems, but only through that of reviving the ancient custom. This is one of the most fundamental traits of pre-industrial societies. It may be useful for the western societies of the twenty-first century to take on board the importance of this frame of mind, which has prevailed in human history from its inception, and which might be a not entirely useless tool for understanding contemporary societies outside the realms of the industrial west. It was only with the advent of the movement known as historicism, as defined by two historians and philosophers, the Neapolitan lawyer Gianbattista Vico (1668–1744) in his *Scienza Nuova*, and the German professor Herder in his *Ideas for a Philosophy of the History of Mankind* (1784–1791), which denied this platonic ideal of the universal values and nature of man, that history was first seen as being culturally driven and created. Historicism claimed that changes and the relationship to the past depend on historical circumstances, a view which meant that, for the first time, a less direct use was made of history in order to explain the present.[64]

The earlier view did not, however, disappear. A different kind of interpretation took its place, a more indirect kind, and it remained influential in terms of looking into the past for solutions to contemporary problems. We can see this in the context of another major political issue: the imperial idea. The idea of empire had its origins during the early medieval period,[65] when Charlemagne and his successors attempted to resurrect the late Roman empire of Constantine and his successors, the epitome of political desirability in their eyes. After the dislocation of the Roman Empire in the west between the fifth and the seventh centuries, periodic attempts were made to revive it – at this stage it was not perceived as dead, only as being in abeyance – the first successful attempt being that of Charlemagne in 800.[66] The theories behind this revival of the imperial idea were to be a constant political and ideological frame of reference throughout the Middle Ages. They did not associate the empire with a country, a nation or even the notion of Europe, but with that of the Christian Roman Empire. The ideal of imperial continuity was posited by the church, which saw itself as the heir to that empire in its spiritual dimension. The essence of what was perceived to be the revived empire was the idea of *res publica christiana*, Christendom, and more specifically Latin Christendom. The medieval obsession with the idea of empire, which came to mean Christian civilisation, was carried on after the disintegration of the Carolingian empire (the last one really to encompass most of western Europe), through the next form of imperial hegemony, which saw Germany and Italy united under the German Ottonian and Salian emperors in the tenth and eleventh centuries, Frederick Barbarossa in the twelfth and Frederick II in the thirteenth centuries.[67]

Although this 'German' empire came to define itself against the rising pan-European power of the papacy, it also regarded itself as the representative of the traditional imperial unity of Christianity and Latinity (*Romanitas* meaning the inheritance of the Roman world). It was approximately at this date that it began to see itself as the Holy Roman Empire. By the fourteenth century the two great conflicting powers of the German empire and the papacy, both of whose ambitions were pan-European and based on the same unifying factors, were beginning to decline, in the face of the gradual rise, between the eleventh and the fifteenth centuries, of nation states, including the kingdoms of France, Hungary, Denmark and Sweden, Bohemia and

Spain. England had been, since the tenth century, the only other major European power, with the empire and the papacy. The quest for a European superpower always remained in the background, periodically coming to the fore, notably after the rise of the Ottoman empire in the East. Political thinkers in the fourteenth and fifteenth centuries were still looking for ways of creating a confederation of European states for peace and defence against the Turks. Others pursued more traditional solutions for the unity of Christendom: reviving the power of the secular empire, as Dante suggested in his *De monarchia*, strengthening the power of the papacy, as Boniface VIII and his successors wished, or even turning the increasingly powerful king of France into an emperor.

All these solutions were stopped in their tracks by the events of the sixteenth century, which saw both the shock and the triumph of the Reformation, which brought an end to 'Latin Christianity', from then on divided. The Reformation and Counter Reformation, and the political struggles which followed them, such as the Thirty Years War, once again led to the search for a peaceful form of European unity. One of the most successful among the solutions, still based on the obsession with the imperial idea, was the conversion of the extremely weak Holy Roman Empire of Germany into one of the most powerful and long-lasting European ones: the empire of the Habsburgs.[68]

The Habsburg family gave its first emperor to the Holy Roman Empire in 1273, and from 1440 onwards it alone held the imperial title continuously until 1806, when the Holy Roman Empire officially ended.[69] Through a policy of wars, and especially of marriage alliances, the Habsburgs expanded first into Hungary (1490), then through the Emperor Maximilian's marriage to Mary of Burgundy (1477) into the Netherlands and Burgundy, where most of the wealth of Europe was concentrated. Maximilian's son Philip the Fair's marriage to Joanna, the heiress of the kingdom of Castile, the death of various heirs and ultimately the discovery of the New World and its treasures, eventually gave to the heir of the Habsburgs, Charles V (emperor from 1519 to 1555), a huge and immensely wealthy empire. It was an 'empire on which the sun never set', as contemporaries had it, extending over most of Europe (Spain, the Netherlands, parts of Italy, Burgundy, Austria, Bohemia, Hungary), as well as the New World.[70] Charles was undoubtedly the head of Latin Catholic Christendom, with a universalist view of his power as heir to Caesar, Augustus and Charlemagne, pioneering the values of Christianity, a universal monarchy encompassing many nations and languages. This was in obvious opposition to the idea of the nation state, by then on the ascendant in the remaining European states.

Charles's ideals were to be defeated by the combined forces of his most powerful enemy, France, and the Reformation. When he abdicated in 1555 his dominions were split between his son Philip and his brother Ferdinand, who reigned respectively over the 'Spanish' area (including the Netherlands and Italy) and the Danubian lands. While the Spanish branch was to decline by the 1650s with the diminishing of its ascendancy over the Netherlands and the seas, increasingly challenged by the rising commercial expansion of the Low Countries and a powerful English monarchy, as well as the Thirty Years War with France, the Danubian branch became the core of the new Austrian empire, which succeeded in defeating the Ottomans and pushing them back from central and western Europe for good in 1683. Despite its diminishing hold on Germany itself, this empire remained the dominant power in central and eastern Europe during the eighteenth century under Maria Theresa and her son Joseph II, and in the nineteenth century under Franz Joseph. It was to maintain this position until 1918.[71] Not even the French Revolution and the Napoleonic Wars could end its cohesion, which was based on values other than those of a contemporary secular nation state: it was a supranational, pluralist, multiethnic, multicultural, multilingual empire, even if it was one that saw itself essentially as the defender of Catholic Christianity; in fact, the very ideas of the medieval empire.

The imperial ideal can be easily traced back to the Middle Ages. From the eighteenth century onwards with the Enlightenment, a parallel idea of European power developed in France and England.[72] The most important element in this gradual development of a secular European ideal of a confederation of states, with common institutions for the 'common good', was the European *feeling*, strong during the cosmopolitan period of the Enlightenment and best represented by Voltaire. This embryo of a pan-European ideal was, however, blown to pieces by the French Revolution of 1789, and its subsequent attempts to 'liberate' other nations from the 'yoke' of monarchical 'tyrannies' of the *ancien régime*, and to introduce the principles of freedom as exemplified in the American and French constitutions. Those were the avowed goals behind the Napoleonic Wars. Napoleon saw himself as a universal emperor, whose purpose was to establish his hegemony not only through conquest but also through the unifying rule of law, in true Roman fashion, as the official successor of Charlemagne.[73] Unfortunately for him, the people whom he purported to liberate did not want to see a *tabula rasa* made of their own traditions, as the French were seen to have made of theirs; nor did they see the French as liberators but as conquerors. Thus, far more than the power of the Habsburgs, the Napoleonic Wars were at the root of the strong reaction which fuelled the rise in nineteenth-century Europe of strong nationalist movements, leading to the spate of uprisings of 1848 and the formation of new states like Belgium, the unification of Germany under Bismarck, and the Italian Risorgimento followed by unification under Garibaldi and Cavour.

The political, as well as conceptual, scheme of things had been either shattered or at least rewritten by the two major events of the late eighteenth and early nineteenth centuries: the French Revolution and, on a different level, the Industrial Revolution. While both changed European society beyond recognition, the new world which came out of them, unsurprisingly, still used the Middle Ages as terms of reference, in some cases much more so than before, but for different reasons and in different ways. Before pursuing the story of political medievalism in the nineteenth and twentieth centuries, some consideration should be given to an even more dominant form of interest in the medieval in European culture.

Strawberry Hill, the Gallery (above) and the Library (below), from Horace Walpole's *Description of Strawberry Hill* (1784). Classicism cast aside. The medieval picturesque in eighteenth-century architecture.

2

Gothic Thoughts

The invention of the medieval genre in literature began, throughout Europe, in the eighteenth century. While a revival of interest in the language of the Saxons, and antiquarian and archaeological studies,[1] developed among both historians and cultured gentry, collections of ballads and romances were made, notably Bishop Percy's *Reliques of Ancient English Poetry* and Richard Hurd's *Letters of Chivalry and Romance*.[2] The latter in particular not only craved recognition for Gothic art and manners, which Hurd claimed to have been superior to any other, but also invested the word 'Gothic' (Gothic ages, Gothic enchantments, Gothic tales, Gothic poems, Gothic romances, Gothic warriors) for the first time with a resonance that was not associated with barbarity but, on the contrary, with the poetry and chivalry of the Middle Ages.

Bishop Richard Percy (1729–1811) was a characteristic example of an eighteenth-century clergyman running a small parish for a long time, who whiled away many hours collecting, translating and editing obscure texts, such as fragments of Chinese literature and some Old Norse poetry in his *Five Pieces of Runic Poetry* (1763). A friend of Dr Johnson, Oliver Goldsmith and David Garrick among others, Percy claimed to have 'discovered', in most romantic circumstances, a manuscript of medieval ballads. He was prevailed upon to publish it, which he did in 1865, as three volumes. These comprised both the 'original' texts and his own additions and interpolated imitations in contemporary style.[3] Medieval ballads had never completely disappeared but had long been regarded as part of popular culture rather than literature, until their value was underlined by John Dryden, Joseph Addison and Nicholas Rowe in the early part of the eighteenth century. The interest in this material intensified with the publication of Macpherson's *Ossian*, alleged to be an authentic medieval text, and by the popularity of La Curne de Sainte-Palaye's work. Percy's edition, which became popular rapidly among the general public, if not always among his own friends like Johnson, contributed greatly to the widespread interest in ballads and their identification with medieval literature. Percy was still slightly embarrassed about what he chose to present as the 'rude songs of ancient minstrels', 'the barbarous productions of unpolished ages', and excused them to polite society on account of their being 'effusions of nature, shewing the first efforts of ancient genius, and exhibiting the customs and opinions of remote ages'.[4] Percy's near contemporaries, such as Thomas Gray, also translated or indeed attempted, Welsh and Scandinavian poetry; his 'Fatal Sisters: An Ode' (1768), a poem about dealing with Norse mythology, was one of his great successes. Unlike Percy, Gray and others had no such reservations about their material, and the popularity of ballads grew to such an extent that Thomas Chatterton, like Macpherson, fabricated a whole set of forgeries to satisfy the new taste with his Rowley and Canynge poems. The revival culminated with Sir Walter Scott (1771–1832) and his *Minstrelsy of the Scottish Border*, Scott himself having been a great admirer of Percy since his early years.

Before Scott, however, the man who more than any other launched the 'Gothic' fashion and changed the meaning of the word from a deprecatory to a praiseworthy one was undoubtedly Horace Walpole (1717–1796), whose influence was paramount both in England and in continental Europe.[5] Walpole was one of the most flamboyant of eighteenth-century figures. Descended from a moderately distinguished family going back to the thirteenth century, he was the younger son of the first Prime Minister and the man generally reckoned to have been the most powerful in England during the eighteenth century, Sir Robert Walpole. The family was based in Norfolk and Chelsea and, despite the indictment of Sir Robert for corruption, followed by his resignation from office with numerous debts, Horace himself was elected MP, and held various crown offices. As a young man, after studying at Eton and Cambridge, he had gone on the Grand Tour with his friend Thomas Gray the poet, and had made numerous friends and acquaintances in Italy and France, notably among the circle of the Encyclopedist philosophers in Paris. On returning to England he embarked on a career of great versatility, being equally active in politics and in the social life of London: he combined theatre, literature, letters and journalism, architectural plans and antiquarian pursuits. These came to the fore from 1747, when he acquired a house in Twickenham, Strawberry Hill. He started rebuilding it in the Gothic style and filled it with a large variety of 'Gothic' objects, meanwhile continuing with his antiquarian researches and tours of England. Work on Strawberry Hill continued through most of his life and in 1774 Walpole published a description of it, to great acclaim. At the same time, he was also pursuing a considerable correspondence with the luminaries of his time, composed memoirs and wrote various works, several set in the Middle Ages, like his play about Richard III and the novel *The Mysterious Mother*. By far his greatest contribution to literary posterity was his novel *The Castle of Otranto* (1764). His ambition was to write a new kind of book, which would belong neither to the traditional romances, nor to the modern novels in the mould of Richardson or Fielding. *The Castle of Otranto* was set during the Crusades, in the south of Italy in the principality of Otranto, and used names familiar to those who knew the historical circumstances of German imperial dominance in that area. Walpole famously first published the book with a preface claiming to bring to the attention of the public a manuscript discovered in an old Catholic household, written by a medieval author. When the novel was published to huge acclaim, Walpole dropped the fiction and acknowledged authorship, thus bringing on his head the critics' ire, who could not understand how 'a refined and polished genius' could become the 'advocate for re-establishing the barbarous superstitions of Gothic devilism'.[6] The public, however, did not quibble: *The Castle of Otranto* became a literary landmark, which subsequently spawned a whole literary genre.

Walpole's medievalism came partly from Shakespeare and partly from his own antiquarian studies, though in general his Middle Ages were more often perceived through the rose-tinted spectacles of aesthetic taste. This taste was displayed with enormous success in *The Castle of Otranto*,[7] soon regarded as a blueprint for the kind of novel later so successfully developed by Ann Radcliffe (1764–1823) and, with considerable changes, by Walter Scott.[8] In *Otranto*, for the first, but certainly not the last time, we come across a tyrannical lord, a gloomy turreted castle, deceitful clergy and damsels in distress. The Gothic novel relied in the first instance on the atmosphere created by the haunted castle and its dungeons, knights in armour, ruinous and terrifying old monasteries peopled with lascivious monks, victimised nuns and cruel inquisitors. As such, it was inevitably drawn into the next step, the supernatural, through the intermediary of ghosts, magic and other manifestations of the otherworldly. It gradually became less imperative to set a novel in the traditionally accepted 'medieval' period, since the emphasis was increasingly on a medieval *atmosphere*, which became almost synonymous with the supernatural, as well as with wildness, fear and gloom, guaranteed to supply the necessary thrill of mystery, wonder and suspense.[9] Like fairy tales, the Gothic novel was set in an atmosphere of danger, pursuit, supernatural occurrences, violence, suspense and love triumphant, and was best read on a wild night with a howling wind, by the fireside. Another parallel with the fairy tale genre was the manichaeism of characters and events: a tyrannical father, a pure, persecuted and virtuous heroine, a villain intent on her destruction, a group of rogues in league with the tyrant, often clergy; and events which took place among Gothic ruins (not classical ones): towering crags, dark crumbling castles where nature and wilderness have taken over from transitory mankind.[10] The story unfolds at extreme times of the

Women's enthusiasm for the Gothic novel. *Tales of Wonder* by Gillray. Women reading *The Monk* by M. G. Lewis.

year and day, in the moonlight, among the agitation of external elements, thunder, lighting, amidst deep forests, terrifying mountains, cataracts and awesome waterfalls. In Ann Radcliffe's *The Mysteries of Udolpho*, as she arrives at the Appenine house of her tormentor Montoni,

> Emily gazed with melancholy awe upon the castle ...; for, though it was now lighted up by the setting sun, the gothic greatness of its features, and its mouldering walls of dark grey stone, rendered it a gloomy and sublime object. As she gazed, the light died away on its walls, leaving a melancholy purple tint, which spread deeper and deeper, as the thin vapour crept up the mountain, while the battlements above were still tipped with spendour. From those too, the rays soon faded, and the whole edifice was invested with the solemn duskiness of the evening. Silent, lonely and sublime, it seemed to stand the sovereign of the scene, and to frown defiance on all, who dared to invade its solitary reign.[11]

In a less talented writer, this could become a collection of clichés, such as:

> the castle; a massy pile of building thrown together by various architects, all irregular and confused; towers jostle towers, and battlement rides on battlement; a dark unhallowed aspect hangs upon it. Time has dressed the walls in sable, and gasping loops and yawning grates, beset the horrid front ... Here the open gallery conducts to each rude tower ... As the strangers approach the gate, the pavement sounds beneath the horses' hoofs and hollow arches multiply the noise ... They cross the drawbridge of the ditch ... the iron studded gates roll rumbling on the massive hinge, and the portcullis, in its passage, harshly grates as the watchmen heave it up.[12]

The interior matches the ruinous exterior: 'The furniture, by long neglect, was decayed and dropping to pieces; the bed was devoured by the moths, and occupied by the rats, who had built their nests there with impunity for many generations. The bedding was very damp ...'[13] A closet with the fatal secret is concealed by a tapestry, whose role is to frighten the innocent heroin, just as the famous Black Veil would terrify Emily in *Udolfo*.

Supernatural beings intervene to right wrongs, especially those done to the bloodline. In *The Castle of Otranto*, the rightful heir Theodore, whose peasant appearance cannot conceal the nobility of character and thus earns him the love of the heroine, Matilda, killed by her father, is announced thus, at the very moment of her death:

> 'What! She [Matilda] is dead?' cried he [Theodore] in wild confusion. A clap of thunder at that instant shook the castle to its foundations; the earth rocked, and the clank of more than mortal armour was heard behind ... The moment

Theodore appeared, the walls of the castle behind Manfred [the wicked father of the heroine] were thrown down with a mighty force, and the form of Alfonso [the ghost of the dynasty's founder], dilated to an immense magnitude, appeared in the centre of the ruins. 'Behold in Theodore the true heir of Alfonso!' said the vision. And having pronounced these words, accompanied by a clap of thunder, it ascended solemnly towards heaven . . .[14]

Those themes are part and parcel of the Romantic movement, which placed heavy emphasis on feelings, on the return to nature, and on the supernatural.[15] The supernatural and the irrational, the triumph of the world of chaos and liberty associated with the wildness of the 'medieval', over order, were used to express the cult of freedom and change. This has been traditionally associated with the mood generally prevalent in Europe after the French Revolution, though it appears to have already been well advanced by the 1740s. In England at any rate, the development of the Evangelical movement which culminated with John Wesley's Methodist Revival is a good example of this emphasis on sentiment and feeling.[16] The supernatural and the irrational, even when they are ultimately shown to have been mere tricks to deceive reason, as Mrs Radcliffe repeatedly did, have long been regarded as a stand against the rational heritage of the Enlightenment and the developing emphasis on science as a corollary of the Industrial Revolution, and against the perceived materialism of the period, to be contrasted with the 'spiritual' dimension of the medieval world.[17] This binary contrast is now increasingly questioned. It is argued that a highlighting of male tender-heartedness and tears was already present from the late seventeenth century onwards, especially in reworkings of Roman themes on stage and in the more extreme forms of religious dissent, while a more general appearance and subsequent 'feminisation' of feeling after the 1740s was only a second wave in the Age of Sensibility.[18] The Enlightenment was, however, by no means as focused on reason as it has been made to appear, and an interest in sensibility and emotion predated Romanticism in drama, poetry and the sentimental novel of which Richardson was the best-known exponent. Moreover, Romanticism, whether in the less extreme Gothic novels or in Coleridge's poetry, often deliberately underlined the role of mind over emotion, or rather of the need to keep affect and sentiment under control lest they become dangerous tools in the hands of an inexperienced individual or crowd. Whatever balance one wishes to attribute to the mind or emotion, even while accepting that the traditional association made between Romanticism and affect may need revising, the fundamental connection which contemporaries saw between feeling and nature, on the one hand, and 'medieval' sensibility, on the other, retains its value in broad terms.

One aspect of this insistence on a return to nature against artifice and convention is the assumption that emotions – love, fear, exaltation, pity and hence tears, and faith – are more 'natural' than reason and intellect. Hence the prevalence of Romantic love and its overwhelming triumph over social conventions. Here is the meeting between the heroine and the hero, believed by all to be a peasant:

> Theodore flung himself at her feet, and seizing her lily hand, which with struggles she suffered him to kiss, he vowed on the earliest opportunity to get himself knighted, and fervently entreated her permission to swear himself eternally her knight. Ere the princess could reply, a clap of thunder was suddenly heard that shook the battlements. Theodore, regardless of the tempest, would have urged his suit: but the Princess ... retreated hastily into the castle ... He sighed, and retired, but with eyes fixed on the gate, until Matilda, closing it, put an end to the interview, in which the hearts of both had drunk so deeply of a passion, which both now tasted for the first time.[19]

Traditionally studies of the social background of the Gothic novel have emphasised the way in which the genre functioned as a manifestation of the values of the aristocratic landed society, where blood and inheritance were the essence of the transmission of name and property, leading to the frequently arranged or even forced marriages by tyrannical fathers of powerless heroines, who could only dream of love and aspire to a free choice not dictated by the necessity of family obligation. To that extent, the Gothic novel set out the conflict between the old aristocratic values of the landed classes, and those of the emerging industrial middle classes, who did not need to rely on either blood or landed inheritance, and whose ideals were more individualistic, aware of the importance of suitably harmonious marriages which would underlie a successful nuclear family.[20]

On a personal rather than social level, also associated with nature and overwhelming emotion in the Gothic novel, was the more direct emphasis on sexual attraction through the exaltation of passion, belonging to the triumph of natural instincts over the laws, conventions and morals of the world. The setting of many of these novels in Italy or Southern Europe, in lush gardens and sun-drenched locations reminiscent of the paradisal and erotically charged gardens of the *Romance of the Rose* or Boccaccio, and the emphasis on 'warm-bloodedness', as opposed to northern coldness, may also reflect the values of nature and instinct as opposed to intellect and frigidity. This is sometimes further enshrined in the contrast of Catholic versus Protestant. Anti-clerical views, which present cruel and dissolute religious figures and inquisitors, have been used to underline many novelists' anti-Catholic feelings; this may be so, or may reflect a shrewd use of cliché figures in the mind of the British public. On a deeper level, however, the setting of most Gothic novels in Catholic countries (Italy, France, Spain, Sicily, even Catholic Scotland) reflects a rising eighteenth-century perception of Catholicism as a form of spiritual Romanticism, more attuned to feelings, emotion and passion.[21] From early on, Walpole rebelled against Richardson's aim of moving away from the 'Catholic improbable and marvellous' towards promoting 'Protestant religion and virtue'. By the time of Radcliffe, Gothicism had ceased to be associated with the notion of Germanic tribes, and was effectively used to describe, in literary terms, events occurring in Catholic countries, in the Latin South which was still ruled by despotic power and Catholic superstition. These attitudes are those of the old feudal order of tyranny, intrigue and superstition, carried out by aristocratic despots like Montoni, in the environment of oppressive castles and convents; it is as though there was in late eighteenth-century England still a fear of losing hard-won freedoms and of being dragged back into the persecutions of Counter Reformation Europe: a strong motivation present in the Gothic novel may be the need to raise the ghosts of Old Catholic Europe in order to exorcise them.[22] At the same time, the hero or heroine of the novel have to clash with these phenomena, and thus reflect their own allegiance to the new order of freedom, enlightenment, and to the sensibility, manners and taste of the eighteenth-century.[23] Such enlightened attitudes are reflected in their religious approach to God, who is beauty and nature, to be approached directly rather than through a clerical intermediary, in the middle of, for example, sublime mountain landscapes.[24]

Two of the most famous writers of Gothic novels were men, Horace Walpole with *The Castle of Otranto* (1764) and Matthew G. Lewis (1775–1818) with *The Monk* (1796). Other men wrote Gothic novels: Thomas Leland, generally regarded as the precursor with his novel *Longsword, Earl of Salisbury* (1762), William Beckford (*Vathek*), and even Shelley (*The Assassins*).[25] Nevertheless, both among the best known and the least known authors, most were women, including the most famous of all, Mrs Radcliffe.[26] Of her six best known novels, three, *The Castles of Athlin and Dunbayne* (1789), *The Mysteries of Udolpho* (1794) and *Gaston de Blondeville* (1826), were set in the Middle Ages, while the other three, though chronologically later, retained the whole gamut of 'Gothic' accoutrements. Five novels take place in France or Italy, as did most Gothic novels,[27] unless the setting was Spain, Germany or Switzerland. With Mary Shelley's *Valperga* (1821) and a myriad of less famous names, such as Clara Reeve (*The Last Baron*), Charlotte Dacre and Sophia Lee, women were predominant among the popular authors who wrote in this genre in a more or less serial way.[28] More importantly still, the genre was much descried by 'serious' authors and readers, mostly male, and regarded as specifically aimed at, and only fit for, female consumption. Jane Austen, whose novel *Northanger Abbey* was a 'take' on the genre, has often been regarded as a critic of the Gothic novel. In fact, Austen was more apt to criticise, as she often did, the *exaggeration* which a diet of such novels could produce, rather than the genre itself. Catherine Morland, the heroine of *Northanger Abbey* is, after all, one of the most 'positive' of Austen's young women, praised on account of her naturalness and spontaneity, or rather lack of artificiality, which was precisely one of the virtues celebrated by the Romantics.

To say that the genre was considered frivolous and only suitable for feather-brained females is not enough. It is important to analyse the reasons why not only was it seen to be so, but also why it did in actual fact command such a following and held such an appeal for women, who both read and wrote it, and by inference, why this provoked such a negative reaction on the part of the men who criticised this phenomenon.[29] Love and emotions, the supernatural (shorthand for *unreasonable, childish, superstitious*), unsurprisingly, were regarded as specifically female traits, setting women aside from the *rational* male, though even a cursory study of both Romanticism and the Gothic novel shows that men too wrote and read such literature. Men were using those same themes and catering for a fast expanding reading audience, whose demands for such literature was a result of what has been called the 'consumer revolution' of the middle classes from the 1790s onwards. Contemporary perception, however, was that the devourers of such novels, through the intermediary of the circulating libraries and of the newly-established and very successful popular publishing houses such as Minerva Press, were women. The dangers of unregulated reading among women was one of erosion of male authority over them, as well as of subversion of the standards of taste suitable for a young girl, thus brought outside the control of her parents or family. The circulating library brought with it images of sexual association through touch, of promiscuity, as well as possible escape from marriage, and thus of possible rebellion against it. Moreover, women writers were not only able to address such issues for other women to ponder on; they could, and did, mix the more restrained and respectable novels with others, rich in sensationalism and eroticism. In addition, they could find a way of escaping the preordained fate of marriage and respectability with potential unhappiness and dependency, since they could earn an independent living. Male condemnation was general:

> We consider the general run of Novels as utterly unfit for you. Instruction they convey none. They paint Scenes of Pleasure and Passion altogether improper

for you to behold, even with the Mind's Eye. Their Descriptions are often loose and luscious in a High Degree; their representations of Love between the sexes are almost universally overstrained.

Or again: 'A young woman, who employs her time in reading novels ... Her mind will soon be debauched by licentious descriptions and lascivious images ... her mind will become a magazine of trifles and follies, or rather impure and wanton ideas'.

More worryingly still for male critics, had the phenomenon been restricted to the upper classes, it could have been contained; but when the fashion reached the 'middling orders of society', then it became a 'great calamity'. Had it not been for the spread of leisure and reading down the social scale, 'females in ordinary life would never had been so much the slaves of vice. The plain food, wholesome air, and exercise they enjoy would have exempted them from the tyranny of lawless passions [as it had] their virtuous grandmothers, and they would not have fallen prey to the first seducer who was ready to take them away from their husbands'.[30] Clearly all the reasons given above by the most virulent critics of the genre can be seen, in reverse, as precisely the reasons why a well-off, leisured, more assured female population would find this literature so tempting and exciting.

Further down the social scale, but in the same vein as Gothic novels, were the romances. Not only did their success not die out when the middle classes found other outlets, but they became the main imaginative resource of the lower classes, and in particular the poorer categories among women, servant girls and other workers, some of whom made up part of the readership of the Gothic novels, and for the same reasons.[31] A well-known eighteenth-century anecdote recounts how a lady sitting in her boudoir was impatiently waiting for the maids to have finished the romance they were reading and then pass it on to her: this was a good indicator of the various social levels of fiction readers, on a par, perhaps, with today's female representative of the Islington *Guardian*-reading 'chattering classes' surreptitiously smuggling away the gardener's copy of the *Daily Mail* from the kitchen table.

The eighteenth- and nineteenth-century appeal of the medieval period as the age of the irrational, of simple faith, of closeness to nature and emotions, manifested itself in the two other medieval-orientated literary genres of the period, Romanticism and the historical novel.

Jean-Jacques Rousseau was the first writer to be regarded as a Romantic by contemporaries, on account of his emphasis on the primitive, on nature (*le bon sauvage* representing the goodness of primitive man before he was corrupted by civilisation), the rights of the heart, the importance of individuality and uniqueness of man, and introspection, all of which figure prominently in *La nouvelle Héloïse*. He was, however, not known for valuing the medieval period, especially on political grounds. It is therefore all the more interesting that, with the taste for the medieval having already become so pervasive, he saw no difficulty in using the story of Abélard and Héloïse as a kind of shorthand for impossible romantic love, and indeed used some medieval imagery too, like the theme of erotic temptation in the garden.

The generation which followed Rousseau in western Europe, the *Sturm und Drang* movement in Germany, then Romanticism itself, was much more attuned to the Middle Ages.[32] In Germany it reacted against the rationalism of the Enlightenment (*Aufklärung*) in several ways.[33] One such way was Pietism, for which the emphasis on religious feeling was more important than theology and ritual, as it was in the contemporary English Evangelical Revival. Another was the call to the national medieval past, its artistic achievements and the use of the national language, by contrast with the learned Latin or the socially fashionable French. The man who represented both was the philosopher Johann Gottfried Herder, originally a Lutheran pastor.[34] He admired Ossian for demonstrating the superiority of primitive, earthy, folk culture, over sophisticated French taste, and he himself edited two volumes of *Volkslieder*. Herder converted Goethe to his ideas and the latter proceeded to write two of the main medievalist Romantic works in the German canon, the play *Götz von Berlichingen* and the *Bildungsroman Werther*, as well as an essay on Gothic architecture in Herder's *Von deutschen Art und Kunst* (1773), regarded as the manifesto of the *Sturm und Drang* movement.

The term 'Romantic' was coined by the next generation of writers, which saw the publication of Friedrich Schiller's plays *Die Räuber* (1782) and *Die Jungfrau auf Orléans* (1801), and the formation of the famous group the *Jenaer Kreis*, including Augustus Wilhelm and Friedrich Schlegel, Friedrich von Hardenberg (writing under the name of Novalis) and Johann Ludwig Tieck. While Schiller associated Romanticism with the pursuit of freedom and Friedrich Schlegel gave it its aesthetics, the philosopher and Jena professor Johann Gottlieb Fichte put forward both the supremacy of the individual self and the ideal of a German united political society, and, through his intellectual position, made Romanticism respectable.[35] Others, like Wilhelm Heinrich Wackenroder, pioneered the revival of Gothic art, writing up medieval buildings and praising medieval, Christian morality as being superior to the pagan classical one.

By far the most influential figure in his dissemination of German Romanticism, in Germany first and subsequently with resounding success in

England, was Friedrich de la Motte Fouqué (1777–1843).[36] A descendant of an aristocratic Norman Huguenot family exiled after the Revocation of the Edict of Nantes by Louis XIV, de la Motte Fouqué traced his ancestry as far back as the Crusades. Like his grandfather and father, he was himself an officer in the Prussian army, who fought against the revolutionary French and against Napoleon. Interested from his early years in Goethe, Schiller and Lessing, he was a friend of Augustus Schlegel, of the philosopher Fichte, and of the writer Jean Paul. De la Motte Fouqué found his inspiration in a mix of northern myths and Germanic legends, in the fake Ossian, the *Minnesänger* and troubadour poetry, as well as in Schlegel's and Goethe's medievalism. Above all, he was an extremely popular writer of legends, tales, and novels of romance, courtly love, chivalry and religion. He was regarded, as indeed saw himself, as a representative of the Christian-German aristocratic culture, both in his life as an officer and a noble landlord promoting the good husbandry of his estate, and as a writer. The work he regarded as his major literary piece, the novel *Der Held des Nordens*, was the first serious rewriting of the Nibelungen material since that of Hans Sachs in the sixteenth century; his novel *Thiodolf the Icelander* (1818) was the first Romantic use the old North Viking myths;[37] and his short story *Undine* influenced countless writers and poets, including Keats in 'La Belle Dame Sans Mercy', E. A. Poe, Tolkien and Edith Wharton, and remains the piece he is still known for today. For his contemporaries and immediate successors, his two *Ritterromane* (novels of chivalry), *Der Zauberring* and *Sintram*, were regarded in Germany and England as blueprints of Romantic literature. He claimed to have a double purpose. The first was that of awakening the German national consciousness through writing about past heroes of the nation, like Charlemagne and Frederick II, their nobility, bravery and loyalty, often in the context of an alleged typical German medieval background, such as free cities and feudal courts. *Der Zauberring* even included an account of the alleged wanderings of the ancient Germanic tribes. The second purpose was that of combining Christianity with the German tradition, claiming to mellow the second through the beneficial influence of the first. The hero of *Sintram*, Folko von Montfaucon, expressed the new German virtues of Christian chivalry, while his father Björn belonged to the older kind of harsher Germanic or Scandinavian hero. Fouqué's novels abound in melancholy, ruins, noble and heroic behaviour, especially when fighting for honour and faith, God and king, while otherworldly mythical and supremely beautiful maidens, like Undine the water spirit of the Rhine, love and help the chivalrous.

From then on German Romanticism brought forth the works of Tieck, Novalis's poetry and his medieval novel *Heinrich von Ofterdingen* and the works of Jean Paul, Hölderlin and Heinrich von Kleist. A good example of the genre is G. A. Bürger's ballad 'Lenore'. It tells the story of the innocent heroine abducted by a mysterious dark rider with only a skull for a head, who saves herself from entombment in a freshly-dug grave by ringing the churchyard bell. It was first translated into English in 1796, becoming part of the staple European Romantic diet throughout the nineteenth century. Most famously of all, Heinrich Heine, in his *Buch der Lieder* and *Romanzero*, developed what we now regard as the standard themes of both Romantic poetry and the Romantic hero: love transmuted into a spiritual experience, the poet as a stranger to the world, the anti-hero, estranged from bourgeois society, haunted by the infinite, peace and renewal through nature, and love to the death. Such themes, especially visible in the doom-laden poetry of Hölderlin, show pessimism about man, readiness to regard poetry as the highest truth, full of yearning, anxiety, loneliness and fascination for darkness and death, as well as for the supernatural and nature in its infinity. Their best known visual manifestation was Caspar David Friedrich's painting, with its feel for a Romantic idea of Christianity and the infinite power of Fate.

From early on German Romanticism had also been nostalgic for the medieval church and spiritual life. For some, this took the form of an interest in folk culture, mysticism and magic, sometimes associated rather dismissively by the likes of Schiller in his later, more bourgeois years, with an attraction of these poets towards the pantheism of the ancient Germans. For poets like Novalis and Heine, nostalgia was aimed at the perceived unity of Christendom in the Middle Ages as the unifying factor in society. Novalis's *Die Chistenheit oder Europa* (1799) underlines this longed-for unity of faith and art: 'Those were fine, magnificent times when Europe was a Christian country, when one Christendom inhabited this civilised continent and one great common interest linked the most distant provinces of this vast spiritual empire'.[38]

This 'omnipresence in life, its love for art, its profound humanity ... make [the medieval church] unmistakable as the true religion'; similarly, Heine also described the 'Age of Faith' as the lost ideal, when 'once, the world was whole ... despite external conflicts, there was an all-embracing unity, and the poets were also whole'.[39] Similar views were put forward in England by Edmund Burke and by Kenelm Digby,[40] and by the French Catholic writers of the early nineteenth century, notably Chateaubriand and Montalembert.

Another aspect of the German Romantic movement, especially in the years after the Napoleonic Wars, in the generation of the *Jungere Romantik* (Clemens Brentano, Achim von Arnim, Joseph von Görres), encompassed more radical attitudes associated with nationalism and the dream of unity of the *Vaterland*.[41]

The Germans shared such views with patriotic, Catholic, Italian Romanticism, with *its* emphasis on Italy's glorious past, in Leopardi's poetry and Alessandro Manzoni's novels and plays (two of which, including the histories of the Lombard queens Rosamund and Theodelinda, were set in the medieval period).[42] At first, in the eighteenth century, Italian interest in the medieval was linked to local patriotism. For example at Sant' Ambrogio of Milan, centre of the Italian Enlightenment, Lombard history was seen as part of the *storia patria* (the history of Italian regional entities, whether united or not). Other aspects were even more specific: Milan in particular had an important issue to grapple with in the eighteenth century with the suppression of its guilds, an obvious medieval leftover, and one which became a *cause célèbre* for reformists. Gianbattista Vico, a Neapolitan lawyer and philosopher, began his work criticising Descartes, and became the first exponent of historicism, a revolutionary understanding of history which moved away from the concept of the universality of human nature, and highlighted the importance of understanding men in their own terms and time.[43] Vico put forward the need for historians to study not only the institutions of these men of the past but also their myths, beliefs and symbols, which were at least as important for the history of 'primitive' societies. Later in the nineteenth century, writers and patriots moved on from using history as part of their *local* past, in their fight for unification and towards the overthrowing of the Austrian alien rule. They started using art to promote Italian national unity, and also the Italian language itself, branded the 'language of Dante'. Major political figures, whose Romanticism normally expressed itself in the fight for independence and struggle for unity through secret societies such as the *Carbonari*, as did Mazzini, nevertheless stressed the cultural aspects of unity.[44]

In Germany nationalist Romanticism manifested itself in the form of a revival of the German national spirit through editions of folk songs, as published by Herder (*Volkslieder*), Görres, or Achim von Arnim (*Des Knaben Wunderhorn*), and of fairy tales (*Märchen*) published by the brothers Jacob and Wilhelm Grimm. The literature of folklore, of which fairy tales were regarded as an essential component, went hand in hand with scholarly interest in the medieval past. In Germany the brothers Grimm were among the greatest Germanist scholars of the nineteenth century. They published philological and literary works, and edited among other texts the Old High German *Hildebrandlied*, which they single-handedly made into the great German national poem. They regarded fairy tales as an important form of memory of medieval popular folklore, an *Urkultur* reflecting the poetry of Germanic origins and the importance of the Germanic past.[45] The pride taken by the Grimms in these examples of what they clearly saw as belonging specifically to the glory of the German tradition is evident in their preface:

> There, within those famed lands of German Liberty, the legends and tales have survived as a near-regular feature of holiday pastimes in some locales, and the people still abound with inherited customs and songs ... wherever writing has not yet disrupted things by importing what is foreign.[46]

Their interest in fairy tales had been shared by eighteenth century French writers, starting with Charles Perrault and various aristocratic ladies.[47] French Romanticism began with the interest in German and English Romanticism taken by two Swiss Protestant writers, Madame de Staël and Benjamin Constant, who admired the emotions and feelings, darkness and passion of the German poets and of Shakespeare. The period between 1825 and 1835 saw the climax of the taste for the medieval in French Romanticism.[48] Among the authors of a plethora of poems, tragedies and novels (fuelled by translations of Walter Scott's novels), the two great exponents of Romanticism associated with a taste for the medieval were Madame de Staël and Chateaubriand. After extensive travel through Germany, when she met all the great Romantic poets including Goethe, Schiller, Tieck, Novalis, as well as philosophers and writers, notably Fichte and the Schlegel brothers, Madame de Staël wrote her much-publicised treatise *De l'Allemagne*, published first in 1810. In it, she placed the origin of chivalry and of the troubadour poetry in the Germanic world of the *Minnesänger*, and she made the Middle Ages the inspiration for a new, moral, spiritual, Christian literature, with a national and chivalric heritage. For her, the importance of the Middle Ages resided in the fact that the period saw the high point of the power of imagination, which she regarded as the most important part of life. This truly Romantic statement became the yardstick by which all Romantic literature and art had to be measured after it was defined in a well-known and repeated form by Chateaubriand: 'imagination is rich, abundant, wonderful; existence is poor, arid, without magic. One lives with a full heart in an empty world.'[49] Accused of anti-French propaganda by Napoleon, who hated her, Mme de Staël defended herself by claiming that she appealed to an older French tradition than the classical one, a tradition that the French had once shared with Germany in the world of Christianity, chivalry and troubadours, and from which they had cut themselves off at the Renaissance.

Exiled to Switzerland, Madame de Staël gathered around her a group of the leading Romantics of the age, notably Augustus Schlegel, who was her son's tutor, and Louis Sismonde de Sismondi, a Genevan historian and philologist, particularly well known for his seminal work on the history of the Italian city republics in the Middle Ages, published between 1807 and 1818. Sismondi defined the general character of Romantic literature as being chivalric, national, popular and Christian, and he was one of the first medieval historians to recognise the difference between the feudal world in its rather brutal reality, and later attempts at idealising it from its own definition of 'chivalry'. His European influence was considerable, on Ruskin and the Shelleys for example: Mary Shelley used his history of the Italian republics, together with Dante, to create in her novel *Valperga* a female character who associates her love for a worthy hero with allegedly republican, freedom-loving views against the tyranny of a *condottiere*.[50] Several members of Madame de Staël's circle promoted a Christian revival based on their perception of medieval religion, at a time which saw great longing for such a revival, after the anti-religious diktats of the French Revolution and the systematic destruction of monuments and churches. Madame de Staël and her friends were handicapped in this attempt by the fact that they were all Protestants. A reviver of medieval Christianity in France still had to be a Catholic. The main French Romantic poet, Chateaubriand, in his *Génie du Christianisme*, published in 1802, was such a figure.[51]

An aristocrat who could indeed trace his family back to the Middle Ages, whose childhood was spent in the family medieval castle in *ancien régime* Brittany, and who became a major political figure in Napoleonic and post-Napoleonic France, Chateaubriand saw the Middle Ages as a metaphor for the violent upheavals of his own life and times in their 'primitive' strength and vigour. *Génie* illustrates the author's return to the Catholic faith, and praises the Catholic Church for the beauty of its rituals, its contribution to art, to freedom and peace. With one stroke, the work created a cult of the Gothic, moulded a religious sensibility suited to the post-revolutionary period by using the perceived poetry and spiritual power of the Christian Middle Ages in order to eradicate the scepticism of the Enlightenment era, contributed to the revival of the chivalric spirit, and to the renewed call for the preservation of medieval monuments ruined during and after the 1789 revolution.[52]

Other French Romantics used medieval themes as a matter of course. Foremost among them was Alfred de Vigny, whose poem *Le cor* was a nostalgic reworking of the Roland story (even though the actual manuscript of the *Chanson de Roland* was not discovered in Oxford until 1832 and published in 1837, the legend had never disappeared from public memory). Alexandre Dumas père in his play *La Tour de Nesle* and in fifteen out of his (admittedly huge production of) historical novels was another exponent of the genre. Even Balzac, who took his inspiration from a totally different perception of the Middle Ages, the popular, robust, Rabelaisian kind, wrote the pastiche *Les contes drôlatiques*.[53] But it was Victor Hugo in his early and middle years, before he increasingly rejected the Middle Ages as his anticlerical tendencies developed, who remains generally regarded as the clearest example of French Romantic medievalism. His phenomenally successful novel *The Hunchback of Notre Dame* (1831), his play *Les Burgraves* (1842–43) and, later on in his life, his mammoth epic *La légende des siècles* (published between 1859 and 1883) were key texts for contemporaries. *The Hunchback of Notre Dame* in particular contributed largely to the rediscovery and the last-minute attempt at preservation of what was left of medieval Paris, and to the fashion for medieval themes and settings among the large number of writers and readers of newspapers serialised novels.[54] Author of the ultimate two Romantic manifestos: the preface to his play *Cromwell*, and his drama *Hernani*, which nearly caused another revolution in Paris, Hugo's Romanticism was equated with torment, the sublime, the flamboyant, the exotic, the grotesque, and ultimately Faustian dilemmas focusing on lightness and darkness and good and evil in human nature. It gradually came to be less and less associated with a medieval setting, in favour of an 'eternal human' one.

Like Théophile Gautier in his essays *Les Jeunes France* ('ce Moyen Age de carton et de terre cuite'), the last of the early French Romantics, Alfred de Musset, also spent much of his life attempting to 'debunk' the taste for the sentimental medievalising of his day. He set his own play *Lorenzaccio* in the Florence of the Medici, underlining the fact that his criticism was only directed at the contemporary taste for the fake, pseudo-medieval, and that his ridiculing was due, not to hostility to the Middle Ages but, on the contrary, to dismay at the debasing of what he saw as the genuine Middle Ages, with their strong, colourful, violent but real nature; as fierce a love for the period, though in opposition with his contemporaries' shallow, prettified version.

Later Romantics continued to set their work in the medieval period. The germanophile Gérard de Nerval, the first French translator of Goethe's *Faust*, also wrote novels set in the Middle Ages: *Le prince des sots, L'imagier de Harlem*, and the play *Nicolas Flamel*, in which he used the inspiration of the medieval mystery play. While his work was an attempt to imitate the Middle Ages of the 'people', his own taste was for mysticism, alchemy, satanism, and the supernatural, which come to the fore in his poetry, as they do in the literature of the later nineteenth-century Romantic and Symbolist writers. They too used medieval themes, but only as one element among many of their esoteric tastes. Joris Huysmans's novel *A Rebours*, with its character's fascination and attempt to rehabilitate Gilles de Rais on moral and aesthetic grounds, is just such an example. After its period of glory between 1815 and 1852 (the years of great revolutions and political changes, until the Second Empire of Napoleon III started), French Romanticism changed course and developed mostly in the direction of the 'fantastical', the supernatural, in literature as, for example, in music, with Gounod's 'Walpurgis Night' in his opera *Faust*.

Like its German counterpart, early English Romanticism too first developed against the perceived rationalism of the Enlightenment and classical art.[55] It, too, had already been notable in terms of its emphasis on emotions and the importance of nature, in the form of melancholy meditations by moonlight in ruined churchyards, which contributed to its nickname of 'graveyard poetry', represented by various poets of the 1740s, such as Robert Young, Robert Blair and, most famously by Thomas Warton's *On the Pleasures of Melancholy* and Thomas Gray's *Elegy in a Country Churchyard*. But early nineteenth-century Romanticism increasingly defined itself in relation to what it saw as the most momentous event in late eighteenth-century Europe, the French Revolution. Edmund Burke, who attacked rationalism and highlighted the importance of imagination, poetry, feelings, the sublime and the beautiful, because they speak to the emotions, was profoundly anti-revolutionary, while contemporary Romantic writers William Blake and then the Lake Poets Samuel Coleridge, Robert Southey and the young William Wordsworth, were in favour of the Revolution, at least at first, when they saw it as representing freedom from oppression.[56] Coleridge's poem *Christabel*, as well as his prose writings, contain a number of references to the medievalist myth of the liberty of the Goths, and the nostalgia for the Middle Ages as the age before the breakdown of mutual dependence of social groups in society, the model for social order and spiritual direction. Other poems also recall standard Gothic themes, such as *The Dungeon* or the reflection on *The Destiny of the Nations*, with lines beginning with 'As though the dark vaults of some mouldered Tower' and continue in the same vein. Even Wordsworth, whose Romanticism focused on nature rather than on medievalism, wrote about the appeal of ruined monasteries and stressed the fact that it was the medieval church which was the 'authentic' English church. His poem 'The Cuckoo at Laverna', an eulogy of Francis of Assisi, provides a good example of the association between medieval themes and his love of nature. Chivalry did get a look in in his poetry in a more general if indirect way, in the same way that it did as a background to the knightly pilgrim heroes in Byron's *Childe Harold* and *Manfred*.[57]

The most radical visionary was Blake, who stated the supremacy of the Sublime, the goodness of nature and the corruption of civilisation, and was in favour of the abolition of all hierarchies, the equality of women and the rule of love. His allegorical style, both in his poetry and in his painting, was, he thought, a return to the great medieval traditions of Dante and Chaucer, whom he was attempting to emulate as a Christian visionary. Blake, who coined the famous phrase 'dark satanic mills', was also the first to place himself strongly in the anti-industrialisation camp, which was to be the rallying cry of so many later writers, philosophers, Pre-Raphaelite painters and William Morris. But the most committed of all to medievalism was Robert Southey, both in his radical and egalitarian period, when he strongly supported the revolution in France (and wrote *Wat Tyler* and then his *Joan of Arc*, about which he was deeply embarrassed later, when his political views moved strongly to the right), and in his reactionary one, when he turned into a monarchist fighting against popular revolt and increasingly advocating control of the masses. Even then, he was still dreaming of the values of social harmony attributed to the Middle Ages and believing that it was the abandonment by the aristocracy of its duty to protect and rule in favour of just enjoying its privileges that was at the root of social disorder and revolution. A life-long medievalist, Southey continued to set various poems in the Middle Ages, as well as his novel *Roderic*, the story of the last Visigothic king of Spain in the eighth century. Despite his anti-Catholic views on nationalistic grounds, Southey was gradually more and more admiring of the role of the medieval church;[58] his nationalistic side, on the other hand, was reflected in his interest in King Alfred. Like almost every person fascinated by medievalism throughout the period covered by this book, but in a particularly clear way in this case on account of his totally radical change of direction, Southey continued to use and adapt the Middle Ages to his purpose, even when that purpose had completely changed in the meantime. The generation which followed Blake, that of Percy Bysshe Shelley and his wife Mary, and Lord Byron in the 1810 to 1830s, were less radical in political terms and more interested in exalting the poetic imagination, except Byron, who kept up the revolutionary idea of the fight for freedom not only in his writings but also in his life. His image of the flawed hero, fighting against social hypocrisy, and for freedom, together with his own glamorous persona, came to illustrate the very essence of the Romantic movement. Nevertheless, both Keats and Shelley used medieval politics to make contemporary points, notably about freedom. Shelley, strongly influenced by Schiller and the German Romantics, in *The Cenci*, his wife Mary in her novel *Valperga*, and Keats in his plays *Otho the Great* and *King Stephen*, did so.[59]

On the whole, there was relatively little straight 'medievalism', as opposed to more indirect reflections of it, in the works of Coleridge, Wordsworth or Byron. By contrast, it became absolutely overwhelming between the 1830s and the 1880, with Arnold, Rossetti, Morris, Swinburne and, towering above them, in contemporaries' views at least, Alfred, Lord Tennyson. Much of this Victorian medievalism in poetry is most specifically associated with the story of King Arthur, Tristan and Iseult, and the issues of chivalry, and needs to be treated as part of that trend.[60] But another aspect of medievalism overtook the Gothic novel in popularity, the historical novel.[61]

Was Walter Scott the first historical novelist? The debate is by no means settled. Leland's novel *Longsword* is set in the Middle Ages, based on a story told by the medieval chronicler Roger of Wendover. But Leland adapted this, picking and choosing what to include and what to leave out. Thus, for example, the original medieval miracle story is left out, as is religion in a general way – a not uncharacteristic eighteenth-century attitude; and Leland's hero is made to behave with the kind of 'progressive spirit' of the eighteenth century in his abhorrence of violence. Here, as in a few other novels set in a later period, for example in Sophia Lee's *The Recess* (1785), great liberties were being taken with the names, characters and events of history. Much more fundamentally, history was used as something 'personal', something in which major events were decided on by individuals in relation to their own affairs and interests. At this point, it was still possible to use the Middle Ages as a period when writers might take liberties with historical truth without well-known facts interfering with their narrative. Because relatively little was known, history could be invented rather than narrated.[62] Historical novelists, who were too far removed from the period in which they set their novels to understand in depth what happened, and possibly had no interest in doing so, wrote history as they believed and indeed wished it to have been.[63]

Walter Scott, rather than being necessarily the initiator of English historical fiction, was certainly a renovator of the genre.[64] *Ivanhoe* (1819) and *Quentin Durward* (1823) were hailed as models of novelty by contemporaries. Scott's knowledge of medieval literature was extensive and those attempting to trace it in his work mention anything from the Tristan stories, Chaucer and Malory to a vast number of romances and ballads, as well as Herder and Goethe's play *Götz von Berlichingen*.[65] What these combined influences brought him was the idea that social unity and a sense of community and good leadership were best exemplified in medieval society, and nostalgia for the order and virtues of that society as he saw it through the medium of chivalry. The way in which Scott's novels brought about a change from the Gothic novel lies both in his different narrative technique and in his creation of fictional characters. The latter not only enabled him to use well-researched and documented material with historical 'accuracy',

Nineteenth-century romancing of the Middle Ages. Knights and damsels: illustration from Sir Walter Scott's *Ivanhoe*.

but also to create secondary characters as heroes, so that he did not have to distort the historical material, but was still able to include adventures, love interests, triumph of good over evil and so on, which it would not have been possible to do with historical characters whose fate was too well documented. He could thus take into account the historical background itself, in terms of politics and society, which, because well researched, *felt* utterly authentic.

This is not to say that Scott's novels were devoid of anachronisms, especially in one respect, that of the divide and hostility which he introduced again and again, for example in *Ivanhoe* and in the *Tales of the Crusades*, between Saxons and Normans; the former all good, the latter all wicked. This line of thought continued through the influence of Scott on Romantic historians, in Scotland and in England, for example in William Hazlitt's *History of the Conquest*, and in France in Augustin Thierry's *History of the Norman Conquest*. Ultimately it contributed to the continuation of the cliché of the Norman Yoke, and has still not ceased to plague historical perception on the popular level, as it did for so long in Hollywood films, for example. Scott's understanding of the issue was not so much a matter of English nationalist feeling against the French Normans; it was part of the whole nineteenth-century attempt to create a blueprint for the idea of 'Britishness', that quality which would enable the conquest and rule of Victoria's empire.[66] Other historical novelists were doing the same, for example Bulwer Lytton in *Rienzi* (1835), *The Last of the Barons* (1843) and *Harold: The Last of the Saxon Kings* (1848), and Charles Kingsley in *Hereward the Wake* (1865). The latter two were yet more rewrites of the Norman Yoke myth, but they were also among the first English novels to deal with the growing myth of the Old North, Scandinavian and Viking past.[67] Apart from de la Motte Fouqué in Germany, only Walter Scott had previously written novels, *The Pirate* (1821) and *Count Robert of Paris* (1831), dealing with these stories. Like Scott, Bulwer Lytton and Kingsley were part of a 'Teutonic' tradition, which saw the Norman Conquest as part of the triumphant march of the British people, or, in some cases, as either a calamity which turned out to be necessary in order to create the new English people, or a success of the British because, despite the Conquest, they had survived and come out stronger. Moreover, the Normans could always be regarded not as French but as Vikings, and therefore of the same 'race' as the Anglo-Saxons. Bulwer Lytton, however, did criticise Scott, partly for historical inaccuracies, but even more because his own sense of the need for the use of documentary evidence led him to go back to using real historical characters, even when it meant cutting through the thick layer of accumulated myth and legend.[68] His novel *Rienzi*, based partly on Gibbon and on Sismondi's history of the Italian city-republics, led Bulwer Lytton to construct characters more attuned to the fourteenth-century people of Rome. Other novelists followed this lead, concentrating on detailed research on medieval documents, some-times, it was said, to the detriment of the book's quality and fluency, as was the case with George Eliot's *Romola* (1863), for which she went to Italy and spent many weeks researching the life of Savonarola and fifteenth-century Florence.[69] Her contemporary, the American Harriet Beecher Stowe, who published in the same year a novel set in Savonarola's Florence, *Agnes of Sorrento*, did not have much greater success. Even Browning, perhaps the least medievalising among the Victorians, wrote in 1840 his verse novel *Sordello* (whose hero is a poet known through Dante and said to have lived in thirteenth-century Ferrara), and made him a kind of proto-Romantic Shelley.

While the historical novel saw a slight decline towards the end of the cen-tury, it never disappeared, as witnessed by the success of Henry Rider Haggard, Arthur Conan Doyle and Robert Louis Stevenson.[70] In particular Rider Haggard and his predecessor G. W. Dasent were interested in what was happening at the northern end of Europe during the Viking Age. Rider Haggard's novel *Eric Brighteyes* (1891) is indeed a 'neo-saga' but it is also, more than the works of his contemporaries, a canvas on which he could paint some of the key themes we find in his other books.[71] Two such themes were the superiority of the 'Northman' (he described his hero Sir Henry Curtis, fighting like his blond Viking ancestors, in *King Solomon's Mines* – Teutonism was still at work) and of the strong Viking women, sexually dominant and possessors of knowledge (like Ayesha in *She*, but also like the contemporary New Woman of the 1890, the type of Nimue or Vivien about whom Victorians were increasingly uncomfortable).[72] On the whole, just as the Gothic novel had increasingly turned away from the historical, to become more and more involved with the supernatural, to the extent of gradually turning into the Fantastic genre of the kind represented by M. R. James's and some of Rudyard Kipling's stories or in American litera-ture by Nathaniel Hawthorne and Edgar Alan Poe, so the historical novel came to be more interested in the 'adventure story' element than in the his-torical part, in parallel with the development of the Boys' Own Paper kind of literature.

Walter Scott's influence remained paramount throughout the nineteenth century, well beyond the English-speaking world. His works were translated throughout Europe, and contributed greatly to the success of the historical novel in France, Italy (Manzoni's *I Promessi Sposi* of 1827 was modelled on Scott's novels, though it was not set in the Middle Ages), Germany (Theodor Fontane), Poland (Jan Potocki's *The Manuscript Found in Saragoza*) and even Russia (Leo Tolstoy), just as translations of Walpole's *Castle of Otranto* had contributed to the taste for the Romantic and Gothic in German literature in the eighteenth century.

3

Romantic Visions

Gothic architecture never disappeared completely in England, possibly on account of what Nikolaus Pevsner once called the innate English taste for the vertical and soaring, rather than the more fundamentally Mediterranean horizontal, in the round, Baroque.[1] While the Gothic had still retained some place at the Elizabethan and Jacobean courts and in domestic architecture, it effected its first serious comeback during the seventeenth-century rebuilding of many Oxford colleges, and even a few Cambridge ones like St John's (library, 1624) and Peterhouse ('Perpendicular' chapel, 1628).[2] A revived taste for the Gothic was behind the major restoration of Westminster Abbey, carried out between 1713 and 1725, first supervised by none other than Christopher Wren, and then by Nicholas Hawksmoor. Inigo Jones, who first used the Gothic in his designs for masques and the stage, later adopted it for various churches in London. His patron, later Bishop Cosin, subsequently took the style up with him to Durham and from there it spread to the north of England.

The main illustration of the seventeenth-century revival of Gothic architecture remains that of Oxford. From the first Oxford buildings, Oriel (1620–42) and University College from 1634, through the Bodleian Library Convocation House and Chancellor's Court (1634–37) and the Great Staircase of Christ Church (c. 1640), to the deliberate imitation of the Gothic in order to match existing architecture in Wren's Tom Tower (1681–82) and Hawksmoor's rebuilding of All Souls from 1716 onwards, the Gothic style continued to coexist with classical architecture. Its most flamboyant manifestation was its imitation of the Decorated style of fan vaulting, as seen, for example, in the Divinity School.

Sir John Vanbrugh, the ultimate 'classical' architect, did indeed design Castle Howard, but, when building his own house in London in 1717, he also used battlements, turrets and a Gothic gatepost. Such a mixture, which rapidly became the fashion, was dominant in the Picturesque style, which happily combined a mixture of elements from various periods as an alternative to pure classicism. A similar mix was displayed in one of the key architectural treatises of the earlier part of the eighteenth century, Batty Langley's *Gothic Architecture Improved by Rules and Proportions* (1747), which attempted to codify the Gothic into orders (a revealingly 'classical' mind frame), but also gave the first illustration of how to incorporate Goth-icising details into domestic architecture. This was to be the trademark of the so-called Gothick style, and its variations in the Rococo, Picturesque and Sublime, which remained dominant until the 1830s.[3]

The first signs of an actual revival of the Gothic,[4] which would consist of building afresh, by choice, in this style, were in fact to be found in landscape architecture. Such features as wilderness, asymmetry, the building of small Gothic temples, mock ruins and other small follies (set up as early as 1717 at Shotover in Oxford), were even more common than we realise, since many were built of perishable materials such as canvas and painted plaster. They were already used on a large scale by William Kent (who had been respon-sible for the restoration work at several cathedrals, for example Gloucester in 1741), before Humphry Repton turned them into indispensable garden features later. This form of architecture was popular with amateur gentle-men architects, who just wanted something evocative of the Middle Ages. By that stage, Gothic was becoming increasingly acceptable as an alternative style, first of all for ecclesiastical, then for domestic, architecture. It was compounded by the Romantic perception of nostalgia and contemplation of the ephemeral:

> In considering a decaying Palace, or ruined Castle, we recollect, that it was the seat of some great lord, or warlike Baron, and recur to the history of the gal-lant actions which have been atchieved [sic] on that spot, or are led to reflect on the uncertainty of all human grandeur, both perhaps, from the fate of its lordly owner, and its own tottering state.[5]

Manifestations of the Picturesque Gothick (a wild rather than classically ordered landscape, a cult of 'ruins' first developed by the Grand Tour, the-atrical trompe-l'oeil) made up the very characteristic English garden from the eighteenth century onwards, and this eventually crossed over to the Continent with great success. It became the 'jardin anglais' in France (for example at Rousseau's Ermenonville, the Bagatelle Garden in the Bois de Boulogne and the Parc Monceau in Paris), in Germany at Wörlitz Castle, in Sweden, Central Europe and as far afield as Russia.

The domestic Gothic Revival on a large scale began with two houses, both restored or rebuilt by gentlemen amateurs: Roger Newdigate at Arbury Hall (begun in the mid 1750s, finished in the 1790s); and Horace Walpole at Strawberry Hill, his house in Twickenham (1747 to 1796). Both attempted to do erudite research in the study of period details, and were influenced by the restoration of Henry VII's chapel at Westminster (and by French Gothic, for example Rouen Cathedral for Strawberry Hill). Both used an elaborate interpretation of the Gothic architectural language, especially in those rooms deemed to be most appropriate for it, the library and the hall. By 1750 Walpole had turned away from a classical taste and proclaimed, 'I am going to build a little Gothic castle at Strawberry Hill' as 'one has a satisfaction in imprinting the gloomth of abbeys and cathedrals on one's house'. Rejecting a friend's offering of a Roman artefact for the house, he assured him that 'I have done with virtú and deal only with the Goths and Vandals'.[6]

Since Walpole not only remodelled the house but, after 1760, actually added to it with new building work, his scope was wider than Newdigate's. The most famous room at Strawberry Hill, partly designed by the owner himself, was the library. Typically, it was approached from the armoury, in which Walpole had placed part of his collection of suits of armour. The library itself had arches filled with stained glass on one side, and Gothic bookcases, designed (from remaining drawings) on the model of the arched doors into the choir of Old St Paul's. The arches could be swung away for those wanting to read those books hidden behind the elaborate carving of the upper part of the cases, along which ran a frieze of medieval motifs. The chimney-piece blended the features of two medieval tombs from Westminster Abbey and Canterbury, and framed a painting on a medieval topic. The most renowned feature of the room was its extravagantly rich painted ceiling, with the Walpole arms in the middle, surrounded by the coat of arms of the families with whom the Walpoles had been allied by marriage, and by the crest and motto of the family. Armoured knights charged across the background, helms and shields defined the corners, all this, like the whole room, painted in strong blues and reds, and glowing with colour from the paint and stained glass. Even the less obviously medieval rooms had some Gothic feature added to them: the dining room, called the refectory, had stained glass, and the Holbein chamber an ecclesiastical-looking chimney-piece. In the newly-added part of the house, Walpole wanted to build a 'gallery, a round tower, a large cloister and a cabinet, in the manner of a little chapel',[7] in Gothic style going from the simplest to the most ornate. The cloister, with its vaulted roof and plain arches, reflected the first; the gallery above, supported by buttresses, was an example of the second. Throughout the house, Walpole displayed examples from his collection of medieval armoury, and added 'Gothic features' such as mock medieval tombs, alcoves for bedrooms, and a general orgy of pointed arches and vaulting. Walpole's reputation as a writer, together with his publication in 1774 and 1784 of the *Description of Strawberry Hill*, which gave detailed recordings of his architectural work for what was effectively the first house to be completely designed and remodelled as Gothic, inside and out, contributed very largely to the renaissance of the medieval Gothic, as opposed to its reinterpretation through the eclectic mix of styles of the early eighteenth century.

Gothic took hold of people's imagination, and this in turn fed into the need for more Gothic designs for furnishings, chairs, bookcases and other pieces, which figured in such treatises as Thomas Chippendale's manual of 1754. The movement grew and even reached architects like Robert Adam, who used Gothic designs for Alnwick Castle in Northumberland in the 1780s. The importance of Alnwick in the history of the Gothic Revival is considerable, since it was one of the first castles to be restored and redecorated in Gothic style, shortly to be followed by others, similarly restored or rebuilt from the mid eighteenth century onwards, both in England and in Scotland. Some such castles belonged to aristocrats who could trace their lineage back to the medieval period, others to patrons who were Roman Catholics, thus highlighting the association made between the Gothic and medieval Catholicism, which would become such a dominant feature of A. W. N. Pugin's life in the following century. Several Catholic families in Oxfordshire, for example at Stonor Park and Milton Manor, Gothicised their houses in this manner. So did many gentry in Ireland, which saw a great enthusiasm for the style during the eighteenth century, perhaps in part for the same reasons. More often than not the revival was due to owners with enthusiastic antiquarian interests. By the second half of the eighteenth century there was already a sizeable group of gentry with such antiquarian tastes, interested in the Middle Ages and in building or rebuilding Gothic country houses.

The infatuation with Gothic architecture was not confined to the aristocracy and gentry, it was adopted by the king himself. In 1800 George III appointed James Wyatt his personal architect, thus enabling him, as Crown Surveyor, to have a great deal of influence in the widespread acceptance of Gothic architecture. Wyatt had worked, controversially, on the restoration of Salisbury Cathedral, then, much more successfully, on that of the chapel of Henry VII at Westminster; later, he was commissioned to Gothicise the royal apartments at Windsor and to work on William Beckford's house at Fonthill. Beckford, famous also as a writer, notably for his novel *Vathek*, had a reputation for being a voracious collector of medieval antiquities. Fonthill used English Gothic as a basis but Beckford also borrowed features from some of his favourite buildings in Portuguese Gothic, the abbey of Batalha and the palace at Sintra near Lisbon. The opening of his house to visitors before its sale in 1822, and the printed Christie's catalogue for that sale, contributed further to the popularisation of the Gothic style. Wyatt died in 1813, but his nephew Jeffry Wyatt (later known as Wyatville) was commissioned to build a new palace in Gothic style at Kew, and George IV later again commissioned work at Windsor, where remodelling in medieval style was carried out, especially on St George's Hall.

Because Windsor was perceived to be the symbolic heart of the British monarchy, Gothic was seen more and more as *the* 'national' or 'native' style of architecture. It was already perceived as such during and after the French Revolution in the 1780s and 1790s, when it was described as the style clearly best suited to the climate and materials of the British Isles, just as the Classical was best suited for the Mediterranean. The most vocal advocate among Gothicists was John Carter (1748–1817), a gentleman and dilettante who wrote more than 380 articles over twenty years in the *Gentleman's Magazine* and contributed a corpus of drawings of English cathedrals.[8] His contemporary John Britton (1771–1857), a topographer, Gothicist and defender of the style as a national feature, carried out major recording work of English antiquities, churches and public buildings throughout the counties.[9] Carter and Britton both advocated a move away from the Gothick, which they regarded as theatrical, inaccurate, a product of imagination and sentiment rather than of archaeological and scientific work. Both contributed considerably to the shift from one to the other between the 1780s and the 1830s. By the 1830s the debate on the nature of Gothic as a national style was also still active, although the theory had been increasingly challenged by the likes of G. D. Whitington, who strongly argued for French origins. The patriotic argument then shifted to accepting these foreign origins but arguing that, nevertheless, it was in England that the style had achieved its perfection and reached its apogee.[10]

By the 1820s the public taste for Gothic was paramount: castle-building and remodelling continued, with architects such as Nash, Smirke and Lugar working in England, and William Atkinson in Ireland and especially Scotland, where Walter Scott had created at his own house, Abbotsford, the new style later known as Scottish Baronial.[11] Castles were built and rebuilt because they were Romantic, picturesque, suggested ancient lineage and authority, drew attention to the owner's generous display of hospitality in the baronial hall, and recollected knights and damsels. Following Scott's example, landowners exhibited heraldry and weapons in great halls and on grand staircases, a fashion partly begun by Walpole. It became all the rage as more and more dealers in London, such as Samuel Grose, began to trade in arms and write treatises on them. 'Armouries and halls full of armour were fast becoming the mid-nineteenth-century equivalent of the sculpture galleries of Georgian country houses'.[12] What these landowners built was of course a modern house, with all the convenience and comfort expected, to which were added various turrets, crenellations and battlements, without any particular interest in authenticity: it was the picturesque skyline which

mattered. Similarly, throughout the nineteenth century, whether in remod-
ellings, as at Hampton Court in the 1830s, Alnwick in 1854–65 or Cardiff
Castle in 1868–85, or when building from scratch, at Arundel Castle in
1879–90 or the extraordinary confection at Castell Coch near Cardiff
(1872–79), comfort was never sacrificed to the taste for medievalism. This
was either a matter of additions to the overall view and silhouette of the
castle, or simply of shaping contemporary objects into a medieval mould,
such as the water-closet in the master bedroom of Castell Coch, built to
imitate King Arthur's throne. The purpose remained 'the preservation of
the medieval character of a house while making improvement conducive to
modern living', an idea which would be embraced with great enthusiasm by
the middle classes too.[13]

The popularity of the Gothic meant that, while in the eighteenth century
the style had been widespread essentially among the aristocracy and the
gentry, the explosion of literature and pattern books of the nineteenth century made the fashion available to the middle classes. They too increasingly
used the same architectural vocabulary to build their suburban villas, in a
combination of imitation of their betters, and of fashion. Books of ornamental design including Gothic furnishings and interiors were written to
cater for the upwardly-mobile middle classes. Their titles are significant in
themselves: E. Gyfford's *Designs for Elegant Cottages and Small Villas
(Calculated for the Comfort and Convenience of Persons of Moderate and
Ample Fortune)* in 1806, or G. Smith's *Repository of the Arts*, which included
designs for such items as a Gothic state bed on a dais and a baby's cradle
with pinnacles and tracery, were aimed at 'making the grander appearance
of a country house available to those who could only afford a cottage'.[14]
The overwhelming number of Gothic houses in the newly-established suburbs of major towns, whether they were built for rising tradesmen or
industrialists in northern towns, or for university dons in North Oxford, is
a clear testimony of the popularity of the crenellated medieval fancies
among the growing urban bourgeoisie. The craze for the style went further
down still, with whole Gothic terraces in areas of London, or the artisan
Gothic village in Highgate, built by Angela Burdett-Coutts to see from her
mansion window.

While new castles and houses were being built, painters and draughts-
men, notably Turner, recorded old ones. Another such recorder was
A. C. Pugin, a French refugee who published one of the first standard books
on medieval architecture, the *Cathedral Antiquities* (1814–35). Even more
important as a reference work was Thomas Rickman's *An Attempt to Dis-
criminate the Styles of English Architecture from the Conquest to the
Reformation*, first published in 1817 but so successful as a textbook that it

was continually reprinted until 1881. Although not quite the first to study the chronology of medieval architecture (this was probably John Aubrey, d. 1697, in his *Chronologia Architechtonica*),[15] he was the first to define it in the terms we still use today: Norman, Early English, Decorated and Perpendicular. Others, like J. C. Loudon, wrote treatises used as far afield as the Russian Court, where a Scottish architect built a Gothic 'Cottage' for Nicholas I's residence at Petershof, and especially in North America, where British cultural influence remained strong. Loudon was recast, to suit American taste, by A. J. Downing in the 1840s and 1850s, and was still used by Downing's colleague A. Jackson-Davies, who designed the best known American Gothic villa at Knoll, part of a group of houses built along the Hudson River valley as an artists' colony. Pattern books were sought after especially in such places as North America or Ireland, where there were relatively few local architects available, but great popular enthusiasm for the Gothic at all levels in society, and where one had to adapt general patterns and materials to native resources. Objects with Gothic ornamentation or made in the medieval style were greatly sought after, including portraits of the owners in medieval dress, medieval-looking chapels and libraries, and generally any kind of Gothic feature. Significantly, in America, the owners, except perhaps for major millionaire collectors like Pierpont Morgan, were indifferent as to whether the objects they owned were actually medieval, or artefacts of the Gothic Revival and Arts and Crafts movements. 'Medieval' was not superior to 'Gothic Revival': what mattered was that the elite which commissioned objects attributed some kind of moral, if not social, superiority to Gothic art, especially in that it meant the opposite of 'factory-made'. Bespoke objects belonged, by definition, to a 'better period', and to own them was to display that superiority.

The price of such popularity was a growing reaction of unease in the second half of the century against the risks of 'debasement' of the style, and a call for greater accuracy in the recreation of medieval architecture and decoration, as well as greater preoccupation with its original religious background. The leader of this movement was the greatest architect of the Gothic Revival, Augustus Welby Pugin (son of A. C.).[16] Born in 1812, he began his career as a talented designer, producing, for example, the greatly praised medieval costumes and sets for a successful opera based on Scott's *Kenilworth*. Widely-travelled, a great collector of antiquities, King William IV's favourite designer of furniture, Pugin was particularly attracted by the late Gothic in its more elegant and delicate form. He remained throughout his life greatly concerned with the need for a scholarly approach, opposing what he regarded as a 'travesty of style' through its popular appeal. Equally, he rejected superfluous ornamentation, which was not there to serve a specific purpose, as he thought it would have done in the medieval period. His ideas were first enshrined in his 1835 book on *Gothic Furniture in the Style of the Fifteenth Century*, and subsequently in his three well-known treatises, *Contrasts: or A Parallel Between the Noble Edifices of the Middle Ages and the Corresponding Buildings of the Present Day, Showing the Present Decay of Taste* (1836), *The True Principles of Pointed or Christian Architecture* (1841), and *An Apology for the Revival of Christian Architecture in England* (1843). These works were written after his much-publicised conversion to Roman Catholicism, and he repeatedly proclaimed his belief that Roman Catholicism was the true representation of medieval Christianity, that an 'appreciation of Gothic architecture was indissoluble from belief in religion', and that the 'excellence of Gothic Architecture was the product of the religious faith of the architects of the Middle Ages'.[17] Hence the implication of the subtitle of his 1836 book, which linked Christian belief to artistic brilliance, that architecture had been steadily declining since the Gothic period, and that this phenomenon was due largely to the loosening up of its links with the Christian faith. Since that faith alone had produced such great architecture, it followed that Gothic was the only genuinely great style in architecture, and the only one to be followed on moral grounds. The point was made most forcibly through a series of contrasting and facing plates under the title of 'Noble Edifices of the Middle Ages, and Corresponding Buildings of the Present Day', notably in the two plates illustrating a Catholic town in 1444, with its saints' names and church spires, and the same town in 1844, where the skyline displays a multiplicity of nonconformist chapels, gas and iron works, a gaol and a lunatic asylum.

Pugin's first major commissions were the remodelling of Scarisbrick Hall, belonging to the Catholic Charles Scarisbrick, begun in 1837, and of Alton Towers (1847–51), home of another Roman Catholic aristocrat, the Earl of Shrewsbury. He remains best known for his work on the most consider-able architectural project of the nineteenth century, the rebuilding of the Houses of Parliament. The old palace of Westminster had been destroyed by a spectacular fire (immortalised by Turner) in 1834, and only Westminster Hall survived from the medieval building. A competition for the new palace of Westminster was won by Charles Barry. Barry was at first assisted by Pugin, who was eventually put in charge of the interior deco-ration in 1844. This included the woodwork, furniture, tiles, carpets, wallpapers, stencilled décor for ceilings and mouldings, metalwork and lighting, all done in fifteenth-century style and, according to Pugin's rules, without superfluous ornamentation and frills. An important innovation, of great consequences for the future, was Pugin's insistence on the fact that

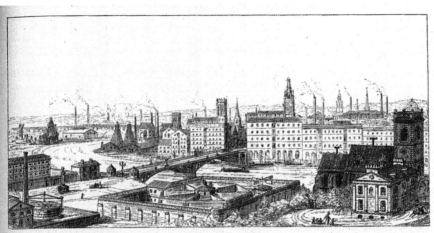

THE SAME TOWN IN 1840.

1. St Michaels Tower, rebuilt in 1750. 2. New Parsonage House & Pleasure Grounds. 3. The New Jail. 4. Gas Works. 5. Lunatic Asylum. 6. Iron Works & Ruins of St Maries Abbey. 7. St Evans Chapel. 8. Baptist Chapel. 9. Unitarian Chapel. 10. New Church. 11. New Town Hall & Concert Room. 12. Wesleyan Centenary Chapel. 13. New Christian Society. 14. Quakers Meeting. 15. Socialist Hall of Science.

Catholic town in 1440.

1. St Michaels on the Hill. 2. Queens Cross. 3. St Thomas's Chapel. 4. St Maries Abbey. 5. All Saints. 6. St Johns. 7. St Peters. 8. St Alkmunds. 9. St Maries. 10. St Edmunds. 11. Grey Friars. 12. St Cuthberts. 13. Guild hall. 14. Trinity. 15. St Olaves. 16. St Botolphs.

The Age of Faith and its moral lessons. Augustus Welby Pugin, *Contrasts*, a Catholic Town in 1840 and 1440.

medieval art was fundamentally based on two-dimensional patterns, *not* on
the standard post-Renaissance three-dimensional perspective. All decorative
items were designed in two dimensions, without attempting to give the illusion of depth or perspective. This wish to discard the by then accepted
system of post-Renaissance perspective shows Pugin to have been one of
the few theorist who actually understood the nature of medieval art. In
addition, it makes him the originator of a major turning-point in western
art, and a precursor of the art of the future in its abstract form in the twentieth century. Following these principles, and with the help of a team of
skilled craftsmen and manufacturers such as Minton and Crace, Pugin's
decorative scheme was revealed when the House of Lords opened in 1847.
The overall theme stressed the medieval origins of the parliamentary system,
with statues of the barons who had made King John sign Magna Carta.
Contributing to the impression of magnificence were the angels modelled
on those from the timbered roof of Westminster Hall (*c.* 1399), a three-part
throne on a dais covered by a carved and gilded canopy (still in use today
for the State Opening of Parliament by the Sovereign), stained glass, pan-
elling, woodwork, and brass light-fittings. The whole edifice caught the
public eye and imagination to such an extent that the model, regarded as
a symbol of the medieval origins of the parliamentary system, was adapted
and reused for Parliament buildings throughout Europe and North America. Pugin's last major project was the preparation of the Medieval Court
for the Great Exhibition of 1851 at Crystal Palace.[18] When it opened, and
on account of the thousands of visitors it attracted, this was a triumph for
him and for the Gothic Revival, and ensured Pugin's reputation after his
death in 1852, as well as his enormous impact on Victorian architects of the
second half of the century.

   Pugin had several successors. The first was his associate J. G. Crace, who,
together with Pugin's son, continued the work at Westminster (the Queen's
Robing Room) and Scarisbrick Hall (the stables), with features increasingly
more continental and 'Flamboyant' in style, and more wedded to the fantasy, if not actual 'story book' element of the Gothic, popular in France
and Germany. The other two were George Gilbert Scott and John Francis
Bentley. Scott, best known for his building of St Pancras Station and of the
Albert Memorial in the 1860s, was deeply involved with the contemporary
reform of church architecture and ritual of the Church of England, being
a major figure of the Ecclesiology movement. Bentley was the architect of
the Roman Catholic cathedral of Westminster. Also involved with the High
Church revival was William Butterfield, whose major projects were the
church of All Saints Margaret Street in London and Keble College in
Oxford, and whose work was the inspiration behind various cathedrals

in the New World, such as Adelaide and Melbourne in Australia, and Fredericton in Canada. The Pugin and Scott tradition centred on the great richness of the Perpendicular Gothic ornamentation. Another, newer tradition, inspired by Ruskin's *The Stones of Venice* (1853), had appeared by the 1850s: polychromy. This followed from the 1820s discoveries that both classical and medieval monuments had been in fact coloured. It prompted both the development of colour in the ornamentation, and that of polychromy within the architectural materials themselves, for example in the use of contrasting building materials such as brick and stone simultaneously. This 'Italianate' Gothic inspiration, seen for example in Oxford at the University Museum (begun in 1855), Keble College and St Barnabas' church, or in the Gothic Museum in Dublin, was represented at its most alluring at All Saints Margaret Street, through the use of red and black bricks in bands, and the alternating coloured stone and marble, deliberately reminiscent of Sienese architecture. The other major architect of the Italianate Gothic style was George Edmund Street, a pupil of Scott, to whom both William Morris and his friend Philip Webb had been apprenticed. Best known for his Law Courts in London in the 1860s, Street too sought inspiration from all over the Continent, going back to the thirteenth and early fourteenth centuries (unlike Pugin's fifteenth-century taste), and using building materials of different kinds to provide contrasts of colours and textures. His contemporary Alfred Waterhouse, who began his career in Manchester in 1856, then moved to London in 1865, was the architect of the town halls in Manchester and Reading, and by 1873 had started work on the Museum of Natural History in London, all on those same principles.

Throughout the century the restoration of medieval buildings had continued apace, sometimes contested in its process and result but seen as an indispensable component of contemporary Victorian culture. By the 1860s and well into the 1880s, most new institutional buildings in England, from schools, post offices, town halls, libraries and hospitals, to mansion blocks, factories, parsonages and churches, were also *built* in the Gothic style. Gothic railway stations expressed in some way the harnessing of the new power, the horses of the new age, within a 'medieval' shell; university buildings similarly harnessed the new learning and skills within the one style regarded as a symbol of cultural superiority, the Gothic. Civic buildings in particular were at the forefront of the trend. Using Gothic architecture in their case, especially in the successful industrial cities of the north, was a way of claiming a tradition of medieval descent, not, in this instance, from the aristocratic and feudal world, but from the merchants and craftsmen of the later Middle Ages, the free cities of Italy, Flanders and Germany, whose wealth was equally reliant on commerce and industry. The Lord Mayor of Birmingham expressed this when he said in 1874:

> We find in the old cities of the Continent – of Belgium, and Germany, and Italy – the free and independent burghers of the Middle Ages have left behind them magnificent palaces and civic buildings – testimonies to their power and public spirit and munificence, memorials of the time when those communities maintained the liberties and protected the lives of the people against the oppression, and the tyranny, and the rapacity of their rulers.[19]

Neo-Gothic buildings included, for example, the Wool Exchange (1864) and the Town Hall (1873) in Bradford, and the Middlesbrough Town Hall (1883–89). The most extensive and often cited example is Manchester itself.[20] Between the late 1850s and 1900, the Assize Court, the Albert Memorial, the Bridgewater Buildings, the Town Hall, the Reform Club, the Prudential Assurance and the John Rylands Library were all built in neo-Gothic style, some by major architects such as Alfred Waterhouse (the Town Hall). In this, the most successful industrial city of the north, using medievalism as a symbol of modernity was a demonstration of the middle-class aspiration to be part of what was perceived as the style of 'culture', as well as serving as a focus for civic pride and the affirmation of a new identity. The use of the Gothic as an illustration of successful British industrial culture in the Victorian era found its most striking expression in the large amount of new Gothic building work outside Europe, in the Empire. A good example of this is Bombay, which went through such a phase of High Victorian Gothic from the 1860s, with key buildings such as the Secretariat, the University, the Post Offices and the Victoria Terminus Railway Station.[21]

This was also the second age of Gothic churches, either built or restored by Victorian architects, some of whom were violently criticised for it by their contemporaries. One needs only to mention anew the way in which the work carried out at Tewkesbury Abbey and Street's restoration of Burford church in Oxfordshire in 1876 prompted William Morris to set up his Society for the Protection of Ancient Buildings, nicknamed anti-SCRAPE. Such restoration was equally vilified by twentieth-century purists, at least until the tide began to turn with the publication in 1928 of Kenneth Clark's *Gothic Revival*, and of Pevsner's work, and the later foundation of the Victorian Society in 1958. This phase of the Gothic Revival was also extremely popular in America,[22] where Venetian-style palazzi were built in New York. Episcopalian churches adopted the Gothic style. Earlier this had remained the prerogative of the Methodist, Baptist and Presbyterian churches, which had created pastiches of the Italianate 'Early Christian' and Byzantine style, as in the Judson Memorial Baptist Church in New York, built between 1888 and 1893. American firms of architects such as Cram and Wentworth, and Maginnis and Walsh, gained numerous commissions to design churches and buildings on university campuses in neo-Gothic style, known in America as Collegiate Gothic.[23] Cram, who had begun his medievalist career as a disciple and admirer of Morris, and had written both poetry and prose on medieval themes, was best known for his commission to Gothicise the cathedral of St John the Divine in New York, and to rebuild the Military Academy at West Point and the campus at Princeton. Maginnis and Walsh were responsible for the Gothic design of many university campuses, including Notre Dame and Boston. Furthermore, designers like the Englishman Charles Eastlake popularised the style to the extent that 'Eastlake furniture' came to be seen as an equivalent of Gothic furniture, and the American revival of the fashion for stained glass, spectacularly displayed by Louis Comfort Tiffany, was an indirect effect of the taste for medieval crafts and creations.

This second phase of the neo-Gothic style, which claimed to go back beyond the refinement of the later Gothic, which had been Pugin's favourite, to the more 'primitive', severe, massive, powerful style of the earlier Gothic, was very much in evidence at the International Exhibition of 1862. One of the main talents to emerge at the Exhibition was William Burges, who had helped design the Medieval Court and whose talent had been launched when he won the competition for the restoration of Lille Cathedral in 1855. Burges was a friend of Rossetti and the Pre-Raphaelites, and a protégé of the third Marquess of Bute, an immensely rich young aristocrat with a passion for the Gothic. He did his best known work for the latter, who commissioned him to restore Cardiff Castle, and to build Castle Coch nearby, with its riot of colours and designs.[24] Both these buildings reflect Burges's eclectic taste, which drew on Assyrian, Pompeian, Arabic, Indian and Japanese inspiration, as well as on fourteenth-century French and Italian Gothic. His great model was the fourteenth-century-architect Villard de Honnecourt's *Book of Drawings*. Burges's francophilia was strengthened by his friendship with one of the main figures of the French Gothic Revival, the archaeologist and antiquarian A. N. Didron, who founded in 1848 the journal *Annales Archéologiques*.

The trend towards both restoration and new building in the Gothic style was not restricted to England. After the wanton destruction of churches that followed in the wake of the French Revolution, restoration was very much at the forefront of the newly-founded Commission des Anciens Monuments in France, for whom Prosper Mérimée was Inspector-General, in charge between 1834 and 1852.[25] Though better known by his contemporaries as the author of the historical novel *Chronique du règne de Charles IX*, published in 1829, and by posterity as the author of the short story *Carmen*, Mérimée's role in French medievalism was essential as the promoter of a vast state-sponsored programme of restoration of castles, cathedrals, churches, town halls and other monuments, which he put in place, and for which he commissioned a full photographic record across France from Gustave Le Gray. He was directly responsible for the restorations of the Romanesque churches of St-Savin-sur-Gartempe and Ste-Foy of Conques, as well as for the cathedrals of Autun, Laon, Strasbourg, the Palais des Papes at Avignon and the castles of Chinon and Blois, among numerous other monuments. His taste for a strict historical and documentary approach to restoration, as well as his preference for the Romanesque over the Gothic, still unusual at this point, made him different in spirit from his otherwise friend Eugène Viollet-le-Duc, probably the best known French architect in charge of restoring and rebuilding medieval monuments.[26] However dubious his romanticizing fantasies may seem now, Viollet-le-Duc's work, for example at the castle of Pierrefonds near Compiègne, was greatly appreciated by his contemporaries both in France and outside it. Now regarded by French audiences as the ultimate example of bad taste nineteenth-century medievalism, Pierrefonds effectively introduced polychrome decoration, the restoration of stained glass and painted furniture inside restored medieval interiors. Viollet-le-Duc displayed great eclecticism in his choice of medieval inspiration, with painted sculpture and paintings from the whole spectrum of medieval art, including that of Norman Sicily. Although, like most medievalist architects of the day, such as Pugin, Viollet-le-Duc also looked to the so-called High Gothic (the thirteenth-century style of Rheims, Amiens and Westminster) as the incarnation of 'medieval' architecture, his purpose was to reconstruct a deliberately idealised building, even when knowing that the said building had actually never looked like that. He made the point in his major theoretical work, the *Dictionnaire raisonné de l'architecture française*: 'To restore a building is not just to preserve it, to repair it, and to remodel it, it is to re-instate it in a complete state such as it may never have been at any given moment'.[27]

Viollet-le-Duc was also responsible for major and invaluable work as the restorer of the walls of Carcassonne, and both the Sainte-Chapelle and Notre Dame in Paris, which was in such a state of decay that it might well not have survived without his intervention. He was also interested in the underlying principles of medieval art, and fought against the idea of simply reproducing it, rather than adapting it to express its own times. Such interpretation ultimately led to the kind of extraordinary mix which is the Gothic-Art Nouveau architecture represented, for example, by Antoni Gaudí's Sagrada Familia in Barcelona, Victor Horta's designs in Brussels and numerous *Jugendstil* then *Sezession* buildings in Vienna and post-Mucha in Prague.[28] Indirectly, though one cannot hold Viollet-le-Duc responsible for the Wagnerian theatrical mood of it, Ludwig of Bavaria's Neuschwanstein was also derived from this French revival. Although much of the Gothic Revival in France consisted of restoration rather than new building in the Gothic style, the latter did occur, for example in the Hôtel de Ville and the church of Ste-Clotilde (1846–1857) in Paris, Ste-Croix in Orléans, and St Nicholas in Nantes (1844–69).[29] About two hundred Gothic-inspired churches were built during the second half of the nineteenth century, many inspired by Viollet-le-Duc, and competitions took place, for example for the commission of the stained glass at Ste-Croix in Orléans.[30] Such new building in the Gothic style was advocated and supported by the two pioneering journals, Didron's *Annales Archéologiques* and the *Revue Générale de l'Architecture et des Travaux Publics*, both fighting against the classicism of the dominant Académie Royale des Beaux-Arts. The predominant influence on the building or rebuilding of churches, especially of cathedrals, remained Hugo's *Notre Dame de Paris*, whose influence both in the literary world and in popular imagination was paramount.[31] Preserving medieval cathedrals became a leitmotif at the end of the century: whether as a symbol of greatness of French art, the expression of the freedom of the people who built it against the oppression of the clergy, or a return to the Age of Faith of medieval Christianity, the cause breached the political and religious divide, and was championed by names as diverse as Charles Baudelaire, Emile Zola, Auguste Rodin, Paul Claudel and Maurice Barrès. It was described in scholarly terms for its iconography by the greatest contemporary art historian Emile Mâle; it also inspired musicians like Eric Satie to write pieces such as 'Quatre Ogives' and poets like Paul Verlaine, who wrote in 1881 'Sagesse':

> C'est vers ce Moyen Age énorme et délicat
> ... Guidé par la folie unique de la Croix
> Sur tes ailes de pierre, ô folle Cathédrale!

(It is toward the enormous and delicate Middle Ages/That my wounded heart must navigate ... On your wings of stone, oh wild Cathedral).[32] In an age strongly influenced by the idea of 'total work' pioneered by Wagner, it was felt to be the symbol of the wholeness of medieval art, the symbol of the French soul and the representation of the art of the community and faith, before commercial imperatives began to rule society. As such, it had to be preserved as a mix of art and religious faith, and not dismantled for political secular purposes, with its component parts ending up as artefacts in museums. These imperatives were repeatedly put forward by one of the great defenders of medieval art and churches, Joris Karl Huysmans (especially after his conversion to Catholicism), in his novels *La-Bàs, En route, La cathédrale* and *L'oblat*.[33] Marcel Proust was equally concerned to defend this heritage, not only when he wrote about churches, from Combray and Balbec to those of his Italian journeys, but also in a more direct political way. His text *La Mort des cathédrales* created a sensation when it was published in 1904, at the very moment that legislation was imminent to establish the Church and State separation:

> one sees the number of deputies who, when they have finished voting for anticlerical laws, leave to tour the cathedrals of England, France and Italy, bring back for their wife an old chasuble to make a coat or a door covering ... haggle with a secondhand dealer over the leaf of a retable, travel as far as the countryside to find fragments of choir stalls that will serve as umbrella stands for their antechamber, and go on Good Friday to the 'Schola Cantorum' ... to listen 'religiously', as one says, to the mass of Pope Marcellus ...[34]

The polemical tone of Proust's article brings forth another issue, which became dominant in late nineteenth-century France. The passion for introducing medieval art into the households of the middle classes, in the form of reproduction objects or fake stained glass, was spreading.[35] The French bourgeoisie could see innumerable replicas of museum objects, tapestries, manuscripts, furniture and others, in the rising number of popular illustrated journals, such as *La Gazette des Beaux-Arts* and *Le Figaro Illustré*. New printing techniques like heliogravure made such reproductions cheap and popular enthusiasm was enhanced by the illustrated articles showing the 'Gothic' houses and studies of famous men who collected medievalia, notably Emile Zola, Anatole France, Pierre Loti and other literary and artistic celebrities. Such indiscriminate collecting prompted debates about the trivialising of medieval art, just as they did at the same time in England. As a reaction to this, writers like Huysmans put forward the model of the discerning collector, des Esseintes or Durtal, who can tell the real from the fake medieval. The trend reached its height in the taste for decorating Parisian cabarets in Gothic style, thus associating the medieval with the nonconformity of students and artists and with the cult of Villon and Rabelais, who were said to be the ancestors of the tradition of the 'chansonniers'. Several such entertainment places and cafés were vying with each other for the most Gothic look, though they were probably all eclipsed by *Le Chat Noir*, the centre of this cult, run from 1881 by the eccentric Rodophe Salis, who dressed the medieval part.[36] Those same students were also in charge of running the medieval 'Feast of Fools' in the Latin Quarter in 1898, with the avowed purpose of reconstructing the atmosphere of Villon's Paris.[37]

But the most evident success of the medieval reconstruction, an ancestor of modern theme parks, came in 1900 at the Universal Exhibition. Two attractions were among the most visited: 'Paris in 1400' (a reconstruction of the Cour des Miracles, supposedly medieval but actually based essentially on Hugo's *Notre Dame de Paris*) and 'Le Vieux Paris: Fêtes, Jeux et Spectacles'. Both were essentially geared towards presenting the pageantry of royalty, as well as incorporating the commercial side of people's activities: visitors could purchase handmade objects by craftsmen working within the set-up, as well as cheaper machine-made objects of daily life. Almost the only missing aspects of this (secular) reconstruction was the presence of the church, at a time when the religious issue was the most contentious in French politics.

Even in Italy it was sometimes felt that the most appropriate style for church-building was the Gothic. The façade of the Duomo in Milan, first planned by Carlo Buzzi (*c.* 1608–1658), was eventually finished by Giuseppe Brentano in 1888; both plans were purely Gothic. In Germany too churches, palaces and 'ruins' were being built in Gothic style for princes across the empire at the end of the eighteenth and beginning of the nineteenth century.[38] The architect Friedrich Hoffstadt (1802–1846), known by his friends as 'Gothicus' on account of his obsession, founder of the 'Society of the Three Shields for the Study of German Antiquity', was the great reviver in Munich of the Gothic style, for the 'maintenance of the purity of German art and its redemption from the domination of foreign art and classical antiquity.'[39] He produced the *Gothic ABC Book: or Principles of the Gothic Style for Artists and Artisans*, highlighting the Christian dimension of Gothic art, to be united to German patriotic sentiment. Others saw in the Gothic the organic 'collective achievements' of the German people. Whatever their political tendency among both princes and theorists, everyone was in favour of carrying out the project which had become a symbol of the German national medieval past, the restoration between 1842 and 1880 of Cologne Cathedral. Architects of the 'Neugotik', for example August Reichensperger (1808–1895), who was famous for defining the style as based on 'religion, fatherland and art', G. G. Ungewitter (1820–1864) and Vincenz Statz (1818–1898), were building churches everywhere. These included small local ones, great civic ones like S. Apollinaris, Remagen (1839–43) and the Nikolaikirche in Hamburg (1863, but based on designs by G. G. Scott), Lutheran churches in the Romanesque or *Rundbogen* style.[40] Meanwhile Friedrich Eisenlohr (1805–1855) built a large number of Gothic railway stations all over Germany. After 1871 the doors were wide open and the neo-medieval was not only prominent but overwhelming in the architectural landscape, in national monuments like the Kyffhäuser, in the restoration of medieval castles, for example that of Goslar, capital of the Salian emperors,

or in the most functional of municipal architecture: town halls, train stations, public buildings, even factories. Austria also had its Gothic Revival
architecture, notably in such buildings as the Town Hall (1872–83) and the
Votivkirche (1854) in Vienna and it is there that the immediate descendant
of that style, as reinterpreted by its creator Walter Gropius (1883–1969),
would emerge in the *Bauhaus*.[41]

Throughout the nineteenth century a range of painters sought inspiration
in an imagined medieval past: Caspar David Friedrich and Albert Böcklin
in Germany, the Pre-Raphaelites and Watts in England, Gustave Moreau,
Odilon Redon and Pierre Puvis de Chavannes in France, and at the turn of
the nineteenth-twentieth centuries, Belgian symbolists like Fernand Khnopff.
This is a roll call of the best art produced during the period; one must never
forget, however, to look at run of the mill, indifferent or 'bad' art, which is
often more revealing of the overall Zeitgeist than that of the more talented,
and therefore, individual, artists.

Not a few among nineteenth-century artists deliberately chose to work
as part of a 'brotherhood', a concept which often owed its very existence
to a Romantic idea of medieval artisans' guilds or religious confraternities.
For the Nazarenes, the Pre-Raphaelites, the group of Russian artists at
Abramtsevo, the Visionists in Boston, the Nabis,[42] and the group of Pont
Aven in France, the Middle Ages stood as a model for the idea of artistic
purity. Medieval art was seen as a model of purity, piety and community, of
humility and anonymity of the artist, unconcerned by money and painting
only for the greater glory of God.[43] The medieval artist was seen as belonging to a classless, pre-capitalistic, non-commercial life, uncontrolled by a
bourgeois society through its commercial values and the official outlets of
galleries or the Salon. The Symbolists and the Nabis declared that to be the
only way to produce an art whose purpose was to serve God or a mystical
idea of the divine. Innumerable attempts were made to create monastic-type
communities of artists, with the artist identified with the ascetic medieval
'monk-painter', whose ultimate model was Fra Angelico. Even Van Gogh
dreamt of building such a community in Arles, with Gauguin as the 'abbot'.
The ideal was implemented in various ways and to various degrees, and
consisted of several features, such as physical separateness (beards, cloth-
ing), some ritual, and the adoption of a monastic style of communal life.
Huysmans, in *The cathedral* (1898), compared this kind of artist to the
painter-monk and the cathedral builder. He was one of the few actually to
create such a successful community when he took over the medieval abbey
of Ligugé and brought there artists to live together like oblate monks. In
some cases, an attraction for the national past and folk art, seen as the real

art of the people which went back to medieval roots, was also a component of the movement. As so often in the nineteenth century, these ideals reflected an avowed revulsion for the materialistic, industrialised and profit-dominated 'bourgeois' world and the desire to escape it through the return to an age deemed to have been purer, more spiritual and more creative on account of the individual production of artefacts and objects of daily life. This trend, proclaimed by William Morris and applied through the Arts and Crafts movement which he pioneered, was far-reaching. It manifested itself in different ways. Among the artists of the community at Abramtsevo in the 1870s it took the form of a return to the Russian medieval folk and rural roots of national art in their quest for national identity. Morris's Kelmscott Press created books modelled on medieval manuscripts. The American Visionists in their aptly-named journal, the *Knight Errant*, saw themselves as the 'new chivalry', in charge of rescuing art and beauty. Two of these nineteenth-century brotherhoods are particularly well-known, the Nazarenes and the Pre-Raphaelites.

The Gothicism of Caspar David Friedrich (1774–1840) belonged to the eighteenth rather than the nineteenth century, to the Romantic movement of Schlegel and Novalis, and of Friedrich's contemporary, the Swiss Heinrich Fuseli.[44] The titles of his landscape paintings are sufficient to give one an impression of what is being attempted: *Ruins at Dusk, The Cathedral, Abbey in the Woods, Church in the Woods, Owl in a Gothic Window, Dreamer in a Gothic Window, Castle Ruins.* Here the emphasis is on ruins, graveyards and abandoned churches in the mist and woods, all belonging to the phase of romanticising the past, turning it into symbols and allegories, and insisting on the beauty of nature and feelings rather than reason and intellect. Friedrich's Middle Ages were more of mood and feeling than a programme of return to the Gothic period, whether in terms of themes or techniques. The Nazarenes attempted both.

The Nazarenes were a group of German and Austrian painters who moved to Rome after 1808, to live in the disused convent of Sant' Isidoro.[45] Their official name as a group was the Lukasbund, referring to the medieval guild of painters (St Luke was the patron saint of painters in the Middle Ages), though they were called Nazarenes by their Roman contemporaries on account of their wearing long beards and long, flowing robes. Not only did they claim to live like a medieval guild, but their stylistic trademark was the return to the 'archaic', 'Gothic' style of Van Eyck and other Flemish painters, of Dürer and especially of Fra Angelico, their supreme model. Apart from the best known among them at the time, the Austrian count Julius Schnorr von Carolsfeld, the other members of the guild were first

Franz Pforr (who died in 1812) and Friedrich Overbeck (1789–1869), while after 1812 the group acquired another two members, Philippe Veit and the more aggressively nationalist Peter van Cornelius. Cornelius returned to Germany in 1819, when the group ceased to exist as such, and only Overbeck remained in Rome. Schnorr had been a well-known painter, employed by various princes including the king of Prussia, for whom he painted a whole series of frescoes illustrating the Nibelungen story in the Marmorpalais at Potsdam. He also illustrated literary works, notably de la Motte Fouqué's *Undine*.[46] Great historical cycles in fresco were one of the favourite media of the Nazarenes and among their best known were the allegories of Germany and Italy on the walls of their convent in Rome. The idea of great historical cycles in fresco was later pursued by other German painters, for example Alfred Rethel (1816–1859) in his Charlemagne frescoes at Aachen, and Hermann Wiscelinus who, between 1879 and 1897, decorated the newly restored imperial palace at Goslar. Great admirers of Wackenroder and Friedrich, the artists of the Lukasbund valued above all 'truth', 'authenticity', as against the artificiality of academic painting, and wished to be inspired by God and to paint with a 'pure heart', living for their art. It was an attempt to associate art and life by resurrecting the period which, for them, had seen such unity between the two.[47] The Nazarenes' influence was widespread among contemporaries as far as Russia, and they had considerable impact on various English painters, including Ford Madox Brown when he visited Rome, and a whole range of Victorian Establishment painters such as William Dyce and Daniel Maclise. Prince Albert was an admirer of the Nazarenes and consulted Peter van Cornelius when the issue of the decoration of the rebuilt Houses of Parliament arose. Overbeck was a favourite painter with the Tractarians during the Anglican Revival. The Nazarenes' influence was to be found in history painting, chivalry stories, and religious subjects, all three being also favourites of the Victorian Establishment.[48]

Victorian mainstream painting had a variety of strands, used at various times. Among them were large-scale historical paintings, social realism (Martineau, Elmore, W. P. Frith), domestic and morality scenes of modern life (James Tissot, Edward Lear, Stanhope Forbes), landscape painting, classical revival painting (Frederic Leighton, Sir Lawrence Alma-Tadema), academic portraits of the Winterhalter type and even, slightly closer to the medieval spirit, fairy paintings and illustrations (notably by John Everett Millais and John Noel Paton).[49] Specifically medieval themes were also very much in fashion. They are found in Benjamin West's paintings of episodes from the reign of Edward III in the King's Audience Chamber at Windsor Castle, in the redecoration of St George's Chapel, in the work of some of

Queen Victoria's favourite painters (Maclise, Paton, Landseer, Leighton), illustrators (Corbould, Franklin, Nixon), and even the photographer Octavius Hill. Particularly prestigious at the time was the work of the indifferent painter Dyce, commissioned by Prince Alfred to decorate the Queen's Robing Room in the new Houses of Parliament with scenes depicting the *Signing of Magna Carta, Edward III and the Order of the Garter* and *The Return of King Arthur*. Also in that room was the *Spirit of Chivalry* by Maclise, an artist otherwise famous among his contemporaries for his illustrations of de la Motte Fouqué's *Undine*. Abroad too academic painting used medieval topics – in France this is usually associated with the glorification of 'la patrie', in the work of the Salon painters of the later nineteenth century, for example François-Louis Dejuinne.

Another aspect of medievalist Victorian painting, originating with the popularity of Walter Scott, was the depiction of 'Merrie England'. The concept defined an age of tradition and social harmony, expressed through the patriarchal bounty of the upper classes dispensing largesse, wassail and mumming to the tenantry at Christmas, or the village festivals and agrarian traditions (maypole, reaping and harvest time, Morris dancing).[50] The nostalgia for 'olden times', felt to have been more harmonious than the present across the social scale, with relations of respective duty, protection and respect between the 'rustics' and landlords, be they 'barons' or monasteries, contributed to a spate of images, paintings or popular illustrations, and major names such as Daniel Maclise, Joseph Nash and Edwin Landseer were among the most prolific producers of such material.

The favourite themes of Victorian painting were chivalry, courtesy and romance, as well as Christian ecstasy and religious feeling. These are to be found in well known works like Watts's *Sir Galahad*, where they symbolise moral and spiritual values. Many less memorable painters, like Paton, painted Arthurian subjects. Another medieval favourite was the Crusades (Millais). At the end of the century and well into the beginning of the twentieth century, medieval themes were still fashionable in mainstream painting by John William Waterhouse and Walter Crane. While using the same subjects, another set of painters and artists, the Pre-Raphaelites, were nevertheless transforming their meaning entirely, in both visual art, poetry and prose.

The very different way in which medieval topics are illustrated in Victorian academic painting and in Pre-Raphaelite painting underlines the differences between their perception of the Middle Ages. The Pre-Raphaelite movement was a loose association, and was regarded as such even by contemporaries. It comprised in the first instance the Pre-Raphaelite Brotherhood, which

only lasted from 1848 to 1853, and included among its founding members
Dante Gabriel Rossetti. It subsequently shifted to a more diffuse movement
including Ford Madox Brown, Henry Holman Hunt and John Everett
Millais, before it was in effect dissolved, and its place taken by a new association of Rossetti, William Morris and Edward Burne-Jones from the late
1850s onwards.[51] These extremely different men, as well as the women
painters associated with the movement, notably Elizabeth Siddall and
Joanna May Joyce, began by sharing some ideals, but eventually went their
own separate ways. Madox Brown, Holman Hunt and Millais became
increasingly closer to mainstream contemporary painting in their choice of
themes and style. Meanwhile Rossetti, Burne-Jones and Morris went in their
own individual ways towards greater aestheticism and new media. More
importantly, and in contrast with most of their contemporaries, Rossetti and
Morris, however different they may have been in the end, did not see
medievalism as an escapist attitude, but as one which used an ancient period
in order to express revolutionary and modern views. They both regarded
their use of the medieval as a modern interpretation, a way of renewing the
art and views of their own time, by removing the syrupy bland moralistic
nature of their contemporaries' output, and returning to the purity and
force of the 'primitive'. The way they carried out their purpose was, however, different. Rossetti sought to transform the alleged Age of Faith and
religion into a form of sacramentalised love or erotic religiosity (the Blessed
Damozel is not an imitation but a reversal of Dante, with the lady in Heaven
longing for her lover on earth in an overwhelmingly erotic mode),[52] while
Morris reinterpreted the medieval through his opposition to the restoration
of medieval buildings and through his socialist stance.

Like the Nazarenes the Pre-Raphaelites also strove for deliberate Gothicism, for the 'archaic' and 'pure' style of Italian painters before the
Renaissance, Giotto and Fra Angelico. Their other great models were
Benozzo Gozzoli, Ghiberti, Masaccio, Ghirlandaio, Memling and Van Eyck,
Dürer, and the frescoes from the Campo Santo in Pisa. Rossetti's understanding of the Pre-Raphaelites' medievalism consisted in highlighting the
absence of perspective and of chiaroscuro, a hard-edge modelling with stiff
and angular attitudes, and emaciated figures,[53] and other pre-Renaissance
techniques. The Pre-Raphaelites' aspirations grew out of the medievalism
of the Romantic movement, and rejected the 'great historical scenes' of
Victorian academic painters like Eastlake or Landseer, even when these
were using medieval themes. The Pre-Raphaelite view was that individual
feeling and the artist's identity had been freer in the Middle Ages than during and after the Renaissance. People's passions had been more intensely
expressed, and one could only express them again in a comparable manner

by using the medieval period as a setting. Hence they tried to revive this 'freedom' as a contrast to the industrial, increasingly mass-produced present of nineteenth-century Britain. The way to do this was to return to medieval techniques, pigments (first oil paints, with the resulting vibrant colours), and media (in particular that of the fresco, church panels and altarpieces), as well as to medieval themes.

Whether inspired by chivalry and love, or religious themes, the work of the Pre-Raphaelites was mainly focused on individual moments and scenes, rather than on narratives, as in Rossetti's *Girlhood of the Virgin* (1848) or Morris's *La Belle Iseult or Queen Guinevere* (1858). Madox Brown (*The Black Prince, Jesus Washing Peter's Feet*) and Holman Hunt (*Rienzi Vowing to Obtain Justice*) and Millais (*Christ in the House of his Parents*) increasingly adopted the spirit of mainstream painting in their historical scenes, chivalry, the Grail themes, even as these became part of the standard vocabulary of Victorian medievalism with Tennyson and Watts. Moreover, they turned to landscape painting and subjects drawn from modern life with moral overtones (Ford Madox Brown's *The Last of England*, Holman Hunt's *The Awakening Conscience*). Even Rossetti, Morris and Burne-Jones, as well as Arthur Hughes, were together involved in the grand work of repainting the Debating Room of the Oxford Union in Oxford with illustrations from Malory's *Morte d'Arthur*. Nevertheless, a strong focus on love, as emotion but also and increasingly as physical passion, was clear from the first, especially in Rossetti's painting and poetry. Some members of the group moved away from this strand and perhaps in the process became more 'respectable', and their painting more sentimental; even their medievalism was more often drawn from Tennyson (*Mariana, The Lady of Shalott*), than from medieval material. Meanwhile the publicly criticised and 'scandalous' love theme came increasingly to the fore in the work of Morris, Burne-Jones and Rossetti from the late 1850s onwards.[54] Lancelot and Guenevere's story (involving passion and adultery) was their favourite medieval theme, rather than Arthur, knighthood or the Grail. Rossetti in particular, who had translated Dante's *Vita Nuova*, depicted medieval heroes in the throes of love, both in his paintings and his poetry. His figures were Lancelot and Guenevere, Dante and Beatrice, Paolo and Francesca, and even sensous imaginary women, in erotic, as well as sometimes exotic, contexts (*The Blessed Damozel, Beata Beatrix, Bocca Bacciata* from Boccacio's *Decameron, Astarté*). Many were based on representations of his wife or mistresses, including the renowned beauty Janey, William Morris's wife. Burne-Jones too used medieval themes in a similarly erotic context, as in his *Laus Veneris* (based on Wagner's *Tannhäuser*) and the *Beguiling of Merlin*, both of the 1870s. Both painters wished to highlight the strength of a transcendental mystery, as well as that of primeval forces: nature, love and sexual attraction, and their glorification of seductive womanhood, offering love beyond the constraints of society's bounds, whether in adultery or as 'free love'. Rossetti's work in painting and poetry grew increasingly closer to the more blatant manifestations of Aestheticism and became a major influence on it, and later on Symbolism, in the art of both England and the Continent.

It has not been uncommon for critics to regard the later work of the Pre-Raphaelites as being in fact the British version of the European Symbolist movement: in 1997, an exhibition held at the Tate Gallery under the title *The Age of Rossetti, Burne-Jones and Watts: Symbolism in Britain, 1860–1910*, made this point forcefully.[55] The influence of the Pre-Raphaelites, especially perhaps of Burne-Jones, on European Symbolism is undeniable. When Burne-Jones's six-piece 'Quest of the Grail' tapestry was displayed at the 1900 Paris Exhibition, its success was considerable.[56] The monastic brotherhood of artists, producing numerous journals with medievalising titles, such as *L'Imagier, Le Saint-Graal, Durendal, Le Trêve-Dieu*, published texts and reproductions of medieval artefacts, or imitations thereof. Above all, the journals disseminated the avant-garde work of Symbolist artists such as Jean Moréas, Redon and Puvis de Chavannes. They publicised these painters' and illustrators' use of medieval topics and techniques, including the flat frescoes and tempera painting, as well as their rejection of perspective, chiaroscuro, and their attempts to return to the 'naïve', hieratic mode of the Middle Ages.

Even more revealing of the common ground of these artists is the presence of certain themes, such as death-in-love or love-in-death, and the sensuous emphasis on women's hair (Rossetti's *Blessed Damozel* and other paintings, Maeterlinck then Debussy's *Pelléas and Melisande*).[57] The choice of medieval allegorical fresco painting like *Inspiration Chrétienne* (1886) by Puvis de Chavannes also has a Pre-Raphaelite history. The similarities are perhaps more of 'feel', of the interest in the beautiful, the allegorical, the otherworldly, mist-obscured mysterious or exotic. These are the characteristics of Symbolist prose and poetry.[58] The 'feel' was especially strong in painting: Moreau, Redon, Félicien Rops and Puvis de Chavannes, then the Salon des Rose + Croix of Péladan, including the painters Roualt and Felix Valloton, in France, Böcklin and Fernand Hodler in the German-speaking world, the Czech Alfons Mucha, and later Fernand Khnopff and James Ensor in Belgium.[59] European Symbolism was indeed a return to the Middle Ages up to a point,[60] but the Symbolists were particularly motivated by the idea of decadence and aesthetic principles of 'art for art's sake'. The closest one may find to Symbolism in England would probably be Oscar Wilde's

Salomé and the illustrations of Aubrey Beardsley and Arthur Rackham. The subject of these works was not necessarily medieval as such (apart from Moreau's occasional forays such as *St George and the Dragon* or *The Unicorns*, or the Pelléas story, or the stylistic inspiration of medieval mille-fleurs tapestries on those created by Vuillard). It was more likely to be either classical myths or allegories such as Dreams, Sleep, Silence, Young Girls and Death, or the very popular Salomé. Other key themes of the Symbolist pantheon were the enchanted 'Celtic' world of fairies, melancholy, wood-land and water; drowning women akin to girl-flowers like so many Ophelias (Wagner's world of Kundry and Klingsor also belongs to that trend); woman as siren, vampire, witch, chimera; the combination of eroticism and death with the Dance of Death, satanism, black masses, Medusa, Oriental inspiration, Pierrot-like figures; and the continual use of particular features like lilies, swans, hair, gems, oriental fabrics, and long-gone myths like the lost city of Ys and Thulé. It is this mood of dreaminess, mists, exotic and vibrant compositions and colours, and above all the overt eroticism and vision, or rather trance-like remoteness, which are still seen as part and parcel of the 'medievalist' dream. Such stylistic inspiration, which saw the continuing use and development of what contemporaries perceived as 'Gothic', remained paramount through the decades of Symbolism, Aes-theticism with James McNeill Whistler, and ultimately the Viennese *Sezession* movement with Gustav Klimt and the Art Nouveau period.[61] Thus the wheel had come full circle and a 'Gothic' revival that had begun life in the late eighteenth century as a rejection of the over-ornate, flowery style of the Baroque and Rococo, and had proposed to do away with anything that was not close to nature and feeling, ended up being itself guilty of the same kind of Mannerist ornamentation and sinuous stylistic complexities as those it had first rejected only a century before. Over the centuries western art and decoration have often known such alternating emphases, from Romanesque to Gothic, from Gothic to Renaissance, from Renaissance then Mannerism to Classical, from Classical to Baroque, and back again.

Even though part of the pre-Raphaelite sensibility, William Morris came into his own in other ways too. Like his contemporaries Morris also sought in medievalism an escape from the perceived crude grime and toil of con-temporary industrial society. He was determined, however, not just to turn his back on the impact of industrialisation and the evils of 'modern' society, but to reform it.

Born in 1836, the son of well-to-do gentry, Morris grew up, in a manner of speaking, with chivalry (he had his own suit of armour made for him before he was ten years old!).[62] As an undergraduate he was entranced by

Malory's work, and his first travels were to see the northern French Gothic cathedrals. He was inspired throughout his life by the writings of John Ruskin, *The Seven Lamps of Architecture* (1849) and especially the chapter 'On the Nature of Gothic' in the *Stones of Venice* (1851–53), in which he proclaimed the superiority of the Christian dimension in art and architecture. Ruskin insisted that the end of Venetian civilisation had come when Venice ceased to have religious faith as its cornerstone and gave way to the pride and worldliness of the Renaissance, and northern Gothic had also lost its medieval purity to Renaissance pride. Ruskin was also most vocal about claiming the freedom of the artist in the medieval world, when he had offered his work to God and had been responsible for the whole of his creation, totally unlike the alienation of the nineteenth-century worker performing the same minute task repetitively, with no interest or pride in the finished product, in an industrial world which did not allow for freedom of creation.

Articled to the Gothic Revival architect G. E. Street in London, Morris proved no great success either as an architect or a painter. His reputation flourished after he founded, together with Ford Madox Brown, Rossetti, Burne-Jones, Arthur Hughes, Philip Webb and another two lesser known figures, The Firm (Morris and Co.), whose purpose was to produce a different kind of decorative art and design.[63] The Firm was engaged in producing surface decoration, wallpaper, textiles (the workers did their own weaving, dyeing and printing), carpets, embroidery, tapestry, tiles, furniture, upholstery, printed cottons and stained glass windows. In a lecture given in 1880, entitled 'The Beauty of Life', Morris expressed his views on art, the people and the soul-destroying nature of contemporary work methods, views which paralleled those of Ruskin in *On the Nature of the Gothic* and in his *Fors Clavigera*. Medieval art alone was both beautiful and free because, unlike classical art which was beautiful but allowed the artist no great freedom, and modern art, which was neither beautiful nor free, being the result of a dehumanised and enslaved working force, it alone let artists and craftsmen unite real and ideal, design and function.[64] Ruskin's anti-utilitarian stance and his belief in the aesthetic and moral superiority of the Gothic, in which he saw an alliance of faith in God and faith in one's own work, had its parallel in Morris's rebellion against the sombre industrial present and its dehumanisation of the worker. Unlike Ruskin, but in agreement with Marx, Morris's stance was less aesthetic than political. His reforming positions combined what he saw as medieval-style designs and patterns based on nature with an attempt to return to a perceived golden age of individual craftsmanship, on a human scale rather than machine-driven, in a fight against the misery brought about by the exploitation of labour in factories. It was also meant to reassert a sense of social solidarity of the kind associated by him with medieval trade guilds. Ruskin himself had attempted to create a Guild of St George to give workers a sense of identity and pride but had failed in this high-minded ideal. Morris's later interest in the medieval period focused more and more on the fourteenth century, the age of communes, guilds and craftsmen as he saw it, rather than the feudal and chivalric. This was the setting for his most famous medievalist novel, *The Dream of John Ball*, and he came to regard The Firm very much as a successful guild. The output of The Firm was prodigious and increasingly sought after: embroidered panels with medieval figures, cartoons for stained glass windows (such as those for *King Richard and Sir Galahad* and for *Queen Guenevere*), tapestry (*The Holy Grail*), painted panels of the legend of St George's fight with the Dragon and his saving Princess Sabra (modelled on Jane Morris) for St George's Cabinet are only a few examples, many of which could be found in the Morris's first home in Essex, the Red House. Built on the principles of a medieval mead-hall and monastic community, with a large hall whose purpose was to promote life in one large room on a communal basis, in an imitation of a medieval utopian world, the house was furnished with handcrafted artefacts by various friends of the Morrises. The whole arrangement provided both an overarching medieval theme (the house was decorated with such artefacts as the marriage casket offered by Rossetti and his wife Lizzie Siddal, shaped like a reliquary and painted with scenes of courtly love derived from Christine de Pisan, and the Prioress's Tale Wardrobe, a wedding gift from Burne-Jones, decorated with scenes from Chaucer's tale), and a medieval network of artistic community and gift exchange. At the same time Morris, Rossetti and Burne-Jones were busy painting Janey Morris in medieval, often specifically Arthurian, guise, as *La Belle Iseult* or *Guenevere*, the Virgin Mary, a saint or Princess Sabra. The Red House has sometimes been regarded as Morris's masterpiece of medievalism in its conception, as well as architecture and decoration. It was mostly in this latter area that it, and The Firm, would become famous for epitomising the new decorative style of Arts and Crafts.

The best-known features of Morris's production were his nature designs of flowers and orchards, which have become the trademark of the style known as Arts and Crafts. This was popular not only in Britain but also in America. Such was the popularity of the designs as wallpaper, cloth and furniture that some came to be used in adverts for commercial products; so it is that we have an advert from the 1890s for toothbrushes, depicting the *Blessed Damozel*. Morris's wife Janey, a passionate medievalist herself, helped him study textile and embroidery by recreating medieval techniques.

Other artists were also designing for The Firm, notably Rossetti and Burne-Jones; the latter's interest in tapestry and stained glass produced some of the most famous decorative patterns of the period using medieval themes, for example in his windows at Christ Church Cathedral in Oxford. Burne-Jones was also associated with Morris's last enterprise when, after having bought the manor house of Kelmscott in Oxfordshire in 1871, Morris launched the Kelmscott Press. It was meant to revive the form of the illuminated manuscript through printed illustrations designed on the model of medieval patterns, ornamental Gothic lettering and decorative borders, in editions, for example, of the thirteenth-century monk Jacques de Voragine's *Golden Legend,* and *Beowulf.* The most famous production of the press was the so-called Kelmscott Chaucer, illustrated by Burne-Jones with eighty-seven plates. Perhaps for the sake of its prudish Victorian audiences, the subjects all deal with chivalry, damsels in distress and such others, the beautiful and moral side of the tales, rather than with any of the rather coarser or openly sexual matter of Chaucer's text.

Another of Morris's successes came from his writings in poetry and prose, such as his novels *The Story of the Glittering Plain* (1891), *The Well at the World's End* (1894), with their fantasy and fairyland elements, and *News from Nowhere,* and above all his political writings. Like his mentor Ruskin, Morris lamented the lost age of individual craftsmanship and the resulting ugliness and dehumanisation of capitalist production. Industrialisation and the division of labour were destroying the pride and joy one should have in one's work, while the 'restoration' of medieval art so fashionable at the height of the Gothic Revival and carried out by the likes of Street were destroying 'popular' art, the achievements of the people of the past. His anti-restoration stance led him to found the Society for the Protection of Ancient Buildings.

> This, then, is the position of art in this epoch. It is helpless and crippled amidst a sea of utilitarian brutality. It cannot perform the most necessary functions: it cannot build a decent house, or ornament a book, or lay out a garden ... On the one hand, it is cut off from the traditions of the past, on the other from the life of the present. It is the art of a clique and not of the people. The people are too poor to have any share of it.[65]

His committed radical socialism led Morris to increasing involvement in the politics of war between Capital and Labour. He became a leading light of the Socialist Party and a social reformer on his own territory, when he designed and had built a group of model labourers' cottages at Kelmscott. The model of his 'craftsmen community' was adopted by artists both in Europe and in America, in the latter case in, for example, Bronson Alcott's settlement at Guitlands.[66] He was also seen as an inspiration for other socialist, Marxist and, in the 1920s, Communist writers, who felt they had discovered early forms of communism and sharing of the means of production in their idealised perception of the economic prosperity of the later fourteenth and fifteenth centuries in England. These centuries were seen as a golden age of representative institutions and freedoms, and bonds of community, like the pre-Norman period. For example, the author of one of the songs written for the socialist movement at the time, 'The People to Their Land', continued to use the Norman Yoke myth well after its scholarly sell-by date, which only confirms how the popular perception of the Middle Ages, and of history in general, has its own momentum, which rarely runs parallel to academic history; a point repeatedly made here and still very much relevant today. The use of medieval events for socialist, and later Communist, political propaganda continued, especially through the adoption of the Peasants' Revolt of 1381 as a model of class struggle. It was used in this way several times, for example by admirers of Langland's *Piers Plowman*, Morris in his *Dream of John Ball*, then Florence Converse in her popular novel *Long Will* (1903), who saw the world of rural and urban rebellion as examples of both proto-Protestantism and proto-socialist manifestation of the oppressed common people. A much later twentieth-century pamphlet describes the rebellion led by Wat Tyler, and ends with the words 'It was perhaps the first time the standard of socialism was raised in Britain' (Paul Foot, 1981) and a 1981 pamphlet of the Communist Party has on its cover an artist's impression of the revolt, with the title: *When the People Arose: The Peasants' Revolt of 1381* (A. L. Morton, 1981). As late as 1986 the opposition to the unpopular new Poll Tax, brought in by the then Prime Minister Margaret Thatcher, was led by one Jack Straw, appropriately and amusingly reminding people of his 1381 namesake who had been one of the leaders of the movement; a coincidence of which both others and himself saw the political profit.

Morris's more direct interest in the Middle Ages remained strong, not only through the Kelmscott Press, but also, especially after his 1870s visits to Iceland, through his awakened interest in northern myths and sagas. He learnt Old Norse and embarked on translations of Icelandic literature, such as the 1877 epic poem *Sigurd the Volsung and the Fall of the Nibelungen*. The Iceland trips probably contributed also to his emerging socialist ideals, through the example of the old northern practices of the folk-mote, with its communal participation of people and leaders in a joint decision-making and conflict-resolving process for the good of the community.[67] By the time he died in 1896, after what he liked to describe as 'a very uneventful life',[68] Morris's fame had spread to inspire a whole generation in Europe, both in

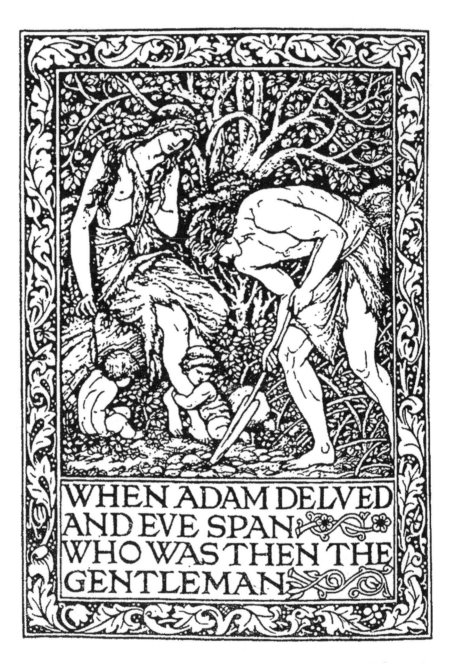

WHEN ADAM DELVED
AND EVE SPAN
WHO WAS THEN THE
GENTLEMAN

Edward Burne-Jones and William Morris, *A Dream of John Ball* (1892), frontispiece to the Kelmscott edition. Victorian socialism, the political heir to the Peasants' Revolt.

art (Rennie Macintosh in Scotland, the *Jugendstil* then *Bauhaus* movements in Germany) and in political reform.

For a group of people as interested in the Middle Ages as the Pre-Raphaelites were, it was impossible not to be confronted at some point with the issue of faith, which had been such an overwhelming aspect of medieval life. When a student at Oxford, Morris's interest in medieval history had led him to be for a while an enthusiastic supporter of Edward Pusey (1800–1882) and to attempt to found, with Burne-Jones, and partly under the influence of the Nazarenes, a monastic order under the patronage of St Galahad.[69] The Pre-Raphaelites were generally thought to have been inclined to be Tractarians somehow associated with the Oxford Movement, which is also referred to as the Anglo-Catholic Revival, advocated by Newman, Pusey and Keble. Burne-Jones and C. A. Collins probably were, and works such as Collins's *Convent Thoughts* or Burne-Jones' Christ Church windows reflect this. Madox Brown, on the other hand, was Evangelical, and his down-to-earth representation of Jesus washing Peter's feet was perceived to be much too gritty and 'realistic',[70] while Holman Hunt, who painted what has probably become the most famous Victorian painting, *The Light of the World* (1851–53), produced simply a mystical work.

Pre-Raphaelitism was not necessarily religious, let alone High Church. Neither were the members of the Oxford Movement necessarily interested in the Middle Ages, at least in the first instance.[71] Their theology was looking back to the 'age of origins' and its alleged purity of doctrine: the apostolic age. On the other hand, in ecclesiological terms, they admired the seventeenth-century Laudian church. For a long time this was Newman's prevailing stance, when he described the Anglican and not the Roman Church as the rightful heir of the Primitive church, because the medieval Catholic Church had added various accretions and destroyed the purity of the church of the origins. Nevertheless, the Anglo-Catholics preserved from the Romantic tradition an attachment to the mystery and the mystical aspects of God and His worship, to the heart rather than the reason inherited from the Enlightenment tradition. They were admirers of the unified church, and of the emotional and aesthetic aspects of worship in the Middle Ages. In this they were the heirs of the Romantic views of the medieval church already put forward by men like Thomas Warton in his *History of English Poetry* (1774–81) and of Edmund Burke's *History of the Revolution in France* (1790), who both highlighted the link between the medieval belief in the supernatural and the imagination and emotions. Newman summarised this in his *Apologia*:

[The Oxford Movement] was a reaction from the dry and superficial character of the religious teaching and literature of the last generation, or century [under the] literary influence of W. Scott, who turned men's minds in the direction of the Middle Ages.

The customs, institutions, traditions, and religion, of the middle ages, were favourable to poetry. Their pageaunts, processions, spectacles, and ceremonies, were friendly to imagery, to personification and allegory ... The very devotion of the Gothic times was romantic.[72]

Burke linked the chivalry he admired with the spiritual life of the medieval church, seeing it at least in part as a religious cult: chivalry was a combination of the 'spirit of a gentleman and the spirit of religion', on which European manners and civilisation have depended for ages. Burke, like Southey a little later, was convinced of the importance of the unity of church and state, and of the importance of the church in moral, spiritual and social terms, as the medieval church had been. The Age of Faith was infinitely preferable to 'this new conquering empire of ... reason' and the 'barbarous, mechanic philosophy ... which banished the affections'.[73] All these Romantic pronouncements in favour of the medieval church contributed to breaking down the anti-Catholic mood in the late eighteenth and early nineteenth centuries, and ultimately enabled the flowering of Anglo-Catholicism.

The Romantic credentials of the members of the Oxford Movement can be grasped from their insistence that feeling and poetry, representing emotion and the affections of the heart, were a much better road to Truth and God, by enhancing the sense of mystery and awe, of the beauty of the divine and of mystical contemplation (Keble and Pusey). Primarily a movement of religious devotion and discipline rather than of doctrinal novelty, High Church Anglicanism was also concerned with reviving the importance of the community of the church over the more individualist Post-Reformation Protestant approach of 'private judgement'. The Anglican Revival was also at the forefront of the renewal of monastic life and missionary work among the poor, notably with the foundation of the All Saints community in London. Because they were confronted by bishops with opposing views, Anglo-Catholic priests often ended up in parishes with a great deal of poverty and unemployment, which led them to champion the cause of the poor; characteristically, one bishop, when talking about the foundation by a militant High Anglican priest of a guild destined to help the poor of London, claimed that it took 'him back to the time of Richard II and John Ball'.[74]

The main exponent of medievalism within the Oxford Movement was Hurrell Froude, who died young, but whose posthumous work *The Remains*

of the Late Reverend Richard Hurrell Froude, published in 1838, was a most
controversial text, criticised by mainstream theologians and bishops of the
Anglican Church for its anti-Reformation stance.[75] Froude produced two
well-known aphorisms: 'Really I hate the Reformation and the Reformers
more and more' and 'The Reformation was a limb badly set; it must be broken again to be righted'. But he did not just dislike the Reformation, he
gradually came to see the church after Edward III as already in decline (he
profoundly disliked Wycliff too), and increasingly admired the nature and
institution of the medieval church and its relationship with the secular
authority. Other Tractarians were less interested in the medieval church,
except Pusey who grew more enthusiastic about medieval writers from the
1840s onwards, when he became leader of the Anglo-Catholic Movement.
Pusey was increasingly interested in the revival of monasticism and in the
outward signs of sacramental worship through the importance of the liturgy,
the sensual beauty of light and a musical revival. This is what has led to our
popular expression of 'smells and bells' as applied to High Church Anglicanism. These reforming practices of High Anglicanism relied largely on the
assumption that they were a return to the medieval church. The use of rich
colours, incense, the revival of cathedral choirs of men and boys, meant to
reproduce the style of medieval monks' psalmody, and the flowering of new
church music and hymns were all meant to bring back the Christian faith
to the people through beauty, a technique previously used with great success by the Catholic Counter Reformation in the seventeenth century. The
ritual was one element of the Romantic 'turning from the head towards the
heart':

> Its roots lay in the desire to turn the churches into houses of prayer and devo-
> tion, where men would let their hearts go outward and upward in worship,
> instead of preaching houses where their minds would be argued into an assent
> to creeds or to moral duties.[76]

After Froude's death, the medievalism of the Oxford Movement came to
the fore in two ways. The first was the founding of the Cambridge Camden
Society in 1839, renamed the Ecclesiological Society in 1845. The second was
the revival, often by men associated with Pusey's increasing ritualism, of
medieval architecture, church furnishings and hymnological tradition.[77]
Building new churches in the Gothic style, as well as 'restoring' medieval
ones, had been already the fashion since the beginning of the century; of
the 174 churches erected under the Church Buildings Act of 1818, three quar-
ters were built in the Gothic style. This was regarded as more conducive to
worship since, unlike the classical style where the emphasis was on the pul-
pit, and which was therefore the preferred form of architecture of the

Evangelical movement, a Gothic church laid the emphasis on the altar. It was thus more appropriate to the reverence and mystery required of the worshipper, as well as giving worship a sacramental focus.[78] The medieval style was associated with the Anglo-Catholic Revival in architecture, where it was used by major Victorian architects, notably Street, Scott and Butterfield. The latter's building of Keble Chapel (1876) and of All Saints Margaret Street, stronghold of the Anglo-Catholic Movement from the 1850s onwards, represented the height of the tendency.

Ritual was another form of medievalism. It revived numerous observances of the medieval church, such as the celebration of the canonical Hours of Matins and Vespers, the emphasis on eucharistic worship, the medieval-style long, elaborate chasuble, and the music. Hymn writers like Dyke, Parry and especially John Mason Neale began a great tradition of hymn writing, and the standard hymn book of the Church of England, *Hymns Ancient and Modern*, published in 1860, was instigated at a meeting of Anglo-Catholic clergy. Also related to medievalism was the revival of plainsong, first used at St Margaret's chapel, predecessor of All Saints Margaret Street. The Gregorian Association was founded in 1871 and the Plainsong and Medieval Music Society in 1888, and Gregorian chant was part of the worship of Anglo-Catholics. The most profound 'medievalist' after Froude's death was the aptly named R. W. Church, who pursued all these principles and who, not surprisingly perhaps, was the editor and translator of what remained for a long time the best edition of Dante's *Divine Comedy*.

It is remarkable that, despite the traditional link between Roman Catholics and medievalist tendencies (as we saw with the castle architecture of great Catholic families), in ecclesiastical terms English Roman Catholics were nowhere near as interested in the Middle Ages as High Church Anglicans were.[79] Pugin deplored this, and not even the fact that the resurrection of plainchant had first taken place at the Benedictine abbey of Solesmes in France, and had become a feature of monasticism there,[80] seems to have moved the English Catholic Church to abandon its Roman Baroque preferences, as well as a much more 'modern', simplified liturgy and church fittings. This contributed to upholding the Anglo-Catholics' claim that they were not innovators. They staunchly insisted that they were not imitating Rome but that theirs was the real Catholicism, the medieval one, that it was the church of Rome which had been corrupted by the Council of Trent, and that the accretions which Victorians associated with Roman Catholicism and so disliked were in fact post-medieval. The Tractarian claim in the 1830s and 1840s was that Anglicanism was a form of Catholicism purged of the abuses and superstitions of Roman

Catholicism, and more attuned and faithful to the 'undivided' church of the early centuries.[81]

Nineteenth-century composers of opera, mostly Italian, sometimes used the Middle Ages to set their plots, in the way they would use any remote and obscure period in time, as good stories on which to project their universal themes (love, revenge). Sometimes a particular plot line had been inspired by a historic anecdote, as had Rossini's *Count Ory*, set during the Crusades, and his *Tancredi*, based on Tasso; Verdi's *I Lombardi*, *Simone Boccanegra*, *Aroldo*, *Giovanna d'Arco* or the even more obscure *Oberto, conte di San Bonifacio*, Bellini's *La Straniera*, and Donizetti's *La Favorita* are a few other such examples. Various pieces of orchestral music were inspired by medieval themes or, at any rate, by medievalist writers like Walter Scott: Mendelsohn's *Fingal* music is one example. Late-nineteenth-century composers also used the medieval theme: the Romantic and Symbolist take on love and chivalry dominated in Debussy's *Pelléas and Mélisande* (based on the play written by another Belgian symbolist, Maurice Maeterlinck), or in Lalo's *Le Roi d'Ys*. The number of operas and musical pieces of all kinds based on Shakespeare's plays have also been innumerable but once again, while these might be plays set in the Middle Ages, such as *Macbeth* or *Romeo and Juliet*, they were at one removed from direct interpretation of the period.[82]

Chivalry, combined or not with the Christian theme of the Holy Grail, is generally regarded as the essence of Wagner's *Tristan und Isolde*, *Lohengrin* and *Parsifal*.[83] Himself a revolutionary (he was arrested and had to flee after the 1848 revolution in Dresden), Wagner's use of the Middle Ages was there from the outset, in his early operas *Rienzi* (first performed in 1842) and *Tannhäuser* (first performed in 1845), this last based on a folk-tale included in the Grimm bothers. *Lohengrin*, whose subject was drawn from the medieval poet Wolfram von Eschenbach, as *Parsifal* was to be later, was first performed in the late 1860s and early 1870s. Earlier, during the 1850s, Wagner had written his *Tristan*, relying this time on Gottfried von Strasburg. He wanted it to be, not a traditional opera, in the nineteenth-century sense, but a 'musical drama', recreating the idea of a complete unit encompassing poetry and drama as well as music, and giving the words and staging equal weight, rather like medieval religious drama cycles. His opera *Die Meistersinger von Nürnberg* was written on the same principles, as were his last work *Parsifal*, and his long-thought about and many years in the completion four-opera cycle of the *Ring der Nibelungen*. The *Ring* was to be the most controversial and highly-charged of Wagner's works in the twentieth century, on whose account he has been accused of practically founding Nazi ideology and justifying German conquest of other races based on the superiority of the Germanic medieval past and heroes like Siegfried.

Like most of his contemporaries, Wagner was both a supporter of Völkism and often antisemitic for personal reasons. But he was not nationalistic in a political way. The driving principle throughout his life was that, although art was not specifically associated with any one country, people or 'race' but embraces the whole of humanity, the German genius had the potential to offer mankind a higher and nobler perception of it. While using a variety of sources of inspiration, this ideal German artist should take the lead in turning art into something universal, thanks to the elusive, mystical quality of the German spirit, which transcends national boundaries. Wagner had little liking for the reality of the 'Fatherland', which he once described thus: 'as for the Fatherland, apart from its lovely ranges of hills, vales and woods, I rather dislike it than otherwise. They are an accursed people, these Saxons, greasy, paunchy, ill-bred, lazy and coarse – what have I to do with them?'.[84]

What was important, by contrast with modern Germans, was this 'German spirit', epitomised by Bach, and which Wagner embodied in Hans Sachs, a spirit which would ensure the *artistic* regeneration of the German people, and hence of mankind,[85] through art, culture and philosophy. It was only to make this possible that Wagner supported German political unity. Not only was he not arguing for German conquest, but he was concerned that nationalism, in the narrow form it took in Germany, had only ever led to the highlighting of the German instinctive lust for conquest, based on 'a false illusion of German exceptionalism, rooted on the ideas of strength and power'.[86] It was this 'German spirit', found throughout the Middle Ages, which had to be reawakened to bring about the renaissance of a 'Holy German Art', and, as a result, the only form acceptable of greatness of the German nation, which would then illuminate the rest of the world.

Wagner used the Nibelungen myth as a philosophical reflection on the role of power, good and evil, loyalty, and ultimately heroic death as a means of salvation and redemption, all of which were in fact by then entirely standard Romantic and medievalist themes. Another medievalist theme was also associating death and salvation, for example in the main scene from Act II in *Tristan und Isolde*, which Wagner described as beginning 'with pulsating life at its most passionate – and end[ing] with the most mystical, innermost longing for death'.[87] The love and death theme was one common to both Romanticism and Symbolism, as was the notion of borrowing and appropriating whatever myths seemed right from a large variety of sources: eastern, Buddhism, Christian with the Grail and the Knights Templar, Essenism, Hinduism, Arabic and Persian mysticism and freemasonry, which

Wagner did for Parsifal.[88] This went even further in the mystical stakes. While apparently returning to the Christian vision of perfection through the quest for the Grail, the mystical redemption through the blood of Christ, *Parsifal* may also be regarded as an indictment of mechanical, ritualistic religion, which can no longer bring salvation. Only a return to the original values of love and compassion, and individual spiritual qualities can do so. Institutional worship is not sufficient for healing and salvation, just as the regulated institutional art of a Beckmesser in *Die Meistersinger von Nürnberg* cannot be great art.

The Romantic ideals embraced by Wagner could not easily make him fit into either a nationalist or a Christian agenda. Just as he was not popular with many contemporary critics, partly on grounds of his music being anti-German, so Wagner, contrary to popular belief, was not popular with Hitler so much through the message of his operas, but only because of the use that could be made on occasion of his more martial pieces. His work was largely 'adapted' by his family, his wife Cosima and various heirs, and it is thus that he was turned into an apostle of German nationalism.[89]

In fact, nationalism was much more marked in nineteenth-century music in the works of Russian composers Borodin (*Prince Igor*) and Mussorgsky (*Boris Godunov*), focusing on a dreamt of Greater Russia. Even Verdi openly promoted a nationalist agenda when he encountered a historical plot susceptible of being interpreted as an encouragement towards rebellion for the purpose of Italian unity. The *Sicilian Vespers*, *Attila* and even *Macbeth* provided stirring arias and choruses singing about freedom. While Wagner's take was that of imagined medieval love, Christianity and chivalry, Russian and Italian opera was a translation into music of nationalism, which is Romanticism in politics.

4

From Aachen to Maastricht

The *ancien régime* in continental Europe and the traditional lifestyle of western society had been severely undermined by the French Revolution, followed by the Napoleonic Wars and, more gradually, by the Industrial Revolution. The overseas expansion of the British Empire also brought about major shifts. All these factors contributed to the progress of nationalism in Europe throughout the nineteenth century. The debate about the origins and rise of nationalism and 'ethnicity' has been very much at the forefront of current historiography in the last twenty years, with contrasting views about its roots in the post-Enlightenment and French Revolution periods[1] or in the medieval and Tudor periods.[2] Although the above-mentioned positions are often irreconcilable, at least there seems to be no doubt that the consolidation of new nation states in the second half of the nineteenth century and at the beginning of the twentieth, for example in Germany, Italy, Belgium, Norway, Romania, Bulgaria and Serbia, strengthened the principle of 'natural frontiers' on ethnic bases, and eventually led to the creation of independent states founded on these principles. Indirectly, it also led to the First World War.[3]

The rise of nationalism around and after 1848 spawned a whole genre of historical fiction whose purpose was to establish a kind of creation myth or origins myth, especially among nations in the throes of finding their identities and defining themselves as nations. Elias Lönrot collected 'folk' material for his great composite poem the *Kalevala*, which became the 'national' text justifying the ethnic past of the Finns, and thus their desire for cultural independence. Ivan Mazuranic wrote the Croat national epic, *The Death of Smail-Aga Cengiijc* in 1846 (significantly just as the volcano of the 1848 revolutions was beginning to rumble across Europe), describing the fight of the Croats against the Turks. In Poland the cultural leading lights of the age, Frédéric Chopin and Adam Mickiewicz, supported the Polish insurrections of 1830 and 1846, and both had to leave Poland and live in exile. Henryk Sienkiewicz (1846–1916), the Polish 'national' writer, made his name with the historical novels *The Teutonic Knights* and *The Knights of the Cross*, exalting the glory of medieval Poland, before winning the Nobel Prize with his best-known novel set in Ancient Rome under Nero, *Quo Vadis*. Even Switzerland, the least aggressively nationalist of European countries, where versions of Wilhelm Tell had been used in the early modern period to support independence from Austria without there being a need to parade such myths later on, had its national text. In 1855 Joseph Viktor von Scheffel published a historical novel entitled *Ekkehard*, set in the tenth-century monastery of St Gall. It had considerable success, was set to music innumerable times, and repeatedly reprinted until the First World War, with the enthusiastic support of the Scheffel Society, the largest literary society in the German-speaking world at the end of the nineteenth century.[4] To this day, even though its popularity has faded away, names of streets, hotels and public places in the town of St Gall commemorate it.

The national or ethnic criterion, which contributed to the formation of national identity through art, was also present in the work of artists and musicians. In Norway, Grieg's *Peer Gynt*, Ibsen's plays and even Munch's paintings contributed to forging a national identity and strengthening the language, part of the strategy of opposing Danish dominance and cultural hegemony, and working in favour of the build-up of a separate nation, eventually born in 1905. Sibelius's musical adaptation of themes from the *Kalevala* played a similar role in Finland at a time when it was attempting to break free from Russia, as did the music of Smetana, Dvorak, Bartok and Kodaly, and Enescu for the Czechs, Hungarians and Romanians respectively, when they were in the throes of defining their national identity. Spain also had nationalist composers, for example Albeniz, Granados and De Falla, focus on vernacular themes. Numerous publications of folktales, whether in Scandinavia or Eastern Europe, vernacular if not actually dialectal popular literature in the form of ballads, stories and poetry in general, and paintings of 'popular' national subjects from peasant culture or national historical events and myths were equally popular for the same reasons. In the Balkans nationalism was strongly promoted by the church (itself an unusual trend since Christianity is supposed to be universal). The Bulgarian Orthodox Church, although autocephalous since at least 1235, came near to a schism from the Orthodox communion in the nineteenth century, when it claimed to be the 'Church of the (ethnic) Bulgarian People', rather than the 'Orthodox Church of Bulgaria'. Particular emphasis was laid on the development of language and grammar as a means of fostering national unity. This went from the creation of a 'new' language, supposedly based on a medieval past, in Hungary, Scandinavia, Wales and Ireland and even in Italy where Dante's 'classic Italian' was highlighted in order to override local dialect, to the development of linguistic studies of vernacular medieval languages, Old French, Old High German, Old Norse, Old Irish and Old English.[5]

The example which most clearly unites all three elements: nationalist revival fuelled by medieval myth, supported by a nationalist Orthodox church and by the renaissance of a unifying language, is Serbia.[6] The medieval kingdom of Serbia, a vassal state of the Byzantine Empire, had reached its political apogee under King Dušan (1321–55), after which it was abruptly dismantled as the result of the Ottoman conquest of the Balkans, suffering a series of major defeats, including one which remained paramount in popular memory (though in fact regarded by contemporaries more as an indecisive victory) at Kosovo in 1389. It represented a crucial moment in the history of the nation since it was not simply a case of diminished power but one of complete loss of political identity as a state. This it only regained in the nineteenth century, when Serbia emerged once more as a nation state. The trauma of Kosovo, combined with the fact that the only element of Serbian identity left over through those centuries was the Orthodox Church, autocephalous since 1219 and very much the single national institution not taken over by the Turks, came to be expressed in the form of the myth of 'Heavenly Serbia', ever present in the national consciousness in the form of the legends and poems relating to Prince Lazar and his heroic resistance against the Ottomans at Kosovo. A large number of such poems were produced, the first being the *Narration about Prince Lazar* by his contemporary Patriarch Danilo III, and the most famous the Serb national epic, *The Mountain Wreath*, by the ruler (both secular and religious) of Montenegro, Archbishop Vladika Njegos (1813–51). They depict Prince Lazar who, given the choice by God, had preferred military loss on the battlefield for the sake of heavenly glory. This explained away the defeat of Kosovo, as well as making the Serbian ruler and his people into champions of moral purity. But Serbia's past, the poems insisted, was not forgotten: this great past would be revived in a great future, in which the Serbian empire would be resurrected, an eschatological theme in which the purity of the Serbian people would eventually pave the way for the expansion of Greater Serbia. This nineteenth-century nationalism culminated in the 1914 Sarajevo assassination of Archduke Franz Ferdinand by a Serbian extremist, and was revived in the nationalism of the 1980s and 1990s, which saw many among the Serbian people and intelligentsia give their support for 'ethnic cleansing' in those areas of the old Yugoslavia which they regarded as part of Greater Serbia. The mood remained the same throughout the two centuries. In 1844 a secret document claimed that:

> The Serbian rulers, it may be remembered, began to assume the position held by the Greek Empire and almost succeeded in making an end of it, replacing the collapsed Eastern Roman Empire with a Serbian-Slavic one [under] Emperor Dushan the Mighty ... The arrival of the Turks in the Balkans

interrupted this change, and prevented it from taking place for a long time. But now, since the Turkish power is broken and destroyed, so to speak, this interrupted process must commence once more in the same spirit and again be undertaken in the knowledge of that right.[7]

In 1989 a major Serbian newspaper published a document underwritten by a majority of intellectuals and churchmen, in support of the then President Milosevic's policies, which included the following lines: 'Since the early Middle Ages, the Serbs, together with their rulers and church dignitaries fighting the Turks, have been the last rampart in the defence of Europe from the Turkish invasion and the penetration of Islam.'[8]

The interpretation of the past by the Serbians is one of the best examples of the use which could be made of the Middle Ages for political purposes, to the extent not simply of distorting history but of turning it on its head. The battle of Kosovo itself had been anything but an evident defeat, as the sultan had been killed and his army scattered; it was later battles which would eventually dismantle the Serbian state. Prince Lazar, rapidly venerated as a saint, had ruled an already declining kingdom in the later fifteenth century, while the kingdom of Bosnia was at its height, and the forces at Kosovo had been a joint Bosnian-Serbian army. The Serbians had quite rapidly become clients and allies of the Ottomans, fighting along them and serving in the Ottoman army, including against the Catholic Bosnians. Even the Serbian epic 'hero' Prince Marko had done so. The Serbian church was re-established in 1557 and was favoured by the sultans as a rampart against Catholic Europe. Serbian nationalism and anti-Muslim attitudes in 1989, and their very virulence, 'may, sadly, be a reaction to the reality of history in which Orthodox Serbs were for centuries the principal Balkan co-operators with the Turkish Empire'.[9] By the nineteenth century, western European attitudes of support for a Romantic ideal of 'primitive' languages and folklore and for nationalistic recreations of the past, especially if they were felt to be helping those nations perceived as the underdog and victim of history, became the allies of the rise in ethnic-based nationalism everywhere in Europe. The result was an large number of literary texts exalting this 'adapted' past, and justifying it to build modern states and expand them.

To a large extent, continental European nationalism had its roots in Germany. German nationalistic movements from the late eighteenth century onwards associated German unity, state and culture with the Gothic Middle Ages. After 1806, when Napoleon put an end to the Holy Roman Empire, various members of the Romantic movement, including Joseph von Görres,

Goethe and Beethoven, who in the first instance had enthusiastically supported the French Revolution, turned around completely. They called on the German people to cast off French dominance and build up a German nation. Almost all such movements, though their agenda and sometimes political views were quite different, appealed to the Middle Ages as their point of reference. 'The Middle Ages, with their "magical, demonic character", thus came to be a source of deeply emotional identification for many German nationalists.'[10] They were idealised as an age of religious commitment, of confessional unity, of a powerful, self-sacrificing faith, and of the development of a Christian-German spirit, as the height of German art and poetry, and as the epoch of German imperial greatness. National hopes and expectations were aroused by the Middle Ages, while contemporary phenomena were measured against them. As the supposed golden age of German history, they affected the self-consciousness of the nation, and their accomplishments were regarded as something to be desired and repeated. Those who linked the national renascence and the fulfilment of national yearnings with the medieval past created traditions and invested the nation with an aura of age and historical profundity.

In the early years of the nineteenth century Schlegel, Novalis and Heine idealised the universal and Christian empire of the Middle Ages. Another contemporary trend, which developed strongly after 1806, was on the contrary anti-universalist, and identified the medieval period with the historical greatness of the German nation and perceived German spiritual, intellectual, social and aesthetic traditions, including Gothic art.[11] The arguments were based on the highly influential work of J. G. Herder (1744–1803), *Ideas for a Philosophy of the History of Mankind,* and that of Johann Gottlieb Fichte (1762–1814).[12] Herder had put forward the idea that every people had an essential, ethnic core (*Volksgeist*), different from that of other peoples. A people was organised in 'nations', each with its own life, history, and identity. The nation was an organism and had a collective personality, and its main unifying factor was its language. Conflicting and competing identities within a nation were a bad thing, to be avoided, and the way to do this was to exclude the elements which disturbed the homogeneous whole. Herder was no German nationalist; on the contrary he was a characteristic eighteenth-century cosmopolitan figure, who favoured the peaceful coexistence of various nations, none of which was superior to another, in order to make for a varied and interesting world. His views led him to underline the value of each culture and nation, which needed to be aware of itself, its value and its proud history. This was why, Herder claimed, the German nation must stop adopting foreign mores and languages, meaning particularly French and Latin, because they were felt to be superior, which was what the Germans had been doing throughout the eighteenth century. They needed to speak German, write and think in German, educate their children in German, and in the glories of the German past and culture. It is easy to see how these two sets of ideas could be put together, not by Herder himself, but by others, for more aggressive German nationalistic purposes. Fichte did so, against the background of the Napoleonic Wars. He glorified the *Volksgeist* as expressed through language, and created a hierachy of 'worthy' and 'unworthy' nations on that basis. Since for him German was the original language (*Ursprache*), it followed that Germany was top on the list of 'worthy' nations, on the basis of its past, best embodied in the Middle Ages.

A succession of writers and political leaders followed across the century, associating medieval values with German national unity, in an anti-liberal (meaning anti-French), anti-secular and pro-monarchical context. Opposition to French centralising administrative and legal policies grew. The lawyer von Allmedingen wrote that 'perfect laws are the beautiful and free forms of the interior life of a nation; they come out of life itself. The Civil Code has not come out of the life of the German people.'[13] The French alliance of government with the rising middle classes of trade, industry and bureaucracy, the beginnings of the Industrial Revolution and, with it, the gradual displacement of the landed base of aristocracy and church, and the emancipation of the Jews, had all been implemented by the 'liberating' French administration. This gave rise to a combination of anti-French and antisemitic feeling. At first anti-French feeling had been translated into nationalist intellectual movements after the 1790s. The foremost representative of this trend was Friedrich de la Motte-Fouqué. He suggested that the historic mission of Germany was to save Europe from revolutionary chaos. His vision of the political order was based on 'the existence of a patriarchal order, God-given differences among social ranks, and a people intimately bound to its dynasty by love, loyalty and obedience'.[14] De la Motte-Fouqué strongly influenced King Frederick William IV and that patriotic prince was the first to speak of an 'organic' German tradition, based on monarchy and Christianity, against the French concepts of revolution and innovation. A significant manifestation of the king's perception, and an attempt at rebuilding the medieval relationship between monarch and his people, was the ceremony of homage to the new king, which he required and received in Königsberg on his accession in 1840. This consisted of a Prussian 'diet of homage', made up of the various estates of the kingdom, who were then confirmed in their privileges (followed by grandiose and glittering dinners and other public festivities, including *tableaux vivants* depicting episodes from the history of medieval Prussia), and of an oath of homage by representatives of the estates, gathered around the throne in the court-yard of the royal palace, to whom the king, in standard medieval fashion, promised to be a loyal, just, Christian sovereign.[15] That year, he had written, in a letter to his brother-in-law Ludwig I, the king of Bavaria, explaining his dream that

> The thirty million Germans at the heart of ... Europe will again *undeniably* constitute the *world's leading nation* ... For on the head of the mightiest German prince, the hereditary President of the [German] Confederation ... I would like to see what is incontrovertibly the world's most important crown, the crown of Charlemagne.[16]

In 1842 Frederick William IV presided over the ceremonies marking the resumption of restoration work on the medieval cathedral of Cologne, the monument regarded as a symbol of the unity of the German people and of the uniqueness of their traditions, which had originated in the Middle Ages.

A parallel, more 'democratic' movement highlighted the achievements of the Gothic age, perceived as a result of the *collective* spirit of ordinary German people. Though hardly to be counted among democrats, Hans von Aufsess (1801–1872), a nobleman with the usual Romantic interest in the Middle Ages, reclaiming Gothic art as German, began collecting artefacts and relics of the past in a systematic way. He founded the Germanisches Nationalmuseum, to which he ultimately left his large collection, as well as the Society for the Preservation of the Monuments of Older German History, Literature and Art, also editing its journal.[17] After 1871 the 'medieval' style came to achieve near-official status in both public and vernacular architecture. Examples of the former are monuments to the heroes of the German past, notably that to Frederick Barbarossa at Kyffhäuser, and the restoration of the palace of the medieval German emperors at Goslar. The purpose was clearly to turn Wilhelm II into the legitimate descendant of the old medieval Reich. The trend continued into the years of the Weimar Republic, which also exalted the German past, this time in contrast to the perceived artificiality of the Classical or Baroque models, being pointedly against the innovations and the perceived modernity of the Jewish and associated socialist group.[18] Thus a variety of political and cultural tendencies were used throughout the century by a whole range of people whose common point was their appeal to the Middle Ages. Such tendencies, all equally unreal, were part of the overall European movement now generally described as 'the invention of tradition', typical of nineteenth-century nationalism. Among these movements, however, none was as long lasting and as successful as Völkism.[19]

The importance of Völkism lies both in its profound impact on German thinking and resulting action, but also in the great influence it exerted on the rising small nations of central and eastern Europe and in the Habsburg Empire. Völkist ideology was based on Romanticism, in its emphasis on man's oneness with nature and rootedness in it, and in the mystical notion of the *Volk* (ancestral people), which defined itself in relation to landscape (mountains, land or soil, trees) and history (heroes, peasants, burghers in small towns), all of which in turn defined themselves in relation to an idyllic medieval past of cosmic and social harmony and unity. Völkism arose from an attempt to reject modernity and progress in nineteenth-century Europe, and its perceived ills, such as industrialisation, urbanisation and alienation of the individual from the community, with its attendant nostalgia for a primitive past of harmony. The movement found a great deal of resonance with historians and writers, such as Theodor Fontane, W. H. Riehl, Paul de Lagarde and Franz Diederich, its main exponents. Riehl proposed to revive a kind of medieval rural utopia, with a society organised in the form of estates and people working in a corporative way, with the workers themselves being assimilated to medieval craftsmen. 'O what a delightful time the Middle Ages were, when everything was learned under the guidance of masters.' [20] Some went as far as to associate the cosmic unity of the *Volk* and its *Geist* (soul), in some mystical alchemy, with pantheism, if not direct paganism, and certainly with an interest in sects perceived to have embodied the essence of medieval mysticism, a mix of Illuminati, Freemasons, Rosicrucians, occultism, alchemy, astrology and other esoteric leanings.

Popular Völkism, unlike Diederich's in this respect, was also generally exclusive about German uniqueness, assuming the attributes of the *Volk* to be unique to a historically superior but repressed German people. Unlike Diederich again, this form of Völkism excluded other peoples from a similar possible ethnic unity and cosmic harmony, for example the Celts, the Slavs and the Jews, and contained the seeds of the idea of the superiority of the German *Volk* over its neighbours. One of its main components was a strong antisemitic tendency: the Jews were seen as epitomising modernity, intellectual and urban interests, as opposed to the emotional link between nature, the land, peasant culture and even mystical Christianity, stripped of the 'corrupting' legalistic influence of the Jew Paul. That kind of Völkism later encountered great success, particularly once it was taken up and turned into a system by Houston Stewart Chamberlain, the great exponent of racial theories, who settled in Bavaria at Bayreuth, where he married Wagner's daughter Eva and started the transformation of Wagner into the apostle of Germanism. Cosima Wagner had begun the process of nationalism with regard to Wagner's work and the Bayreuth festival. Chamberlain and Eva, then Wagner's daughter-in-law Winifred (both of whom were English), who took over from Cosima the Wagner cult at the festival from the 1920s onwards, turned Bayreuth into a shrine of 'Germanness' and ultimately consecrated the Nazification of the festival, largely resting on Winifred's personal friendship with Hitler.[21]

The other trend of Völkism, Diederich's, remained alive too and had considerable impact on central and eastern European writers, philosophers and politicans, many educated at universities in Berlin, Jena, Dresden, Heidelberg or Vienna. They too adopted the ideas of national and ethnic unity, of the link between the land and its peasants, and of the rooting in the soil and history of the people. Their stance was against modernisation, urbanisation, industrial development and the ever-increasing impact of international capital, a stance which thus often included antisemitism, on account of the perception of the Jews as representatives of this modern capitalistic world. An example of this can be found in the Magyar Nepiés movement, represented by writers such as Laszlo Neméth or Gyula Illys, author of *People of the Puszta* in the 1930s. By the beginning of the twentieth century and beyond the First World War, Völkism, or national variations of it, was the dominant movement throughout the vast spaces and numerous populations of Germany and further east as far as Russia. In a derivative form, it was also to be found elsewhere, for example in Italy, where it was supported by a dispossessed church, and where politicians, even while uniting Italy and bringing it in line with the Industrial Revolution, believed that liberalism, capitalism, private initiative and the market economy had been generated by Protestantism, and that they should be fought against and destroyed for causing all the injustices and problems of the modern world,[22] choosing to ignore that it was good Catholic Italian bankers, merchants and craftsmen who had invented capitalism in the Middle Ages. America also had its representatives in the 'agrarian' literary school led by Allen Tate and Robert Penn Warren, who made a case for the rural way of life of the Deep South as an alternative to the industrial capitalism and left-wing policies of the North.

Throughout the nineteenth century interest in the medieval period among historians continued to expand, as history was increasingly transformed into a university discipline. The editing of texts from the Middle Ages was now carried out on a vast scale, no longer part of a church agenda but part of the new job of recently founded scientific societies, the *Monumenta Germaniae Historica* from 1826 in Germany, the *Rolls Series* in England after 1854, the Surtees Society from 1835, the Camden Society after 1838, the Roxburghe Club, and a whole variety of other Royal or Imperial Societies throughout central and eastern Europe.[23] This was itself related to the rise of nationalist feeling and the interest in the 'origins of the nation'. The same impetus applied to the writing of academic history, increasingly focusing on aspects of the medieval past felt to illustrate the glories of national origins. Examples of this are Augustin Thierry's *Chroniques des temps mérovingiens* (1840), Michelet's history of France, and the works of Friedrich von Räumer, who taught medieval history in German universities, which were, by then, the best in Europe.

By the first half of the nineteenth century in Germany and France, and by the mid nineteenth century in England, medieval history was increasingly in the hands of academic historians rather than in those of the men most directly involved in making current history, mostly lawyers and politicians. It became more and more the domain of university studies.[24] The main academic historian, perhaps the greatest of nineteenth-century medieval historians in England was William Stubbs, holder of the Oxford Regius chair from 1871. A most prolific editor of texts in the Rolls Series, and writer, author of two works still on the history syllabus today, *Select Charters* (1870) and the *Constitutional History of England* in three volumes published in 1874, 1875 and 1878, Stubbs was a Tory and a holder of the 'Teutonic heritage' theory. While agreeing that parliament had not existed as such before 1265, he nevertheless held that English national liberty was the sum of individual liberties as had first belonged to the Anglo-Saxons. He mixed nationalism and history, but did so less than his contemporary, E. A. Freeman, whose *History of the Norman Conquest* in six volumes (1867–79) is now best remembered on account of the author's proto-'Aryan' views, coupled with antisemitism (in his view the French, descendants of the Normans, were 'semites' – a view which might have made his contemporary Dreyfus smile). Freeman's book revived the controversy on the Norman Yoke and the free Saxons, and he spent a large part of his life debating this and fighting against his contemporary J. H. Round, who saw the Norman Conquest as the instigator of feudalism.[25] This time the debate saw less emphasis being put on constitutional matters and more on nationalism.

Medieval history did not in fact become an exclusively academic discipline, with little engagement with contemporary ideas, until the end of the nineteenth century, in England at any rate. As a result it became increasingly divorced from the public political debate. Throughout the Victorian era, it was still used as it had been before, by sixteenth-century Parliamentarians and eighteenth-century Romantics or Whigs, in order to examine and mostly to criticise contemporary failures. Both Tories and Liberals appealed to the medieval constitutional or economic ideals to promote either an agrarian and paternalistic programme, or the need for constitutional, economic and social reforms. 'The authority of the Middle Ages was used to validate both freedom *and* order, egalitarism *and* hierarchism, liberalism *and* conservativism, self-expression *and* self-sacrifice.'[26] Among the most vocal representatives of the age were William Cobbett and Thomas Carlyle. Cobbett was a yeoman from southern England, who saw the traditional and, to his eyes idyllic, way of life in to which he had been born (with cottage industry and the general prosperity of the rural classes), destroyed by enclosures and industrialisation. His nostalgia was fuelled by his sympathy for Catholicism and the awareness of the social role of the medieval church in its perceived responsibility of support of the poor. On this basis, he stated (sometimes deliberately distorting his evidence) that the Middle Ages had seen a populous and prosperous England, where the people were defended by both the church and the lords who regarded it as their obligation to be socially responsible for their dependants. By contrast, contemporary Victorian society had witnessed a decline in population, civil liberties, a rise in crime, materialism and selfish *laissez-faire*, which had led to the decline and unhappiness of English society. His solution was a return to the system of small landholdings, where everyone was a producer and took pride in their work, against the rise of capitalism, an 'agrarian Utopia under the guidance of a benevolent church and gentry'.[27] Cobbett was not alone in seeking the revival of rural England through the return to small landholdings, the principle of responsible wealth (duty in return for wealth and privilege of the aristocracy, the principle of *noblesse oblige*), the fight against the injustice of the Poor Laws and the workhouse system, and the return to holidays, social harmony, order and leadership, and religious bonding.

The Young England group did so too.[28] Its members were committed landowners who dreamt of resisting the modern world of utilitarianism, rationalism, atheism and social alienation, and of reviving their Romantic vision of the Middle Ages with its chivalry, religious mystery, patriarchal leadership, and understanding of emotion and imagination. Most came from the upper classes and landed gentry, and had similarly nostalgic, past-aspiring views. Disraeli was the best known representative of the party, and his medievalist inclinations in his youth had led him to write historical novels like *Tancred*. He distanced himself from the group and its ideas after his political career took off, and became less of a nostalgic medievalist, but his legislation as Prime Minister, through a variety of Public Health Acts and laws aimed at preserving English rural society, shows that he had not given up completely on his dreams of reform for the improvement of the working people's lives.

Another medievalist historian and writer came from a very different background. Born in Scotland, Carlyle had first-hand knowledge of the

Industrial Revolution and its effects.[29] Strongly influenced by the German Romantics including Fichte, the Schlegels, Herder and Novalis, Carlyle saw contemporary poverty and exploitation as a result of the lack of leadership of the ruling classes, who had abandoned the function which justified their existence and which had made the Middle Ages such an age of heroes. Carlyle's search for heroes translated into his essays on *The Nibelungen Lied*, *Heroes and Hero Worship*, *History of the Norse Kings* and, above all, in *Past and Present*, based on a medieval chronicle of the abbey of Bury St Edmunds by Jocelyn of Brakelonde. In it Carlyle used the example of the stern but just, caring and responsible Abbot Samson to prove the benefits of the strong power of a beneficent leader.

France also saw an outstanding use of history in the cause of patriotism, first around the 1830 revolution, and again later, after defeat by Germany in the Franco-Prussian war of 1870. By the late nineteenth century the medieval past had a wide appeal, both in terms of scholarly research and popular awareness. It had ceased to be simply a matter of picking and choosing from a 'shop of unworn accessories' whatever was picturesque and colourful, but was now claiming to want to know the historical 'truth'.[30] The reason for this medieval revival was linked with patriotism and the 1870 defeat. Both the defeat and the ensuing Paris Commune were perceived as a result of the fragmentation of French society between the two great conflicting demands of turning France into a secular republic, and the French Catholic awareness of its historic role as the 'eldest daughter of the church'. Each party blamed the other for the defeat, and each party also appealed to the medieval past as the time of national unity and French hegemony. Again, both parties reclaimed two national heroes, Joan of Arc and Roland, as models for the French ability to overcome temporary defeat and regain its greatness. Joan of Arc in particular was the perfect example of conflicting models: Catholics emphasised the religious origin of her calling, while secular republicans depicted her as the popular victim of church and clergy. Both heroes were invoked in literature, poetry, on the stage and in opera, and in a large number of uninspired works, some of which encountered great success on patriotic grounds.[31] Lithographs and engravings, increasingly cheap to produce in great numbers, illustrated their stories, and those of other great heroes of 'la patrie' in their moments of glory (Clovis, Charlemagne, Hugh Capet, St Louis, Philip the Fair and Etienne Marcel in particular). Such illustrations, accompanying the text of schoolbooks, which by then incorporated the Middle Ages as part of the basic syllabus, were published in great numbers, originally at Epinal in Lorraine, which had been lost to the Germans, and were thus known as 'images d'Epinal'. Their introduction in the by then compulsory school textbooks, and in an expanding number of cheap illustrated publications, made them even more widespread for propaganda purposes. The term is still used in modern French, in a derogatory way, to describe a cliché of popular history.

Patriotism was also at the forefront of scholarly debate. Historians like Michelet and Guizot, and especially Gaston Paris (1839–1903) and Numa Denis Fustel de Coulanges (1830–1889), highly respected for their historical work, initiated a trend of anti-Germanist studies. Fustel's own field of study, which was the Germanic 'invasions' of Gaul in the early Middle Ages, was very much at the forefront of the debate; the author, a defender of the Roman origins of the French people (as opposed to the Frankish Germanic ones), saw his views discussed by a wider audience rather than just a specialised one of academic historians.[32] Paris, who had spent time in Germany as a student, was more interested in medieval French language and literature than history. He edited poetry, Chrétien de Troyes and *chansons de geste* (he was the inventor of the term, as he had been of *amour courtois*) and, without being as openly anti-German as Fustel, gave public lectures in 1871 exalting French patriotism as being on a par with Roland's sacrifice.[33] Scholarship was brought into the service of the much needed national rebuilding of confidence, and was used across the republican-Catholic divide. Numerous history chairs and journals, including the still running *Revue des Langues Romanes, Romania* (to counteract the German periodical *Germania*) and *Le Moyen Age* were founded, as well as the Société des Anciens Textes Français, the Ecole des Chartes and the Ecole des Hautes Etudes.[34] Partly as a challenge to the supremacy of German scholarship in medieval philology and history, and founded on acute Germanophobia, one of the greatest editors of medieval texts (in particular of the Tristan legend), Joseph Bédier, insisted on the late, clerical, learned origins of Tristan, as opposed to the German theories of a popular, oral, Germanic origin. His purpose was to reclaim for French culture a text which many felt had been hijacked by German culture, via Gottfrid of Strassburg and, in more recent days, by Wagner. Similarly, well-known historians, including the revered Fustel de Coulanges, and some periodicals such as *La Revue des Deux Mondes*, in effect 'descended into the street' in the 1870s: between 1871 and 1876, nearly 25 per cent of its articles was devoted to the Middle Ages. At a time when history was in the process of becoming more of an 'ivory-tower' academic discipline, this was a reversion to the centuries and decades when it had been part of a public debate that sought to understand the past in order to adapt it to contemporary problems and formulate solutions to these. Popular audiences were deeply involved in these debates, learnt about the Middle Ages from popular journals and from the explosion of museums and galleries consecrated to medieval art, notably the recently opened Musée de

Cluny, the Musée des Monuments Français and the medieval galleries of the Louvre. The debate took on a new dimension as the new century began, as the issue of the separation of church and state came increasingly to the fore, eventually consummated in 1905. For Catholics, the defeat and the troubles of fin de siècle France were a form of divine retribution for Napoleon III's abandonment of the pope in 1870 during the unification of Italy: France had lapsed from its role of 'eldest daughter of the church', and needed to repent and return to Mother Church. The renewal of the medieval pilgrimage tradition, especially after the beginning of popularity of Lourdes, would put the country again where it belonged, under the protection of the Virgin Mary. The newly-founded order of the Assumptionists was very active in promoting Catholic renewal, notably through its extremely popular illustrated journal *Le Pèlerin*. The order's given duty was the 'Crusade for the delivery of the Holy Father and the salvation of France'; as a result of recent disasters, Catholic France had to remember once again its allegiance to Mary; a 'France which remembers its traditions [is] the France of Charlemagne and of St Louis that takes up its cross, walking toward God in whom salvation lies.' Meanwhile, under the influence of Victor Hugo and Viollet-le Duc, the appropriation of the medieval as representing democracy, the working people victimised by the church, and the attempt to set up the anti-clerical republic as the heir of this alleged medieval freedom, was equally strong in its propaganda. In his famous article in *La Revue des Deux Mondes* in 1872, Fustel de Coulanges expressed this dichotomy:

> Each person makes his own, imaginary Middle Ages ... and each person forms his faith and his political credo according to the error he has chosen or the error to which his education has bound him. There are as many ways of considering the Middle Ages as there are political parties in France: it is our historical theories that divide us the most.[35]

While continental Europeans used their medieval past to construct a national identity focused on a mythic ethnic origin, the English made use of the Middle Ages in a more complex manner. The first to use the Anglo-Saxon past were the Elizabethans John Bale and John Foxe. Both were particularly interested in the existence of a national church and people. Bales sought to justify the creation of an English state church by reference to that Anglo-Saxon past and Foxe in his *Acts and Monuments of These Latter and Perilous Days* (1563), popularly known as the *Book of Martyrs*, stressed Protestantism as a way of returning to 'the church of Augustine'.[36] The list of texts in which this line was defended well into the eighteenth century is long: a characteristic example, revealed by its title, is George Smith's *The Britons and Saxons Not Converted to Popery: or The Faith of Our Ancestors*

Shewn to Have Been Corrupted by the Romish Church, and Restored to its Ancient Purity by the Reformed Church of England (1748). Bede's history in particular was often used as a basis for the origins of Englishness and the greatness of England as a Protestant nation fighting Catholic Europe and the tyranny of the papacy. That same Bede, however, had been edited by Thomas Stapleton in the mid sixteenth century while he was a Recusant refugee in Louvain, in order to associate the 'primitive' English Church with the church of Rome and Roman Catholicism. (A line which, incidentally, Bede would have been much more likely to approve than Foxe's!). An interest in the Anglo-Saxon past continued throughout sixteenth-century chronicles and histories, and is in evidence, for example, in Spenser's *Faerie Queene*, which first saw King Arthur glorified as a symbol of united, Protestant, Englishness under the rule of a 'good' sovereign.[37] Throughout the eighteenth century and into the early nineteenth, the theme of Englishness and English roots in the medieval, and notably the Saxon, period, was a commonplace of literary production, examples of which can be found in a variety of often indigestible epic poems or plays, of which one can mention, purely as examples, William Taylor's *Wortigerne* (1799) or Chatterton's *Goddwyn and Aella*. William Taylor, who was above all a scholar and linguist, belonged to the group of revivers of Old English studies, all part and parcel of the search for a 'national character', closely connected with the original, 'Teutonic' language and literature.[38] Studies in and of Old English in England, in the tradition of Junius and Nowell, as well as of Old Norse, were pursued for purely philological purposes by George Hickes (his *Thesaurus* was published in 1701) and later eighteenth-century scholars.[39] Translations of the eddic poems and of the first sagas had begun in earnest by the end of the eighteenth century, especially with the work of Samuel Laing (1780–1868), whose influence on later novelists and poets such as Carlyle and Longfellow was far-reaching.[40] The use of Old English, and subsequently of Old Norse, to create a kind of Teutonic myth began, in fact, in Germany, with the Schlegel and the Grimm brothers.[41] Plays such as *Earl Goodwin* by Ann Yearsley (1791) and *Edwy and Elgiva* by Fanny Burney (staged in 1795) reflect this trend.[42]

The interest in promoting the common 'Teutonic' past was further increased after the French Revolution, when the mood was one of distancing English politics from the French style of government. Anti-French political feeling contributed to reinforcing the idea of a common 'Germanic' heritage, but one centred on Scandinavia rather than Germany itself. George Stephens, a scholar who eventually emigrated to Scandinavia, was the best representative of both the interest in the Old North in Victorian England, and of anti-German feeling, which reached fever-pitch after the annexation of Schleswig-Holstein by Germany from Denmark in 1864.[43] Stephens put into his admiration for the Vikings a variety of features to which he could relate the society of his own day: their spirit of entrepreneurship; their non-feudal society based on a 'constitutional' monarchy in which the king exercised power because it was given to him by the people; their democratic system of law and justice; and their strong oral culture, which he contrasted with the, to his eyes, feeble Anglo-Saxon one that had been taken over by the church. He claimed that the Vikings had, in fact, saved Anglo-Saxon England, and reclaimed the North as part of Anglo-Scandinavian, rather than Germanic, culture. These themes were illustrated in his best known work as an author, the play *Revenge: or Woman's Love* (1857), a story set in the days of King Edgar and the Vikings, whose heroine Rowena became a Victorian icon. A whole range of other scholars went on translating sagas and the eddas, notably George Dasent and Benjamin Thorpe. By the middle of the nineteenth century, the language, religion and myths of the Old North had become known and gave rise to a huge industry of poetry, prose, scholarly lectures, folklore studies and Scandinavian travel.[44]

The Victorians 'invented' the Old North as a subject, reclaiming it as part of the English past. Nevertheless, the great hero of Englishness from the six-teenth century onwards was undoubtedly King Alfred.[45] Perceived as a lawgiver, the father of the British constitution and of the navy, the founder of the English nation and the preserver of its liberties against the Danish invaders, his exalted status was already clear in the two earliest texts recounting his life, Robert Powell's in 1634 and Sir John Spelman's in 1642–43. Both writers were royalists, and for a long time Alfred was to be, in a sense, a Tory icon: he was, for example, the model of choice of Prince Frederick, the son of George II, an opponent to his father's Whig policies. Encomia of Alfred abound in the works of Burke, Hume, Gibbon and Wordsworth. Two epic poems entitled *Alfred*, by J. Cottle and H. J. Pye, appeared within a year of each other in 1800 and 1801,[46] and a host of other historians, both scholarly and popular, as well as playwrights, poets and even composers wrote about him. In 1740 Prince Frederick commissioned a play about Alfred from J. Thomson and D. Mallet, with music by Thomas Arne; it was performed for his birthday and its title to glory remains the finale, officially entitled 'Grand Ode in Honour of Great Britain', better known as 'Rule Britannia'. Significant of his popular appeal and perception was the building of a mock castle named King Alfred's Hall at Cirencester Park in Gloucestershire between 1727 and 1732, with an inscription by the creator to the 'virtuous Alfred', contrasting his reputation with that of George II, of whom the owner disapproved. Another inscription to Alfred, on the tower at Meanwood near Leeds, a kind of folly erected in 1787 'to the memory of Alfred the Great, the Wise, the Pious and Magnanimous, the friend of Science, Virtue, Law and Liberty' reiterated that same theme.[47] Alfred was equally praised abroad, by Voltaire and the Encyclopedists as a model of a good ruler to be followed by French kings, by Mirabeau (and thus Revolutionary France), and by Grillparzer as well as other German-speaking authors. In fact, for a long time the best-known biography of the king was German, written by Reinhold Pauli in 1851. Between 1800 and 1901, which turned out to be the height of the Alfred cult with the celebration of the thousandth anniversary of his death,[48] there had been three statues of him, twenty-five paintings (not counting innumerable illustrations) and over one hundred literary works, novels, poems, plays, children's books as well as academic and popular histories. His popularity was due in part to the availability of sources, especially of the medieval biography by Asser popularised through translations by J. A. Giles and J. Stevenson, even though this biography had had numerous interpolations in it from the time it had been first published by Matthew Parker and Henry Spelman. The greatly popular but entirely apocryphal stories of Alfred and the cakes and Alfred's foray into the Danish camp were two such interpolations. Biographies and literature were only one form taken by the veneration for Alfred. Through often misunderstood, misinterpreted or extrapolated versions of the sources, he came to be regarded as the founder of the English nation and defender of the land, the founder of the empire, the founder of Oxford University or, at any rate, of education in England, the founder of the navy, of parliament, of representative government, the constitution, local administration and the jury system, a good king concerned with his responsibilities for his subjects (such as not burning their livelihoods!), and even a 'captain of industry'. Moreover, he was equally praised as an obedient child, a model scholar, a pious and just man, a good husband and father, keen on self-improvement and possessing a heap of other Victorian virtues which turned him into a saintly figure. This image of the perfect 'constitutional' monarch and enlightened king was especially potent when he was described as the precursor of 'good' monarchs like William IV and Victoria: contemporary history books with titles like *Alfred to Victoria: Hands Across a Thousand Years* illustrate this trend. In 1848 the celebration of a thousand years from his birth in Wantage was a still relatively modest affair. But the 'cult' of Alfred rose to unparalleled heights during the second half of the nineteenth century. He was depicted from then on in an amazing number of pictorial images and illustrations, sometimes as a monumental figure but more often within the framework of historical scenes with enormously long titles, such as *Alfred Submitting his Code of Laws for the Approval of the Witan* (John

Bridges, lithograph of 1847), *Queen Judith Reciting to Alfred the Great, when a Child, the Songs of the Bards* (Richard Westall, watercolour, 1799), and hundreds of others in the same spirit. During the 1901 celebrations, his achievements were highlighted not just locally but nationally and internationally: the 20 September was made a national holiday, representatives from Britain, France, Germany and all the colonies were at Winchester, as were the mayors of major cities, representatives of the navy and empire, academics, ambassadors and industrialists, to take part in the events and to watch the unveiling of Alfred's statue.

By the later eighteenth century the cult of Alfred had become part of Whig political culture. In the early nineteenth century it was established beyond party lines, as it were, and he could be both adopted as an overall national hero and become the object of more detached scholarly study. This was the first great age of monumental scholarly studies of Anglo-Saxon England. Sharon Turner's *History of the Anglo-Saxons* (1799), which was the first modern history of its kind, and remained one of the most influential, exemplified such accounts throughout the nineteenth century. Other major historians, Henry Hallam, Joseph Bosworth, Benjamin Thorpe, John Mitchell Kemble and Bishop Stubbs, were important authors in the field.[49] Kemble (1807–1857) in particular, who was a regular correspondent and enthusiastic supporter and translator of the Grimms in England, played a major part in the dissemination of the Alfredian cult in his own works.[50] Through these scholars' studies, not only Alfred but the Saxon past, became the blueprint of national consciousness. In his inaugural lecture as Regius Professor of Modern History at Oxford in 1840, Thomas Arnold claimed that:

> We, this great English nation, whose race and language are now overrunning the earth from one end of it to the other, – we were born when the white horse of the Saxons had established his dominion from the Tweed to the Tamar [revealingly excluding the Welsh, Cornish and Scots!]. So far we can trace our blood, our language, the name and actual divisions of our country, the beginnings of some of our institutions. So far our national identity extends, so far history is modern, for it treats of a life which was then and is not yet extinguished.[51]

Interest in Alfred and a few other Anglo-Saxon kings such as Edmund was not restricted to upper-class consciousness and academic isolation, but became a widespread phenomenon. People gave their sons the names of Anglo-Saxon kings, which become increasingly frequent in nineteenth-century censuses, at first in families with some bookish connection (stationers, teachers), but increasingly as far down the social scale as agricultural labourers. This went so far that, unlike the Stuarts, who claimed descent from Edward the Confessor, and could therefore also claim a saint as a patron, the Hanoverians preferred to claim their descent from Alfred, regarded as the founder of English liberties. The 'Norman Yoke' debate, which had been at its most powerful as a political tool during the Commonwealth, and had remained popular with the Whig radicals of the 1790s, was revived by the American, and then the French Revolutions. In America it had been used by Thomas Jefferson for example, who had incorporated into the Declaration of Independence the myth of Saxon freedom, claiming it for the Americans. Later he was to use it to argue that American Indians should be 'colonised' by English Americans just as the Britons had been by the Anglo-Saxons.[52] Medievalism in America was also used, as it was in England, by completely opposed political and social groups, both claiming to find the roots of their identity in it: the aristocratic society of the South, as well as the 'industrial' society of the north-east coast and Boston. It could justify both a conservative, literally 'feudal' hierarchical organisation representing patriarchy, paternalism and stability in the Deep South, and the radical, socialist, corporate trade unions in the North, which saw themselves as a form of latter-day medieval guilds.[53]

The Saxon freedom versus Norman Yoke myth was not only a symbol of British patriotism against the French, as well as of Whig political ideas. It was also a Whig appropriation of national history and an ideological appropriation of the medieval past and was absorbed fully into popular perception. It evolved from a political principle (defending Anglo-Saxon liberties), and a scholarly concept (unity of the free Saxons with their Germanic roots) for Kemble and later Freeman, to a popular perception which, from Walter Scott onwards, would remain paramount in the English-speaking world down to twentieth-century Hollywood films.

By the 1850s a strong Anglo-Saxon and English national consciousness had developed, focused on heroes like Alfred, based on the religious roots of the Anglo-Saxon church, the legal roots of common law in Anglo-Saxon legislation, the interest in Old English, and the consciousness of the unity of the 'Germanic' race. It is all the more interesting, therefore, to see how and why the concept of Englishness ultimately became unravelled.[54] The attempt to dilute and suppress such *English* historical consciousness was deliberately engineered as a result of pressure by the Victorians, whose aim was to create a sense of 'Britishness' instead. This 'sacrifice' of Englishness to Britishness came either as a form of compensation for the loss of independence and of real political power of Scotland, Wales and Ireland, or on account of what was perceived to be of greater importance to the nation, its imperial position. In the latter case, the need was to stress the Britishness of all subjects anywhere in the world. This has continued until recently. Its most obvious manifestation have been the lack of national symbols, such as a flag or a national anthem (both the Union Jack and 'God Save the Queen' are symbols of Britain, not England), and an absence of English nationalism and of an English origin myth. Even men like Kemble and Freeman ultimately gave in, and claimed the *Anglo-Saxon* past as part of the *British* past. Towards the end of the nineteenth century and in the early twentieth, when the main enemy was no longer France but Germany, Britishness came to be seen as even more appropriate: Englishness was to be avoided, on account of its cousinship with Teutonism. This solution served its purpose for all the time that the British Empire was in existence, and subsequently too, as long as the Union is still in place. While the empire has all but disappeared, and the Union may be on its way out with the increasing devolution of power to Scotland and Wales, it will be interesting to see whether Britishness too is fading away.

Some signs point already in the direction of a revival of English nationalism. What began at first as just manifestations of football hooliganism has rapidly escalated into much more generally popular stances of Englishness in the last two or three years. Witness the greater popularity of the St George flag (now apparently allowed for car stickers with ENG, *as well as*, if not yet *instead of*, the Union Jack and GB), the celebration of St George' Day as a popular National Day, the use of 'Land of Hope and Glory' (also 'British' but perceived as a sign of 'Englishness' now) as an addition to 'God Save the Queen', just as the Scots and the Welsh make a point of using 'Flower of Scotland' and 'Land of Our Fathers' at public events, and the pointed association of Shakespeare with St George – he was born on 23 April 1564, the saint's day in the calendar. A Royal Society of St George exists, and advertises in magazines with a traditional County audience, with the slogan: 'Do You Love England?' Its advert continues thus:

> Are you proud of your Country and her glorious history and heritage? Then why not become a member of the Royal Society of St George? You could take an active part in our determination to safeguard England *and Englishness* [my italics], to revitalise our nation and restore decency and integrity to our daily lives.

St George as a symbol of Englishness has revived, again 'by popular demand', mainly as a football icon in the twenty-first century – unsurprisingly still as the 'man of the (English) people', so to speak. For the first time since the mid nineteenth century, a renewed sense of *English* national pride and unity has come to the fore, even if only on such occasions as the

Football World Cup and the Queen's Jubilee on 2002. The very fact that a debate around the decision made by an American conductor to remove such staple patriotic fare as the 'Rule Britannia' and other popular singalongs from the Last Night of the Proms for reasons of political correctness, *could*, and *did*, rage throughout the Summer of 2002 is in itself significant. The monarchy has been the ultimate manifestation of British patriotism in the last 150 years, and never more so than on major public occasions such as royal weddings, funerals and especially, of course, coronations. The combination of a state church which had regained its ritual and ceremonial stature between the 1890s and 1910s, and had benefited from a major musical revival with great choirs and composers (Parry, Stamford, Stainer), with a monarchy whom medievalist Victorian stage-masters had returned to what was perceived as the glory and pageantry of the Middle Ages proved unbeatable. Significantly, one of its main musical supports was Elgar, composer of the aptly-named *Pomp and Circumstance*, containing the unofficial 'hymn' 'Land of Hope and Glory'. (It may be no coincidence that Elgar, whose name was in fact Edward Greening, should have chosen to adopt a pseudonym based on the Anglo-Saxon name Ælfgar.) [55] Already in the late 1930s, the German historian Percy Schramm was contemplating the English monarchy with nostalgic awe:

> Everything at Westminster remains as of yore, while Aachen and Rheims [the German and French medieval royal capitals] are desolate. There is no longer an 'Imperator Romanorum'. Even the Habsburgs and Hohenzollerns have had to lay aside their imperial titles, and the Crown, sceptre and robes of the old imperial treasury are gazed at as exhibits in a museum ... There is hardly a country that has succeeded in so continually adapting her medieval institutions as to avoid their overthrow ... Indeed it is one of the symptoms of our age that countries, in the enjoyment of newly-awakened powers, create an entirely new form of state, and consciously throw the past aside. In the midst of these scenes of construction and destruction, no tokens of the past remain in existence save the Cathedral Sancti Petri at Rome and the Choir of King Edward at Westminster. [56]

Both the Habsburg Empire and the European ideal first formed during the Enlightenment had survived with difficulty the aftermath of the French Revolution and the Napoleonic Wars. [57] The imperial ideal, as well as the European one, retained their attraction, and both re-emerged, on a worldwide rather than purely European level, either as a real form of supranational power through colonialism, or as an ideal in the form of international socialism. In this respect, too, the First World War represented a watershed.

The demise of the last European imperial power with the dismantling of the Habsburg Empire at the end of the war meant that the European ideal had to be constructed anew in a different from, first as a unified and pacified Europe, then as a new ideal of unity through economic and political links. The first imperative was to avoid another disaster like the Great War in future. Various options were proposed and examined, most famous immediately after the war being Aristide Briant's *Memorandum*, – and the great pan-European movement of the 1920s Coudenhove-Kalergi Plan. The failure of these movements, and of the American-supported League of Nations, was due in no small measure to Nazi and Fascist hostility, and to English indifference, the former on nationalistic grounds, the latter because of predominantly Commonwealth interests. The lack of a solution was only too obvious with the outbreak of the Second World War and its aftermath, the formation of the two blocs and the Cold War. Germany's gradual reconstruction after the war thanks to the Marshall Plan enabled west European powers to attempt various forms of integration on a smaller scale. Customs Union, Council of Europe, Coal and Steel Community, Defence Community and Atomic Energy, all came into being in the 1950s, providing limited associations of common interest.[58] Thanks to Jean Monnet and Robert Schuman the Treaty of Rome, which founded the European Community, was signed by France, Germany, Italy, Belgium, the Netherlands and Luxemburg on 25 March 1957. It established a common policy on various trade issues, economic benefits and defence, and provided some common institutions. In 1972 the Community was enlarged to include Britain, Eire and Denmark, and was gradually extended to Spain, Portugal, Greece, Finland, Sweden and Austria, forming the European Union in the 1990s. With the end of the Communist bloc (which had had its own economic union, Comecon) and the reunification of Germany in the 1990s, the European Union aimed at becoming not only a single market, but also a free circulation zone, with common legislation, European institutions at supranational level, and, since 2002, a common currency. This was the ideal set out in 1992 in the Treaty of Maastricht. Perhaps one might reflect on the fact that Maastricht is a city set in the very heartland of Frankish rule in the eighth and ninth centuries, those same Franks who were Charlemagne's people. The ideals set out in 1992 would have been completely understood by Charlemagne, and by his successors like Frederick II or Charles V. Such ideals were at the back of their minds for the three ministers who first pushed forward European integration in the 1950s, Robert Schuman of France, Alcide de Gasperi, Prime Minister of Italy, and the German Chancellor Konrad Adenauer: these three men probably had in mind to recreate one day a modern version of 'Christendom', as had been the spiritual and political union of the West under Charlemagne.[59] Such aspirations and ideals may even have pierced through the not uncommon europhobia of many early twenty-first-century Englishmen: in June 2002, the President of the European Union, Romano Prodi, was awarded an honorary degree by Oxford University. In his speech (in Latin, the 'universal' European language, as is still the rule on these occasions), the Chancellor of the University began by quoting Signor Prodi himself: 'For the first time since the Roman Empire we have the opportunity to unite Europe', and continued to praise the honorand for his concern with European unity.[60]

But at the end of the twentieth century, nationalism, the other political force which also claims medieval roots, was far from dead. Twentieth-century nationalism came in two different forms. The first was represented by the two main political movements between the two world wars: Nazism and Bolshevism. In contrast, the third such movement, Italian Fascism, hardly used the Middle Ages at all, focusing its historical propaganda either on the present, on the Roman past, or on the Renaissance. It was the age of the *condottieri* which was used by the Fascists, turning these into heroes fighting for the unity of Italy like so many proto-Garibaldis. The age of the *condottieri* was perceived, if anything, as anti-medieval, turning its back on the irrational, mythical, dark ages, which were an institutional and political mess with no centralised state or law – a long-enduring view of the Middle Ages in Italian culture. The main cultural propaganda tool used by the Italian government was the film industry.[61] Over the whole Fascist period, only four films set in the Middle Ages were produced – every year between 1939 and 1942 alone, Italian studios produced respectively 50, 83, 89 and 119 films. Best known of the four was *La corona di ferro*, begun before the war and, actually, an openly pacifist film – when Goebbels saw it, he hated it and regarded it as hostile to the regime – in 1942 the director of Italian cinema happened to be sent to the Yugoslav front, in the thickest of the battle, where he promptly died.

Why did the Nazi and Stalinist regimes made such use of the Middle Ages? It is not sufficient to argue that they automatically choose what they would regard as the most 'glorious' period in their national history. Rather, one should inquire into why it is that both German and Soviet propaganda actually regarded the Middle Ages as their 'best' period. Concepts of territorial and ethnic integrity were obviously paramount in both cases: both Russia and Germany had been at their most extensive geographically and at their most unified and dominant at that time. Völkism, with its return to medieval roots, the primitive German society, close to the soil, in Nazi Germany, was another reason. Nazi and Stalinist propaganda, in their complex and myriad ways, are both considerable fields of study in their own right. The best way to illustrate the use made by both regimes of the Middle Ages is to examine the way they dealt with it in the newest medium at their disposal, film.

The parallel between the attitudes of the two regimes towards the film industry is striking. In both cases there was a need to build up a national film industry to fight the impact of 'foreign' films (American in the Soviet Union, French in Germany), which provided a large part of popular entertainment through adventure film and glamorous stars.[62] Despite what we now regard as the golden age of classical German cinema during the Weimar Republic, with the films of Fritz Lang and Friedrich Murnau in particular, such films were hardly competition for foreign films as popular entertainment in the 1930s and early 1940s. Both Lenin and his successors in the Soviet Union and Goebbels in Germany were aware of the value of the new medium for propaganda purposes, but both were also aware of the fact that propaganda functioned best when mediated through entertainment. Both regimes set up special state departments, a People's Commissariat in the Soviet Union and a Ministry for Propaganda in Germany, to deal with the issue, and the way in which their task was defined is eerily similar:

> The cinema, more than any other field of our work, needs public support. The cinema is not merely a medium of agitation and propaganda, but it is a powerful and key factor with the aid of which we shall raise the masses to a higher cultural level ... [the organisation] should do much to transform the cinema into a real weapon for the cultural influencing of the masses'; [it is to become a] weapon of class enlightenment for the proletariat, for the education of masses.[63] (Soviet Union)

Lenin himself, who regarded cinema as the 'most important of all the arts', and who was adamant that it could not be apolitical, had defined his views on the subject when he stated that, 'in the hands of the Party it must be the most powerful medium of Communist enlightenment and agitation'.[64]

> Film is one of the most modern and far-reaching ways of influencing the masses today ... skilfully produced film propaganda could educate public taste according to the dictates of the Party.[65] (Germany)

Both regimes based their film propaganda on two main elements. The first was the fight against the 'enemies' of the regime. There were two kinds of enemies, those outside and those within. Outside enemies were the Mongols or Germans in Soviet cinema, the Slavs and the English in Nazi cinema. Inside enemies were the anti-Bolsheviks fighting for bourgeois values against the triumphant rise of the Communist masses in the Soviet Union, and

Jews in Germany. The second common element to both was the cult of an individual hero, either through the exaltation of Hitler himself, notably in the famous *Triumph of the Will* (Leni Riefenstahl, 1933), or the more indirect cult of Stalin through the association made between him and heroes of Russian history, notably Tsar Ivan the Terrible. In fact, Stalin specifically commanded Eisenstein to make this film, after the director's years in the wilderness between 1938 and 1946. Both cinemas ultimately tried very hard to support a revival of national feeling in the 1930s through the medium of history. A number of their films dealt with other periods perceived as those of great national pride, and focused on Peter the Great, for example, or on Frederick the Great and Bismarck in Germany. A few, and significantly these are among the most successful in propaganda and public recognition terms, specifically engaged with medieval themes.

If we first look at the Nazi version of the 'medieval', one of the most striking facts is what it does NOT contain: that is any films associated with the Niebelungen myths, either in the old 'Germanic' form or indeed in the Wagner version.[66] The only film on the subject was Fritz Lang's two-part epic (*Siegfried* and *Kriemhilde's Revenge*), produced at the height of the Weimar Republic; there would not be another until the mid 1960s. Hitler and Goebbels appreciated the Niebelungen epic and Lang's *Siegfried*, with its glorification of a German national hero and myth to counterbalance foreign culture and communist internationalism, and both admired Wagner, supported the Bayreuth Festival, and the way in which Wagner's heirs turned it into a monument to Hitler and Nazism. But Lang's *Kriemhilde* no longer concentrated on either the German past or a tragic and romantic love story; instead it denounced unblinking reverence of a hero, fanatical love for a leader and the overwhelming desire for revenge which leads to the destruction of a people. The heroes of the film were the 'Germanic' Burgundians, represented as the master race because civilised, opposing the savage, eastern, small and dark Huns of Attila; but the message could be interpreted differently. The film was regarded as too dangerous for the people since, ultimately, it suggested that total obedience to an absolute ruler can only lead to tragedy. Using Wagner's music as an accompaniment to parades or as part of the sound-track for the *Triumph of the Will* was one thing, using the *Ring* itself, like using Nietzsche, was too dangerous for mass consumption. The turnabout is revealing in the light of the early associations of Nazism with the Germanic past through the founding in 1923 of the Thulé Society (whose ideas were later taken up by the Nazi party and government).[67] The purpose of the society was to promote the *Ahnenerbe*, the worship of the ancestors, with an agenda of Teutonic and chivalric themes, as expressed in so-called medieval ceremonies at the castle of Externsteiner.

The young Hitler had been a member of the society, whose emblem was the swastika, later adopted for other purposes. Part of the society's brief was to return to the worship of the old Germanic gods of the legend, while using the Teutonic Knights and the Knights of the Round Table as models, and its main claim was to have traced the descent of the German people as warriors from the fabled Atlantis and Thulé. Other Nazi associations with the medieval past were with Charlemagne (Hitler was an admirer; Himmler, with a greater historical culture, was against Charlemagne on the grounds of his repeated victories over the Saxons). Himmler, whose father had been a professor of medieval history, was also a member of the society. He founded a fantasy Grail castle at Wewelsberg, complete with a 'convent' of thirteen 'knights' and the 'Spear of Destiny', presumably meant to have been the famous Holy Lance of Charlemagne and later emperors. Himmler's model medieval emperor was Henry I, and he had an imperial reception arranged for his visit at Quedlinburg, the old capital of the Ottonian and Salian emperors in the tenth and eleventh centuries.

What Nazi propagandists mostly turned to again and again was the Völkist theory, with its concept of 'blood and soil', and hence of the role of the peasant, most closely attached to the German soil and roots, and to the primeval forest. In this context, the two most representative films in Nazi cinema, characterised by examples of 'charismatic leadership, an emphasis on race and the *Volk* and the dream of national unity',[68] are *Blut und Boden* (*Blood and Soil*), a documentary made in 1933, and *Ewiger Wald* (*Eternal Forest*), made in 1936.[69] Both films illustrate this mystical connection between the elements of the *Volk*, its roots in the German soil and the forests which, in the distant past and by contrast with industrialisation and bourgeois Jewish-led contemporary culture, had enabled the 'pure' German spirit to prosper. Both have peasant heroes, and their message is the longstanding relationship between man and nature, the unity of an 'organic community' as it had been throughout its history, notably during the happy period of the Middle Ages, with its peasants, craftsmen, artists (associated with Gothic churches), and Teutonic Knights. Bringing back this unity might involve fighting all those who attempted to deny it, and who attacked the peaceful German people – hence the nationalist agenda.

Nationalism was also the main agenda of Soviet cinema and of its incursion into the Middle Ages. *Ivan the Terrible* was made in two parts in 1944 and 1946, largely at Stalin's request, because he wished to see himself portrayed in the tradition of a tsarist hero fighting against the boyars in the sixteenth century. It was directed by Sergei Eisenstein on account of the success he had had with his previous film but one, made in 1938, *Alexandr Nevski*.[70] *Nevski* is the most potent example of cinema reworking and reinterpreting the Middle Ages for a specific political, nationalistic, purpose. 'My subject is patriotism', Eisenstein is reported to have said. He continued:

> The themes of patriotism and natural defence against the aggressor is the subject that suffuses our film. We have taken a historical episode from the thirteenth century, when the ancestors of today's Fascists, the Teutonic and Livonian knights, waged a systematic struggle to conquer and invade the East in order to subjugate the Slav and other nationalities in precisely the same spirit that Fascist Germany is trying to do today, with the same frenzied slogans and the same fanaticism.[71]

His didactic purpose, of educating Soviet audiences in the spirit of the new nationalism of the 1930s, was part of the need to foster anti-German propaganda, to provide the masses with a model epic designed to combat the menace of Fascism and to arouse them in preparation for war. Its subject, the thirteenth-century defeat of the Teutonic Knights by the Russians led by Prince Nevski, was to be a precursor of the struggle, renewed in the late 1930s, of the Russian people against their German oppressors. Moreover, the Russians, naturally brave, heroic and true, represented the 'real people'. Their leader Nevski, though a prince, nevertheless belonged to these secular masses, being a 'man of the people', by contrast with the German knights, who represented the greedy cruel aristocracy, associated with the power of the church. Numerous signs identify the message to the audience, leading them to recognise, in the portrayal of Nevski, the cult of Stalin, and in the Teutonic Knights, Russia's Nazi enemies. Eisenstein's blatant and avowed patriotic and class manipulation of history allowed him openly to change it, to the extent of obliterating the fact that the real Nevski had in fact been an ally and puppet of the Mongols, in other words a traitor to Russian interests for his own political purpose, and that he had repressed several popular rebellions, in alliance with the great boyars.[72] The message of *Alexandr Nevski* was hammered at the audience not only through the subject-matter, but also and very potently through the cinematography and the musical score, written by Prokofiev. Nowhere is this as obvious as in the most famous scene in the film, the Battle on the Ice. Symbols identify the opponents of this battle between East and West, for example the Latin cross of the Teutonic Knights. The balance between the musical themes, eastern and western, at first mixed during the battle, sees the eastern theme representing the Russians take over gradually, as their victory approaches.

If Nazi and Soviet cinema were the most conspicuous users of the medieval for nationalistic purposes, they were not entirely alone in their choice. Patriotic films were produced elsewhere, especially around the time of the two world wars. The producers and directors used whatever themes could be harnessed to exalt the national past and help with popular morale. One such example came from English studios, with the film *A Canterbury Tale* (1944), directed by Michael Powell and Emeric Pressburger (the latter himself a Hungarian refugee).[73] Powell himself described the film as an illustration of 'why we fight', a reflection on the values for which England stood: to understand these, one had to return to the medieval pastoral roots of the country of Chaucer, to counter the attempt to destroy it through materialism, greed and war. The spiritual pilgrimage of the characters leads them to understand these values of the countryside, its rhythms, crafts and people, and to represent them as the essence of England and Englishness, the source of national strength, with its appeal across party lines. The film was released with the accompanying text:

> *A Canterbury Tale* is a new story about Britain, her unchanging beauty and traditions, and of the Old Pilgrims and New. As the last scene of the picture fades away, to those who see it and are British there will come a feeling – just for a moment – of wishing to be silent, as the thought flashes through one's mind: 'These things I have just seen and heard are all my parents taught me. That is Britain, that is me'.[74]

Nationalism did not die with the end of the Second World War, despite its more muted appeal in mainstream Europe, which had witnessed the horrors it had produced during the first half of the century.[75] It remained a constant feature on a smaller scale, mostly within existing nation states where minority ethnic groups attempted to negotiate a more autonomous existence, notably the right to use their language and religion freely. In many cases such nationalisms had stressed the ethnic-linguistic element: Catalan from the 1850s, Finnish and Gaelic from the 1860s, and Basque, which saw the foundation of a national party and the adoption of the name 'Euskadi'.[76] These movements were fairly low-key, and their constituencies were sometimes entirely different: while the Basques had mass support in the years after the First World War, as had the Irish, Catalan nationalism was more representative of the intellectual middle classes. Catalonia gained autonomy from Spain and developed into a successful economic and political entity, whereas the Basque case, where there are only eight per cent of Basque-speakers, with an agenda for independence and violent military action, is still today an unresolved issue. Similar national movements, the Scottish, Welsh, Breton and Flemish ones, for example, only emerged after the Second World War. In some cases, nationalism led to peaceful reform, as in Wales and Scotland; in others, it led to ethnic minority fighting against the centralising power of the state for Bretons and Corsicans in France, and to linguistic warfare in Belgium. More recently, in the 1990s, other linguistic nationalisms have re-emerged in ex-Soviet-dominated eastern and central Europe.[77] There too the issue is being argued on the basis of 'medieval' tradition, as it is in Hungary and Romania.

Two particularly destructive forms of warfare and terrorism, with the parties waging war both claiming medieval roots to their conflicts, have dominated the twentieth century, and have yet to be entirely resolved. In the case of both Ireland and the Balkans, the nationalist agenda specifically has claimed to be one of return to the imaginary status quo of a golden age, set in the Middle Ages. In Ireland the identification was one of the 'Celtic' (meaning Roman Catholic) past of freedom from English conquest. In the Balkans, the identification of the Orthodox Serbs with the past glories of the kingdom of Greater Serbia before the battle of Kosovo in 1389, was used to justify fighting traditional enemies, Catholic Croatians or Muslim Bosnians and Kosovars, a unifying national cause, whose rhetoric was convincingly delivered and widely received. These two examples are a perfect illustration of the complete irrelevance of the actual historic situation at any given time. Ireland was conquered by the English, naturally themselves Catholic at the time like everybody else in western Europe, during the twelfth and thirteenth centuries, in the full flowering of the Middle Ages; there were, between the sixteenth and the nineteenth centuries, as many Protestant 'Celtic' (meaning Irish) men and women as there were Catholic ones in Ireland. The creative interpretation of Serbian resistance to the Ottomans as it was depicted in post-battle of Kosovo history and literature has already been mentioned. Historic facts have no, or very limited, importance. It is their interpretation, misuse if need be, which really counts. It may be of no small significance that it is possible to use the medieval period so flexibly: it is still sufficiently close for some major facts to stick in peoples' minds and to become myth, but is too remote and vague for most people to inquire closely into. This is a crucial factor in the study of perceptions of the Middle Ages, especially in the twentieth century, and one that occurs again and again. It applies with particular virulence to this most elusive but all-pervasive concept, the 'Celtic' myth.

5

The Celtic Bandwagon

Lampeter is a small town in rural West Wales. It was a favourite spot for the culture of the flower-power age, and is probably one of the few remaining places in the UK where one can find not one but several small shops selling a mixture of Indian cotton skirts, incense joss sticks and cards with Celtic mythical stories, usually owned by otherworldly-looking fifty-something ex-hippies. These days, many of them have been replaced by an influx of New Age Travellers, no doubt attracted there by a combination of the well-known tradition of 'alternative' life-style, relatively low property prices, and considerable, if sometimes amused, local tolerance. Its university has profited, over the years, from this trend. It may be one of the few in Britain where the Students' Union asked the vice-chancellor and authorities to allow room on university premises for its Pagan Society, on a par with other religious groupings, *and got it.* This came in the form of a venerable old tree standing near the main quadrangle, now permanently festooned with pieces of paper expressing pagan worship of some kind. Indeed the university's recruitment prospectus now underlines the Welsh druidic and mythological roots of the area, and university departments offer courses on druids and Celtic Christianity which invariably fill the classroom.

As a concept, 'Celtic' covers a mix of the non-Christian or pre-Christian sacred (replacing, incidentally, the 1960s, 1970s and 1980s taste for eastern spirituality and other guru- or swami-led cults), nature-worship with its mother-earth goddess cult, witchcraft, supernatural communications, natural health and therapies, organic food, ecological concerns, sexual freedom, arcane and secret cults like the Rosicrucians and the Golden Dawn. The mix is generally perceived as being an anti-establishment, anti-rational, anti-capitalist stance in our money-ridden contemporary society. Sometimes deliberately, but most of the time through ignorance or indifference, this concept of the Celtic bears very little relation to what it claims to revive. It has little to do with the Iron Age Celts as scholars have attempted to reconstruct their world through archaeological studies of the Halstatt or La Tène cultures in Europe.[1] Neither does it have much to do with our current understanding of pre-Roman Britain, early Christian Ireland and Wales, which were the first forms of 'Celtic culture' to have left some historical and archaeological evidence. We know only too well, having seen it repeatedly in this book, that historical evidence is of no relevance to the issues discussed here – hardly worth getting worked up about *that*. So, again, the question is not, why choose a concept anchored in the past, but why choose this particular label to define the kind of exceedingly popular mix described above?

By the beginning of the twenty-first century, almost every aspect of human life in the western world is part of the 'free for all' of the public sphere of discussion and negotiation, except for two: death and Christianity (which can be closely associated in relation to the afterlife). While religious observance is anything but discreet in the context of other religions, Islam and Buddhism for example, Christianity in the West is in retreat, and the human instinct towards the sacred has to be accommodated elsewhere. Islam and Buddhism are possible and successful alternatives. Celticism is another, which can be used, perhaps unconsciously, as a pretext to distance the practitioner from what is perceived to be an Establishment-associated, empty, hierarchical, traditionally repressive and ritualistic Christian faith.[2]

Such associations are anything but new. In the wake of the Reformation in the sixteenth and seventeenth centuries, Archbishop Parker and the Irish Anglican Bishop James Ussher were already attempting to establish Anglicanism as a part of the ancient British tradition, which was deliberately set apart from, and against, Roman Catholicism.[3] The latter was perceived as a powerful, repressive and ritualistic institution, no longer embodying the spiritual expression of the age of faith closest to the founder, namely the early centuries of Christianity. The myth of the Celtic Church began as a Protestant attempt at finding an alternative form of Christianity, purer and more 'authentically English' than the Catholic, Rome-led and 'imposed' medieval church. This myth was wielded by the Reformers as a propaganda tool for their desired re-establishment of that pure Christianity through the Reformation. In the nineteenth and early twentieth centuries, the myth of the Celtic church was reinterpreted as a 'kinder sort of Christianity ... suited to modern liberals: tolerant, decentralised, unworldly, intensely creative and closely associated with nature'.[4] It has been part of the dynamic of Christianity over twenty centuries regularly to seek such spiritual renewal against perceived decline and secularisation, and against the wealth of the institutional church, in new, charismatic returns to the sources of the faith. Medieval movements, such as monasticism, then the mendicant friars, 'heresies' and fringe religious associations, the Reformation, the Catholic Counter Reformation with its Jesuits and Carmelites, the English Puritans, eighteenth-century revivalist movements (Quakerism, Wesleyan Methodism and German Pietism), nineteenth-century nonconformity and twentieth-century charismatic movements like Pentecostalism have all been such examples. Because of the dominance of Christianity in the West, these reforming trends were traditionally channelled within the Christian tradition; since the 1970s they have no longer felt the need to stay in it. Sometimes people abandon Christianity altogether. Sometimes they press for reform from the inside in the traditional way, through evangelical renewal movements or prophetic warnings of impending doom. In 1959 W. M. Miller, an American writer and author of the much talked about novel *A Canticle for Leibowitz* created a world set in a post-nuclear age, in which mankind is saved by the only form of order still surviving, based on the strength of the church and a new liturgy, in the form of the Albertion Order (founded by the medieval master Albert the Great). Other writers feel sufficiently strongly about the old order still and create a world which rejects it completely by demonising it, as does Philip Pullman in his trilogy *His Dark Materials*. Here is a work which ends up reading almost like the product of a good old anticlerical and institutional evangelical tradition (and is his choice of writing a 'trilogy' not significant of the medievalist tone of so many works of fiction discussed in this book – for three is regarded, by definition, as the magic, prime number, both Celtic and Christian?). For others within the churches, Celtic Christianity has been suggested as an antidote to the 'spiritual crisis of the West'.

Celticism, now called by some 'Celticity', came into being as a result of the Romantic movement which, just as it sought in some cases in Roman Catholicism a form of liberation of the human body and heart from the perceived combined repressiveness of Puritanism and Reason, came to think of the pre-Christian past, first the Greek and Roman, then the Celtic, as another and even better source of such liberation. There one could find a host of by now familiar Romantic aspirations: a love of undomesticated nature, an exuberant and irrational relationship with the supernatural of 'Celtic' folklore, an obvious manifestation of 'good primitivism', to be found and recorded in the form of folk tales and great narrative cycles (Irish stories, the Welsh *Mabinogion*, the *Gododdin*), failing which one could always invent them as did the 'Ossian' poet James Macpherson in the 1770s. Historians throughout the nineteenth and twentieth centuries studied the 'Celtic Church', opposing it to what they saw as the more dogmatic, worldlier and hierarchical 'Rome'-inspired church of early Anglo-Saxon England. They contrasted accounts of saintly figures like Cuthbert, with his humility, love of nature and other-worldliness, and of places of learning and magnificent artistic production, such as the monasteries of Lindisfarne and Glastonbury or the Welsh and Irish centres which gave birth to manuscripts like the Book of Kells, with the power-building and prosaically administrative impact of the church set up by Roman bishops in England.[5] The Irish and Welsh came to be seen as the epitome of simplicity of spiritual life and ritual, purity of soul, in fact as no less than the precursors of the Primitive Methodists and other evangelicals of the Victorian era. Such perceptions have remained paramount until today, when not only do we see large numbers of books written to extol the virtues of the simple, austere and pure form of Christian belief and practice, but also when courses on 'Celtic Christianity' are among the most popular for students of history and theology, whether in universities or in adult education classes, regardless of the fact that academic historians have quite firmly eliminated the myth of the 'Celtic church' in terms of historical scholarship.[6]

In the early times of the Celtic revival, there was as yet no particular distinction between the 'Celtic' and the 'Germanic' sides, both being entwined in some sort of concept of 'popular' deep roots, opposed to the Establishment's 'foreign', artificially imposed, 'Latin' element; an emotional, natural, primitive response to the world, as opposed to the non-indigenous intellectual one. During the nineteenth and early twentieth centuries, this construct was expressed in relation to 'Celtic Christianity' during the Anglo-Saxon period, a notion which relied heavily on a literal reading of Bede's *Ecclesiastical History*. Bede appeared to contrast the simple asceticism and other worldliness of St Aidan and St Cuthbert with the hieratic and hierarchic church either imported from Rome or in conformity with Roman traditions, as exemplified by Augustine of Canterbury, Archbishop Theodore and Wilfrid of York. Concomittantly, a great deal was made of the enthusiasm of the Irish and British, the 'original' and 'uncorrupted' Celtic populations of the British Isles, for learning and art. Their production in these areas was highlighted, as a sign that 'real', that is to say, Greek and Latin culture, had been preserved nowhere else in Europe as it had been in Ireland, from where it was later exported by Irish missionaries throughout Europe. These views emphasised the cultural and spiritual impact of Ireland, to the extent of implying that without it the western world would not have been what it is now. They were promoted by a host of British and Irish scholars in their histories of the Irish church, Irish saints and Irish monasticism. It was through such successful books that this perception became established in the popular mind.

The interest in all things Celtic led to the revival of allegedly pagan culture, through the editing of literary texts, real (*Mabinogion*) or imaginary (*Ossian*), the revival of druidism by William Stukeley and others in the late seventeenth and early eighteenth century, and the revival of supposed popular Celtic manifestations. Of the latter, the two most obvious, pertaining to the attitude now generally defined as the 'invention of tradition', were the Highlands 'revival' in Scotland, and the creation of a Welsh national past.

The 'invention' of the Highlands mythology was largely the work of the English or of Lowland Scots. It began after the definitive defeat of the Jacobite Rebellion in 1745.[7] For the first time Highlanders, associated with the rebellion, needed no longer be seen as despised robbers and bandits, which had been the traditional view of them by Lowland Scots as well as by the English, but as a Romantic primitive people, the image of Rousseau's 'noble savages'. A combination of Walter Scott's enthusiasm for the Scottish past, and Queen Victoria's romantic views of Scotland and preference for Balmoral as her home, contributed to the success of the kilt as the Highland dress (the kilt had been in effect 'invented' by the Lancashire industrialist Thomas Rawlinson in 1727 for practical purposes, namely the need for his miners to wear a more suitable form of dress in the mines than their long tunics), and the subsequent mythology of tartans and clans, which made the fortune of both the cloth industry and various authors writing treatises such as *Costume of the Clans*, from the 1820s onwards.

The Welsh, on the other hand, had been in the habit of 'inventing the past' since Geoffrey of Monmouth in the twelfth century. As a people they saw themselves as heirs to the mythical Brutus and the Trojans, and King Arthur. The Welsh Tudor family in the sixteenth century also claimed descent from the legendary king Cadwaladr. But the medieval bardic culture of Wales, with its messianic and prophetic tradition, and indeed the Welsh language itself, were in decline from the sixteenth century onwards. A revival of both was sought by a few enthusiasts during the eighteenth century, most of whom were members of the Welsh Society in London. The first manifestation of this revival was the attempt by the Welsh Society of London to reinstate the Eisteddfod, the last, insignificant one having taken place in 1576, by which time it was a dying institution. It was at first an amateur contest in 1700, since there were no bards left; then a more traditional one in 1780. The Eisteddfod only really took off after 1815, when it was once again back in Wales, supported by a militant Welsh gentry and clergy. The first revived Eisteddfod in Wales was held in 1819 in Carmarthen, under the patronage of Bishop Burgess of St David's, otherwise known as the great Anglican reformer of the Welsh church. Such ecclesiastical involvement was particularly significant since the occasion also saw the introduction by Edward Williams of the Gorsedd of Bards. Williams was a mason from Glamorgan, better known under his assumed name of Iolo Morganwg, who single-handedly invented neo-druidism with its lore, ceremonial and dress while he was still in London in 1792, and subsequently set up 'cells' of bards all over Wales. A great deal of the myth and legends of the druidic past, which made the druid not an 'arcane obscurantist, who indulged in human sacrifices, but the sage and intellectual defending his people's faith',[8] was due to Iolo's inventions and later forgeries supporting them, but this clearly fed a popular taste for myth-making. 'What had been a joke earlier in the eighteenth century was transformed into something sublimely serious by the Romantic vision',[9] and mini Stonehenges were set up all over Wales.

Furthermore, the Celtic past was increasingly supported by the interest in Celtic languages, first developed by the French Breton Paul-Yves Pezron, who investigated the common origins of Welsh and Breton and took them back to the first European language, which, in his views, was Celtic.[10] His theories were pursued in Wales by Edward Lhuyd, then in Germany by G. W. Leibniz (1646–1716) who, in his *Collectanea etymologica* (1717), was the originator of the tradition of Celtic studies. The whole Celtic myth allowed the Welsh to gain a view of their history which was not only grandiose but also different from that of the English. Various other 'rediscovered' or 'invented' elements contributed further to the awareness of Welsh differ-ence. One was the turning of the standard Welsh dress, which had been that of the country people of the 1620s, and thus clearly obsolete by the 1830s, into a Welsh national costume. Another was the appearance of national heroes like Owain Glyndŵr, the last rebel ruler of Wales in the fifteenth cen-tury, who became a pioneer of Welsh nationalism; and of various symbols of nationhood, notably the creation in 1856 of one of the first pieces of music in Europe to be used as a national anthem, 'Land of our Fathers'. Most important, however, was the revival of the Welsh language, in particular in relation to the rise of nonconformity. The Bible and the liturgy of the Anglican Church had been translated into Welsh in 1588, and were in cur-rent use. But Welsh was increasingly used for the production of tracts and other literature of nonconformity, especially Methodism. More and more a whole new culture arose after the second Methodist revival which associated Welsh and Wales with hymn-singing, Chapel and the dry Welsh Sunday.

English opposition and the attempts to keep the Welsh revival within the church, and to focus on cultural rather than political action, had the effect of reducing the gap between nonconformists and 'patriots', and of arousing political radicalism and anti-foreign, which is to say anti-English, feeling. Symbols of Welshness were increasingly used to vindicate this: best known was the reintroduction of the Welsh medieval Red Dragon as the national emblem, replacing the more 'subservient' three plumes of the Prince of Wales. The revival continued in the twentieth century with Welsh, and in Ireland Irish, as languages to be studied in school and compulsorily used side by side with English in the administration from the 1960s onwards, thus also contributing in no small measure to nationalist interests, for whom the Celtic concept became a rallying cry against the English.

Pan-Celticism works in different ways in these two countries. Scotland makes a point of political independence based on a past medieval and early modern state, but supports it with artificially constructed symbols (the St Andrew's Cross flag, kilts and tartans, all of which would have been incomprehensible to the Scots of the past before the nineteenth century), while it did not preserve such aspects of culture as the Gaelic language on a large scale. Wales on the other hand, which was never a truly united state even at the time of its pre thirteenth-century independence, works in practice much more as a nation held together by a national language and culture (singing, rugby, Eisteddfoddau). From the moment that 'Celticity' became an issue in the eighteenth century, the balance has constantly shifted between the political and the cultural. This bore no relation to such historical elements as the length of time that individual countries had been 'subjected' to the rule of non-Celtic states. Ireland was de facto conquered by the Anglo-Norman kings by 1169. Scotland had become a vassal state of the English Crown in 1291 but recovered its independence until the official union of the two crowns in 1603 under James I. Wales was in principle ruled by the English since the late twelfth century but had constant successful rebellions which allowed its own princes some degree of autonomy until the last one was defeated around 1415. Brittany was not officially incorporated into the kingdom of France until 1488.

By the time the issue of Celticism was brought to the fore in the eighteenth century, the unifying factor linking together the revival was language, of which the development of Celtic philology and studies was the manifestation. Societies for the revival of Celtic language, music and traditions flourished, and took on some of the elements 'invented' by men like Walter Scott and Iolo Morganwg (language revival, music, Gorsedd of bards and others), which subsequently migrated to Cornwall and Brittany. In 1900 the Celtic Congress was founded as a representative of the pan-Celtic idea.[11] While promoting the notion of a common past and a common future through language and education to create a 'Celtic identity', it also had a political impact, in particular in Ireland, where it supported Irish independence and found a voice through one of its supporters, Eamonn de Valera. The Celtic Congress was gradually supplanted after 1961 by a rival organisation, the Celtic League, founded by Alan Hensall, who wanted a more clearly political platform for independence on account of what was perceived to be a deteriorating situation in Brittany, where the French government was totally opposed to linguistic autonomy. Ironically, the great opponent to this was Général de Gaulle, as usual favourable to increased centralisation. Ironically because he was the descendant of another Charles de Gaulle, who was regarded by many Celticists as the great rival to Lhuyd in his scholarly pioneering of Celtic Studies, an ancestor of whom the Général had made much use for election purposes in the west of France earlier in his career. The Tudors too had made much of their Welsh ancestry to gain support. Henry Tudor called his son Arthur, but by the time he held the reins of power in his hands though, government was firmly based in London. His descendants strengthened this tradition of centralisation.

In the 1970s Celtic festivals took off, the best known being the Celtic TV and Film Festival, first set up in 1979, followed by the now annual and hugely successful Lorient Festival in Brittany and the pan-Celtic Festival at Killarney in Ireland. One of the key performers at successive festivals, and the initiator of a vast trend of renewal of Celtic music, was Alan Stivel, 'Celtic harp' player and composer, notably of the *Symphonie Celtique*, who launched the fashion for instruments and music regarded as embodiments of the Celtic 'soul'. These are now only too often regarded as the kind of soothing background music to be found on self-healing CDs and in alternative medicine centres and shops. While political autonomy has remained elusive in Brittany, it has translated into something more tangible in Wales and Scotland, in the form of devolution, decided upon, however, from Westminster. The way in which this has affected the two countries concerned is revealing. Wales was the most reluctant to go for the political option, clearly quite happy with the level of autonomy achieved through the progress of Welsh teaching in education (it was granted equal status with English in 1967) and the use of the language in administration and everyday life, for example in Welsh newspapers, the successful TV channel S4C with its popular Welsh programmes including the soap *Pobol y Cwm*, and a Welsh film industry. Scotland's Gaelic language, from being already only spoken by a very small minority, and despite evening classes offered, is in decline, and though there is the *de rigueur* Scottish soap, it is obvious to most observers that Scottish individuality is based on a desire for political statehood rather than on the more diffuse sort of Welsh association of nation with language and culture. One manifestation of Scottish political myth-making is its allegedly long-standing historic pro-European stance (the 'Auld Alliance'), notably with France, crystallised by romantic views of Mary Queen of Scots supported by the French (the whole idea predicated on opposition to the English). Scottish historians themselves may regard this as a combination of rose-tinted spectacles and wish-fulfilment, but it has become part of the 'construction of nationhood' for the Scots and, at least to that extent, a bonus for the European Union. Whether a historic Celtic identity can be said to be a common factor in Wales and in Scotland, as well as in Ireland, Cornwall, Brittany and the Isle of Man, is a moot point. Historically, until modern times, being Welsh, Irish, Highland Scot or Lowland Scot would have been the prime means of ethnic identification. The Celtic 'nationalistic' renewal of the twentieth century in particular may have changed this in favour of broader awareness of this newly-found identity. Claims have been made, however, that at least in part, such an identity is more often projected upon the 'Celtic peoples' by outsiders, notably English and American, in an unconscious desire of identifying with and admiring a romantic concept to which they can aspire and find exotic. This can certainly be demonstrated in at least one instance. Eighteenth- and early nineteenth-century Lowland Scots (like Walter Scott) regarded themselves as 'Teutonic' and most certainly not belonging to the primitive, Gaelic Highlands, regarded as romantic, but also rather savage, uncouth and anything but law-abiding. There was no great Celtic fellow-feeling between Edinburgh and the west of Scotland.

From the second half of the twentieth century 'Celticism' began to manifest itself not only through thousands of books on art, myth, fiction, TV programmes and now Internet sites, but also increasingly through the notion of 'Celtic spirituality'. Some Christians continue to relate to it, often entranced by the exotic Irish religious poetic texts found in a variety of books of 'Celtic Prayer' and used by mainstream churches. A particular favourite is the popular Irish prayer known as 'Patrick's Breastplate', couched in an archaic language made popular precisely through its exotic and ritualistic, mantra-like quality. The fact that it is said to have been written by St Patrick himself, and thus much closer to the 'age of the founder' and 'the primitive church', is in itself revealing of the only too common and characteristically Christian tradition of 'going back to the sources of the faith' whenever people feel that it has moved too far away from its 'pure', non-institutional roots.

On the whole, Celticism is now less and less associated with the Christian revival of the Victorian and later evangelical movements, and more and more often with the idea of 'paganism'. This includes an assortment of esoteric notions taking in self-proclaimed pre-Christian Celtic religion and philosophy, from druids, witches and warlocks, to New Age mysticism, closeness to mother-earth and goddesses of fertility, soft drugs, organic food, natural products and green issues. Some of these manifestations can be seen in the revival of allegedly pagan rituals carried out by specifically-named pagan societies, from the small Lampeter one to the world-wide Internet groups and sometimes purportedly scholarly groupings using the 'classical' tag of Roman and Greek cultural studies. Magazine articles with titles such as 'I am a Full Time Witch' are frequent and an Internet search for the word Celtic produced 956,000 websites at the time of writing this chapter (this number will undoubtedly have increased by the time this volume is published). The 1960s rebellion led to a search for alternative lifestyles, in many cases looking back, like the Romantics and Victorians, to a pre-industrial golden age. The apparent triumph of 1980s and 1990s capitalism and the equally apparent death of political ideologies and religious systems is now in turn leading (when it does not turn into religious fundamentalism) to widely-held concern about the increasingly visible destruction of the planet, and hence to a desire for re-establishing a more harmonious and gentler relationship with nature and ecosystems. On the basis of the love of nature apparent in Irish poetry (or, at any rate, a healthy respect for nature's potential for causing harm to men when dealt with harshly), Celticism is at the forefront of the models used by westerners worried about overt materialism, about the damage caused by savage industrial exploitation of land, forest and sea, and by the prospect of an apocalyptic post-nuclear age.

Two aspects of the Celtic pagan revival, both of considerable influence since the 1970 and 1980s provide a good indication of these associations. One is the revival of druid and 'wicca' cults, the other is the popularity of New Age Travellers.

Serious practising druids now seem to agree that, while their name and origins refer to forms of prehistoric religious life, twentieth-century 'druidry' actually began with the eighteenth-century revival by Iolo Morganwg and William Stukeley, and even more specifically in the twentieth century with the founding of various druidic orders, notably by George MacGregor-Reid and Ross Nicholls.[12] The author of what now seems to be the standard introduction to the subject, Philip Carr-Gomm, was himself the re-founder in 1988 of the main druid organisation today, the Order of Bards, Ovates and Druids (OBOD), which acquired four thousand new members between 1988 and 1996. From the eighteenth century the interest in druids was restricted to groups of Christian gentlemen, and was often well entrenched in the Establishment, rather like the Freemasons or Rotarians (after all, the Queen is a patron of the national Eisteddfod, and the current archbishop of Canterbury was a frequent participant in druidic ceremonies in Wales). Druidism was better integrated than 'wicca' (witchcraft), with public and picturesque ceremonies in daylight, at prescribed intervals, as opposed to those of 'pagans' and 'witches', more likely to be private, secret and nocturnal. While both cults profess to share a similar view of the sacred, based on the worship of gods and goddesses associated with nature, sacred trees and animals, and identical festivals, differences arise from the more 'cultured' nature of druidism, including its association with Arthurian myths. Merlin is regarded as the archetypal druid, and occasional ceremonies are aimed at reviving the spirit of King Arthur and Merlin. A self-styled King Arthur Uther Pendragon took the fight for the freedom to worship at Stonehenge to the European Court of Justice, as he explained in an interview ('as King Arthur said to the *Guardian*').[13]

Druidism had begun in the eighteenth century. While it grew as a movement, and partly stemming from a similar anti-Enlightenment and scientific rationalist attitude, a whole set of secret societies and orders were also founded, prominent amongst which were the Rosicrucians, theosophy and the Hermetic Order of the Golden Dawn. Most of them mixed inspiration from the Middle East, Ancient Egypt, Buddhism, Hinduism and Prehistoric, Celtic, Anglo-Saxon, Norse and Greek and Roman paganism. The latter had been celebrated throughout the late eighteenth century and the Romantic period in Germany and England, reaching a high during the 1890s. Its contention was that Christianity had proved itself inadequate to satisfy man's needs, while paganism was a happier, more positive religion, which celebrated the natural world, contributed to freeing the flesh and to renewing primeval contact with the archaic life-force. This exalting of the natural, of the irrational, of nature perceived as the feminine, led poets and artists to focus on resurrecting the worship of pagan divinities associated with wild nature, excitement and sexuality (Pan), the countryside and the woods, the night, the moon (Diana) and especially Ceres or Demeter, the Corn Mother, seen as the archetypal earth-mother goddess.

In parallel with literary developments, historical research from Herder and the Schlegels onwards was constructing a theory that primitive religions were the embodiment of truths pertaining to an instinctual understanding of the rythms of nature and life, all now lost through 'too much civilisation'. Nature became feminised and was perceived as one great female entity at the root of all religions, the primeval goddess. These theories were subsequently put forward in an exceptionally successful popular manner by two best-sellers, James Frazer's *The Golden Bough* (published in a condensed popular version in 1912) and Robert Graves's *The White Goddess* (1946). In addition, nineteenth-century scholarship was also greatly interested in folklore, again at the instigation of German historians keen to find in popular customs the survival of 'original', meaning 'Germanic', pagan rites for fertility and rites of passage. This interest in folklore was adopted with great enthusiasm in England in the late nineteenth century. Nostalgia for a fast-disappearing rural England consolidated the view that by studying the traditions of the countryside one gained access to the old, pre-Christian religion, which had maintained itself there until at least the seventeenth century, among people who, under a veneer of Christianity, were in reality deeply pagan. Despite the fact that most of these traditions went back no earlier than the eighteenth century, major trends in scholarly orthodoxy until the 1970s went on seeing these customs as living fossils from pagan Antiquity.[14] A similar equation of 'old religion' and paganism was proposed by students of witchcraft, who now claimed it, for the first time, as an example of survival of pagan practice, whose devotees were persecuted for it, especially because they were independent women, in the great witch-hunts of the (supposedly) medieval and (genuinely) early modern period. This was the theory of the greatly acclaimed and highly-regarded writer Margaret Murray, in her popular and influential books written between the 1920s and 1950s, of which the best-known was *The Witch Cult in Western Europe* (1921). Together with Alesteir Crowley, another writer on witchcraft and founder of the Ordo Templi Orientis, Murray was the theoretician on whom the revived witchcraft movement, or 'wicca', relied in the twentieth century.

The 'wicca' movement, with its prehistory in the fabled New Forest coven of 1940, was in effect founded in the following years by a retired civil servant from India, the self-styled druid and wicca Gerald Gardner. Gardner was also a prolific writer, author of the bestseller *Witchcraft Today* (1954), as well as of the original 'bible' of wicca ritual, *The Book of Shadows*. He ultimately retired to found a wicca museum and 'training' centre on the Isle of Man. His vision, which he shared with the druid movement, namely the celebration of the sacredness of natural features, was more insistent on the importance of the feminine principle in the world, the great goddess or mother-earth, all-round woman as maiden, mother, wise woman, giver of life, healer and embodiment of the Grail. The elements of worship he proposed were largely inspired from a combination of Murray's and Frazer's theses, and from secret society practices like the freemasons, the Golden Dawn and Crowley's Ordo. They included ritual initiation, use of circles, pentagrams and triangles, invocation of spirits and a whole range of beings from Hebrew angels to Egyptian deities via figures from Celtic mythology, medieval romances and sixteenth-century *grimoires*, drawing of divine forces into one of the celebrants, and cult impedimenta of swords and knives. The content of this 'fertility religion' coalesced during meetings to celebrate the four festivals or sabbaths (the four major Celtic feasts), with leaping of fires, covens of thirteen, the importance of female devotees and the worship of the Horned God and the Great Goddess. This secret worship was carried out at night in nakedness, highlighting the link between sex, nature, magic and flight. Such a mix of practices, drawn by Gardner from a large variety of sources, included features clearly imported from the hundreds of standard accounts of witchcraft trials in early modern times in Europe and America as described by Murray, and still part of academic orthodoxy until the 1970s, when it was finally put to rest. A new generation of scholars showed to what extent many of these alleged practices were often imposed upon the women thus tried, many illiterate and voiceless and made to confess to practices which may have only existed in the heatedly erotic imagination of their frustrated misogynistic inquisitors. They were in any case not old pagan rites but parodies and inversions of Christian rites. Gardner's wicca religion was enormously successful and spawned a whole range of later groups around various people, such as his disciple then opponent Doreen Valiente, and Alexander and Maxine Sanders, whose house in London was a hub of 'alternative' culture in the 1960s. In a letter of 1914 Crowley first articulated the definition of wicca:

> The time is just right for a natural religion. People like rites and ceremonies, and they are tired of hypothetical gods. Insist on the real benefits of the Sun, the Mother-Force, the Father-Force, and so on, and show that by celebrating these benefits worthily the worshippers unite themselves more fully with the current of life. Let the religion be joy, but with a worthy and dignified sorrow in death itself, and treat death as an ordeal, an initiation ... in short, be the founder of a new and greater Pagan cult.[15]

From the 1970s onwards the wicca movement saw considerable expansion in America, where it was not only still reliant on Murray's views, but pushed them much further in the direction of feminism, stating that

> witchcraft had been the religion of Europe before Christianity and of European peasants for centuries after. Its persecution in the early modern period had therefore been the suppression of an alternative culture by the ruling elite, but also a war against feminism, for the religion had been served by the most courageous, aggressive, independent and sexually liberated women in the populace ... To gain freedom, modern women needed, therefore, to become witches again.[16]

For the radicals, witchcraft was a 'religion conceived in rebellion, with the greatest toll of martyrs in the history of any faith, and which could only be true to its nature when fighting oppression'.[17] In addition, the adepts of green movements saw the destruction of the planet, mother-earth, the ancient deity venerated throughout Europe, the goddess, threatened by modern technology, while her 'devotees were pitted against patriarchy, militarism and ecological destruction'.[18] The feminist and ecological trend combined with the interpretation of wicca as a tool for self-fulfilment, and the realisation of human potential, to create an even more successful strand defined by Starhawk, a Californian feminist, in her book *The Spiral Dance* (1979). This strand reached its culmination with the publication in 1982 by the wiccan high priestess Marion Zimmer Bradley of her bestseller *The Mists of Avalon*, which brought together the myths of the 'old religion', with its feminist tone, with those of Arthur, Merlin and Celtic lore. English wicca groups meanwhile had reacted against the American glorification of the irrational, occult counter-culture and ultra-feminism. The new generation of wiccan high-priestesses, notably Leonora James and Vivianne Crowley, and the American Margot Adler, were academic-trained women, who admitted that wicca had been built on a pseudo-history, that the attempts to link it to either ancient paganism or the witch-hunts were a fantasy, but that this did not detract from its value as a 'new' religion, paganism being an ideal religious trend in the context of the present non-traditional multicultural societies. It has been claimed that wicca, as a new religion, is the only one that the English can be said to have offered the world rather than received from others.

Increasingly, modern practice attempts to eliminate the words *witch* and *witchcraft*, and even *wicca*, to replace them with what is perceived as the essence of the new movements, paganism. This defines itself as consisting of three principles, as set forth by the Pagan Federation in 1989:

> love of, and reverence for, and kinship with, the natural world; a positive morality based upon the discovery and development of each person's true nature, providing that this is done without harming others; and an active acceptance of both male and female divinity.[19]

To say that these reflect considerable eclecticism would be an understatement. Similar principles can be found in half the religions of the globe, monotheistic or animist, and paganism includes systems, deities and ideas drawn from 'the cultures of ancient Greece, Egypt, Rome, Mesopotamia, Ireland and Wales, and of the Anglo-Saxons and the Vikings, the folklore of the British Isles, the structures of prehistoric monuments, Hinduism, Buddhism, eighteenth- and nineteenth-century Celtic Romanticism, native America, and the modern earth mysteries and radical feminism'.[20] At any rate, wiccans and pagans themselves are quite content to admit this, if not to glory in it, as Adler described the 'most authentic and hallowed Wiccan tradition – stealing from any source that didn't run away too fast'.[21] Journals like *The Wiccan* (from 1994 renamed *Pagan Dawn*) and *The Cauldron* were at first the main link between wicca and pagan groups. Increasingly there are, since the foundation of the Pagan Federation in 1988, annual conventions, TV and radio debates, academic conferences such as the international one held in 1996 at Lancaster University on 'Nature Religion

Today', pagan chaplains in hospitals, universities and prisons, magazines, tapes and divinatory systems. The explosion of the Internet has added to these pagan bulletin boards, commercial services, usernet newsgroups, mailing lists, and officially recognised web pages on druids, Celtic paganism, myths and legends, magic and shamans.

So what makes both druids and wicca, or more generally paganism, so popular? There are enough orders of druids to fill a *Druid Directory* in the UK, France, and especially America, where the New York City Library is said to have the largest collection in the world of druidic literature. An off the cuff calculation yields something like 6000 practising pagan druids and 10000 practising witches in Britain alone, which means, in addition to these 'clergy', something like 100000 non-initiates who follow pagan beliefs and practices.[22] Who are they? The phenomenon appears to be associated mostly with the upper levels of the working class and the lower levels of the middle class. They include no people with inherited titles or wealth, no people of great wealth generally, of political importance, no professionals or academics, but also no factory workers, miners or farmers. Mostly they are artisans, shopkeepers, service industry and financial services people, owners of small businesses, employees of local government and artists. Common to many of these occupations are a large amount of independence and self-organisation, and a definite interest in self-education through individual reading as well as further education or studies as mature students. The nearest comparison in sociological terms is with the development of the house church movement, the fastest growing (possibly the only growing) in British Christianity.[23]

What do people find in this new religion, which satisfies the same needs as does the whole 'Celtic' revival in fiction, music and its other manifestations? Perhaps one can see it through the evolution of the druid movement. The druids saw themselves at first as a religious order, with a set of rituals but also a tradition of learning that had to be studied for many years. A major figure of druidism wryly said that from the 1960s onwards druidism saw an influx of people more interested in paganism and in saving the environment. Increasingly in recent times, people have joined with no interest or willingness to make the effort of studying in depth, who just feel 'spiritually attuned' to these movements and fascinated by their rituals.[24] This 'spiritual kinship' is clearly associated by them with a series of perceived Celtic beliefs in the sacredness of the natural world and a pervasive search for both theirs and the earth's salvation through unity with nature and with a distant mythologised past. The best way to describe this movement is to allow it to speak for itself.

We believe that Neopagan Druidism has an important role to play in the future

of Neopaganism and the survival of the earth ... If we can attract enough people who are willing to dedicate their time, energy and money ... [we] can save
the Earth Mother, create a global culture of prosperity and freedom and usher
a genuine 'New Age'.[25]

To contemplate the flowing curves and spirals of Celtic art, the pouring out of
forms in vigorous, organic swirls, is to get a glimpse into the way the early Celts
perceived the web of life ... a perfect, precarious balance between the orderly
and the unbounded.[26]

In the ancient Celtic world of my Scottish and Irish ancestors, there was a deep
and abiding awareness of the divine ... the contemplative and earth-centred
practices of a neglected – but still available – Celtic spiritual tradition.

On the next page, the same writer describes himself as 'someone working in
both the field of ecopsychology and in the resurgence of Celtic spirituality',
and as a psychotherapist, 'akin to the sacred wells and oak groves at which
[his] Druidic forebears worshipped', his 'client becomes like a shrine ...
energy is exchanged, in some cases healing occurs.[27] This is because, he
explains, what people suffer from in the world of today is the 'Common
Wound of the Soul', which is in effect no other than the Holy Wound of the
Arthurian Wasteland theme, which can only be healed by the presence of
the Grail.[28]

Yet another writer, who ends her short biography with the statement that
she runs a shamanic practice, talks of her spiritual journey, which took her
to Scotland. There, 'a place whose heathered moors and mountain streams
speak to my soul, a place where the spirits of the wind soar on eagles' wings
in the high and wild places ... I had responded to a call that was so strong
within me I could not ignore it', began her awareness of the importance of
the goddess, the feminine principle of life, from which mankind had separated itself for centuries. She continues:

As the great wheel turns and we fast approach the twenty-first century,
humankind lives with the menacing results of that separation. Our history tells
of the long and painful journey that we have taken together as a result of our
denial of the divinity of the feminine and our focus on an all-powerful God.
The consequences of this have brought us to a point where, through the para-
noid denial of the Divine Feminine, we have the weaponry, the technology and
the power to destroy ourselves and all life on earth.[29]

A summary of the spirituality of neo-paganism is perhaps best provided
through the second half of the main wicca 'prayer', 'The Charge', rewritten
by Doreen Valiente:

I who am the beauty of the green earth, and the white moon among the stars, and the mystery of the waters, and the desire of the heart of man, call unto thy soul, arise and come unto me; for I am the soul of nature, who giveth life to the universe. From me all things proceed, and unto me all things must return; and before my face ... thine inmost divine self shall be enfolded in the rapture of the infinite. Let my worship be in the heart that rejoiceth; for behold, all acts of love and pleasure are my rituals and therefore let there be beauty and strength, power and compassion, honour and humility; mirth and reverence within you.[30]

Note in this text the vaguely familiar language of the Old Testament, including the Song of Songs and the Psalms, in an imitation of the forms of the Authorised Version and the Elizabethan Book of Common Prayer, all of which provide friendly grounding on which one can feel both at ease if brought up in this tradition, and exhilarated by the replacement of the 'outside' divine (male too) with a personalised self-divinity suitable for an age of individualism and obsessed with self-knowledge.

These texts indicate clearly enough what lies at the root of the fascination with 'nature cults': a mixture of nostalgia for a romanticised version of both a personal and national past, a diffuse sense of the sacred world and the role it can play in what is the equivalent of the 'salvation of one's soul' (not in the next world but in terms of peace in this one), and the salvation of the earth from the polluters and destroyers, in true millenarian style. In addition, the strong emphasis on the feminine, the goddess, associated with life but also with emotion and intuition, as opposed to the perceived tyranny of male reason, aggression and destruction, proves once again, as it did during Romanticism and the post-Enlightenment world, of huge appeal.

A not dissimilar agenda is also part of the aspirations and lifestyle of New Age Travellers, seen in particular in its two key components: the festivals and the nomadic life.[31] Travellers see themselves as belonging to a historical tradition which associated the notions of freedom, nomadism and revolt. For the generation of young people in the Sixties, the inspirational book by J. J. Jusserand made the Middle Ages wayfaring life a model of emancipation from hereditary and social constraints, and the 'freedom of the road' an attractive lifestyle.[32] Heirs of the hippies and other movements begun in the Sixties, the Travellers saw their numbers rise steeply from the 1980s onwards, partly in reaction to the money-making, rat-race 1980s, but fundamentally inspired as a group that saw itself as carrying on the vagabond lifestyle of medieval wandering players and musicians, going from fair to fair. A whole range of concepts influenced them: peace

movements, green trends, anarchist ideas, the gypsy life, the idea of popular revolt against the Establishment as taken from such historical
movements as Robin Hood and the Levellers and Diggers of the seventeenth
century, a positive view of ancient British and Celtic culture and the myth
of 'Avalonia', and ultimately paganism. Although not necessarily religious,
New Age movements have adopted a diffuse spirituality based on personal
development, the 'sacralisation of self' as one writer put it.[33] Also part of
this lifestyle are the communes, an interest in alternative therapies and
pre-modern forms of knowledge: astrology, earth mysteries, ancient healing techniques, simple communal living in a rural environment. 'As a
form of spirituality, the New Age makes use of ... forms of rejected
knowledge as an alternative to modern, scientific, rationalist beliefs and
rejects their hegemony'.[34] Many Travellers are even less specifically religious
and more interested in the lifestyle and its main social manifestation,
the festival, with its own 'religion' of hedonism, music, drug culture and
general carnivalesque aspects. This latter trait is yet another link with the
perceived medieval roots. The festival is not only the heir of the medieval
fair, with its exchange of goods, services and entertainment, but also the
most obvious manifestation of a similar inversion of social norms. Just as
in the Middle Ages it reflected a challenge to the social and ecclesiastical
order, so it now reflects a challenge to official culture, with its defence of
decorum, respectability, low-level noise and cleanliness, and the culture
of work and time-keeping. These values are opposed by a culture of entertainment and play. In addition the festival, like the nomadic lifestyle, allows
for a loss of the old identity based on class, gender, name, personal past,
which can be replaced by a new identity with new names or groups (tribes).
This new identity is obtained in the same way as it was for medieval pilgrims, through membership of a group of elect, grounded in a shared
emotional experience of trials and tribulations, communion en route to a
sacred site, where both a personal renewal and a new communal identity can
ultimately be achieved. The first major festival took place in the early 1970s
at Windsor Great Park, but was subsequently closed down. Stonehenge took
over between 1974 and 1984, a site of great importance and mystery, invested
with huge spiritual and emotional value by Travellers as well as druids and
other devotees of pagan cults. After it too was closed down by public pressure and by the Heritage lobby, which regarded the annual celebrations
there as a risk to the archaeological site, only local meetings continued to
exist, with the exception of the annual Glastonbury Festival. This has now
become a much more commercial venture, and has even achieved the ultimate integration into the acceptable social scene through being broadcast by
the BBC.

The clearest example of New Age associations with the medieval and Celtic is made manifest by the creation of an image of the countryside which places the movement firmly within the English Romantic tradition of a myth of rural idyll, Arcadia, the place of freedom and mystery. Above all, it is the place of separation from the modern, industrial, alienated life, with a rejection of that life for the quest of a more 'authentic' one of self-discovery: the pilgrimage of New Age Travellers is not a pilgrimage to a shrine but a sacred journey into a sublime, wild, mysterious inner landscape. It belongs to the tradition of the Picturesque, the Sublime, the Romantic quest for the authentic of Blake, the Lakeland poets or Cobbett. Life on the road, associated with such spaces as fields, country lanes, common land, woodland, water, sacred sites, all preferably in remote areas of the Celtic 'fringes' (Wales, Scotland, Cornwall), not only reconnects with this utopian Arcadia but helps return to an earlier, Celtic, British, later marginalised 'ethnicity' waiting to be retrieved. This identity is itself based on a recreation of Englishness, not in a narrow political nationalistic sense, but drawing on the cultural tradition of Romanticism, which proclaimed it to be more authentically English, of Celtic and Saxon origins, incarnate in the rural, pastoral, way of life, being destroyed by alien elements.

Travellers construct, out of a Romantic English tradition, a vision of the countryside that fits with their values and their beliefs and is suited to the sort of lifestyle they have chosen to adopt. The idea of the rural as a source of authenticity is paramount to their vision of the landscape.[35] Ironically, of course, this vision comes into direct conflict with the perception of the countryside of the Heritage industry, tourism, agribusiness or suburbia – hence the conflicts around Stonehenge, and the rejection of Travellers in rural communities, where they are often most strongly resented by wealthy townspeople who have abandoned a city life for the sought-for 'peace and quiet' of a country house and garden.

The 'Celtic' factor, present in the nationalist and political sphere,[36] is a strong element in the cultural sphere too, through fantasy fiction,[37] and heroic fantasy films.[38] It is also an exceptionally successful retail concept. The market for books as well as objects associated with a 'Celtic' label is exceptionally large. A rapid survey of some of the publicity material describing the contents of books on these themes is revealing. Here are a few quotes:

Celtic Britain's landscape can in some ways be explained, and in other ways will always remain a mystery. The fact that aspects of Celtic structure survive today is a testament to its mysterious power. Its spiritual beliefs, art, oral traditions and monuments have left us a rich tapestry of the past that can still be explored today ...

The story of Celtic Britain', a book of 'voyage ... into the oral history, myths and known events of the Celts and their past [when the Celts held sway over ancient Britain], [the Celts whose story] is soaked in sensuality, tragedy and gore ...

again

The Dark Spirit, a fascinating and provocative look at the weird and frightening aspects of Celtic culture ... bringing together the cast of macabre characters from history and folklore [the author] shows that the Celts' dark spirit remains deeply ingrained within the fabric of western society ... a deliciously unsettling volume ...

and finally, as well as most significantly, two of the countless books about Merlin,

often seen as a subversive, a maverick ... does he not perhaps represent a vital part of our forgotten selves and of the magical world-view that we are rediscovering, allowing us to dream of a healing identification with the landscape and all its creatures?

At any rate, 'an enthralling magical quest, for all those entranced by Celtic lore and landscape'. A CD entitled *Celtic Legends* defined itself thus:

The Celts believed that true fulfilment could only be achieved when you find the central harmony of mind, body and spirit. This ... collection ... can help you achieve this harmony, as well as feel enthused and uplifted ... themes include ... Celtic dawn-which is inspired by the close Celtic connection to nature.

Nowadays, so-called Celtic spirituality has an enormous impact. As an ideological concept it emerged through books, festivals of alternative culture like Glastonbury, classes in meditation and public lectures by groups like the Centre for Self-Awareness, replacing, or at any rate rivalling with, the 1960s and 1970s eastern or Buddhist interests. One particular publisher has in a recent catalogue a series of 'Celtic titles'. It includes books entitled *Celtic Alphabets, Celtic Borders, Celtic Decoration Kit (or Make Your Own Designs with Rubber Stamps), Celtic Design and Ornament for Calligraphers, Celtic Illumination, Celtic Patterns Painting Book,* and a whole series of introductory manuals to Celtic Design, from a *Beginner's Manual to the Dragon and the Griffin, Illuminated Letters, Tree of Life* and others. This is only one series among several from just that one publisher. A second contains titles such as

The Celts: First Masters of Europe, Celtic Heritage, and yet another series, on 'Mythology, Philosophy and Religion' (a kind of syncretism itself extremely revealing of the diffuse perception of the spiritual at the start of the twenty-first century), offers *Celtic Secret Landscapes, Celtic Heritage, Celtic Saints, Dictionary of Celtic Myths and Legends, Celtic Mysteries: The Ancient Religion,* and, by extension, *Exploring the World of the Druids, At the Centre of the World: Polar Symbolism Discovered in Celtic, Norse and other Ritualised Landscapes, Merlin and Wales: A Magician's Landscape* ('an enthralling magical quest for all those entranced by Celtic lore and landscape') and *Gods and Goddesses of Old Europe.* A rapid trawl through book catalogues reveals innumerable books on the Celts, the druids, Celtic goddesses, pagan Celtic Ireland: *The Celts: The People Who Came Out of the Darkness, Holy Places of Celtic Britain, The Celtic Heritage, Celtic Britain, Creatures of Celtic Myth, The Celtic Heroic Age, Complete Guide to Celtic Mythology, The Encyclopaedia of Celtic Myth and Legend,* and so on ad infinitum. Previously such interest might have been occasional among scholars of the 'Celtic church' or 'Celtic saints', or for historians of early medieval Ireland.[39] There are now numerous titles on the market which incorporate the word Celtic for perfectly sound historical reasons when they deal with the Iron Age peoples of Europe, or when they attempt to analyse modern anthropological trends, for example *The Atlantic Celts: Ancient People or Modern Invention, Celts and Christians: New Approaches to the Religious Traditions of Britain and Ireland.* But, as a selling point, the word is now essentially confined to pagan Celts, and other 'primitive', earthy, feminine-friendly, 'natural' cultures. The English-speaking world has no monopoly on the trend, and Brittany in particular is another major actor in the Celtic renaissance. A popular French writer, Jean Markale, who defines himself as a 'celtisant', produces numerous books of historical narrative about myths and esoteric matters, especially about the (by him renamed) Breton King Artus, Celtic women and, being French, Celtic cuisine – 'le chaudron celtique'. It is entirely consistent with the syncretism already encountered that he should also be interested in writing about the druids, the Grail, dragons, Atlantis, as well as the historical but increasingly mythologised Cathars and Templars.

Celticism has also become an outstandingly successful retail concept, linked to the Heritage Industry. Bookshops named *The Celtic Experience* or *The Celtic Dawn* abound in Europe and North America. One does not need to look exclusively at such specialist retailers; mainstream Heritage concepts too are sucking the Celtic vein dry. This applies to everything from the reproduction of museum objects to mock-Celtic objects of the kind sold by the greatest heritage retailer in Britain, *Past Times.* Every one of their catalogues has a section entitled 'Celtic Treasures', or 'Celtic Art', in which one finds objects ranging from brooches, torc bangles, rings, crosses, lockets and other jewellery, some specifically associated with perceived 'Celticisms', like the locket 'inscribed with an Irish blessing', of the 'may your cup overflow with health and happiness' kind. The sales pitch repeatedly mentions 'interwoven Celtic motifs ... thought to symbolise the eternal thread of life', 'the gemstones and metalwork of treasures such as the shrine of St Patrick's Bell ... recalled in [our] exclusive silver-plated necklace' or 'necklace ... based on motifs from the seventh-century Book of Durham [sic]'. A 'locket with a joyous Celtic blessing' or 'interlace Celtic patterns from the ninth and tenth centuries' on a gold ring are sold side by side with other 'Celtic treasures' such as 'tree-of-life' pens, bookmarks, scarf clips, Book of Kells ties, nightdresses, Lindisfarne tunic and trousers sets, throws and cushions, aromatherapy sets, something called a St Kilian candle and Celtic prayer candle plate, or Pendragon leather travel accessories, organiser and cuff-links box. A clear indication of the thinking behind this is summed up in the write-up for the Celtic Aromatherapy Pomander: the buyer is invited to drop fragrant oil 'in this deep blue Celtic style ceramic pomander, and enjoy the soothing scent of a more tranquil age'. Another way of saying the same thing is the constant allusion to famous and slightly esoteric items such as the Books of Kells, Durrow or Lindisfarne, and the specific tie between the ancient and modern, meaning 'you too can benefit from the natural fabrics, colours, stones and even, by implications, blessings, associated with the style', as in a throw described as 'decorated with a traditional knotwork design ... the warm blues evoke the colour of early Celtic fabrics produced using natural dyes such as woad', 'in Celtic symbolism the fine knotwork designs ... represent unity and eternity', or again 'our silver-plated bangle is reminiscent of the torcs worn by high status Celts'. The latest catalogues have new mottoes associated with specific pages. Celtic Art is defined as 'Sacred knotwork designs, symbols of eternity', and a special page is consecrated to the 'Celtic Christmas: a mystical midwinter celebration of fire and light', clearly an allusion to a perceived 'traditional' festival of a pre-Christian period, relating to an age of nature (presumably with the subtext of 'in opposition to the modern-day commercialised Christian festival'). A similar subtext of pagan Celtic festivals is implied on T-shirts advertising the 'Celtic year celebrations', to be found commonly on market stalls across the British Isles.

Past Times is only one among the retail players in this field. Others too use the concept, as does a popular mail-order store promoting the sale of 'Claddagh' rings, 'a symbol of love ... and loyalty', engraved with the words: 'with my two hands I give you my heart and crown it with my love'. This intriguing object has had great commercial success, due, one suspects, not only to its slightly exotic appeal. It purports to be a kind of informal engagement ring (though in its 'original' incarnation, in Ireland, one supposes engagement to have been anything but informal, in a society where betrothal was far more binding than our engagement); perhaps for that reason, it allows a male population increasingly commitment-shy of marriage to make a symbolic and appeasing, but not necessarily binding, gesture in that direction.

On a slightly different level, but with the same mixed subtext, and creating both an audience and a phenomenal success, is another form of Heritage repertoire: the Celtic theme park. Allusions to Celtic elements are incorporated into such attractions as the 'Crystal Quest' in the Cheddar Gorge complex: a fantasy adventure in which 'Mordon, the Lord of Darkness, has imprisoned the daylight. You must enter the underworld, challenge the Dragon and find the Crystal'. Two of the best known Celtic theme parks are Celtworld in Waterford in Ireland and Celtica, described as 'one of Wales' leading attractions'. Its motto is 'Experience the world of the Celts'. The Celtica Experience defines itself thus: 'A journey of discovery, portraying the Celtic spirit ... Discover the origins of the Celts and experience life in a Celtic Iron Age village before you venture into the mysterious Vortex to see Celtic Wales today through the eyes of Gwydyion, the Druid's young apprentice.' The experience is set around such themes as Celtic beliefs ('See where the druids made offerings to their gods – if you dare'), Celtic events ('join us to celebrate a Celtic festival'), not forgetting the Celtic souvenir shop, teashop and other amenities. English Heritage's brochure for Cornwall, entitled *Castles, Celts and Kings*, promises 'mystery, myth and magic', notably at Chysauster, an ancient settlement of Celtic Cornwall. One can currently find on the Internet a whole variety of other similarly themed outfits, such as the travel agent Astral Tours, providing one with information about the 'real' England through guided tours to such highly significant 'spiritual' places as Stonehenge and Glastonbury, the two high-places representative of 'Celtic roots', annually celebrating a 'reconstructed' Summer Solstice, and the ultimate great fair of alternative culture.

While one might explain the attraction of the whole concept in the same way as one might have explained the attraction of eastern religions previously, through the absence, in an increasingly secular western society, of spiritual fulfilment and emotional religious involvement through institutional Christianity, this does not explain the shift from such alternative religious choices as Egyptian cults, Buddhism, Islam or Christian Scientism, say, to Celtic interests. Such a shift may be further enhanced by what is perceived as a return to our own deep popular past, in some mythical golden age before it was destroyed by an oppressive and authoritarian Christian Church – a reaction not entirely unlike that of the revivalist movements of the past but, this time, free from the need to remain nominally Christian and thus able to choose what it sees as a more indigenous 'religion'. One of the main advantages of this choice is of course that anything belonging to Celtic prehistory is essentially constructed on often imaginary evidence from a culture which left few written historical records, and therefore all kinds of modern images can be projected onto it, with nothing to contradict them. On the rare occasions when some evidence is available and can be discussed, it is usually so sketchy and flexible that popular interpretations, however extravagant they may be on occasions, still win hands down. In this sense, the panderings of the academic establishment to this interest, unless it is done specifically for the purpose of explaining the tenuous link between popular perception and scant historical evidence, is on occasion mercantile, in an age when students are customers and universities have to vie with each other in a market, and to use degrees and modules to attract extra numbers of students away from rival institutions. Little surprise then that one university should advertise itself in its prospectus not only by its stunningly beautiful natural environment and high degree of academic excellence, but also with the words: '[the area] is also a land of myth and legend: they say that a cave near Ystrad Ffin was once home to [the Welsh Robin Hood], while Merlin, wizards and other wise men are reputed to be sleeping under the hills and in caves, waiting for recall'. The association of these two concepts is not fortuitous: Celticism on its own has its attractions at the end of the second millennium but, since the end of the first, it has been almost always paired up with that greatest of western European myths: King Arthur, the Knights of the Round Table and the Quest for the Holy Grail.

6

King Arthur

'Royalty and Romance, Wizardry and Betrayal.' Thus does English Heritage define, in shorthand, the appeal of Tintagel Castle, of Arthur's Camelot, of his Knights of the Round Table Gawain, Lancelot and Percival, of Guenevere, and the Quest for the Holy Grail, all living side by side with the wondrous deeds of wizards and fairies: Merlin, the Lady of the Lake, Morgan-le-Fay. To most men and women from the fifteenth century onwards these names and myths are what, above all, defines the Middle Ages.

Arthurian myths are complex to unravel. The story began with an obscure ninth-century entry in a chronicle, the *Historia Brittonum* (for a long time known under the name of 'Nennius'). This mentioned a sixth-century British war leader who had waged war against the Saxons in twelve battles (a characteristically symbolic medieval commonplace), including Mount Badon or Badon Hill, and was victorious with the help of an image of the Virgin Mary painted on his shield. The story was repeated in another set on Welsh annals, with even less detail given, but with an additional entry for a battle at Camlann, and a companion of Arthur called Mordred.[1] From these modest beginnings, the tale was expanded and written up in an entertaining manner by the twelfth-century writer Geoffrey of Monmouth, who brought into it the name of Arthur's father, Uther Pendragon, those of Guenevere, and of his nephews Mordred and Gawain, and the death of the king who retreated to the Isle of Avalon. But it had even at this stage remained a story of battles and military conquests (Arthur was said to have fought and been victorious over various peoples and leaders, as far as Rome!). On that basis, however, and with the addition of later, Anglo-Norman developments, such as the Lancelot and Guenevere love story, and eventually the addition of the Holy Grail from French sources such as the romances of Chrétien de Troyes, the composite myth caught the imagination of the whole 'civilised' western world. Innumerable stories, poems, romances and other literary forms were created between the late twelfth and the fifteenth centuries by such poets as Wace, Hartman von Aue, Gottfried of Strassburg, Wolfram von Eschenbach, Marie de France, Chrétien de Troyes, the Gawain poet, and countless *trouvères*, *troubadours* and *Minnes-änger* from the Atlantic to Central Europe, until it found its final and most impressive medieval expression in Malory's *Morte d'Arthur* in 1485. The narrative evolved from being the account of an alleged king of the Britons fighting against the Saxons, a king who thus later became a hero of Welsh independence, to encompassing every aspect of vernacular medieval culture in defining and refining the ideals of chivalry and courtly love, and eventually adding to them the Christian interpretation of the quest for perfection and salvation in the form of the Holy Grail, at first said to have been the cup of the Last Supper and later also identified with the vessel which received Christ's blood on the Cross.

In addition to this material, as a kind of substratum to both the culture of chivalry and the Christian quest, the story kept what is still perceived as its 'Celtic' mystery, the 'matter of Brittany' as it was called in the Middle Ages, through its incorporation of a pre-Christian set of characters, both human and inanimate: the wizard Merlin, the good and bad fairies, the Lady of the Lake, Morgan, the enchanted forest of Brocéliande, the all-powerful sword Excalibur, Camelot, and a host of minor figures perceived as embodiments of the natural world. With such a wealth of stories, completely flexible and adaptable, comprising at will bravery in battle, romance and passion, mysticism, myths of regeneration, enchantment, good and evil, and many other facets of human behaviour and hopes, it is not hard to see how this might have become the essential myth for the times during the Middle Ages. Its last propagator, but by far the most complete in putting together all this material as a coherent whole, was Malory, and, although no new editions of the *Morte d'Arthur* were available between 1634 and 1816, it was on his work that post-medieval generations relied most.

And rely they did. Since then the story, with all its ramifications, has never ceased to appeal, to be transformed, staged, rewritten, put to music, painted and represented. It was never lost or forgotten, even at times of interest in other figures of the past. *L'histoire du San Greal* was published in France in 1516, while in England Henry VII, in order to strengthen his hold on the throne, was already using his Welsh Tudor ancestry to claim descent from Arthur, in the process also naming his eldest son Arthur.[2] It was under his aegis that the 'Round Table' (in fact a thirteenth-century artefact) was displayed at Winchester and repainted in the Tudor colours of green and white.[3] When Malory was writing, he was already feeling that the age of chivalry was coming to an end; it did in fact linger into the 1620s. Arthurian-themed tableaux were incorporated into royal pageants under Elizabeth, for example during her royal progresses in 1575 at Kenilworth, and in 1590, when a masque used the theme of Merlin incarcerated in a rock, and ended with Elizabeth rescuing him and re-establishing order, a propaganda tool whose message could not fail to be understood.[4] Chivalry continued to find an expression in the devotion to Elizabeth, the Virgin Queen, notably as she

1. Dejuinne François-Louis, *The Baptism of Clovis at Reims, 25 December 496*. The medieval foundations of the national Catholic past in Prance. (*Château de Versailles et de Trianon*)

2. The Adventures of Robin Hood. The Middle Ages in Hollywood.

3. John Waterhouse, Manchester Assize Courts, 1859, from Charles Eastlake, *A History of the Gothic Revival* (1872). Urban civic pride: reviving the values of late medieval burghers and merchants.

4. Sir Edwin Landseer, *Quuen Victoria and Prince Albert as Queen Phillippa and Edward III at their Bal Costumé, 1842*. Victorian medieval escapism. Viewing the Middle Ages in comfort.

5. President Slobodan Milosevic of Yugoslavia. Arousing nationalist passion in 1980s Serbia: the myth of Kosovo.

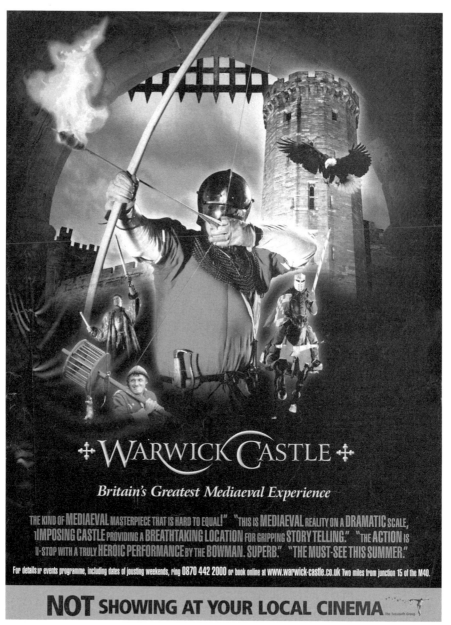

6. Warwick Castle, Britain's Greatest Mediaeval Experience. Experiencing the medieval in the twentieth-century re-enactment and the Heritage Industry. (*Madame Tussaud's*)

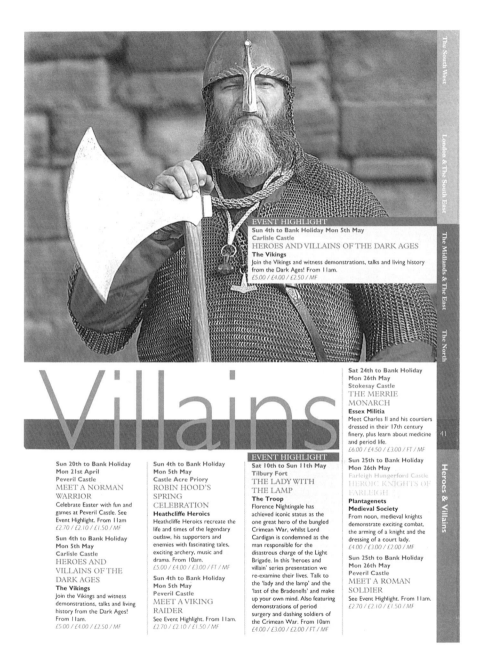

EVENT HIGHLIGHT
Sun 4th to Bank Holiday Mon 5th May
Carlisle Castle
HEROES AND VILLAINS OF THE DARK AGES
The Vikings
Join the Vikings and witness demonstrations, talks and living history
from the Dark Ages! From 11am.
£5.00 / £4.00 / £2.50 / MF

Villains

Sat 24th to Bank Holiday
Mon 26th May
Stokesay Castle
THE MERRIE
MONARCH
Essex Militia
Meet Charles II and his courtiers
dressed in their 17th century
finery, plus learn about medicine
and period life.
£6.00 / £4.50 / £3.00 / FT / MF

41

Sun 20th to Bank Holiday
Mon 21st April
Peveril Castle
MEET A NORMAN
WARRIOR
Celebrate Easter with fun and
games at Peveril Castle. See
Event Highlight. From 11am
£2.70 / £2.10 / £1.50 / MF

Sun 4th to Bank Holiday
Mon 5th May
Carlisle Castle
HEROES AND
VILLAINS OF THE
DARK AGES
The Vikings
Join the Vikings and witness
demonstrations, talks and living
history from the Dark Ages!
From 11am.
£5.00 / £4.00 / £2.50 / MF

Sun 4th to Bank Holiday
Mon 5th May
Castle Acre Priory
ROBIN HOOD'S
SPRING
CELEBRATION
Heathcliffe Heroics
Heathcliffe Heroics recreate the
life and times of the legendary
outlaw, his supporters and
enemies with fascinating tales,
exciting archery, music and
drama. From 10am.
£5.00 / £4.00 / £3.00 / FT / MF

Sun 4th to Bank Holiday
Mon 5th May
Peveril Castle
MEET A VIKING
RAIDER
See Event Highlight. From 11am.
£2.70 / £2.10 / £1.50 / MF

EVENT HIGHLIGHT
Sat 10th to Sun 11th May
Tilbury Fort
THE LADY WITH
THE LAMP
The Troop
Florence Nightingale has
achieved iconic status as the
one great hero of the bungled
Crimean War, whilst Lord
Cardigan is condemned as the
man responsible for the
disastrous charge of the Light
Brigade. In this 'heroes and
villain' series presentation we
re-examine their lives. Talk to
the 'lady and the lamp' and the
'last of the Bradenells' and make
up your own mind. Also featuring
demonstrations of period
surgery and dashing soldiers of
the Crimean War. From 10am
£4.00 / £3.00 / £2.00 / FT / MF

Sun 25th to Bank Holiday
Mon 26th May
Farleigh Hungerford Castle
HEROIC KNIGHTS OF
FARLEIGH
**Plantagenets
Medieval Society**
From noon, medieval knights
demonstrate exciting combat,
the arming of a knight and the
dressing of a court lady.
£4.00 / £3.00 / £2.00 / MF

Sun 25th to Bank Holiday
Mon 26th May
Peveril Castle
MEET A ROMAN
SOLDIER
See Event Highlight. From 11am.
£2.70 / £2.10 / £1.50 / MF

7. English Heritage 'Heroes and Villains' programme, 2003. The twentieth-century learning experience: recreating the Middle Ages. (*English Heritage*)

8. Past Times 'Medieval Gifts'. 'Medieval' objects of desire for a 'better' life in late twentieth-century advertising. (*Past Times*)

was fighting, through her knights, the Catholic enemy. The last tournament took place in 1624, ten years before the last edition of Malory for nearly two hundred years was published.[5]

Even though Malory's text itself was not available, his stories were used through memory, adapted romances and other indirect knowledge. One of his first indirect successors was Edmund Spenser, a great admirer of Langland's *Piers Plowman* and of Chaucer, both authors repeatedly reprinted in the sixteenth and seventeenth centuries. Spenser's *Faerie Queene*,[6] written in the tradition of Middle English romances and drawing heavily on Ariosto, uses the character of Arthur as a prefiguration of Gloriana, the perfect queen (clearly referring to Elizabeth herself), turning Arthur into a hero of English national identity and defender of the Protestant church. This 'spirit of nationalism' used historiography to promote the greatness of the English Protestant nation.[7] To that extent it might have more than puzzled the Welsh Geoffrey of Monmouth, whose hero was a British king fighting the Saxons. The versatility of the myth, with its successive and inclusive interpretations, was in fact ideal for its potential use on either side of the ideological fence, as medieval themes have so often been over the last four hundred years. Sir Philip Sidney, whose work, notably *The Arcadia*, and indeed whose very life as he saw it, and as it was made sense of by his biographer and his contemporaries, was meant to personify the virtues of chivalry.[8] Sidney epitomised an understanding of chivalry which went beyond the simple literary culture to be an essential part of contemporary social relations.[9] James I, another king needing to establish himself on the throne of England, as Henry VII had done, also used the Arthurian myth extensively, even writing plays himself, but above all by supporting the production of Arthurian court masques, the best known of which was written by Ben Jonson in 1609.[10] This association with the Stuarts, which they so strongly promoted, made Arthur less popular officially during the Interregnum, especially as the Puritans disliked and despised romances. John Milton, their poetic mouthpiece, who had originally planned to write an epic poem about Arthur, turned against it for that reason and used Genesis instead as the theme of *Paradise Lost*. The last manifestation of the Stuart link was Dryden's libretto for Purcell's opera *King Arthur*.[11] Written before 1688, it was not performed until 1691, by which time James II had been displaced by the Glorious Revolution. Although the text had to be adapted in order to make it palatable to the new regime, the myth remained associated with kingship. William III was indirectly glorified through Arthur by Sir Richard Blackmore in his two epic poems *Prince Arthur* (1695) and *King Arthur* (1697), in which the author drew an explicit parallel between the freedom-loving Gallic lords and the Huguenots, who appeal to Arthur alias William against the tyrannical King Clotar alias Louis XIV.[12]

The sixteenth century had seen the use of the Arthurian myth for 'nationalistic' purposes by the Tudors, and the seventeenth by the Stuarts. It had underpinned the ruling dynasties, serving as a model for the monarch as a defender of England and of Protestantism, and as a model of chivalry for the aristocracy. By the eighteenth century another dimension came to be added, at a time when national history and the search for, or construction of, national identity acquired unprecedented importance. King Alfred and Robin Hood, two other medieval heroes, belonged to this tradition, which sought to find the glorious foundations of national identity in the Middle Ages.[13] The Middle Ages, it was claimed, had given birth to the political system, had established the foundations of the economic and social order, and had seen the origins of an English empire. 'Englishness' in the eighteenth century would be defined as the embodiment of the free-born defence of the rights of the people, especially when set against the definition of 'Frenchness' (the great enemy) as tyranny.[14] Arthur illustrated this tradition, and his prowess as a military leader made him especially popular at a time of more or less constant military conflicts with France, in which England was engaged throughout the century. These produced the need for successful military heroes and knightly virtues, to serve as models for soldiers and officers, or to boost the nation's morale when things went wrong on the battlefield, as they did during the American Rebellion. Significantly the victors in that particular instance were rapidly coming to claim Arthurian status themselves. By the end of the century the newly-independent American colonies also put their successes into an Arthurian and chivalric framework.

Everybody could claim to be the heir to Arthur and his knights, on entirely similar grounds: martial prowess *due to* the justice of their cause in God's eyes; or defeat *despite* the valour of a knightly army. The high point of Arthurian myth usage was during the Revolutionary and Napoleonic Wars, when the story of Arthur's Return, a neglected aspect of the legend, was put forward to explain England's victories over Napoleon. A not-inconsiderable literature at the time strove to show that the new, or rather the returning Arthur, was none other than Wellington himself (whose Christian name, significantly, was Arthur). One among numerous example of the heroic poetry of the period praises British soldiers fighting in the Peninsular Wars:

> Thy ruby Cross aloft they raise
> Thine ancient star of Victory

They emulate our ARTHUR's days
And ARTHUR's self again they see.[15]

On those grounds alone Arthur's popularity was at its height by the 1820s.

Such an attitude was further consolidated by the support of George III, who saw medievalism, and chivalry at the heart of it, as an ideological buttress for the monarchy.[16] His son, George IV, also used the theme, having had himself painted as the Black Prince and turning his coronation in 1821 into a magnificent Gothic banquet at Westminster Hall, with all guests in period dress, an event immortalised by the painter William Turner. A similar 'medieval' style prevailed for his visit and Scottish coronation in Edinburgh the following year, which inaugurated the royal taste for the perceived Romantic Highlands lore and dress, to be launched so successfully as medieval by Walter Scott.

In the eighteenth century, even before Romanticism and the newly-resurrected appeal of the Gothic took them over, the myths of chivalry had been gradually transformed, from deeds of glory carried out by such perfect knights as the Chevalier Bayard, to the understanding of chivalry as a kind of noble calling to turn young men into *gentilshommes* in *ancien régime* France and *galant'uomini* in Italy. To the traditional virtues of bravery and noble conduct in battle were to be added a rounded education in the ways of the world, generosity, ease of conversation, polite and respectful behaviour to all, and permanent readiness to defend the weaker members of society, notably women. These ideals, partly inspired by such models as Castiglione's *The Courtier*, were taken up by European salons and courts from the seventeenth century onwards. They put forward urban, courtly and polished virtues, far removed from the rustic and rough English attitudes of Fielding's Squire Western. While one school still associated the gentleman with rights of birth and old-style military or at least sporting virtues, and defined manliness as a mixture of physical strength, sexual and drinking prowess, gambling and fighting,[17] the other was beginning to highlight the social graces and virtues of education and character above those of birth. By the mid eighteenth century, after the publication of Bishop Percy's *Reliques*, Hurd's *Letters of Chivalry and Romance* and Grose's *Treatise of Ancient Armour and Weapons* in 1786, and the translation into English in 1779 of de Sainte-Palaye's *Mémoires de l'ancienne chevalerie* and *Histoire littéraire des troubadours*, the English gentry at any rate had access to a whole range of materials and information relating to chivalry, as well as to artefacts and visual traces of it in the landscape.[18] While aristocrats were being guillotined in France, their counterparts in England and the rest of Europe became ever more romantically aware of the ideas of chivalry and generally of the Middle Ages, seen as an age of respect for kingship and church, an age of simple faith and devotion to sacred values seemingly under threat from the revolutionary French. This was the background to Edmund Burke's all too-famous lament that chivalry is dead: deploring the fact that, as he would have wanted it, there were not 'ten thousand swords [leaping] out of their scabbards' to defend Marie Antoinette, he went on to claim that

> The age of chivalry is gone. That of sophisters, economists, and calculators, has succeeded; and the glory of Europe is extinguished for ever. Never, never more shall we behold that generous loyalty to rank and sex, that proud submission, that dignified obedience, that subordination of the heart, which kept alive, even in servitude itself, the spirit of an exalted freedom. The unbought grace of life, the cheap defence of nations, the nurse of manly sentiments and heroic enterprise, is gone! It is gone, that sensibility of principle, that chastity of honour, which felt a stain like a wound, which inspired courage whilst it mitigated ferocity, which ennobled whatever it touched, and under which vice itself lost half its evil, by losing all its grossness.[19]

Gradually the type of rather boorish English squire gave way to the continental type of gentleman, who had to display education, manners and a noble character. Unlike the European model, on account of the importance of arcadian ideals of the English elite, which still saw its life centred around the country house, this ideal did not turn the gentleman into an urban figure, but on the contrary reinforced the country appeal, as well as the premium set on excellence in country pursuits. This became the model for the nineteenth-century 'English gentleman', to be exported with great success to continental Europe and America in the nineteenth century.

By 1800 the influence of the chivalric model had already become so pervasive that it was present, perhaps unconsciously, even in the mind and work of one of the allegedly most anti-Romantic of English novelists, Jane Austen. Some critics have called her novels romances based on the 'knight in shining armour getting the girl in the end'. Whether one agrees with this interpretation or not, the fact remains that a close look at, for example, *Pride and Prejudice*, is sufficient to show, in a very subtle way, how the behaviour of Darcy, expecting to gain his woman *vi et armis* just by being an aristocrat, is condemned by Lizzie Bennett who, in effect, does exactly what the ladies in the age of *courtoisie* were trying to do in order to turn a brute into a knight, by educating him in the language and art of courtship. Darcy clearly comes to see this as he tells her how much her response to his first marriage proposal, when she called him 'ungentleman-like', had 'tortured' him. Neither could the other overtly anti-Romantic novelist, Thomas Love

Peacock, resist the trap of chivalry, even as he chose to make fun of it in *The Misfortunes of Elphin* (1829).[20]

It was left to the nineteenth century to revive the Arthurian and chivalrous myth in a major way. Keats's *La Belle Dame Sans Mercy*, Coleridge's *Christabel*, Tennyson's *Idylls of the Kings* and Robert Browning's *Childe Roland to the Dark Tower Came* remain familiar to many. The images of Guenevere, knights and damsels by Rossetti, Burne-Jones and William Morris are also recognisable by all. But it is still be useful to carry out a tour of other, more obscure, English, continental European and American man-ifestations of the myth, and to see how it came to be transformed and interpreted in this context, before we can watch it being once again recast, with a completely different emphasis, in the later twentieth century.

It is generally conceded that Scott's success is due to his offering his thou-sands of readers his own version of the Middle Ages. This succeeded in captivating them and inflaming their imagination for several reasons. It was presented with great immediacy and vividness. It was totally different from their own lives. But, at the same time, it presented them with a mirror that could be made to express particular virtues which they felt their own age badly needed to find again. Throughout the first thirty or so years of the nineteenth century Sir Walter Scott was the most famous and most popular living writer anywhere in Europe.[21] His influence, through his novels and poetry, and by his lifestyle at Abbotsford on the Scottish Borders, where he effectively invented both the Highlands as a culture and the Scottish Baronial as a model for architecture and interior decoration, was paramount both in Britain and on the Continent, where his work was very widely trans-lated. His first successes were in poetry, with the publication of ballads in *Minstrelsy of the Scottish Border* in 1802–3, based on his Jacobite sympathies. This was followed by a whole series of other poems including *The Lay of the Last Minstrel*, *The Vision of Don Roderick*, *Marmion* and *The Lady of the Lake*, all published between 1805 and 1809, and then by his first novel *Waverley* (1814). Only some of his novels, however, were set in the Middle Ages. Of these *Ivanhoe*, *The Talisman*, *The Tales of the Crusaders* and *Quentin Durward* were most famous. Although he only wrote one 'Arthurian' novel, *The Bridal of Triermain* in 1813,[22] he became totally iden-tified with the age of chivalry. In the wake of his writings, noblemen were encouraged to build 'medieval castles' and furnish them with grandiose and intensely uncomfortable wooden carved furniture and weapons on the walls, and to make romantic gestures and perform dashing deeds, while young ladies could dream of gallant knights and courtly love. Meanwhile they could all read about passions, feuds, battles, loyalties divided, all set in castles with drawbridges, portcullises, armour-hung halls and high tables on dais, set among remote lakes, mountains and forests, and of knights and ladies engaged in tournaments, feasting, Christmases with Yule logs, mumming and Lords of Misrule, happy peasants dancing around Maypoles and various other manifestations of an imaginary Middle Ages with its heroes, Arthur and his knights, Richard Coeur de Lion, Ivanhoe and the rest.

While it has been often said that Scott single-handedly invented the tourist industry of the Highlands, with its tartans, clans and bagpipes, he arguably also invented the concept of Merrie England,[23] further developed by the likes of Cobbett and popular prints. Most importantly, Scott created a list of virtues, including bravery, loyalty, hospitality, respect for and protection of women and social inferiors, with a resurgence of the notion of feudal relations based on an exchange of loyalty and protection between a lord and his subjects, respect for honour and the given word, and refusal to take advantage of one's enemy except in a fair fight. His knight could probably be summarised in a few words, those describing his hero Lochinvar in the poem of that name in *Marmion*:

> So faithful in love, and so dauntless in war
> There never was knight like the young Lochinvar.

These became not simply feelings in books, but served as models for Victorian young men in their lives, who adapted these rules of chivalry to transform them into the norms of conduct for the English gentleman. The concept of the English gentleman came to be absorbed by young men as part of their education from very early on, through the pervasive influence of literature, pictures and observations of others, and persisted well into the twentieth century, in such a character as Dorothy L. Sayers's fictional Lord Peter Wimsey in England. The ideal was equally admired and copied on the Continent (in the same way as the Scottish Baronial architectural style was to be so influential on neo-Gothic castles such as the Koenigsbourg fortress in Alsace), and was still a powerful model in early twentieth-century Paris, in some of Proust's characters, for example the Guermantes family and the Baron de Charlus.[24]

Walter Scott's medievalism remained nevertheless always on the side of the imaginary: medieval knights and castles were, ultimately, *things of the past*, if of a glorious and golden past. One could at best borrow and adapt their virtues. Scott's contemporary, Kenelm Digby, an Anglo-Irish gentleman, was to see things differently, and for a long while his views of the Middle Ages and chivalry, as he defined them in his book *The Broad Stone of Honour*, were prevalent.[25] Hardly anyone now knows – or reads – Digby, partly because of his indigestible style; for his contemporaries *The Broad*

Stone of Honour was a revelation and a bedside book. Digby developed a great enthusiasm for the Middle Ages. He embarked on an European tour aimed at visiting places with Romantic chivalrous associations, such as Pierrefonds, Bayard's castle, Chillon in Switzerland and the castles of the Rhine, including Ehrenbreitstein, which gave him the inspiration for the title of his book. Significantly, *The Broad Stone of Honour*, published in a first edition in 1822, and expanded to five volumes between 1847 and 1876, had as its subtitle: *Rules for the Gentlemen of England*. For Digby chivalry did not simply belong to the past: he converted to Roman Catholicism because he saw chivalry and the church as inseparable, and dated the decline of the former from the Reformation. Above all, he specifically encouraged his readers to adopt a code of behaviour that would make them effectively behave like knights. This had to be a permanently valid code, and in his mind the two concepts of knight and gentleman became interchangeable. While Scott saw the gentleman as deriving from the medieval knight, with some civilising features, Digby saw chivalry as the supreme good, and he saw it as a reality in his world, fighting the forces of evil, rationalism and utilitarianism, triumphant in the 1820s. Young men throughout Britain took this to heart. Digby's influence was paramount on Wordsworth, Ruskin, Burne-Jones and Morris, and his book became a gospel of chivalric behaviour among young men of all social ranks for the next fifty years at least. Another such gospel was Charlotte Yonge's novel *The Heir of Redclyffe* (1853). Like Digby, the author was a disciple of de la Motte Fouqué, who had been the first to associate chivalry and Christianity in *Sintram*. Yonge also made her hero a model of chivalric behaviour inextricably bound up with Christian faith.

The numerous young men who read Digby and Yonge, most of whom did not become artists and poets, included many members of the upper classes who went into political life between the 1820s and 1840s.[26] Whether claiming to be Whigs, Radicals or part of the Young England movement, of which Disraeli was a co-founder in his youth, they all used the Middle Ages to justify their political stance. Some were rich landowners with radical sympathies and Gothic castles, such as Edward Bulwer Lytton at Knebworth from 1844. Alfred Tennyson inherited Bayons Manor in 1835 and immediately proceeded to change his name to Tennyson d'Eyncourt (claiming this family as his medieval ancestry) and to add numerous fortifications, battlements, and a great hall complete with minstrels' gallery to the place. Often these aristocrats' medievalism was essentially made up of romantic nostalgia for a pre-industrial age, for a Saxon England under a beneficent monarch protecting the rights of parliament and people, and benevolent landowners looking after their dependants. Members of the Young England movement were mostly wealthy but socially responsible landowners, reacting against Peel's 'Toryism without principle',[27] who were hoping to help bridge the gap between rich and poor in Victorian England, and recreate a sense of both local and national community. Even when they later became Tories, some of these men, including Bulwer Lytton and Disraeli as Prime Minister, continued to protest against the nefarious effects of the Industrial Revolution, increasingly visible by then in its overcrowding, poverty and disease in towns, and child labour and smog, which had put an end to the Golden Age they dreamt of. The most trenchant summary of this view was stated by Disraeli in his youth novel *Sybil*, though in his later life he became more anti-medieval than he had been during his idealistic youth: 'the people of England were better clothed, better lodged, and better fed just before the Wars of the Roses than they are at this moment'.[28]

Apart from being prompted to political action by romantic views of the golden age in terms of organisation of society as they imagined or wanted the Middle Ages to be, and besides reading novels and poetry, which inspired their code of conduct, the upper classes found another means of recreating the medieval world of their dreams, through re-enactments of medieval tournaments, jousting and feasting.[29] In 1714 William Stukeley, the antiquarian, had already taken part in a 'medieval banquet' at Hampton Court, in which the diners were serenaded by minstrels while they ate. George IV's coronation had involved massive festivities, with courtiers in medieval and Tudor costumes. Victoria's coronation in 1838 was on a much more modest scale, and thus created a feeling of disappointment for all lovers of pageantry, so much so that, a few years later, to make up for it, the newly-married queen gave a fancy-dress ball at Buckingham Palace, in which she and her husband wore their version of the costumes of Edward III and Queen Philippa.[30] The ball, with its enormous expense and two thousand guests in medieval costume, had probably been Albert's idea: he had been brought up in the age of German Romanticism, notably with the books of de La Motte-Fouqué which he contributed to making popular in England in the 1840s. Underlying the theme of the ball was the idea that the court of Edward III had seen the climax of the English Age of Chivalry, so that the new Queen and her Consort could be said to have brought about a revival of that great age. Later Albert was increasingly involved in schemes associated with medievalism, whether through his patronage of artists and the decoration of the Houses of Parliament (he was the chairman of the commission in charge of this), or by having himself represented in portraits and statues in the guise of a medieval knight, and Victoria as a medieval queen or medieval damozel. The change is revealing: no longer was the medieval used simply to depict or commemorate medieval events, scenes or people, even kings; it had acquired the power to symbolise the chivalrous qualities of a man, in short, the successful application of the code of chivalry to the English gentleman.

Victoria and Albert were not alone in recreating a medieval scene. From the late 1820s various aristocrats staged mock tournaments for their entertainment at their country houses, such as that of Firle Park in Sussex in 1827. Stimulated by this, the Earl of Eglinton decided to stage a major tournament in 1838, complete with coats of arms, pavilions and pennants, a Queen of Beauty and other such accoutrements, at his castle in Scotland.[31] The tournament attracted a huge crowd, whose participants were drawn from the English and Scottish aristocracy; many people travelled to Eglinton Castle from all over Britain, and the event drew attention throughout Europe. It ended up as a fiasco, on account of very bad weather, but it nevertheless had the effect of producing a large number of souvenirs, mementoes, books, plays, popular music and pictures. These presented an idealised version of the event and thus contributed to the spread of the taste for medievalism.

Outside England and Scotland chivalry and its manifestations was also alive and well. Frederick William IV of Prussia organised in 1829 the Festival of the White Rose, on the occasion of the empress of Russia's birthday.[32] Before marrying the tsar she had been Princess Charlotte of Prussia, Frederick William's younger sister, and had returned home for the occasion. Both siblings were ardent admirers of de La Motte-Fouqué, and Charlotte had adopted the medieval name Blanchefleur (Chrétien de Troyes's heroine in his romance *Perceval*) with the white rose as her emblem. The main attraction of the festivities was a tournament, complete with knights in armour, heralds, homage, coats of arms, and prizes for victors. Neither was this, a royal tournament, a unique revival of the medieval tradition; builders and owners of neo-Gothic castles liked to have such events in their grounds, for example at Laxenburg near Vienna or at Löwenburg near Kassel.

America was also swept by the spirit of chivalry.[33] There too 'straight' retellings of Arthurian and chivalry stories were written, strongly influenced by Walter Scott. Thomas Bulfinch's *The Age of Chivalry: or Legends of King Arthur* (1858) and *Legends of Charlemagne* (1862) were among Tennyson's own favourites, while Sidney Lanier's *The Boy's King Arthur* (1880) and poetry like James Russell Lowell's *Vision of Sir Launfal* (1848) became staple educational fare. Indirect knowledge of chivalry might take the form of an aloof awareness of their own superiority among the self-styled aristocracy of the Deep South, with the usual accompaniment of tournaments, duels and a certain formality of human relations which came to be seen as gentleman like behaviour. With it went the justification of slavery, also on the basis of feudal precedent.[34] Medievalist taste sometimes took the form of literary circles interested in chivalry. One such called itself the Knights of the Square Table, around Ralph Waldo Emerson (1803–1882) in the north.[35] An interest in Dante and Chaucer and in medieval myths, such as the discovery of America by the Vikings (the myth of Vinland) as an alternative origins myth to Columbus, all contributed to Longfellow's medievalism.[36] He was the founder of the Dante Society in America, and his *Tales of the Wayside Inn* were written in imitation of Chaucer.[37]

The spirit of chivalry in a most peculiar form was then adopted by the literature and myths of the western and of frontier culture. From the time of Thomas Jefferson, who was a great believer in the myth of Saxon liberties,[38] comparisons were made between the natives of North America and their civilisation and the 'progress' brought to them through laws, religion and so on by the conquerors moving further and further west through the continent. Increasingly throughout the nineteenth century, and still in the twentieth, the conquest of the Far West began to be perceived as the American Middle Ages, and parallels between the Arthurian and chivalry myths with the world of cowboys were part of the subterranean streams of American psyche in literature and then in film.[39] The Far West disliked central government and took the law into its own hands to right wrongs, and it exalted simplicity of faith, which recalled many traits of the medieval chivalrous ethos as understood by contemporaries.[40] Many of the tools and technologies of the American frontier, including log cabins, wagons, the ubiquitous jeans (originally from Genoa, where the fabric was made as sail cloth), and the lonesome brave stranger, the fellowship of men fighting enemies and nature, belonged in the first instance to the European Middle Ages. Moreover, the admittedly rather peculiar chivalric code of the cowboy, a man of justice, fighting attackers and defending and honouring the ladies, in short a 'good guy' against the 'bad guys', who do not respect any of these codes, was also linked with this inheritance.

Medievalism permeated through to the middle and working classes of Victorian England.[41] It was assimilated by the Fabians and Socialists like Charles Kingsley, who tried to educate working men in the spirit of future knights, combining intellectual development and physical activity. It was at the root of the education provided in the newly-created public schools such as Rugby and Clifton. Increasingly over the century, these attempted to inculcate physical ideals in young gentlemen through sport and, even more importantly, moral values based on team spirit (fellowship) and chivalrous behaviour (honesty, not cheating, losing gracefully, playing the sport for the sport's sake). All of these were passed on to young men through specially written literature, notably *Tom Brown's Schooldays* by Tom Hughes, who incidentally also wrote a life of King Alfred. With such books, and poetry like Sir Henry Newbolt's extremely popular *Vitaï Lampada* (Newbolt had been educated at Clifton) and ideals which identified being a gentleman with games, patriotism, the British Empire, and King and Country, these men were despatched to various parts of the world to govern the Empire. The development of imperialism enabled them to become 'knights', who went to the colonies to keep the borders safe, and to help those who were less fortunate than themselves in not being British. Public service became their sphere of action, in which they could either go abroad and 'fight against the forces of nature, produce abundance, redeem inferior peoples from slavery, superstition or unjust rulers, and give them peace and a wise and firm government',[42] or stay at home and fight against the internal enemies: poverty, ignorance, exploitation, drink and disease via missions, institutes, halls and societies, through which the middle and upper classes channelled money and energy into various worthy projects in the poorest areas in northern industrial towns or in the East End of London.[43] Popular novels expatiated on these models and virtues: the best known belongs to the latter part of the period and was written by J. Lockhart Haigh under the only too transparent title of *Sir Galahad of the Suburbs* (1907), but it was only one of a long string of such pieces already in fashion long before. The reward of these 'Knights of Empire', for they were taught to despise money (or had enough of it in the first place), was to worship the queen as their lady, to gain orders of knighthood (whose number greatly increased in the later nineteenth century), and to behave like worthy imitators of St George, the patron saint of England but above all of knights.

For centuries in England the popular imagery of St George had actually been much more important than that of Arthur.[44] Arthur had, even in the early nineteenth century, only the literary glory, while the crown, chivalry and knighthood, the army, popular fiction, popular traditions and iconography, down to the naming of pubs, retained George as a favoured 'cult'. As the nineteenth century unfolded Arthur began catching up on the popular front too: horses, as well as ships, were increasingly named after Arthurian characters; themed fancy balls and entertainments, for example balls and children's toy theatres, evolved around them; the production of knights and Merlin toys grew; and, as popular tourism began to take off especially in Wales, Arthurian sites, castles, caves and other natural beauty spots became frequently visited landmarks. While St George remained the official 'patron saint' of chivalry and gentlemen, as well as a popular figure and one often illustrated, his literary reputation and even representation suffered a minor eclipse during the second half of the nineteenth century, partly because the Arthur story could be adapted and constructed to fit many more complex relationships and social microcosms. It could present Camelot as the

Robert Baden-Powell, *The Young Knights of the Empire*. Boy Scouts – a school for future gentlemen.

embodiment of a perfect human political grouping, and make a political point. It created a model for those thirsting for the spiritual through the Grail quest. Last but not least, it provided the romantic reader with both an adventure story and a love interest through the story of Lancelot and Guenevere. A large number of images of St George and the Dragon became once again available in the 1890s, however, when he returned to the fore as an icon for the Empire and for chivalry.

This ethos of chivalry was also purveyed by various organisations of a paramilitary nature for boys, the most famous by far being Robert Baden Powell's Boy Scouts. Baden Powell's definition of the Boy Scouts, for whom the ideals, rules and codes, even insignia of chivalry were essential, was that of 'Young Knights of the Empire.' 'St George is the patron saint of cavalry and scouts all over Europe'. The scoutmaster is regarded as a knight and 'these are the first rules with which the old knights started and from which the scout laws of to-day come ... A knight (or scout) is at all times a gentleman.'[45] St George is invoked indirectly in the famous first rule of the scouts, usually incompletely quoted: 'Be Always Ready, with your armour on.'

St George came very much into his own in the early twentieth century, as part of First World War mythology.[46] Traditionally a warrior saint and the medieval patron of Edward III and the Order of the Garter, and still regarded as such in romances and by Spenser, the popular St George came once more to the rescue of English soldiers during the war in the form of the 'Angel of Mons', the divine messenger to the soldiers fighting the Germans, in a text by Arthur Machen, *The Bowmen*, first published in the *Evening News* in 1914.

Those future gentlemen who in the years around 1900 had imbibed during their formative years the code and manners which would make them recognisable as gentlemen and members of the elite were to be the generation that would disappear in the war. Significantly, their epitaphs were all couched in the vocabulary of chivalry: 'a gallant man', 'a chivalrous officer', 'he played the game like a gentleman'. Here is an example of an epitaph for a young man who died during the war, symbolic for the relative anonymity of the modest soldier it remembers as much as for its wording:

> His Country Called: He Answered
> Old England to Defend.
> Mid Shot and Shell He Never Swerved;
> Faced Duty to the End.
> When Death is Near and All Seems Night,
> May We Like Him Say 'It's All Right'.[47]

Together with so much of aristocratic Europe, the ideals of chivalry died in the carnage of the First World War.[48] The code and manners which were their outward signs did not, however, for a long while. When Neville Chamberlain's pronounced his famous dictum that 'Mr Hitler was not a gentleman', he was counting on his contemporaries understanding just how crushing a judgement this was meant to be – Chamberlain had been educated in the pre-1914 tradition. In many countries of Central and Eastern Europe, such outward signs of what is regarded as gentlemanly behaviour had still not died out after years of Communist rule. There, a man's upbringing included such basics as letting women through the door first, holding their coats open for them, or continuing the practice of hand kissing. These, however, belonged to another aspect of the chivalrous ethos, that of courtly love.

After the excesses of the Gothic novel, it was Walter Scott who, once again, first returned to the original references to Lancelot in *Marmion*. By 1820 there were already three editions of Malory in print, including one with a famous preface by Robert Southey. This was the edition read by Tennyson as a young boy. He in turn became the author of a complete rewriting of medieval romance.[49]

The literary and representational craze began in the 1830s. Tennyson's first set of Arthurian poems, 'The Lady of Shalott', 'Sir Launcelot and Queen Guenevere', 'Mort d'Arthur' and 'Sir Galahad', appeared in 1832 to tremendous acclaim. In 1837 Lady Charlotte Guest produced her seven-volume translation of the *Mabinogion*. The 1850s were full of Arthurian lore, from Rossetti's Arthurian paintings of 1855–59, Morris's paintings of 1859, the illustrated Tennyson with engravings by Rossetti, Holman Hunt and Maclise, Watt's *Sir Galahad*, to the Oxford Union redecoration with Arthurian themes by Rossetti and Burne-Jones. There were two completely different and opposing attitudes to the interpretation of the whole story, which clashed essentially on the issue of Lancelot and Guenevere.[50] One was the line taken by Tennyson, and most contemporary Victorian painters like Dyce, a favourite artist of Prince Albert. This was a fundamentally moral approach, in which Arthur and his knights epitomise the virtues and moral stance which contemporaries should model themselves on, these being essentially fellowship, purity, honour, mercy and generosity to the vanquished, protection of the weak and of damsels in distress, and virginity followed by fidelity in marriage. Tennyson's line became increasingly visible as he completed the last six of his *Idylls of the Kings* between 1859 and 1873. Here is the depiction of the perfect knight or English gentleman. His duty and joy are:

To reverence the King, as if he were,
Their conscience, and their conscience as their King,
To break the heathen and uphold the Christ,
To ride abroad redressing human wrongs.
To speak no slander, no, nor listen to it,
To honour his own word as if his God's,
To lead sweet lives in purest chastity,
To love one maiden only, cleave to her,
And worship her by years of noble deeds,
Until they won her; for indeed I know
Of no more subtle master under heaven
Than is the maiden passion for a maid,
Not only to keep down the base in man,
But teach high thought, and amiable words
And courtliness, and the desire of fame,
And love of truth, and all that makes a man. (*Poems*, 1836–7)

From that perspective the issue of Lancelot and Guenevere, namely that of adultery, was a major difficulty. It was at first condemned by Tennyson, who makes it the root of the downfall of the Round Table fellowship and of the happy reign of Arthur. Eventually Tennyson changed his mind slightly and produced what was in effect an acceptable version by suggesting that the affair had in fact been only slander. The phenomenal success of both Tennyson and this particular perception of courtly love was, however, paramount in shaping the ideals by which Victorian gentlemen were driven, and the manner in which they should behave in love. Such behaviour was to be based on the man's faithful service and devotion to his lady, often in a platonic way, to the extent of obeying her and devoting his life to her in all circumstances and through all manner of trials, as medieval knights were reputed to have done throughout the literature of the troubadours and of courtly love. This produced a spate of very odd patterns of behaviour, such as Ruskin's famously unconsummated marriage and, some have suggested, Disraeli's devotion to Victoria. It also allowed a large number of women, both in the upper and middle classes, unsatisfied within their loveless marriages, to satisfy their hunger for romance, in which the trappings of courtship and worship were actually more important than the consummation of an affair, while they were still being given no other role models than those of pure virgin or virtuous wife and mother.[51]

As against this official Victorian line, we can also find the exact opposite interpretation of the story of Lancelot and Guenevere's love. This is enshrined in Algernon Charles Swinburne's poetry, Morris's 'Defence of

Guenevere' and Rossetti's unfinished 'Defence of Lancelot'.[52] It is adapted to another comparable couple in Matthew Arnold's 'Tristram and Iseut'. In these, as in Rossetti's and Morris's paintings of Lancelot and Guenevere and of Tristan and Iseult, there is no condemnation of adultery. Quite the opposite: an exaltation of love, of the sexual and erotic, seen as self-justifying. Rossetti in particular, who celebrated erotic passion within medieval literature in his paintings of Dante and Beatrice or of Paolo and Francesca, was condemned and vilified for his sensuality, or 'fleshiness' as his most outspoken critic called it, which was regarded as a trade mark of the Pre-Raphaelites. What he and Morris in particular offered was a justification of love in its own right, identified with beauty and 'right', love understood as physical passion, as when the Guenevere of Morris's poem, naked and bound at the stake (itself an extremely erotic image) claims:

> See my breast rise,
> Like waves of purple sea, as here I stand;
> And how my arms are moved in wonderful wise . . .
> See through my long throat . . .
> And wonder how the light is falling so
> Within my moving tresses . . .
> Will you dare . . .
> To say this thing is vile?

The importance played by hair in a Victorian context cannot be too strongly emphasized. Whether used as a symbol of female sexuality and erotic appeal when flowing and unbound, or of chastity when tressed, hair reflected the fascination of men with the two aspects of womanhood, virgin and chaste or fallen and seductive, Madonna or whore, Eve or Mary Magdalene.[53]

The other female icon of nineteenth-century Romanticism was Iseult (later increasingly called Isolde, because of the celebrity bestowed on the story by Wagner). The couple which she forms with Tristram (or Tristan) is a more or less exact parallel one to that of Lancelot and Guenevere. She is the wife of a king (Mark of Cornwall), said to have been Arthur's brother or cousin, and she falls in love with one of the 'knights' at court, the king's nephew Tristan. Nevertheless, the differences between the two stories are revealing. Mark was accepted from the first as a purely imaginary figure, and none of the complex issues of national past, warlike qualities or leadership of a group of knights were ever associated with this particular story. It was no more, it would seem, than a love triangle, however doomed, and its appeal was precisely that of the impossible fulfilment of the most extreme and powerful kind of romantic love, sublimated in the form of a love philtre, said to make such love irresistible. The story was known, and referred to, in the poems of the troubadours of Provence, as the archetype of unhappy and passionate love. Despite its supernatural and poetic elements, popular with the Celticists, despite its links with medieval provençal culture and its allegedly Cathar associations, it is still revealing that this story should have become popular only from the Romantic period onwards. It was then that, for the first time, poets, artists and musicians felt it incumbent upon them positively to exalt human and physical love as a sacred passion, beyond the bounds of the common stigma of adultery.[54] The success of Wagner's opera *Tristan und Isolde*, after its première in 1865, added a metaphysical dimension to the story, focusing as it did on the themes of love, death, atonement and renunciation.[55] The popular appeal of the myth of the star-crossed lovers can be seen from the speed with which it became part of the common vocabulary of love for even the most rustic of suitors. The apparently rather simple-minded peasant-boy Nemorino in Donizetti's opera *L'elisir d'amore*, who is in love with the landowner's daughter busy reading the story of Tristan and Iseult, is happy to purchase from a quack doctor what he claims to be the 'elixir of love', none other than a bottle of the love philtre of Queen Iseult. Proof of the hero's gullibility? No matter. More significantly, if needed, proof of how far and wide into the popular imagination the knowledge of the lovers and their tragic story had reached.

Variations on the theme of the doomed lovers were pursued by Arnold and Swinburne, though their perception was both more and less philosophical. Arnold's *Tristram* argues that even in the most perfect of love there can be no happiness or fulfilment, only grief, passion being nothing but an all-consuming 'furnace' (a traditional medieval topos, incidentally), while detachment and philosophy alone can provide such happiness. Swinburne's poetry was regarded as even more shocking and degenerate than Rossetti's. Swinburne was a life-long medievalist from childhood, an accomplished scholar with a profound and comprehensive knowledge of medieval history and literature, as well as a translator and even writer of medieval pastiches, a great admirer of the forms of provençal troubadour literature as well as of Dante, Villon and Chaucer. Between 1857 and 1896 he produced a large corpus of poetry and prose set in the Middle Ages, from his earliest 'Chronicle of Queen Fredegund' to the 'Tale of Balen', through poems like 'Queen Iseult', 'Rosamond', 'The Queen's Tragedy' (Iseult again), 'Chastelard', 'St Dorothy' and 'Tristram of Lyonesse'. Some individual poems belonging to these cycles are often the best known of his corpus of work, especially the 'Laus Veneris', using the same theme as Wagner's *Tannhäuser*. Swinburne was a great admirer of Wagner, as he was of Hugo. A friend of Rossetti and Burne-Jones, but immensely contemptuous of Tennyson (he wanted his Tristram not to be 'mistaken for his late Royal Highness the Duke of Kent, or Iseult for Queen Charlotte, or Palomydes for Mr Gladstone'), Swinburne's medievalism was nevertheless in some sense more 'Victorian' than theirs in its attempt to provide an overall, systematic and unified vision of the world of the Middle Ages with their political, social and spiritual values. At the same time it was also even more extreme in its directly sensual and mystical nature, which the poet saw as being no less than a reinterpretation of the medieval tradition. Fatalism, the impossibility of separating love and death, the first being only ultimately fulfilled in the second, led to an exaltation of love in its own erotic right as the only possible goal in life:

> Do thy will now; slay me if thou wilt
> Yea, with thy sweet lips, with thy sweet sword; yea,
> Take life and all, for I will die, I say ...
> Take ... my flower, my first in June,
> My rose, so like a tender mouth

The two medieval women who say this to their lovers are clearly 'medieval châtelaines rather than ... Victorian Angel[s] in the House'.[56] 'Publicly obscene' and 'unclean', said the critics, of the man who would clearly show the way to the next generation of poets and artists, steeped in Aestheticism, but also to the New Woman of the 1890s, vilified for her independence.

From the early nineteenth century, one has only a very occasional inkling of a model of womanhood that is not that of the medieval damsel in distress. The Tennysonian model only accepted two versions: the pure virgin, virtuous wife and mother (or the girl being allowed to die of love while still knowing her place, like Elaine); or the danger woman, the harlot who seduces and kills men, like Vivien or Nimue. In between, but clearly belonging to the second category, is the adulterous wife, the Guenevere who is a distraction for men, corrupting them by making them more interested in sex than in their role in the public sphere of life and duty, war and politics, and who, in the end, by undermining the fabric of society based on the family unit, brings destruction to the male world of Camelot.[57] Throughout the Regency period and later, women novelists such as Jane Austen, George Eliot, the Brontës or Mrs Gaskell had already been undermining the model. Popular culture followed and presented alternative models too, again using the medieval period for that purpose. Historical novelists and poets, for example Felicia Hemans (1793–1835), Letitia E. Landon (1802–1838), and later Edith Nesbitt (1858–1924) wrote historical novels in medieval settings in Sicily, Rome, France and Provence, as did Elizabeth Barrett Browning (1806–1861), whose medievalism in her medieval novel and poem *The Romaunt of the Page* and *Aurora Leigh*, was of the tongue-in-cheek variety. What they had in common, however, was their treatment of female characters, increasingly removed from the cliché of the languishing damsel, the woman who needs a man. They are all shown to be heroines who function independently of male protection, and were often themselves heroic.[58] The combination of sexual power *and* intellectual knowledge was precisely what had prompted the repeated assault on the figures of Morgan and Vivien, the women who successfully destroyed Arthur and Merlin specifically through their ability first to seduce, then to overpower, them through their learning acquired from a *book*, a kind of knowledge which belonged to men. Victorian illustrators of the story, Frederick Sandys (*Vivien*, 1863), Burne-Jones (*The Beguiling of Merlin*, 1874–76, and several other later watercolours on the subject), relished the type. Even the French illustrator of Tennyson, Gustave Doré, highlighted the lethal combination of these two attributes, sex and learning which, by right, ought to have been the respective sphere of women and men. When learning was usurped by women, who should have restricted their sphere of influence to beauty and sex, Victorian men saw only ensuing chaos.[59] The paramount example of the medieval independent-minded, assertive heroine was Maid Marian, who lives and fights in the forest, alongside her lover Robin and in the company of men, regarded in some sense as almost the heir of the warrior queens of the British like Boudicca.[60]

Even though the eighteenth century was the high point of the use of the Arthurian myth in politics and history writing, such use did not cease in the nineteenth century. Since the twelfth century a strong historiographical tendency had led towards an anglocentric vision of the history of Britain in which Wales, Ireland and Scotland became subsumed, historically speaking, into one common past, perceived as being dominated by England and English institutions. Arthur represented the unity of the kingdom under the aegis of a national hero belonging to England's past, but could also be used to promote and support the role and importance of the *British*, meaning 'Celtic' side of British history, as a representative of the Welsh or British component of the kingdom. At a time of great expansion of Celtic studies, philology, poetry and history, partly under the influence of German scholars, partly as a deliberate political attempt to promote Britishness in an age of imperial expansion, Arthur was a handy mix of several models, and could be used to support the unity between Celt and Saxon and Welsh and English.[61] Characteristically, ways were found to avoid showing that, historically at least, Arthur had fought against the Saxons. Similarly, although the newly-developed keenness for historical 'accuracy' perforce led to debates about the origins of both Arthur and Arthurian literature in a French past, ways were found to overcome the problem of each country claiming the honour of being the original Arthurian land and language, mostly through learned debate demolishing the rival's claim. That it should only have been possible to deal with the historiographical issue in this way, on the basis of national histories (including the question of whether Arthur was French or English) is a good reflection of the nationalistic bias of nineteenth-century history or literary studies which laid claims to strict 'objective' detachment. That there might have been a common 'Celtic' culture in the early medieval period, or, for that matter, a common Anglo-Norman one across the Norman then Plantagenet 'empire', was not contemplated. Either solution would have made the debate entirely redundant, since it would have been irrelevant which part of these areas had first produced the characters of the myth or its literary form. Within a nineteenth-century context of tensions with France on various issues, not least the expansion of the two respective world empires, thinking in terms of a common history and cultural unity would have been extremely difficult. The contemporary rivalry in expansionist terms and the role of Arthur in it were by no means alien to one another.[62] The Arthurian myth, with its own associations with overseas imperialism, came to be adopted by the supporters of foreign expansion of the empire. They kept alive Arthur and chivalric models as part of Britain's imperial ambitions, opposing the less glamorous anti-expansionist, 'stay-at-home' parties, the supporters of the defence of one's own territory rather than the risks of foreign adventures, a faction which began to rise in influence after the débâcle and shock of the Indian Mutiny of 1857. Another fascinating twist of the story is to be seen in the most famous Arthurian work of the early twentieth century, T. H. White's Arthurian tetralogy of the mid 1930s, *The Once and Future King*. Here not only is the Arthurian myth again making references to the return of Arthur, but this and the story itself are used specifically to support the defence of England and the values of Englishness at home, against Nazi Germany.

In the twentieth century the emphasis changed again, away from the issues of courtly love and physical passion, which, unlike in the nineteenth century, were themselves increasingly available and mentionable commodities, no longer debated as matters of morality. The ever-flexible Arthurian myths took on two different lines of development, one scholarly and one popular. The first saw the publication of hundreds of books, journal articles and collected papers concerning themselves with the origins, development, influences and literary criticism of the medieval Arthurian corpus of texts, their transmission and afterlife. Among them were such literature scholars or archaeologists of early Britain as R. W. Chambers, Leslie Alcock and Richard Morris. These activities included the setting up of an *International*

Arthurian Society (IAS) with its bibliography and newsletter, conferences on Arthurian topics, books, articles, dissertations and theses, dictionaries, ency-clopaedias and bibliographies, and numerous periodicals, such as the journal *Arthurian Studies* and more recently *From Avalon to Camelot*.[63] In the United States, in particular, both university courses and schools pro-grammes focusing on Arthur have seen a phenomenal development in recent decades. The expansion of Arthurian studies as an academic disci-pline has been gigantic, though not always even in quality. Where these studies have dealt with text criticism, the impact of the stories on medieval *mentalités* and archaeological work on late Roman Britain, they had and continue to have the most impeccable scholarly credentials.

During the twentieth century Arthurian myths moved very firmly to Amer-ica. American writers were fascinated by them and adopted them directly, indirectly, or even caustically with a subversive purpose. The first example of the subversive rewriting of the myth comes from the later nineteenth cen-tury with Mark Twain's *A Connecticut Yankee at King Arthur's Court* (1889).[64] It is one of three novels by him, as well as several short stories, to have a medieval theme. Twain's attitude to the medieval period was one of simultaneous rejection and attraction. In the first instance there was his dual criticism of both the Middle Ages themselves, and of the medievalist revival of the nineteenth century. For Twain, as for his models of historical writing which were clearly spiritually attuned to the Enlightenment, the medieval period was bad on account of the political system of the monarchy, of the feudal aristocratic world which regarded itself as superior to its contempo-raries, of courtly love which encouraged women's lewd behaviour and undermined the authority of men and family, and of the power of the church and Catholicism. All these were also features of the world of the Deep South, in which Twain had grown up, and which he criticised for its perceived aristocratic and agrarian class structure, oppression, taste for duels and feuds, and for the mock castle architecture of its mansions. He also abhorred the medieval revival taste of the Deep South, what he termed the 'Sir Walter Disease', the influence of Scott, which had contributed to per-petuating the unrealistic model of the chivalrous, romantic and ultimately defeated character, stuck in a 'culture of defeat'.[65] Ostensibly, especially in *A Connecticut Yankee*, Twain wished to celebrate the ethos of progress and middle-class values, energy, prosperity, entrepreneurship, pragmatism com-bined with sentimentality about women and family life. These reflect the image which Hank Morgan has of himself as the self-made Yankee, a firm believer in progress, optimistic about the future, and trusting in the power of knowledge, by which he means technology. Moreover, while in the first drafts of the book the character is only interested in business, in the final draft he is shown as a reformer, attempting to bring to the world of sixth-century England constitutional theories of justice, equality before the law, representative government, separation of church and state, and free trade. Hank is the American 'common man' who is, however, a 'capitalist hero' of the new world, the American Adam. Twain's own description of the book in his autobiography is as 'an attempt to contrast ... the English life of the whole of the Middle Ages with the life of modern civilisation – to the advantage of the latter, of course'.[66]

While using the Middle Ages as a means to present his political views about his own world, Twain was nevertheless himself deeply attracted by medievalism. As a child he, too, like others in the Deep South, had read Lanier's rewriting of the Arthurian stories, as well as Malory and Scott. He spent his life hankering after the past, fascinated by the history of his family and its alleged aristocratic lineage in Virginia, commissioning a Gothic house in Hartford (Connecticut), where he finally settled, and using constantly the stock motifs and conventions of medieval romances. Even courtly love found its place in his writing, in the Romantic Tom Sawyer's devotion to Becky as his lady. The comparison of chivalry with childhood, of the Middle Ages with the childhood of civilisation as opposed to the present as its maturity, led Twain to describe it as primitive and ignorant, but also as a symbol of innocence, freedom and imagination. The paradox is ultimately resolved in the increasingly sombre and pessimistic ending of *A Connecticut Yankee*. Hank's name is an abbreviation of Henry, the most common royal name in medieval England – a significant dent in the apparently democratic system which he sets up. His choice of name for himself, (Sir) Boss, is clearly meant to call to mind the name used by the great corrupt industrialists and robber barons of nineteenth-century capitalism, who exploited the labour force that Twain was defending. Ultimately, the society 'reformed' by Hank is defeated and wiped out by a stock exchange-type speculation, reflecting the rapacity of industrial and *laissez faire* capitalism with its corruption, and Hank's technology of war, which he has seen as progress, destroys his newly created world. Having started as a paean to the world of modern America, the book ends as an indictment of it, while the world of the knights has been extinguished, with nothing else found to put in its place.

The 'straight' retelling of the myth needs not be mentioned more than in passing, to record the existence of large numbers of medievalist novels, literature for children and now fantasy and film. Twain had, however, opened the floodgates for the production of a large quantity of interpretative Arthurian literature in America in the twentieth century, which focused on a variety of issues either discussed by him or new, notably anti-medievalist feelings, the North-South divide and general political use of the myth. One of the writers most frequently associated with such a reinterpretation of Arthurian myths was John Steinbeck.[67] He retained throughout his life a 'straight' interest in Arthur, too, and he came to England to research and write his *Acts of King Arthur and his Noble Knights* (1958–59). Most of his work uses the Arthurian theme indirectly, especially in the form of the Grail Quest and the Knights of the Round Table. The best known for this are *Cup of Gold* (1929), *Cannery Row* (1945), *The Winter of Our Discontent* (1961) and, above all, *Tortilla Flat* (1935), of which the author wrote:

> the book has a very definite theme ... I have expected that the plan of the Arthurian cycle would be recognised, that my Gawaine and my Launcelot, my Arthur and Galahad would be recognised. Even the incident of the Sangreal in the search in the forest ... The form is that of the Malory version, the coming of Arthur and the mystic quality of owning a house, the forming of the round table, the adventure of the knights and finally, the mystic translation of Danny [who] corresponds with Arthur. [I] can only think of the Round Table as having existed in Salinas, California, around the turn of the twentieth century.[68]

Influenced both by the novels of Sidney Lanier and John Erskine, and by the rejuvenation of Arthurian poetry and prose by T. S. Eliot and E. A. Robinson's Arthurian trilogy in the 1920s, Steinbeck used simultaneously the adaptation of the 'straight' myth (notably in the analogy between the cowboys of the Wild West and the medieval knight errant), and a 'deconstruction' of the Arthurian myth and chivalric ideal, aimed at showing them to be fundamentally flawed.

One of Steinbeck's best known contributions to the American Arthurian scene was his association of J. F. Kennedy with Arthur.[69] In an interview with the *San Francisco Chronicle* in 1960, Steinbeck was the first to set side by side the images of Kennedy and Arthur. Through this, and later through other media such as the musical *Camelot* (which premiered less than a month after Kennedy's election, and which the President used in his speeches), the Kennedy-Camelot link became one of the potent uses of myth in American politics. 'To many Americans, among them [Kennedy], both Arthur's Camelot and the new administration represented an ideal world – one filled with hopes and dreams'.[70] Kennedy himself loved it, had been influenced by its message, and used it to suggest a parallel between him and Arthur, which was so successful that it eventually turned the Kennedys into America's 'royal family' for years to come. The association became so common both then and later that, for example, a book of photographs by Jacques Lowe, a

The Arthurian myth explained to children.
Walter Crane, 'Sir Galahad is Brought to the Court of King Arthur' (1911).

friend of the Kennedys, was published in 1996 under the significant title of *Camelot: The Kennedy Years*. The mythical link was further strengthened by the assassination, the 'sacrificial offering of the prince of Camelot to the forces of bigotry, irrationalism and fanaticism'.[71]

The story becomes even more fantastical, with a string of 'legends' which highlight Kennedy parallels with Arthur, his death and future return. Suggestions were made that the dead President was preserved in a vegetative state in a variety of secret places (a Washington military hospital, Onassis's island) until such time as the doctors could resurrect him. Only his wife has access to these places – incidentally, a way of explaining and excusing her remarriage: obviously, if Jackie had married Onassis only to finance her husband's recovery and keep his secret, then she could continue to be regarded as a noble lady worthy of her lord, instead of a woman who rebuilt her life.[72] Other major writers who also made indirect use of the myth were F. Scott Fitzgerald, whose Gatsby can be read as a modern knight, and William Faulkner in *Mayday*.[73] Arthurian connections have even been claimed for Raymond Chandler in several of his novels, most conspicuously the evocatively named *The Lady in the Lake*, with Marlowe being another modern incarnation of the medieval knight.

The appeal of Arthurian myths to American audiences is often based not on their medieval roots but on their discovery, second-hand, through works of popular fiction such as T. H. White, Mary Stewart's *Merlin Trilogy* (1970–79), comics like *Prince Valiant* by Hal Foster, and film. Arthurian and chivalry themes were used extensively from the very early part of the twentieth century, especially in children's books like Lanier's *The Boy's King Arthur* and Howard Pyle's *The Story of King Arthur and his Knights* (1903), a classic greatly admired by F. D. Roosevelt.[74] Arthuriana was also used in youth movements for children and teenagers, with the Knights of King Arthur, founded by W. B. Forbrush in 1893, and the Knights of the Holy Grail, founded by P. E. Powell, both nonconformist ministers.[75] Forbrush's books, *The Knights of King Arthur: How to Begin and What to Do* and *The Round Table: The Order of the Knights of King Arthur and its Affiliated Societies. A Handbook for Leaders*, explained the purpose of the organisation for boys aged thirteen to sixteen, at a time when 'they are said by psychologists to be in the knightly period'. They suggest the creation of 'Castles' (non-secret fraternities under the control of the local churches) and of leaders called Merlins, with awards such as the 'sacred honor of the Siege Perilous' given for 'athletic or self-sacrificing attainments'.[76]

The Arthurian literature of Pyle and Steinbeck, the teenage organisations, and magazines like *Harper's Young People* (which changed its name to *Harper's Round Table: or The Young Knight*) continuously passed on the same set of messages, aimed at ensuring the creation of the model young American male, virile and strong in character, but also having the Arthurian virtues of chivalry, courtesy, respect for women and Christian values, and above all, the American ethic of respect for family, duty and hard work. Through such personal endeavours, rather than through inherited titles and wealth, would one come not only to be successful, but would indeed be *like* King Arthur and his knights. America promoted the 'democratisation' of the Arthurian myth, whereby everyone who behaved like Arthur could symbolically *become* Arthur, whose true nobility comes not from his power and status but from his human qualities.

Ideals of knighthood did not cease to appeal once Americans emerged out of their teens. A plethora of 'Orders', with connections to secret societies and especially to Freemasonry, which itself experienced a great revival in the early twentieth century, were available for joining, with names like the Order of the Golden Cross, the Knights of Pythias, the Knights of St Crispin (a cobblers' union, another kind of medievalism, since St Crispin was the patron saint of that trade in the Middle Ages) and, particularly important after its foundation in 1869, the Noble and Holy Order of the Knights of Labour (generally known as the Knights of Labour).[77] This was in fact a trade union of workers, a very successful one since, within twenty years, it included one in five of all American workers. The ethos of medievalism influenced the Knights of Labour in their titles, ritual and publications, such as W. K. Tisdale's *Knights' Book*, which claimed descent for the knights directly from Hugh Capet, and dealt with such themes as 'Chivalry and Knighthood in the Middle Ages', 'The Passage of Arms' and 'The Battle for Honor and Renown'. Above all, it reflected the association in the workers' minds between medievalism and anticapitalism, even antimodernism, which so worried them in the rapidly-expanding industrial world of America, as it had worried their predecessors in a similar context in England. A contemporary poem reflects only too well the mindset of the potentially exploited workforce; addressed to the knights, it wishes that

> Fair ladies of honor come crown these brave knights
> God help them to gain men and women their just rights.[78]

On a different level, but still placing a knight in the context of modern problems and enemies of America, was the hero of Hal Foster's cartoon or comic *Prince Valiant*.[79] In the first years of its publication after 1934 it was very clearly geared towards fighting Fascism and Nazism, in the thinly disguised form of the end of the Roman Empire, with its decadent emperor Valentinian (illustrated as Mussolini), attacked by the Huns (whose leader was in turn illustrated as Hitler). Though not a knight of the Round Table,

Prince Valiant fights alongside Gawain and Tristram, with the help of the Singing Sword – all these allusions to Arthur, Excalibur and chivalry would have been more than transparent to contemporary readers invited to identify good and evil in their own time.

The first half of the twentieth century in England had its large share of 'straight', realistic, often patriotic retellings of the Arthurian story. A large number of plays on the theme had been produced in the late 1910s and 1920s by Arthur Symons, Laurence Binyon and John Masefield, among others,[80] and an equally large number of novels were written, the best known among them being Charles Williams's *Taliesin through Logres* and John Cowper Powys's *A Glastonbury Romance* and *Porius*.[81] The most popular was T. H. White's series *The Once and Future King*, published for the first time as a set in 1958 but begun in 1938, the last properly 'Victorian' treatment of the story.[82]

By the 1920s the indirect approach, the use of the symbols of the Grail, the Wasteland and the Fisher King to allude to modern themes of power and men's use of it, war, destruction and renewal, and people's understanding of history and society, had begun to mark a different approach to the story, notably in T. S. Eliot's revolutionary work *The Wasteland* (1922) and James Joyce's *Finnegans Wake* (1939).[83] Not dissimilarly, more recent writers who reworked the Arthurian myth, for example by placing Arthur's return during the Blitz (Donald Barthelme) or by ridiculing the Grail knights and turning the Grail itself into the ultimate weapon (Thomas Pynchon's *Gravity's Rainbow*, 1973), also reused the myth for contemporary political as well as metaphorical purposes.

Use was made of Arthurian themes elsewhere than in America at the end of the twentieth century. For example, in the (then) German Democratic Republic, playwrights like Tankred Dorst and Christoph Hein turned the myth on its head by attempting to show that, like all utopias, Camelot was doomed from the start, could not be reformed, and must, by definition, fail – a parable which could be also used by critics of Marxism.[84] The versatility of the Arthurian stories had proved itself again and again, not only for the purpose of entertainment or, as in the nineteenth century, to define relations between men and women or particular values expected of the European gentleman, but this time and at an even deeper if more indirect level, in a philosophical context, redefining social relations, political aspirations and conflicts, and ultimately metaphysical powerlessness.

Arthurian interpretations of the last thirty years rely on those themes which have made this most versatile of myths popular from the beginning: adventure, magic, love and romance, bravery, brotherhood, nobility and treachery. They have also added to it another dimension. The story offers an irresistible entry into their own preoccupation for those with arcane interests in the Grail, occultism, paganism, astrology, esoterism and associations with the Rosecrucians, Knights Templar, Freemasons and a variety of other obsessions in a world which feels only too deprived of preordained certainties.

The character of Arthur himself, as opposed to the overall themes of chivalry and the Round Table, in the literature for adults, children and teenagers (now more politically correctly known as Young Adults) in the twentieth century, has been the subject of hundreds of books, with other art forms, high and low brow, in even greater profusion. A few key themes run through most of them. First is the 'quest for the real Arthur', with books on the sixth-century British leader who fought the foreign invaders of Britain, Saxons and Picts, as in Rosemary Sutcliff's *Sword at Sunset* (1963), Mary Stewart's trilogy *The Crystal Cave* (1970), and a wave of non-fiction literature.[85] The hidden agenda in most of these works is the national 'Celtic' one, returning Arthur to his Welsh roots by showing him as the leader of the British people fighting the invading Saxons. This is Britishness in the twentieth-century meaning of the word: the oppressed Celts fighting against an English oppressor, transposed into a different space and time yet entirely identifiable as such. The 'Celtic roots' of Arthur are reclaimed by both nationalistic Celtic writers, in Britain and in France and by those who like to associate the 'Celtic spirit' with the various aspect of esoteric interest, all of which are brought together in the pantheist myth of return to the deepest folk origins of some sort of 'eternal' nature and ancestral worship. Indirectly related to this trend is the apocalyptic and millenarian anti-war message for which the myth is used, with its emphasis on the futility and waste of it. This became paramount in the second half of the twentieth century which, after two world wars, saw itself facing the nuclear threat. From Laurence Binyon's *Arthur: A Tragedy*, written after the First World War, and T. S. Eliot's *The Wasteland*, to the allegorical quest of *Apocalypse Now*, the message is the same. Science fiction and fantasy literature and film, for example the films *The Dark Crystal* and *Mad Max*, adapted the myth of the brotherhood of the Round Table to gangland or futuristic models. Comics like *Camelot 3000* recast Arthurian characters as modern heroes fighting against aliens. The extravaganza of the *Sword in the Stone* rock concert saw Michael Jackson performing as a visored knight in shining armour with an electrically-glowing sword. There are large numbers of re-enactment societies and other gatherings of enthusiasts of Arthur, Dragons and 'Dark Ages Britain'. Added to an explosion of Arthurian tourism around Britain and Brittany, the myth has been dragged along every possible path from the sublime to the ridiculous.

Popular taste has also created a rapidly expanding need for Heritage sites and artefacts. English Heritage's brochure about Tintagel presents 'King Arthur's legendary birthplace', 'a marvellous family experience of mystery, myth and magic'. Not far away is the 'Arthurian Centre', with its 'Grail Trail' and 'the site of King Arthur's last battle of Camlann (c. AD 540)', a battle occasionally re-enacted by the 'Northern Mercenaries' group, with side shows, 'archery, living history, merchant stores, weapons displays, medieval dancing ... battles and parades'. A rival attraction is at Corris (Powys) in Wales. Here we have 'King Arthur's Labyrinth', with tales of the 'fight of the dragons and the foretelling of the coming of Arthur, the giant Rhitta, the head of Bendigeidfran, the flooding of Cantre'r Gwaelod and the bells of Aberdyfi, the battle of Camlann and the death of Arthur, and the cave where Arthur sleeps', while the craft centre next door has working craftsmen and women including a potter, a jeweller and a candlemaker selling their produce. Even in Scotland, various contenders for the much coveted title of 'real' Camelot are equally popular, as are their European equivalents like the *Son et Lumière* play *Lancelot du Lac* in the 'Forêt de Brocéliande' in Brittany. We are once again in the middle of the contemporary identification of Arthur with the Celtic world and its connotations of ecology, mysticism and supernatural. In Tintagel there is a 'King Arthur Bookshop'. It advertises the sale of 'Arthurian, Celtic, New Age and general books, Celtic designed jewellery and gifts, Myth and Magic' – all printed in a 'Celtic'-style font. Such bookshops are also present in large numbers in Glastonbury, a site originally associated with Arthur since the medieval period (where it was already venerated as his and Guenevere's tomb after being 'discovered' by the monks), and also with the supernatural and supposedly pagan prehistoric connotations of Glastonbury Tor, on which, every year, Travellers from all over gather for the ultimate alternative festival. It is no surprise to see for example that Glastonbury, a medieval monastery (which, however, claimed a legendary foundation by Joseph of Arimathea two thousand years ago) and Stonehenge, a Neolithic and Bronze Age site of which almost nothing is known (except that it obviously dates back to three thousand years), should both be placed in the same category on grounds of spiritual pagan nature worship.

More extreme in this line of thought, and more dangerous perhaps for their popular esoteric appeal, are the large number of books creating a kind of melting pot of the 'occult', incorporating every 'mysterious' aspect of the European tradition. The Templars, alchemy, the Kabbalah, Rosicrucians, Freemasons, Satanism, the Dead Sea Scrolls, the Turin Shroud and Joseph of Arimathea are used to surround the myth of the Holy Grail.[86] Such a treatment of the Grail had already been part of various kinds of fascist ideologies, and serious Nazi scholars were told to find the Grail itself, as well as the Ark of the Covenant, Atlantis and other archaeological dreams – Indiana Jones may not have been real, but the themes underlying some of the films were! A similar theory, together with some rather debatable associations with the concept of race (now more prudently named 'lineage') has been put forward by some who identify the Grail with the sacred bloodline of the Merovingian kings, supposedly originating in the offspring of Jesus and Mary Magdalen, washed ashore in Gaul and preserved at Rennes-le-Château. A large amount of ink has flowed, both in Britain and in France, over such theories and refutations thereof. In the overtly materialistic and intellectually uncensored world of twenty-first-century Europe, the thirst for spiritual nourishment, mystery and apocalyptic fears combine to create the right climate for such ideas to thrive.

Analysing the changes brought to the twentieth-century understanding of Arthurian myths means underlining once again how this, the most flexible and rich of European streams, can be used to highlight particular aspects of contemporary society and culture. The Victorians saw chivalry, courtly love and sensuality triumphant, which were at the forefront of their preoccupations (possibly because their direct and open discussion was less well accepted). The twenty-first century, in contrast, uses the myth to focus on the least discussed of human issues today, one which despite two hundred years of triumphant rationalism and science refuses to go away: the spiritual. Having re-emerged with a vengeance in what is perceived as a particularly materialistic age, it has returned both by the front door, in this instance through the appropriation of Arthur, Merlin and the Grail by the Heritage world, and by the back door, through the New Age rebelliousness, somewhat romantically labelling itself as such through its association with the 'Celtic world.'

7

Medieval Inspirations

The use of the Middle Ages in historical fiction has been long standing, from nineteenth-century exponents like Walter Scott to Melvyn Bragg and Bernard Cornwell in the 1990s. It was part of a tradition of historical fiction with a rich thread throughout Europe, from Alexandre Dumas père through the early twentieth-century Norwegian writer Sigrid Undset in her novels *Kristin Lavransdottir* and *Vigdis*, Maurice Druon's *Les rois maudits* and Jeanne Bourin's *La chambre des dames* and Robert Graves's *Belisarius*, to Umberto Eco. Medievalism in the European cultural tradition has been a component of the Romantic movement. One key element, belonging to both, was an interest in the supernatural, the irrational and the inexplicable. This same fascination with the supernatural, often specifically associated with a medieval setting, was a major component of the nineteenth-century Fantastic genre, represented in Germany by works like E. T. A. Hoffman's story *Das goldene Krug*, in England by M. R. James's tales and Wilkie Collins's novels, and in America by E. A. Poe's stories.[1] It may be no coincidence that an interest in 'ghost' stories should have been strong in nineteenth-century English and American literature, in the Victorian era which insisted so much on the pursuit of science and progress. Victorian Gothic in literature flourished by replacing the traditional castles and abbeys as places of terror with the urban industrial landscape of dark alleyways, slums, opium dens and fog. The cosy domestic space was taken over by the new villains of the urban and scientific world: criminals, mad scientists who create artificial monsters, dangerous foreigners from far-flung corners of the empire, and ghosts which recall the dark secrets of the family's or the individual's past.

The end of the period saw a further transformation of the Gothic, which became obsessed with the idea of decadence. This interest in the darker side of the mind combined with the fear of decay, chaos, rupture and fragmentation, even of the self, at the core of novels such as Oscar Wilde's *The Portrait of Dorian Gray*, R. L. Stevenson's *Dr Jekyll and Mr Hyde*, and H. G. Well's *The Island of Dr Moreau*. Typically, the fascination with this twilight world was then transmuted into allegories of the fin de siècle in the restless and anxiety-ridden world of the late Austro-Hungarian monarchy in the novels of Gustav Meyrink's *Golem* (1915) and *Walpurgisnight*

(1917), Franz Kafka's *Castle* and *Metamorphosis*, and Leo Perutz's super-natural tales. Some critics have gone further and defined 'magic realism' in the twentieth century as equally heir to the 'medievalist' tradition. As an eminently international literary trend, magic realism acquired a maturity of its own in the work of, for example, Heinz Ewers, Dino Buzzati, Julio Cortazar and José Luis Borges and, more recently, Angela Carter and José Saramago.[2]

The late twentieth-century French tradition of non-academic medieval-ism has been less philosophical and weighty, and is expressed above all in the proliferation of historical novels. The foremost representative of the genre is Jeanne Bourin.[3] She also writes cookery and children's books on medieval themes, and claims that she would have liked to have lived in the Middle Ages, 'when the balance between the spiritual and the physical was greater, and when the love of God led to love of his creation', 'quand nos aïeules étaient libres' (when our ancestresses were free).[4] Her professed purpose is to fight the idea of the Middle Ages as the 'dark ages', and to have people, including children, learn about their past and '*terroir*'. The attraction of a return to one's deeper roots is the avowed reason for the success of the books. But, beyond the pleasure of accurate knowledge about everyday medieval life and a well-written, emotion-filled, identification-provoking read, they also provide a feeling of security and comfort, in contrast to a worrying present with its overwhelming problems. History is here perceived through the medium of private life, where emotions are paramount, and these usually long 'saga' novels focus mostly on female characters, to whom twentieth-century feelings and perceptions are allo-cated, as well as a working life and freedom which all make them seem 'modern' to the reader's mind, while they nevertheless function on a back-ground of exotic period detail and archaic language. Bourin's main market, by choice, is women and children. While her books have been called 'women's' or 'Summer' novels and regarded as escapist entertainment (echoes of the Gothic novel perhaps?), they are both a successor to tradi-tional historical novels from a feminine angle, rather than the traditional 'knights' adventures', and a result of the kind of interest which is at the root of the success of the historical, and specifically medieval, crime novels and fantasy fiction.

The attraction of the medieval as a way of discussing the modern continued throughout the twentieth century. Dante remained a major source of inspiration for twentieth-century poets, as he had been for Blake, Byron and others in the previous age, as a model for prophetic and allegorical literature, anticlericalism and even the ideals of a free, united Italy.

In the twentieth century Ezra Pound, T. S. Eliot, J. B. Yeats, Louis McNeice, Samuel Beckett and Seamus Heaney in the English-speaking world claimed affinities with him.[5] Ezra Pound translated Guido Cavalcanti's *Canzone* (into *Middle* English, deliberately), but he also wrote poetry which he wanted to model on that of the troubadours, notably Bertrand de Born, on the Italian poets of the *dolce stil nuovo*, on Dante, and on Chaucer.[6] Almost every major and minor poet included medieval-themed poems in their work, witness 'The Lady with the Unicorn' by Vernon Watkins. The twentieth century continued to make use of the Middle Ages in the theatre too, starting with Maeterlinck's *Pelléas and Mélisande* and the plays about St George. T. S. Eliot's *Murder in the Cathedral* (1959) adapted Thomas Becket's story to show the continued relevance of martyrdom for one's beliefs, and Eliot generally used the theme of pilgrimage or quest through-out his work, as we have already seen with *The Wasteland*.[7] Religious drama itself had a major revival,[8] not only directly with the Mystery Cycles of York, Chester and Wakefield being once again alive every year, but also in radio drama, such as Christopher Fry's *Boy with a Cart* (1939), recounting the story of the Saxon saint Cuthman, and his *The Lady is not for Burning*, set in the 1400s. Perhaps most in tune with the original style of late medieval plays mixing the religious, the chivalrous and the farce tradition was the work of the openly French Catholic playwright Paul Claudel, especially *L'annonce faite à Marie*, *La jeune fille Violaine* and *Le soulier de satin*, writ-ten between 1892 and 1943.[9] Medievalism and Roman Catholicism had been closely related in some cases in the nineteenth century, for example by Chateaubriand and by Pugin. In the earlier part of the twentieth century medievalism became a manifestation of the intellectual Catholic revival on the Continent, sometimes in combination with a rather dreamy right-wing nationalism of the kind advocated by Charles Péguy, the French poet who identified Catholicism with the deep-seated roots in the French past, and defined the Middle Ages as the period which had produced the best of French culture on account of its religious nature. France was not alone in pursuing this association: so did Hilaire Belloc in English, and the Catholic Chesterton, best known for his Father Brown stories,[10] who also depicted the Middle Ages as an ideal period on account of its religious feeling and the overwhelming influence of the church. Possibly the most famous poet of the Catholic revival, who used Middle English vocabulary and versification style, was Gerard Manley Hopkins, a convert who became a Jesuit in 1868.[11] Apart from medieval stylistic inspiration, Hopkins was also deeply attuned to the philosophy and theology of the Middle Ages, especially St Augustine and the fourteenth-century theologian Duns Scot.[12]

One of the figures most frequently identified with the Catholic revival in

France was Joan of Arc. As a nationalist heroine since the nineteenth century, especially after Michelet, and as the symbol of France during its fight to regain Alsace after the Franco-German War of 1870,[13] she performed a similar function during the First World War and was used in film propaganda. A large number of indifferent French writers and poets wrote works featuring Joan, especially between the two wars, when she was hijacked by the French Catholic nationalist Right – a place she has not lost today, when she is still regarded as the 'patron-saint' of the Action Française movement and Jean-Marie Le Pen's National Front party. George Bernard Shaw in his play *St Joan* and Jean Anouilh in his, *L'alouette* (1953), highlighted Joan more as a heroine of the people and what we might term a 'freedom fighter' than as a Christian martyr. Already in the nineteenth century she had migrated to America as an image of the popular heroine fighting for freedom, an example of the 'common man', of fight against oppression and a kind of first 'republican'.[14] This was Mark Twain's picture of Joan. She retained this high status in American literature and especially, from very early on in the century, in American film.

An almost exact parallel trajectory was that of Robin Hood, another nationalist, populist 'freedom-fighter' both in England and later in America.[15] His figure too came to be much diluted and simplified within American culture – gone were, for example, the traditional English view of Maid Marian as his lover, also an outlaw living in the forest with him and his men as an equal – to the extent that the story could be transformed into children's books and films. The only remaining characteristic of the legend was the image of the rich man wronged by authority, who ran away and went 'native'. Sympathising with the ills of the poor, Robin turned his anger to the righteous purpose of 'robbing the rich to give to the poor', and defended the country while its rightful and allegedly 'good' leader was away, and those in power abused it for their own profit. Both of these themes have, within American culture in particular, both a biblical resonance of rich and poor, rightful and usurping power, and also chime in with the western themes of the lone enforcer of justice of the Wild West.

Back in Europe, and rather more weightily, in the later twentieth century German writers in turn went back to the Middle Ages, this time in a totally reinterpretative mode. The songwriter Walter Biermann's texts about political oppression and exile have been associated with the tradition of the *Minnesänger*. Other poets' preoccupation with the parallels between the Black Death and AIDS, and spiritual healing, already encountered in the context of natural and holistic medicine, were also associated by them with medievalist themes.[16] Another example of a rewrite was the proto-feminism which some have attempted to identify in the work of medieval nuns such as Hildegard of Bingen, Mechtild of Magdeburg and Hadewijk of Brabant.[17]

Three works of fiction in the English-speaking world have become the embodiment of medievalism across the twentieth century: C. S. Lewis' Narnia books, J. R. R. Tolkien's trilogy *The Lord of the Rings* (and sundry associated prose), and Mervyn Peake's trilogy *Gormenghast.* The trilogy mode itself is significant, and numerous modern fantasy and science fiction works have been written in three volumes, presumably on the grounds of the mystical significance of the number three (a very ancient Indo-European and Old Testament concept, significantly though quite unnecessarily now associated in popular culture with the 'Celtic' world). The first two works are predicated on the author's creation of a mythical world,[18] inhabited by a mixture of humans and creatures of indeterminate species, part-animals, part-human, with fantastical characteristics of speech, dress and behaviour, as well as traditional fairies, witches, wizards and elves. These evolve in a complex imaginary world, sometimes in fairyland in Narnia, sometimes in the intricate geography of peoples and places constructed as Middle Earth, Lothlorien, Gondor, Rivendell or Mordor in Tolkien. Narnia is a relatively simple world, in which the medieval is integrated mainly in terms of its fabled monsters and values, and despite the sad and heavy price to be paid by the heroes in the Last Battle, ultimately leads to the some kind of triumph of good over evil in a fundamentally Christian context.[19] Tolkien was deeply Catholic, but interpreters of his work are at odds about whether his world and his philosophy were Christian.[20] Only one sees in it a profound Christian message, based on the parallels between Christ and the Elf King, the change of Gandalf from grey (the old man) to white (the new man), and the progression of the debate about kingship in *Lord of the Rings* from Germanic to Christian in the last two volumes.[21] It took on board what might be regarded as some sort of primeval myths and archetypes of mankind, which the author attempted to retell and rework as his predecessors over the centuries had done. Foremost among these predecessors were the early medieval poets: 'Tolkien ... was pre-eminently aware of *his* source-texts, like *Beowulf,* or Snorri's *Edda,* or Layamon's *Brut,* as the work of individuals like himself, who used old stories for contemporary purposes just as he did'.[22] His medievalism rewrites rather than just repeating traditional themes such as the quest, with its long and dangerous journey, the struggle of the hero with the help of supernatural forces, the victory of the hero, the triumph not just of good over evil, but of the spiritual over the material (the ring representing the forces of power and destruction). Allegory, myth and eschatology were brought to contemporary audiences by someone who was a medieval scholar by training. From early on in life Tolkien had been deeply interested in philology and linguistics, had learnt Old English and Old Norse (he came to love the latter through reading Morris's translation of the sagas), and he maintained these interests throughout his life. In his first work, *The Silmarillion*, he invented a specific language. He spent as much time as on this as on the writing of the stories, and it was largely behind the creation of a whole new mythology; he then went further by proposing various forms of these languages, notably several elvish languages, not just one.[23] Using both his own taste and his professional knowledge, he presented those eternal themes in the widely popular guise of Old Norse and Anglo-Saxon traditions, thus contributing in no small measure to perpetuating the popularity of these traditions. It is partly because he did so that current writers can produce books with titles like *The Real Middle Earth*, in a not unusual inversion of interest and knowledge going *from* contemporary fiction *to* history; the above mentioned book by Brian Bates is introduced in one place with the following lines:

> The imaginary world created by J. R. R. Tolkien in *The Lord of the Rings* was largely based on the English civilisation of the Dark Ages. Drawing on the latest historical and archaeological research, this accessible account examines the importance of folklore and belief in witchcraft in this mysterious society. For the Anglo-Saxons and Vikings, the English landscape was a home to dragons, elves, dwarves and demons – a place where spells had real force ... forgotten mythical legacy of sacred rivers, plant magic and fantastical creatures, bringing back to life an enigmatic civilisation ... compelling investigation of a culture as enchanting as Tolkien's fictional version.[24]

Here we see Tolkien as the twentieth-century equivalent of Walter Scott: the new gateway into the Middle Ages through popular fiction (and now film).

Tolkien had an additional purpose, which became even more important in his eyes during the 1930s and 1940s, when he saw the whole Germanic world which he knew so well through his scholarship being hijacked for the nefarious aim of creating a German 'aryan' superiority. His aim was not only to correct this by emphasising the common Germanic and 'Celtic' literary and cultural past, but also very emphatically to create a 'mythology for England'; in his own words to 'make a body of more or less connected legend, ranging from the large and cosmogonic to the level of romantic fairy-story – which I would dedicate simply: to England; to my country'.[25] Patriotism, in the form of his love for England, was often mentioned by Tolkien. The Hobbits and Middle Earth represented, through their inns and gardens, what he 'loved best about England', and he described

Sam Gangee as a 'reflection of the English soldier, of the privates and batmen I knew in the 1914 war'.[26]

The *Gormenghast* trilogy works in a different way. Although its adaptator for a BBC series a few years ago wanted to give the scenery a vaguely oriental, Chinese, feel, on the grounds of Peake's having spent his childhood in China, and apparently 'deliberately ... ensured there were no pointed Gothic arches anywhere in sight',[27] I personally have not come across anybody for whom the whole world, castle and characters of Gormenghast can be anything but 'Gothic' and 'medieval'. Most would agree that the dreamlike, allegorical world of the first two volumes of the trilogy must exist either in some past time, or in a dimension parallel with ours. There is no geographical location or indeed, crucially for a world which has made the observance of the ritual of the past its very *raison d'être*, no history. Time is confused, with a 'Gothic medieval edifice: cobwebs, shadows, sinister goings-on in a feudal system', lit by torches in which a lord with the significant name of Sepulgrave is given injections against microbes and the murderer Steerpike is paid a salary.[28] The writing encourages the confusion between the animate and inanimate, ghosts are sometimes alive while the humans are dead, and while some characters like the hero Titus change over the years, others remain perennially the same, doing exactly the same things. It is a dead world, one in which darkness, loneliness, disharmony, isolation and desolation dominate. It is indeed another world, a parallel one but certainly not a happy one: life has stopped, and only decay and death bring changes, unless one leaves it, as Titus does by the end of the second volume.[29] As so often with the themes which can be slotted into the 'medievalist' pattern, there have been attempts to interpret this world in terms 'relevant' to our times.[30] Some have seen it as a kind of Kafkaesque allegory of any ageing modern human institution in which tradition and the respect of formal observance have become more important than people. Others, notably the BBC adaptators, decided that, since Peake wrote in the 1940s, having seen a charismatic nobody who was also a loner made his way to the top by burning books, murdering people, imposing his will and ultimately destroying a whole way of life, and saw his portrait of Steerpike as an illustration of Hitler; at the same time it was also possible to define Steerpike as the man who embodies the virtues of liberalism and egality, against the dead aristocracy of the castle.

Indeed, whatever one's views of the characters may be, it is only too obvious that the real 'hero' of Gormenghast is not a person but the castle itself. Like in the Gothic novel, or indeed in Kafka for that matter, the Gothic ethos of the castle dominates the world, landscape and lives of Gormenghast. It, too, in its way, has a gravitational pull that none can resist, for good or evil, not in an active or even menacing way, but just by *being there, forever*. The Gothic fantasy of the castle is particularly exaggerated in Autumn and Winter, when

> crumbling . . ., looming among the mists, [it] exaled the season, and every cold stone breathed it out. The tortured trees by the dark lake burned and dripped, and their leaves snatched by the winds were whirled in wild circles trough the towers. The clouds mouldered as they lay coiled . . .[31]

Such surroundings contribute to the 'self-contained otherness' of the Gormenghast world and enthrals the reader. Ultimately, the castle is also the determining factor in the characters' relationship with the issues of freedom, identity and individuality, initiation, change and growth, separation from the community, a desire to return to nature beyond the artificial, and the rebellion of youth. Real, grotesque, repellent or pathetic, the characters are the castle's prisoners, as they are of the empty rituals which govern its life, with the exception of Titus, the Romantic rebel, and the Faustian Steerpike, who both escape it. But the illustration of their world is one which expresses a kind of Middle Ages gone mad – was this Peake's deliberate view, or the product of his imagination, fed on the culture of the Gothic tradition, and using it, as so many before him, to 'place' his allegory in an existing framework of fantasy?

The new literary genre of fantasy fiction is entirely different from historical fiction like Walter Scott's or contemporary novels set in a deliberately 'Celtic', but nonetheless genuinely medieval context, such as Stephen Lawhead's trilogy *The Celtic Crusades*. The origins of the genre may be taken back to William Morris's prose, for example the stories he wrote and had published by the Kelmscott Press, such as *The Story of the Glittering Plain* and *The Well at the World's End*. Other twentieth-century examples through which the genre acquired its credentials include Mervyn Peake's *Gormenghast* trilogy and Tolkien's *Lord of the Rings*, neither of which, however, fully belongs to fantasy fiction. The genre is also different from the Fantastic, whether Victorian or modern with magic realism. The Fantastic functions on the basis of the supernatural gradually or suddenly breaking into the everyday, and remaining unexplained, whereas fantasy fiction is predicated on the creation of a completely different, parallel, supernatural or magical world, as so many current writers create for escapist purposes. At its best, the genre produced Tolkien or Philip Pullman; at its worst, a plethora of run-of-the-mill fantasies meant for rapid consumption.

Fantasy fiction invents myths, legends and characters situated in a world before time, doing heroic deeds and achieving impossible tasks with the help of magical creatures (beasts, demons, magicians and others). These illustrate the importance of man's understanding of, and working with, the natural world and its members, which ultimately brings about wholeness and happiness. Many of these fantasies include, or at the very least allude to, Arthurian myths and the Grail legend. A significant twentieth-century change has been the transfer, within this genre, from an interest in chivalry to an obsession with the 'spiritual' side of the story, the Christian Grail legend or the ever-popular 'Celtic' myth. In Stephen Lawhead's Arthurian trilogy *Pendragon*, Marion Zimmer Bradley's *The Mists of Avalon* and, more recently, Bernard Cornwell's *The Grail Quest* the emphasis is on either 'Celtic Christianity' or on Merlin's world of nature and magic. Fantasy fiction more generally comprises hundreds of novels from the pen of contemporary writers such as Anne Rice, Ursula Le Guin, Stephen Lawhead, Robert Jordan, David Eddings, Robert Holdstock, Mark Chadbourne and numerous others, with titles such as *The Wheel of Time* (made up of books like *The Dragon Reborn, Lord of Chaos, A Crown of Swords*), *The Death Gate Cycle, The Belgariad, The Malloreon, Everien, The Age of Misrule* (which claims to refer to 'an ancient Celtic myth'), the *Prydain* series, the *Song of Albion* and others, with their heroes, places or gods' names with a Celtic resonance, from Sauron and Galadriel to Nynaeve, Aviendha, Amyrlin, Caemlyn, Ilian, Torak and Belgarath.

The point of these is for the authors deliberately to suggest an association in the readers' minds with what is widely perceived to be a world before time, a world of supernatural creatures, powers and heroes, a world of wonders and exotic, fabulous myths and legends, in which there is a distinction between good and evil, and where good triumphs, love and heroic deeds are rewarded, and all is well with the world. Like Arthurian fantasy, this category appeals, not as one might have assumed in the first place to teenagers, but often to an adult audience. It finds in them an escape from daily drudgery and a too-rational surrounding world, and a way of thinking about major life issues not always addressed by mainstream fiction, as well as colourful characters in exciting life-threatening situations. Fantasy fiction functions in the same way as the original fairy tales did, before men like Charles Perrault and the Grimm brothers drew out their teeth to make them into children's literature. Both teenagers and adults read this literature for 'escapist' purposes. But, in addition, adults often marvel at the perceived 'historical accuracy' of the reconstruction and at the 'modernity' of the characters – the latter being very much the author's own imaginative contribution to the anachronism. Moreover, the genre has the ability to be non-gender specific, appealing to both men and women, unlike other popular literature like westerns or bodice-rippers and romances. The combination of entertainment, bonding with major themes of perpetual human interest, and the apparent historical veracity of the best of these novels explain their success for an adult audience reassured that it is reading something instructive as well as imaginative and fun, rather than just 'trash' – perhaps a deeply-buried puritanical instinct seeking some excuse rather than accepting the notion of purely hedonistic pleasure. This interpretation may be supported by the fact that fantasy fiction originated, and is still overwhelmingly read, in the English-speaking world, where the ethics of puritanism or of conformity, and a strong work culture, predominate. Such an attitude could also explain, in part at least, the success of crime fiction.

Does the trend of fantasy fiction and murder mysteries also appeal in continental Europe? While it does so in Germany, in France and Italy, for example, less is made of historical murder mysteries, even though the tradition of historical novels is alive and well, and writers such as Zoë Oldenbourg, Régine Pernoud, Maurice Druon and Jeanne Bourin in France, and Umberto Eco and Valerio Manfredi in Italy remain popular. There is, on the other hand, in these countries a great demand for, and provision of, good 'academic' history, written by the great names in the world of medieval research like Georges Duby, Jacques le Goff, Carlo Ginzburg, books deliberately not 'talking down' to the audience but written in a sufficiently approachable way to make the subject a popular one. This may be due to the frame of mind which, in France and Italy and in those countries of central and eastern Europe which took their educational structures from them, allows and encourages people of various backgrounds to see themselves as 'intellectuals', on the basis of what was for a long time a solid general culture acquired at school and continued through reading, philosophical and political debate in the public arena. One could account for the way in which people in public life there have often been able to express some sentiment or other with reference to a commonly understood medieval past. Among the best-known examples are expressions which have become part of popular parlance. When Bismarck's famously claimed that 'We will not go to Canossa', Germans knew it was shorthand for 'We will not humiliate ourselves asking for mercy', referring to the Emperor Henry IV's political penance and public humiliation by the pope. The French routinely describe their wealthy capitalists as 'barons d'industrie', unlike our more neutral 'captains of industry.' Jack Straw's remark about England as the country founded in 1066, previously mentioned, shows an attempt to follow suit, despite its unfortunate connotations for an Anglo-Saxon historian, but such medieval references are still rare – only too often the most common understanding of the expression 'it's positively medieval' in English continues to be a derogatory one. An example of the muddled thinking relating to the concept of medieval is provided by another newspaper article, which deals with the alleged iniquities of one Richard Marker, whose family has owned the estate of Combe, in Devon, since 1846. Mr Marker, so far regarded as the local squire, was said by the author of the article to have served eviction notices on twenty-eight tenant families from the village of Gittisham in order to sell the houses on the open market. According to one village inhabitant, 'it is extraordinary behaviour in the twenty-first century. This is more like the eighteenth and nineteenth century [sic]. Even in feudal times there was some chivalry'; another inhabitant, however, describing how devastated the villagers were about the perceived end of their community, says that 'we thought the feudal age had ended.'[32] So, is the feudal age one of chivalry, that is to say one in which landlords act responsibly towards their people, or one of tyranny, in which they oppress them by selling their houses from under them? Clearly, opinions are divided.

The Christian context of the medieval period, and its artistic manifestations, were revived in other art forms. A festival was created around the cycles of Mystery Plays every year at York. Medieval music took off in the 1970s, from the popularity of Gregorian chant both live and in recordings, to the birth of a large number of choirs, orchestras and 'consorts', whose aim was to recreate anything from the court music of Spanish kings to the full cycle of the monastic day ritual and even, more recently, to Byzantine music.[33] To all intents and purposes, medieval and Renaissance music are in fact subsumed into one, under the label of 'early music', which enables its scope to widen to madrigals, Counter Reformation masses, and even operas up to and including Monteverdi and Purcell. The musical world took the medieval revival very seriously, and studies have been made and published over the years about the reading, interpretation and performing of medieval music, while increasingly medieval or sixteenth-century masses by composers such as Guillaume de Machaut, Guillaume Dufay, William Ockheghem and Orlando di Lasso are used as permanent features of the more high church cathedral choirs such as Christ Church in Oxford or Wells Cathedral. Such liturgical music was a source of inspiration for earlier twentieth-century composers, such as Olivier Messiaen, Francis Poulenc or Leoš Janáček in his *Glagolitic Mass*. A later twentieth-century opera composer who went back to find inspiration in the medieval corpus, notably in the story of Gawain, was Harrison Birtwistle. His opera *Gawain* used the Arthurian myth, while another work, *The Last Supper*, included musical references to polyphony and plainchant. The medieval musical tradition was, however, not restricted to a 'high-brow' audience. In the 1970s and 1980s the group Steeleye Span, one of the first to adapt medieval songs to the world of country and pop music, had great success. More recently, other groups, for example the Medieval Baebes, and the pop group Enigma, who produced a hit recording mixing modern rythms with a basic plainchant background, have continued this tradition of successful adaptation.

Painting and architecture too retained a medieval flavour, to various degrees. Late Victorians who painted well into the 1920s, 1930s and even 1940s were still 'medievalising'. In the 1970s architects who must obviously have greatly enjoyed playing with their Lego cubes as children or building sandcastles, were producing pastiches of medieval castles with ramparts and portcullis, which gave us for example the Robinson College building in Cambridge. In a less obvious but perhaps more interesting way, the pervasive presence of the Middle Ages enabled painters such as Pierre Matisse, Marc Chagall and John Piper to use medieval media and techniques, like stained glass. They continued the tradition of biblical interpretation, use of light, and adaptation of themes found in medieval churches to great effect, for example at St Rémy in Rheims (Chagall), St Paul de Vence (Matisse) and Iffley parish church (Piper). These artists pursued the tradition of interpretation and reinvention of the Middle Ages which had been the defining aim of the best among nineteenth-century exponents of medievalism. A similar kind of reinterpretation has been used by architects, especially for the building of churches and chapels, for which a medieval flavour seemed to be particularly suitable. The architects' choice in this respect was by no means exclusively Gothic, but turned to the style increasingly popular with the more minimalist feel of the later twentieth century, the Romanesque. Vaulting and stained glass may have been retained and reworked, as we see in so many contemporary chapels (Vence, St Benet's Hall in Oxford, Frank Lloyd Wright's churches in America), but the simplicity of lines, the plainness, lack of superfluous adornment, and the in-the-round feel of many such places refers deliberately to the pre-Gothic period, which is now perceived as being more uncluttered and therefore spiritually more elevating.

In the 1970s and 1980s a new kind of fiction grafted itself on to the genre of the historical novel. This was the philosophical novel set in a historical context, of which Hermann Broch's *Virgil* and Christoph Ransmayr's *The Last World* were two successful representatives. Both these novels were set in the Roman world, focusing on aspects of the lives of Virgil and Ovid respectively, and both were meant to be a reflection of the two poets on their world and, indirectly, on our own. While the audience for these books was limited and essentially 'high-brow', another such novel burst upon the world in the early 1980s, this time revolutionising the genre and opening it up to a huge readership: this was Umberto Eco's *Name of the Rose*, first translated into English in 1983. Eco's innovation was the introduction of a murder mystery, complete with detective and assistant in time-honoured fashion, in the form of an elderly fifteenth-century friar and a young monk, and including dastardly plots and even a love interest, all apparently within a 'straight', intellectual novel, which did not 'talk down' to its readers but on the contrary took for granted their ability to transpose themselves into intelligent arbitrators of difficult life issues. Moreover this was done in a complex language which was made to resemble as closely as possible the way of thinking and talking of people brought up in the context of a medieval monastery, up to and including their easy shift between Latin and the vernacular, and between theology and other daily activities. The impression of mild strangeness which this gave to the novel, making it seem slightly unusual and exotic, but not so much that one would not recognise enough of the still vaguely familiar memories of one's schooldays Middle Ages, only added to the quality of the narrative and the writing, ensuring a huge worldwide success for its author, and making a new genre respectable for anyone ready to follow in his footsteps.

It might be argued that one of the reasons why it was so easy for Eco to bridge the gap between 'serious' fiction and the detective genre was because by that stage the latter had already gone a long way into becoming respectable. The genre had become a medium for social comment and debate, through the American *noir*, the novels of Boileau-Narcejac in France, the Italian political *giallo* with Leonardo Sciascia or Fruttero and Lucentini, and increasingly in Britain, with authors like P. D. James, Ruth Rendell, Reginald Hill and numerous others. The rise to respectable, 'middle-brow' literature of the detective story, and its popularity in the last decades of the twentieth century, may be explained in part at least by the fact that the 'naturalistic' novel has been demoted from mainstream fiction, with a few exceptions of popular writers like Joanna Trollope, or of thrillers, psychological shockers, fantasy fiction or bodice-rippers (the latter four still regarded by many as 'popular' genres rather than 'literature'). Post-Joycean style, and French *nouveau roman* writing, placed little value on narrative, on a story-line. The latter, many would argue, has taken refuge in detective fiction, where contemporary social studies can be centred around a story.

It is entirely possible to use a contemporary setting for a murder mystery, and many writers do so. Quite a few nevertheless choose historical settings, for the purpose of adding local colour and an element of escapism. While the so-called 'middle-brow' literary category does not really exist in continental European literature (detective fiction there can often be used for political purposes, as in Italy with Sciascia, or even in Latin America with Mario Vargas Llosa), it now encompasses the historical 'whodunnit' in the English-speaking world with great success, as a form of thoughtful entertainment. A wide range of historical periods has already been used, from Ancient Greece and Egypt, to classical Rome, Elizabethan England, Renaissance Italy, Georgian, Victorian and Edwardian England, nineteenth-century Egypt, Belle Epoque France and many others; the list is growing daily. The fact remains, however, that no period has been used by quite so many, and with such variable success, as the Middle Ages. Why?

One obvious explanation is that the first really successful novels of this kind, written by the doyenne of the genre, Ellis Peters, were set in the twelfth century.[34] Her 'Brother Cadfael' stories were successful not only as books: they spawned a whole line of TV films, a medieval theme park, the Shrewsbury Quest, and a whole range of related artefacts. But what of the other 'medieval whodunnits'? Apart from the Cadfael books, set in Shrewsbury in the 1130s and 1140s, during the civil war between King Stephen and the Empress Matilda, the number of series written between 1990 and this year has now gone into double figures. They are set, chronologically, in seventh-century Ireland (Peter Tremayne), in the years after the Norman Conquest (A. E. Marston), again during the civil war between Stephen and Matilda in the mid twelfth century (Robert Gellis), in twelfth-century Kent (Alys Clare), in the late twelfth and early thirteenth centuries during the reign of Edward I (P. C. Doherty, Bernard Knight, Michael Jecks), during the Crusades (James Patterson and Andrew Gross), in the 1340 and 1350s in Cambridge (Suzanna Gregory), the 1360s in York (Candace Robb) and the late 1370s in London (Paul Harding), and several series in the fifteenth century in Oxford (Margaret Frazer), London (M. M. Pulver), on the Canterbury pilgrimage with Chaucer (Doherty again), in the West Country (Kate Sedley) and in southern England (C. L. Grace, yet another pseudonym of Doherty). Recently new series have stretched even further geographically, and English-speaking writers have expanded their field to encompass other European locations: mid twelfth-century France and Normandy (admittedly then belonging to the English crown) in Viviane Moore's novels, late thirteenth-century Spain with a returning Crusader at the time of the Spanish Reconquest and the beginnings of the Inquisition in Michael Eisner's books, as well as Catalonia (Caroline Roe) and, even more exotically, sixth-century Byzantium (Mary Reed and Eric Mayer), and Jerusalem and Byzantium during the Crusades in Alan Gordon's novels. Some stalwart already established writers like Doherty have branched out even further away, to thirteenth-century China for example. What do these books have in common?

A first comment is prompted by the very choice of period setting, and the exponential increase in the number of books set in the last two centuries of the Middle Ages, on account of the greater number of sources available then, compared with the Early and High Middle Ages. From this self-explanatory fact stems a second comment related to the chronological time frame chosen by most authors. With few exceptions most novels are set in periods associated with 'major events', the kinds of memories that one might be expected to recall from one's school days: war, political crises, or other forms of civil or religious turmoil. This comment, of course, assumes that schools in Britain still teach medieval history these days, an increasingly rare occurrence and one which may not be entirely devoid of significance in terms of the rising tide of popularity of a period increasingly known not through study but through the intermediary of the 'leisure industry' of books, film, Heritage centres and re-enactment fantasies. This applies to seventh-century Ireland and northern England, for example with the 664 Synod of Whitby (Tremayne), Domesday (Marston), the civil war between Stephen and Matilda (Peters, Gellis), Simon de Montfort's rebellion (Doherty), the Crusades (Gordon, Patterson and Gross), the Hundred Years War (Robb), the Black Death (Gregory), the Canterbury pilgrimage, and several of the allegedly well-known medieval European historical myths. It also attaches itself to particularly exotic events and locations, such as the Crusades, the Inquisition, and Venice, Byzantium and Jerusalem. The settings are not accidental, since these are the events that most readers are likely to recall, however remotely and vaguely. In the same way, most novels are situated in suggestive places: London (the court at Westminster, the City, the Tower), Oxford (the university, the civil war), York (the archbishop and the Minster), Cambridge (the university again, but also the wool trade), even Shrewsbury (so close to one of the cities central to the fortunes of the war, Chester), Normandy, Moorish Spain, Venice and Jerusalem, or in imaginary locations connected with suggestive contexts, such as the Canterbury road. They are also centred around well-remembered names, especially Chaucer's. Some exceptions occur, especially in the more recent books, for example Sedley's West Country, Jecks's Devon and sometimes Knight's work. It is entirely insufficient to claim that the reason for both time and place chosen is dependent only on the existence of the sources, or even on the importance of the events mentioned. This is fiction; hence it is the personal element and the story, with its characters, which matters. The books could theoretically be situated in any period or place, and the information is available to the same extent; more recent novels are again a case in point of it being possible to do just that. We are therefore back to the issue of appealing to the reader by drawing them into the plot through an expected surface familiarity with the events and places, particularly if these places have both historical and aesthetic connotations on a large scale today, as all those above-mentioned do. This is the first way in which the reader is hooked, by being made to recognise elements vaguely familiar but still sufficiently alien to be seen as colourful and slightly mysterious.

The second unifying element of these novels is the detective character chosen by the author. Fidelma, Frevisse and Helewisse are nuns, abbesses or prioresses, Cadfael, Æthelstan and Theophilos are monks, Father Hugh is a priest, Gervase Brett and Hugh Corbett are royal clerks, and Crowner John, Bailiff Simon Puttock, and John the Eunuch are in royal or imperial service. Roger Chapman is a relapsed monk. Owen Archer, though an ex-captain of archers, is in the service of the archbishop of York. Francisco Montcada, a Crusader, is involved with an inquisitor who is a Cistercian monk, and Sir Richard Straccan, also an ex-Crusader, is a 'bone pedlar', selling relics to the monks. The overwhelming preponderance of the clergy in all its forms is patently due to the fact that so many of our medieval sources come from the church, that is was for so long essentially the clergy who were literate, and thus, one is led to think, that they were the people we know most about. In addition, one might expect members of the clergy, because they had the best education, also to have had the best chance of putting together clues in a logical fashion and of thinking their way to the solution of a murder. Nevertheless, another element contributes to the choice of the clergy: the wish to add specific colour to a period which has always been regarded as one of dominance of the church, and to include a key factor which contributes to the impression of 'otherness' in relation to our own time, while still dealing with what is remembered and not totally unfamiliar ground. Even when the detective characters become slightly more diverse, as they have done in some recent novels, they retain this 'otherness' which makes them special. This is made up of their social position (rich merchant, bailiff, sheriff and other officials, including a Constantinople palace eunuch, representing royal power) or their cultural affiliations (the physicians Matthew Bartholomew and Kathryn Swinbrooke, the blind Jewish doctor Isaac of Gerona, or, for that matter, Chaucer himself). These positions give them access to knowledge, writing and law, and hence reasoning and deduction powers commensurate with their role as detectives. To that extent they are still associated, through work or personal friendships, with the clerical group.

Other elements contribute to the overall dominant 'known-yet-exotic' factor in medieval detective stories. One such element is the English-foreign issue, inherited from the still popular myth of the Norman Yoke, which translates into hostility between the 'native' Saxons and the Norman 'conquerors'. Although the concept has a long history, it is also one with renewed appeal in the late twentieth century, as it corresponds to the pre-occupations of a multiethnic and multicultural society. We find this obsession with ethnic differences, mostly between Celtic and Saxon (Tremayne, like many readers over the centuries, misinterpreting Bede) and Saxon and Norman (Marston and Peters). At least Peters, while keeping to the traditions inherited from a fundamentally nineteenth-century education, nevertheless posits a rather subtler ethnic distinction, involving less the opposition between Saxons and Normans than the nature of a border society, between England and Wales.

Another revealing factor is the importance given by writers to female characters (Tremayne, Robb, Frazer, Gellis and Grace). These exceedingly emancipated women are portrayed as being almost the norm in medieval society, doing the same jobs, for example, lawyers or doctors, and being their equal socially and intellectually, sometimes indeed ruling over them. Even in the Anglo-Saxon society, where women, by and large, played a more prominent social, economic, cultural and even political role than they did at any later time until the twentieth century, they were rarely quite as independent as they are portrayed by several of these writers. This may be partly due to their own deliberate wish to perceive medieval society as more egalitarian than later periods, and hence a clear precursor of our own. At the very least, presenting it in such a way is a good ploy to ensure popular success for the book, in keeping with contemporary feeling.

Similarly, the choice of the Middle Ages for reasons associated with what might loosely term eco-friendly attitudes (in this sense inheriting the Romantic view of the 'return to nature') is part of the attraction for both readers and writers. Here, as with the 'Celtic spirit', what appeals is the perceived common ground between the medieval and the contemporary, with the latter endorsing natural medicine, organic food, animal welfare, and the nostalgia for values perceived as good but now gone forever, such as social solidarity or a sense of the sacred to be found in nature.

So, what of the much sought after 'historical accuracy'? Some authors insist on mentioning sources, in using titles and words linked to the period, even going as far as to mix English and whatever language seems required by the period; most try to ensure that the names they choose are appropriate, though few except Ellis Peters really succeed every time. The overall idea is to use major events as a background on which to depict daily life from medieval sources, while filling in the gaps with characters, events and features from the authors' imagination. Some writers make mistakes even on factual matters, and many are certainly taken in by clichés, or deliberately cultivate those because they make a better story. The 'Celtic church' and the

English, the Saxon and Norman divide, the Crusaders, and the Inquisition, are all standard themes. The very concept of accuracy, we have seen time and time again, is a chimera. Accuracy cannot exist even when most of the factual information is as appropriate as it is possible to make it. This is because generally the writers' perception of the period is overruled, indeed has to be left out, in order to make the book palatable and interesting to readers. It almost inevitably means projecting twentieth-century attitudes and moral issues onto medieval characters. The treatment of women is an obvious example. Another is the issue of punishment for a crime, essential in detective fiction. To take one example: unsurprisingly since we live in a completely secular society, punishment has to be through either the judicial process or, possibly, through accident or suicide. Contemporary readers would hardly consider penance or pilgrimage a sufficient form of punishment for a crime like murder, whereas this could have been the case in a fundamentally Christian society, where the implications of crime, repentance and penance were not simply on the level of personal conscience, but also of social unity. Once again Peters comes closest to twelfth-century views in *Monk's Hood*. Adaptations of this kind are entirely understandable, indeed necessary for the modern writer and reader, and the whole issue of 'historical accuracy' is a red herring. It is of no importance to the reader, who is the consumer of detective stories; the only claimants to it are some well-intentioned but often misguided authors, who see it as a matter of honour.

What really matters is the way in which the period is depicted and perceived. That perception is of a world of cruelty, injustice, violence, intolerance, poverty and filth, while at the same time people are made to hold values seen now as lost: neighbourly help, permanent love, closeness to the natural world. The outcome means that the reader can feel at the same time superior ('they knew no better'), nostalgic, and interested in a form of entertainment which is strange but not totally unfamiliar, from the vaguely recollected events which have become part of the national collective memory, and the places still to be seen. This is what ensures the success of the medieval detective story, as it also does, in part at least, that of another new twentieth-century art form, film.

8

Camelot Goes Celluloid

The study of history and cinema is a rapidly expanding topic, still greatly indebted to the pioneering work of Pierre Sorlin.[1] The possibilities of cinema for the purposes of political propaganda have been recognised by political leaders very early in the history of the medium. A film like *Alexander Nevski*, engineered to be part of the Soviet propaganda of the 1920s and 1930s, is an example of such use of the Middle Ages. The message of such 'political' films is quite transparent, and their directors deliberately used and manipulated medieval themes for openly nationalistic and political reasons.[2] Another category of films which is not relevant to this discussion is that of Shakespeare adaptations. They cannot be said to display modern views of the Middle Ages, since they contain two layers of interpretation, first Shakespeare's, then the director's take on Shakespeare. They, too, like Shakespeare's plays, are thus less a modern understanding of the medieval period, but reflect, in the first instance, Shakespeare's views.[3]

There were, according to K. J. Harty, the latest and most complete compiler of films about the Middle Ages, nearly six hundred such films between the first, George Méliès's *Jeanne d'Arc* in 1897, and 1996.[4] These films are broadly divisible into the two categories, referred to from now on as 'Hollywood' films and European 'auteur cinema'.[5] Before discussing which films belong to which genre, a by no means inflexible division, it must noted that the categories overlap strongly at least in the case of the large number of films made by the Americans as co-productions with Italian studios in the 1950s and 1960s, at the time when the 'sword-and-sandals' line had become somewhat exhausted, but the taste for historical films had not. Hence the production, often with Hollywood directors like Richard Siodmak, and with some American actors, of about fourteen films between 1954 and 1969, on topics related to the more glamorous aspects of early medieval Italian history: Goths, Lombards, Justinian and Theodora, and other subjects with potential for heroic deeds against various 'barbarians' in the form of Huns, Mongols and Vikings.[6] These Italian-American films are not particularly interesting as such, and belong to the general swashbuckling adventure and love story format. While many deal with the standard medieval themes popular throughout western culture (Arthur, chivalry, Robin Hood, Ivanhoe), many refer to specific topics familiar to the Italian schoolchild, such as Marco Polo, Dante or the Medici , as well as to the end of the Roman world and the fight against various barbarian peoples. This may have been due in part to national sentiment, and in part to the possibility of offering the viewer clear-cut heroes and enemies, an ideological message which permeated the American film industry itself during the years of the Cold War. The message was one of defending the values and freedom of the civilised, usually Christian, nations against the non-believing, dangerously militaristic barbarians of the twentieth century (mostly coming, as usual, from the East).[7] Hollywood money strongly influenced Italian studios, and numerous Italian pot-boilers were sub-products of the American film industry. Italian cinema meanwhile and at the same time was also producing a very different kind of films, also set in the Middle Ages, directed by Liliana Cavani, Roberto Rossellini, Franco Zeffirelli, Mario Monicelli and Pier Paolo Pasolini.

It was precisely in the 1950s and 1960s that most of the classic all-American films about the Middle Ages were also made. Some themes, or rather, enemies, were those which had been made known via the Italian sub-products: *Genghis Khan* or the *Vikings*. But most Hollywood films concentrated on the more specifically 'Anglo-Saxon' area: *The Adventures of Sir Galahad* (1950), *Ivanhoe* (1952), *The Knights of the Round Table* (1953), *King Richard and the Crusaders, Prince Valiant, Quentin Durward* (all in 1955) and after a short break *Lancelot and Guinevere* in 1962, *The Warlord* in 1965 and the musical *Camelot* in 1967. The Viking theme was not altogether abandoned, with *The Long Ships* in 1964. These were all traditional swashbuckling narratives in 'medieval picturesque' mode. Three of them, *Ivanhoe, The Knights of the Round Table* and *Quentin Durward* were made by the same director, Richard Thorpe, and in all of them one of Hollywood's leading men, Robert Taylor, was the main star. Thorpe, like Anthony Mann (*El Cid*) and other directors at the time and in that category, normally specialised in adventure films (set in any period) and westerns. American studios ceased to be interested in the Middle Ages for more than a decade. In the early 1980s Hollywood again took up the medieval theme, through the co-production with a British director, John Boorman, of *Excalibur*. For most of the 1980s and early 1990s, partly as a result of the success of *Excalibur*, Hollywood's interest shifted to films belonging to the 'fantasy' category, which was becoming popular in the book world too. *Dragonslayer, The Sword and the Sorcerer* and various *Conan the Barbarian*-style concoctions, which 'raped the mythology of the Dark Ages'[8] with their form of syncretism of Dark Ages culture, incorporating Viking, Mongol, Germanic, even archaic Greek themes, were made chiefly for entertainment and thrills, complete with old-sounding names, fights and pounding music. Not before the mid 1990s did Hollywood return to more traditional medieval topics, Arthur and his knights and other chivalry films or Robin Hood. Altogether Hollywood produced a total of just under sixty films set in the Middle Ages, of which nearly half were multiple takes on the same subject: Ivanhoe, Robin Hood, Joan of Arc, *A Connecticut Yankee at King Arthur's Court*, *The Hunchback of Notre Dame*, Richard the Lionheart and the Crusades, Genghis Khan, the Vikings, and a large number of variants on the Arthurian story and the knights of the Round Table. Other topics used by the studios were the *Hundred and One Nights*, the Lombards, Marco Polo, Lady Godiva, *Quentin Durward*, El Cid, the Moors in Spain, Thomas Becket, Good King Wenceslas, Lochinvar (from Walter Scott's poem), the Pied Piper of Hamelin, Wilhelm Tell, François Villon, the *Decameron* and William Wallace. To these have to be added both the historic fantasy film category, and the 'medievalist' science fiction such as the Star Wars trilogy. Many of the standard topics were of course common to both Hollywood and the European film industry. Overall one can count approximately nine versions of the *Hunchback of Notre Dame*, thirteen of Wilhelm Tell, about twenty films on the Vikings, over thirty five on Robin Hood and well over fifty on the Arthurian and Round Table story (without counting the more general 'chivalry' films), not forgetting the large number dealing with Joan of Arc, Ivanhoe, Quentin Durward, Tristan and the over ten versions of *A Connecticut Yankee at King Arthur's Court* (the latest in date adapting the story to turn Hank into a little Black American girl).[9] These became in effect international topics, with films made by the British, French, Italians, Germans, Spanish, Americans, Russians, even some by the Swiss, Portuguese, and in Hong Kong.

European cinema had its own pot-boiler historical films, especially British and Italian. Many were not set in the Middle Ages but, for example, during the Tudor and Stuart period in British cinema during the 1930s and 1940s,[10] or as sword-and-sandals (Roman period) films in Italian cinema. These periods were presumably perceived by producers and directors to be more appealing to wide audiences on account of a common historical culture acquired through school and general popular knowledge. But some of it applied to the Middle Ages too: many films made in the 1960s and 1970s in Britain, sometimes with Hollywood support, were of the traditional kind, such as *Ivanhoe*, at least five *Robin Hood* films, *The Black Knight* (1954), *The Siege of the Saxons* (1967), *The Viking Queen* (1967), *Pope Joan* (1972), *The Thief of Baghdad* (1978), *Gawain and the Green Knight* (1973) and its later remake by the same director, Stephen Weeks, under the title *The Sword of the Valiant* (1983). Early on, before and immediately after the First World War, there had been some films set in the Middle Ages too, on more unusual themes, for example the *Last of the Saxons* about King Harold (1910) and the *Last King of Wales* (1922), as well as four versions of *Jane Shore*, a successful eighteenth-century play based on a story set during the fourteenth century. Even during the period of Hollywood dominance one encounters occasionally more unusual films, such as the three on Thomas Becket, of which two (1951, 1964) were based respectively on T. S. Eliot's and Jean Anouilh plays; *The Servant* (1953), based on a contemporary play about Joan of Arc, and the Polish-directed though English-produced *Gates to Paradise* (1967) by Andrej Wajda. More recent films are still straightforward historical narratives, but often cover interesting and unusual topics, such as *Stealing Heaven* (director Clive Donner, 1989, on Abélard and Héloïse), *The Anchoress* (director Chris Newby, 1993, the story of a fourteenth-century anchoress) and *Hildegard* (1994, on the life of Hildegard of Bingen).

The French also produced their own 'straight' versions of medieval stories from very early on. Before and around the time of the First World War, there was a large 'medieval' output, some drawn from Shakespeare (Edward IV, Richard III and the Princes in the Tower), some co-produced with the Italians on suitable topics of mutual interest (Pope Boniface VIII, Cola di Rienzo, the Black Death in Florence, Paolo and Francesca from Dante), some on more specifically French 'national' subjects (the Knights Templar, the Hundred Years War, the fourteenth-century poet François Villon, and the Merovingian king Dagobert), and some rather unexpected ones like *Griseldis* (1912; based on Chaucer's Knight's Tale), the Scottish-themed Robert Bruce, and the adaptation of a then very popular novel, *Le miracle des loups* (1924). The French film industry continued to finance the occasional plain narrative historical film on the Hundred Years War (1961), the *Chanson de Roland* (1970), the Year One Thousand (1985), William the Conqueror (1987), as well as the usual reworkings of the Round Table and chivalry films. Overall, these films, though sometimes superior in quality, were nowhere near as numerous as Italian ones.

By 1993 there were already well over 155 Italian films set in the medieval period, even leaving out those which adapted Shakespeare plays like *Macbeth* and *Romeo and Juliet* or operas set in the Middle Ages like Donizetti's *La Favorita*. This was itself a relatively small percentage of the output of Italian cinema. This output of run-of-the-mill swashbucklers and romances is awesome. Even before the First World War, twenty-one films were made, including two of Joan of Arc, three based on Dante and three on the Borgias (regarded as part of the Middle Ages), with the rest spread out between the French king Louis XI, the Lombard king and queen Alboin and Rosamond, the last Italian emperor Conrad Staufen, the doge of Venice, the Cid, Tristan, Siegfried, Parsifal, Francis of Assisi, and the story of Pia de' Tolomei based on Dante. Subsequently, and until the late 1940s, there were more films about Francis, the Borgias, Tasso's *Gerusalemme Liberata*, Attila, Boccacio, Anthony of Padua, Ivan the Terrible, the Lombards, three films about the Visconti of Milan and two about the Pazzi Conspiracy and Julian of Medici, and films based on literary texts or popular stories, two on the *Due Foscari* and one on Genoveva of Brabant. From the 1950s onwards we have again multiple remakes of the same topics: Ariosto's *Orlando*, the Saracens, and the popular literary story of the Baker of Venice (*Il fornaretto di Venezia*) three times each, Genoveva four more times, Francis, and the Vikings, five times each (the latter mostly co-produced by Hollywood, like the two films about the Tartars), Alboin and the Lombards six times and no less than thirty romantic love and adventure films. In addition to these, numerous other topics were dealt with only once.[11] This extraordinary variety of subjects shows just how much residual knowledge of the period and of popular literary classics on the part of contemporary audiences was taken for granted by the film industry in Italy, even of relatively obscure topics. Nevertheless, the Middle Ages were still regarded as a rather more esoteric proposition than other historical periods, even in Italy, and especially in French cinema (about forty films, of which one erotic – on a par with the four Italian versions of the Decameron, similarly used), Germany (about ten films), the Soviet Union (about twenty films) and Scandinavian cinema (about fifteen, or sixteen if one counts Dreyer's Joan of Arc, a French production). This may explains the popularity of the medieval period with the 'auteur' cinema.

Until the 1980s European auteur cinema dealing with medieval topics was limited. It came essentially from the Italians, the French, the Scandinavians, a few British and a few Russian directors, thus seemingly not following any specific pattern. German auteur cinema was strong in the 1970s and 1980s, but it was not interested in the Middle Ages. After the 1920s and 1930s, which saw five films set in the Middle Ages, the only two 'medieval' films made in Germany were a *Till Eulenspiegel* (1956), Harald Reinl's *Die Niebelungen* in the 1960s in two parts (an entertainment historical pot-boiler of little interest though it was modelled on Lang's earlier film),[12] *The Fire and the Sword* (another pot-boiler on the Tristan story in 1981) and Hans-Jürgen Syberberg's nine-hour-long *Parsifal*, effectively a Wagnerian piece. The English produced rather more. Apart from the standard films mentioned previously, major auteur films set in the Middle Ages were *The Lion in Winter* (director Anthony Harvey, 1968), *Alfred the Great* (director Clive Donner, 1969), *Robin and Marian* (director Richard Lester, 1976, an Anglo-American production), *Monty Python and the Holy Grail* (directors Terry Gilliam and

Terry Jones, 1975) followed by the Monty Pythons' *Time Bandits* (1981) and, separately, Terry Gilliam's *Jabberwocky* (1977), Terry Jones's *Erik the Viking* (1989), and John Boorman's *Excalibur* (1981, but produced with Hollywood money). After Eisenstein the Russians only made two films with medieval associations, of which the best-known is Andrei Tarkovski's *Andrei Rublev* (1966). Another player in world cinema joined the club in the 1950s when Akira Kurosawa began his career with *Rashomon,* followed by the *Seven Samurai, Kagemusha* and *Ran,* all set in the medieval Japan of the samurai. His films were of considerable importance, not least for the influence they had in stylistic terms on western directors. Meanwhile, even as the Italian industry was mass producing historical films, often with American money, the greatest of contemporary Italian film directors used the period in a completely different way. One after another they brought out Rossellini's *Francesco, giullare di Dio* (1949), Cavani's film on Francis and Monicelli's *L'armata Brancaleone* in 1966, upon which followed Monicelli again with *Brancaleone alle crociate* in 1970, Pasolini's *Decameron* in 1971 and his *Canterbury Tales* in 1972, the same year as Zeffirelli's film on Francis of Assisi.

The two major European cinematic traditions using the medieval period by choice throughout were the Scandinavians and the French. First came Benjamin Christensen's *Häxan* (1921), which influenced Ingmar Bergman, and Carl Dreyer's revolutionary *Passion de Jeanne d'Arc* (1928), followed by Bergman's *The Seventh Seal* (1957) and *The Virgin Spring* (1958). More recently we had Michael Meschke's *Skärseld* (1975), Gabriel Axel's *Prince of Jutland* (1994) and Liv Ullmann's *Kristin Lavransdatter* (1995). Scandinavian cinema continually used the medieval period for its reflection. So did French cinema from its inception, indeed one of Jean Méliès's short films was about Joan of Arc. Later on, to cite but a few, came another Joan of Arc in 1926, Marcel Carné's *Les visiteurs du soir* (1942), Robert Bresson's *Le procès de Jeanne d'Arc* (1963) and *Lancelot du Lac* (1974), Nina Companeez' farce *Colinot Trousse-Chemise* (1973), Eric Rohmer's *Perceval le Gallois* (1978), Bertrand Tavernier's *La Passion Béatrice* (1987), André Delvaux's *L'oeuvre au noir* (1988, a Belgian director for an adaptation of Marguerite Yourcenar's famous novel), and *The Hour of the Pig* (an Anglo-French film directed by Leslie Megahey in 1994). One could add to these two 'cult' films, both great popular successes, one the European co-production of Umberto Eco's *The Name of the Rose* (dir. J. J. Annaud, 1986), the other the comedy *Les visiteurs* (1992) which, although set in modern days, transports two medieval characters into the present, a sort of Mark Twain in reverse.

A broad analysis of the interpretation of a few key themes will make the distinction between Hollywood productions and European ones more imme-

diately obvious. From Hollywood cinematography four classic representa-
tive films spread across the chronological range provide good case studies.
These are the 1938 *Adventures of Robin Hood* (M. Curtiz) *The Vikings*
(R. Fleischer, 1958), *El Cid* (A. Mann, 1961) and *First Knight* (J. Zucker, 1995).
The following themes appear throughout these films: the choice of names,
the battle scenes, coronation ceremonies, the king's court and castle, the
king's council, tournaments, feasting, the peasants, women, and religion.
One can thus compare them across the century on a one-to-one basis.

People's chosen names and titles are often anachronistic and mix periods,
according to how exotic and appropriate they sound: one such example is
Robin Hood's 'bishop of the Black Canons', possibly impressive-sounding
but definitely non-existent in any church hierarchy. Battle scenes in all four
films are represented by the sea attack and the castle attack in *The Vikings*,
the ambush in the forest in *Robin Hood*, the attack on Valencia and the
memorable battle against the Moors in *El Cid*, and the battle against the
usurper of Lyonesse, in which King Arthur displays his 'battalions' and 'reg-
iments', in *First Knight*. What do they have in common? The obvious answer
is the huge number of people, acting together like a twentieth-century army
under command, banners flying, rousing music, the expected Viking horns
and various colourful 'uniforms' (rather akin to *Star Trek* ones in *First
Knight*[13]). Fortified castles abound, and attacks on them are standard: witness the fourteenth century-type castle under Viking attack in *The Vikings*,
itself a story set presumably during the ninth century. As it happens, and
unfortunately for the director, Vikings did not attack castles, and such a
stronghold as that seen in the film would not have existed in the ninth century, but such details as the small matter of conflating images separated by
five hundred years is hardly going to stand in the way of a good fight. What
it all has to amount to, of course, is a medieval 'clash of the titans', in which
the 'good' army is triumphant. It is no coincidence that Mann, for example,
was essentially a director of westerns, and brought a similar 'good guys –
bad guys' equivalent of a shoot-out to the film. Coronation ceremonies,
King Aelle's in *The Vikings*, King John's in *Robin Hood* and King Alfonso's
in *El Cid*, provide another opportunity for vast displays of pageantry, colour,
large numbers of attendants in 'court dress', uniformed trumpet-blowing
equerries, long processions into big halls, and strangely dressed priests mut-
tering Latin incantations in the background. Similar such displays are
presented when the action focuses on the king's court and castle: magnificence reigns everywhere, at Aelle's court, at that of the king of Castile at
Burgos, at Nottingham Castle and even in sixth-century Camelot, the latter
looking like an impressively-lit Manhattan at night. There are some sub-
themes associated with the king or ruler: his council, his faithful and

rejoicing (or groaning) subjects, court feasting and tournaments and jousts. The king's (or Viking leader's in *The Vikings*) council can be either formal, conducted with strange rituals displaying the advisers' love for their king and sitting at the Round Table (*First Knight*) or a rather more 'pagan' and unruly affair among the Vikings. It usually involves two sets of advice, one from the younger, wilder and more adventurous element, and one from the wiser, older heads – the ruler's positive or negative status depends, for the audience, on which type of advice he chooses to follow. Needless to say, they are all men. Feasting is another significant theme, where the display of large amounts of food, including sundry large animals being roasted on spits, can be used to show royal popularity, or greed, or social cohesion through sharing food, drink, and entertainment (the latter of a sometimes deliciously 'savage' kind, such a plait-cutting with an axe, a favourite Viking pastime, we are led to believe). Finally, the most glamorous and indispensable element of pageantry must be integrated somehow: hence the tournaments or jousts, popular entertainment of the aristocracy under the sunny Nottingham skies (*Robin Hood*) or, two hundred years before it was performed as such, as a means of conquering a city in eleventh-century Spain, the jousting complete with caparisoned horses, knights in coats-of-arms and ladies' tokens.

Not surprisingly, it turns out to be rather less easy to isolate examples of other themes. Peasants (or any other groups except kings and nobles), rarely appear in these films and when they do, they are usually shown as either rejoicing over a hero's victory or fleeing from the advancing armies. *The Vikings* shows good examples of both. Women, that is the aristocratic heroines (peasant women are indistinguishable from the men in the previously-mentioned category), may be individually spunky and opinionated, but in practice their role is to wait in the castle, confiding in their ladies-in-waiting and worrying about their men. An exception to this (by 1995 Hollywood has taken on board some of the social changes of the 1960s and 1970s) is the Guenevere of *First Knight*; at the start of the film, she is the reigning figure in the kingdom she has inherited from her father, and it is only when she finds herself unable to defeat her rival that she flees to seek the help of a man, King Arthur. Although, like most of her predecessors in films, she too acts as a clothes-horse, being made to change outfits and parade a different one in every scene, she is, nonetheless, allowed to attend the odd royal council. By and large, Hollywood steers clear of religion, except to add local colour: occasionally the films show good or bad priests, a church background for a woman praying for her hero, the frisson of pagan religion with a seeress casting runes in *The Vikings*, and the occasional 'message for religious tolerance' when *El Cid* fraternises with the Muslim leader.

The one rite of which much is made is the Viking funeral at the end of the film, not because it is perceived as religious (being pagan), but because it enables a good director and a good cameraman to end on an amazing *Gotterdämmerung* finale, with all the panache of a colourful, exotic note.

The primary purpose of the Hollywood film industry is to entertain. Escapist fantasies require colour, music, costumes, general glamour, exoticism and pageantry, all key elements of these films. The entertainment is all the more enjoyable and successful if it is more or less in tune with the audience's vague school memories of the period, hence the coats of arms, knights, Viking helmets, castles, boars roasted on spits, royal crowns, Latin chanting and so on – directors made the Middle Ages of their films match the audience's expectations. In addition, the director was primarily the executor of the studio's policy. These not only required grand scale love and adventure in a romantic, idealised spectacular but they also had to make the film acceptable to all. Thus it needed to cater for the 'lowest common denominator', with a suitable moral line and an optimistic ending. The Middle Ages of these films are often no more than a background for adventures, plots and actors who could be set anywhere and at any time, in a kind of 'Pre-Raphaelitism filtered through the glossy pages of Vogue'.[14] Naturally, as a studio product the film carried the message of the studios, whose aim was both to reflect and to shape American public opinion.

On a general level, the message reflects the obligatory triumph of good over evil: Robin Hood over bad king John; El Cid over the usurper and bad king of Castile; Arthur, Guenevere and Lancelot over the usurper and bad king of Lyonesse. The political common factor itself is meant to signify that good power is all right, only bad rulers are to be ousted. But there are specific moral implications too. *Robin Hood* is a prime example of some of these.[15] Two themes dominate the film in the background. The first is the forcefully and repeatedly drummed in hostility between 'Normans' and 'Saxons', historically nonsensical in the thirteenth century when the plot is set. This still common view, left over from Walter Scott's inheritance and the Norman Yoke cliché, focuses on the contrast between the bad king, John, and his courtiers the rich aristocrats, who are all Normans, and whose purpose in life appears to be to oppress and starve the Saxons, the good, brave but impoverished 'natives' of England. Robin de Locksley is said to be a Saxon, hence his rebellion and popularity with the masses. Much is made of his support for the faraway, and therefore almost by definition *good*, King Richard the Lionheart, so much so that one almost fears that one will be told that Richard was a Saxon, too, unlike his brother, and that John had usurped the crown of England against the law! The film, made in 1938, at a time when Nazi conquest of Europe threatened, pits the good, resistant natives against a foreign oppressor who has conquered their land, and who is referred to through the parallels drawn by the studios between the strict hierarchy of power and stiffness of the Normans and those of the Nazis. The film was a subliminal message to be conveyed to the peoples of occupied Europe. There may even be a more personal note here since the director, Michael Curtiz, was a Hungarian Jew who had emigrated to America, and was thus even more fiercely anti-Nazi.

A second major theme in Robin Hood, while pursuing the contrast between good Saxons and bad Normans, takes it further. The Saxons are simple folk, living a healthy outdoor life in the country, feasting together in friendship amidst woods and rivers. Their very clothes are made in colours recalling nature, the green of the trees and the brown of the earth: they represent primitive rusticity, purity, honesty and wholesomeness. By contrast, the Normans dress in rich unnatural colours, they feast at court with a lavish display of greed, conspicuous consumption, decadence and corruption. The line taken could almost be that of seventeenth-century Puritan preachers against court life or of eighteenth-century Rousseauist idealists, but it represents in fact the values of Middle America, fearful of urban decadence and corruption, and seeing itself as the depositor of a traditional, country-based wholesome lifestyle. The film is set in a society in which, on the surface at least, distinctions of class and wealth are less important than individual virtues and worth – the hero is the prime mover behind major conflicts and changes. This theme reflects the American 'democratisation' of medieval myths like Arthur and the Knights of the Round Table, who are successful because of their personal qualities rather than on account of their birth and circumstances. Moreover, despite the political undertones of the film, Robin Hood's main purpose is no longer the popular and legendary task of 'robbing the rich to give to the poor', but has turned into a personal vendetta against the sheriff of Nottingham, who is his rival in love.

Two later Hollywood films about Robin Hood, John Irwin's *Robin Hood* and Kevin Reynolds's *Robin Hood, Prince of Thieves* (both 1991), show many similarities with the classic 1938 film. However, they were preceded, and clearly influenced, by two British television series.[16] The first was *The Adventures of Robin Hood*, produced and shown in the late 1950s as family viewing; the second, consisting of twenty-six episodes, was shown between 1984 and 1986, under the name of *Robin of Sherwood*. In the first series, often relying on familiar episodes from traditional ballads, Robin, unlike his Hollywood aristocratic and royalist counterpart, is no earl or even knight, but the son of a forester, who behaves like a gentleman. Some republican overtones occur, though mostly associated with Continental figures. Above all, Robin's concern for social justice is noticeable, possibly a reflection of the contribution of left-wing American refugees from McCarthyism working within the British film industry at the time. *Robin of Sherwood* most clearly shows Robin as a peasant helping the dispossessed and marginalized.[17] The series is particularly concerned with ecology and nature mysticism, and has a strong interest in pagan movements, witchcraft and New Age cults,[18] presenting the outlaws as peace-loving pagans rather like medieval hippies, while the sheriff uses black magic. It also introduces the character of Nazir, the Saracen warrior. All these features attempt to reflect a multicultural, multi-religious, as well as an anti-Thatcherite, Britain. It may be of some significance that in democratic America Robin Hood should be above all a royalist and aristocratic figure, while in Britain, he has come to be portrayed as a socialist peasant rebel with republican leanings, as in *Robin of Sherwood* or in Richard Lester's film *Robin and Marian*.

Several of the elements from the British television series must have had considerable influence on both Irwin's and Reynolds's films. Irwin's makes Robin's actions motivated, not as traditionally shown, by patriotism and fidelity to Richard the Lionheart, but by a political and social 'conscience'.[19] It gives the director an opening for a 'realistic' depiction of the hardships of life as an outlaw, with poverty, hunger and disease. The ideal of social justice did not really appear in medieval ballads about Robin Hood, and had only been added to the legend in post-medieval texts known as 'garlands', as had the love interest of Marian, and the temporal displacement of the story from the fourteenth to the early thirteenth century. It had been present in the 1938 film, which attempted to establish in its American audience's minds a parallel between Robin Hood's redistribution of riches and F. D. Roosevelt's New Deal, with Wall Street rich businessmen who had despoiled the poor during the Great Depression getting their just deserts.[20] Reynolds's film on the other hand, presumably heavily influenced by its star Kevin Costner, goes back to the more traditional model, despite its device of adding an 'innocent abroad' figure in the character of Robin's Saracen friend, and despite creating a Marian-figure who may be regarded more of as a 'career woman' than a delicate maiden. Its main feature, which makes it close in tone to Costner's previous film *Dances with Wolves*, is a strong ecological message: in both films a 'nobleman' abandons by choice his familiar sophisticated social environment, to live with more 'primitive', more 'authentic' people who are closer to nature and who bring about his conversion to the cause of the poor and the desire to lead them in their fight against power and institutions. Some adaptations to our age and its main preoccupations since 1938 have clearly taken place: social justice, environmental concerns, feminism have been taken on board, an understandable feature since Hollywood directors and studios continued to play a part as a driving force behind ideological and moral crusades. But the main narrative line of these films is the same, as is their message of a pure and good natural world versus a decadent civilisation, some plot devices (the attack on the convoy in Reynolds's film descends from the western attack on the stagecoach or train by Indians), and the unsubtle characterisation, especially of the 'baddies' like the sheriff of Nottingham.

Mirroring the Saxon to Norman opposition inherited from Walter Scott and highlighted in other films like *Ivanhoe*, a similar device of enmity between a savage group of conquerors and the native people and king, the first led by a traitor and spy who defected to them, is at the heart of *The Vikings*. Made in 1958, when America was in the throes of the Cold War, it was described by Kirk Douglas himself (playing the Viking hero) as a 'Scandinavian western'.[21] Ultimately the young Viking leader fails and is redeemed by the generosity of his enemy (who also turns out to be his half-brother), but only because he could not bring himself to kill this half-brother: the redemption comes from his respect for family ties and shared blood. Heroic he may be, but he represents brute force and pagan values, ultimately to be conquered by Christian heroes and morality. Note the way in which the script makes the two heroes half-brothers against their will, with the conquering 'bad' one eventually redeemed by the 'good' – a blueprint for America's future, perhaps?

Are any of these themes represented in European films and, if so, how? One unifying feature within the 'European' cinema style is common to most films in stylistic terms regardless of theme or period: the 'minimalist' approach. Grand set pieces, battles, jousting on a grand scale or court pageantry are usually missing. There are few people around (no Hollywood budgets there), few and almost exclusively natural colours: white, brown, beige and tan, almost no background music, and, as my students would say, lots of talk and very little action. The characters are rarely heroes, and spend their time agonising over their feelings and motivations. *Andrei Rublev*, *Lancelot du Lac*, even the older ones like *Les visiteurs du soir*, are cases in point, even though the themes they address may be different every time: redemption by God, the duties of chivalry, the conflict between love and honour, or the role of God in artistic creation. A good summary of the visual expression occurring in this kind of film can be found at its most revealing in the Danish director Gabriel Axel's *Prince of Jutland*, a Danish-British production of 1994. The film has a plot, a very convoluted one at that, being in fact the original Danish story of Hamlet, very close to the literary background and style of the original text of the thirteenth-century chronicle of

Saxo Grammaticus, set some time during the Anglo-Saxon period. It was not the first of Axel's films to use the medieval period: in 1967 his *Red Mantle*, one of the first Scandinavian films to attempt an adaptation of the world of the sagas, displayed already many of the features that we later find in *Prince of Jutland*. Axel used the story to reconstruct as closely as possible the feel and atmosphere of the early medieval period. Minimalism is extreme: plain, dun colours, of natural wool and earth (which makes the unique appearance of a purple velvet cape as the sign of royal status all the more potent), a 'kingdom' which is the size of a few villages and whose king knows all his subjects by name, a king and advisers who are all local farmers, a palace which is a big farm, though it has the large wooden hall of saga memories. The emphasis is on essential aspects of medieval life, however presently unfashionable, such as hunting, killing your enemies in a brutal fashion, and paying blood-money, all shown non-judgementally on screen. When the main character arrives in England, the real historical contrast in wealth is made clear, with the English ruler's castle made of stone and feasts with a wealth of food and drink, and even music (in a film which has almost none in the background at all). The character of Hamlet is involved in a battle, a million years removed from Hollywood ones, a 'great' battle opposing two 'great' armies of approximately thirty people on each side, and in which every below the belt and unchivalrous means at their disposal is used by the soldiers, including propping up dead men in the fog, knifing enemies in the back and killing or stealing their horses. There is in all this a message, of course, rather than just someone making a film to show how right he can get his historical material. The message is for the viewer to see the period as 'it was', warts and all, and to admire the way in which strong-minded men managed to put together a country under such circumstances. Another probably characteristically 1990s side of the film is its understated but clear ecological message. This is not so much the return to nature of the Romantics, then of Hollywood, but one of love of natural colours, earth, woods and water, and the perceived solidarity and wholesomeness of the village community in its shared intimacy and political consensus.

The point of the previous comments is obviously not to criticise Hollywood films for their lack of 'historical accuracy' – with historical film as with historical novels this is irrelevant. Despite any claims to do so, almost no film set in the past is actually 'accurate', whatever this may mean. In the case of the Middle Ages, only one of all the films mentioned, *Prince of Jutland*, came as close to period details and atmosphere as one could hope to get. This was, one might add, to the detriment of its success, which was not great when the film was released in the UK. When I screened *The Vikings* and

Prince of Jutland back to back to my students of medieval history, by way of contrast between a Hollywood fantasy production and a European 'histori-cally accurate' film, they, like the mainstream audience, claimed to see the merit of the latter but found it slow and tedious, while the former was, to cite one of them, the 'kind of film that got them interested in the Middle Ages in the first place'. What needs explaining are the choices made by the studios or the directors about how and why they chose to recreate the Middle Ages in a particular way.

One way of making these choices clear is by doing a point by point com-parison between films dealing with similar themes. Two subjects in particular are revealing: the treatment of Joan of Arc;[22] and that of the Arthurian and chivalry material. Two early films about Joan of Arc were produced in America. The first, made in 1916 and directed by Cecil B. de Mille, was based on Schiller's play, and its avowed purpose was to persuade Americans to join in the First World War.[23] In order to arouse the audi-ence's interest and to make the point that the American and the British are on the same side, it invents a love story between Joan and a British soldier.[24] The other, much more famous film, was directed by Victor Fleming in 1948 (after the Second World War) and starred Ingrid Bergman, who reprised the role she had created on Broadway in Maxwell Anderson's play *Joan of Lor-raine* (1946).[25] Anderson was a 'rebel' writer, a 'liberal intellectual', who had been involved in writing about the need to fight for justice in the wake of the Sacco and Vanzetti affair, and would be again associated with works against the Mafia and gangsters, and racism. *Joan of Lorraine* was centred on issues such as the role of history, the gap between ideal and action, the pos-sibility or otherwise of political action which would not lead to compromise and, very specifically in this play and in reference to the war, fraternisation and collaboration with the enemy – it surprised nobody that Bergman, who was also known for her liberal political views, should have created the part on Broadway. Anderson was asked to write the script for the film, but almost nothing of his play was left by the time it had been adapted as a piece of Hollywood hagiographic imagery. Fleming gave the audiences the Middle Ages they expected, with glamorous set pieces: warfare western-style, a grand coronation scene, manichaean characters and the elimination of any religious content to the story. Significantly Bergman played the part again, this time under the direction of her new husband Rossellini, who in 1954 filmed the oratorio *Jeanne au bûcher*, with a text by Paul Claudel and music by Arthur Honnegger.

   After the 1926 French Marc de Gastyne film about Joan as a national hero-ine, as she was indeed to be used by the 1930s Right in France, two other films were made about Joan of Arc in France, Carl Dreyer's *Passion de Jeanne d'Arc* in 1928[26] and Robert Bresson's *Le procès de Jeanne d'Arc* in 1963. Both showed little interest in the story of the fight against the English, being concerned essentially with Joan's trial. Dreyer was the first to have read the full transcript of the trial, which was what interested him. Historical detail was not his business. He did not try to produce a historically accurate film like a costume drama, in fact he almost eliminated any period reference, 'de-historicised' the film to concentrate on an abstract vision of Joan's passion and martyrdom, through an extremely minimalist, formal, pure style which would be a visual pointer to Joan's own purity and sanctity.

> A thorough study of the documents from the rehabilitation process was nec-
> essary: I did not study the clothes of the time, and things like that. The year of
> the event seemed as inessential to me as its distance from the present. I wanted
> to interpret a hymn to the triumph of the soul over life.[27]

The purpose of creating this 'out-of-time' style was precisely to show how contemporary Joan's quest for an absolute truth was. What he hoped to achieve, as Bresson was to do again later, was a mystical, uncluttered approach, which was his perception of the Middle Ages. Finally, to add to the corpus, we have another two films, the American Otto Preminger's *Saint Joan* (1957), an adaptation of G. B. Shaw's play, and the French *Jeanne la Pucelle* (director Jacques Rivette, 1994). Two new films about Joan were both released in 1999, both Franco-American productions, one directed by Luc Besson (*The Messenger*) and one by Christian Duguay (*Joan of Arc*).[28] Both have, predictably, a strong feminist slant and an even stronger anti-religious one: the first deliberately makes Joan a neurotic obsessive traumatised by the (imaginary) rape of her sister into religious mania, while the second turns her into a female 'hero of the people', in a 'rational atheist, Marxist-populist strain'. Others have used Joan to make various points, starting with *Das Mädchen Johanna* (director Gustav Ucicky, 1935), whose script was allegedly written in part by Goebbels himself, and which neglected Joan's story in favour of exalting the Dauphin's cunning and leadership, as a thinly-disguised Hitler.[29] In 1970 the Soviet Gleb Panfilov also used the story, through the intermediary of a Russian actress rehearsing the part, for polit-ical purposes.

Another major theme which can be compared on a one-to-one basis to show the contrast between American and European film is that of Arthurian and chivalry stories.[30] Pageantry is a key element in Hollywood films, from Richard Thorpe's in the 1950s to *First Knight* in the 1990s. Hence the need for big crowd scenes: battles, court, feasts and tournaments, and clothes shows for the female cast. The tournament and jousting are staple fare.[31] The purpose of such a tournament may, incidentally, be to help with a just cause (to defeat the Normans, to gain the city of Calahora), but essentially its role is to confirm the hero as such, and to allow him to gain love or the lady's hand. The scenes must include such devices as symbolic colours (the white arms) and the masked knight. What is shown in these films is usually the late fifteenth-century version of the jousting, with its one-to-one fighting, the spectacle, the costumes, the ladies' tokens. Whether set in the twelfth century in *Ivanhoe*, the eleventh century in *El Cid* or the sixth century in an Arthurian context, they all work on this model. There are other specific Hollywood factors. The story of Arthur and the Round Table, in Hollywood terms, is fundamentally about power: having it, losing it, recovering it – an entirely secular fight for a kingdom. Any religious dimension, whether in the form of the quest for the Grail or of the supernatural powers of Merlin, Morgan and others, is normally eliminated, and Merlin himself is no more than a 'wise' old counsellor and warrior. Christian morality, however, is all powerful: issues like Arthur's illegitimate birth, the incest with his sister, Mordred's parricide and, of course, the adultery of Guenevere and Lancelot, are either not mentioned, are skimmed over or are depicted as slander (an old Tennysonian reflex). While this may seem understandable in the era of studio dominance and moral code in Hollywood, in 1995 it reflected a new trend showing those same studios buckling under renewed American Christian fundamentalism, with its insistence on 'family values'.[32] The perception of women as either good, because obedient and pure, or wicked, because wilful, underhand and power-hungry witches, is often a corollary of this, even to Walt Disney's interpretation of Merlin, which has only one woman in the film, as the 'baddie'.[33] The male-dominated world reveals to what extent these films are nothing other than traditional westerns set in the Middle Ages. American literature often reflected Arthurian myths in the western genre – film does the same in reverse. It has often been said that the American Middle Ages in Hollywood terms was the conquest of the Far West. From the western came the style of warfare with attacks by wild riders (the Picts attack like Indians), the male bonding of knights sitting together at night by the fire singing, the importance of a man's horse and weapon, the friendship between men which is more important than love and women, and even the lone stranger coming to save the town or kingdom (Lancelot, who is French – like Hollywood's 'Latin lovers' types – riding into Camelot). Another important, and to European minds rather unusual, aspect of the story is its 'democratic' line. Just as in American Arthurian literature, in film too one sees the Round Table as a group of equals, of which any one can become a member if they are good enough, regardless of birth, as Lancelot does in *First Knight* or William Thatcher in *The Knight's Tale* (director Brian

Helgeland).[34] Thatcher is shown to be of low birth but as chivalrous as the best of knights and therefore worthy of being one.

Last but not least in the ideological pointers of the Hollywood production is its political message. Joan of Arc had been used for that purpose during both wars, the Vikings during the Cold War. The Cold War had also been present in a transparent way in the most politically loaded American film of the 1950s, *The Black Knight* (director Tay Garnett), in which the McCarthyist themes of the 'red scare', patriotism, anti-Communism and the fear of the 'traitors within', as well as virulent antihomosexuality are on the agenda.[35] Robin Hood had made the point about fighting foreign invaders to preserve one's freedom, and so did *Braveheart* (director Mel Gibson, 1995), where it is the English who are the conquerors (of Scotland). Another Robin Hood film in 1991, like *First Knight*, also refers indirectly to the first Gulf War. *Robin Hood, Prince of Thieves* shows a friendly, 'civilised' Muslim, by contrast with the 'bad' ones fighting in the East, while *First Knight* uses the example of Malagant, dark-haired, dark-skinned, living in a world of dark caves, not respecting authority or civilised behaviour in either love or politics, unlike the blond-haired Lancelot and the brilliantly-lit Camelot, as a transparent allusion to Muslims and Arab countries and what has been called the 'pax Americana'.[36] The most recent Hollywood offering, the 2004 *King Arthur*, makes a point about the studio's insistence on historical authenticity by 'demedievalising' the film and setting up the story in Roman Britain, in a sombre and gritty style presumably meant to make away with the glamorous props of the Round Table, Guenevere and the Grail, and even with Christianity altogether since Arthur alone is a Christian while his companions are pagans. The contemporary political message nevertheless comes through very strongly. Arthur and his 'knights' – the anachronistic name is preserved – represent the American values of freedom, self-determination, equality and male companionship. They are helping the 'natives', here the Picts but they could, of course, stand in for any Native American or other oppressed minorities, against a colonial power. Even religion is represented as a matter of personal choice, though in the end Arthur's Christianity still emerges as the most civilised. For Touchstone studios, history is all right in its place, but it must not interfere with current politics. Further political allusions, this time to fighting totalitarian regimes as well as lawless ones, are equally transparent in another recent, if indirect, incarnation of the Arthurian and knightly myths in the *Star Wars* trilogy, with its Arthur/ Percival hero Luke Skywalker, his fight against the Empire with the help of the Force, his new version of the Grail and his all-powerful laser-sword.[37]

A political message has been identified as the main undercurrent of *Excalibur* too, a film made with American support and Hollywood-style special effects, but directed by John Boorman, whose contribution as auteur comes through.[38] Even while he purported to do little but adapt Malory, he simplified him (for example by conflating characters like Morgan and Vivien, Morgan and Arthur's sister, Arthur and the Fisher King, Percival and Galahad), and used other texts, from the thirteenth-century Robert de Boron and Chrétien de Troyes to Wagner. Here no secret is made of illegitimacy, incest and parricide, nor of the adultery which is pointed to as the reason for the end of the Round Table fellowship, for the loss by Arthur of his sword of power and hence of the unity of kingdom and earth, and for the start of an age of misery, winter, sterility and devastation. The issue of the spiritual is not skirted either, whether in the form of the powers of Merlin and pagan witchcraft, or the quest for the Grail, whose success alone can bring back unity and prosperity to the world. To that extent it represents a quest for the harmony of the universe, in an attempt to reconcile science and mysticism in the sort of religious syncretism already seen rise to such heights with the success of the 'Celtic' and pagan movements in the 1980s. In what might be regarded as an 'anti-modern' way, though one entirely consistent with Malory's medieval world, the film also deliberately took issue with the perceived individualism and self-preoccupation of the 1980s, by showing the quest for the Grail as an attempt by the individual to find, not himself or herself, but a place in relation to the universe, society and destiny. Attempts have been made to read in *Excalibur* an apocalyptic undercurrent, which has been sometimes identified as a kind of post-Vietnam feeling, combined with the search and desire for a strong ruling hand, and some have seen the film as symptomatic of America under the presidency of Jimmy Carter. Perhaps one could rather see a way of turning around the myth of chivalry to reveal the modern ideology of violence, while highlighting the beauty of uncontaminated nature and the importance of the Grail less as an achievement than as a quest.

The contrast with the treatment of Arthurian themes in two major French films is considerable. Eric Rohmer's *Perceval le Gallois*, another literary adaptation following right in the footsteps of the director's previous adaptation of Kleist's short story *Die Marquise von O*, saw Rohmer once again working on the equivalent of a *Bildungsroman*, an initiation from childhood to maturity.[39] The hero in this story is a forest child who meets some knights and is so overwhelmed by this experience that he wants to be like them. He gradually acquires a moral education through chivalry, learning to distinguish good from evil through his peregrinations, and finally finds self-knowledge and spiritual enlightenment. The film was to be a faithful rendering of Chrétien de Troyes' romance *Perceval*, but also a Book of Hours brought to life, reproducing the colours and scenes of illuminated miniatures. Rohmer's choice was to create as *unreal* a world as possible, by using the original Old French text, by the artificial device of a theatrical production and especially by a simplified, completely stylised space, with its non-existent perspective and symbolic woods (the trees are artichoke stalks), moors (a pile of sand) and water (some broken glass), even while the costumes and objects are faithfully rendered. This deliberate choice of depicting the Middle Ages as a cultural construct, an 'out-of-time' space, purposefully shows the Grail quest to be part of a different reality than the everyday one, and underlines the role of mysticism and initiation in the medieval world.

Robert Bresson's *Lancelot du Lac* also incorporates very little of the traditional 'realistic' material of chivalry films.[40] It begins at the end of the story, when the knights return from the quest, in which they have failed to find and bring back the Grail. They see this failure as punishment for their own lack of unity, fighting against each other, defeated rather than invincible. They become aware of the gap between ideal and reality, and despair at the failure of the latter, which not even faith can compensate for. It is their anguish and despair at being no more than an anachronism, empty shells only distracted by empty rituals like tournaments, while awaiting their death and the death of their world, which drives the film. All this is shown by the visual set-up: the film is a long series of discontinuities, always focusing on details and never on the (lost) whole of unity. The images are fragmented, fighting or the tournament are depicted as inarticulate shots of broken bodies, horses' hooves, the noise of metal striking against metal, with a heavy, fleshy feel made real by the weight of the weapons, the smell of blood, the mud, the heavy breathing of the fighters, expressing the loss of unity of the knights as people and as a group, once it is clear to them that they have failed in their quest. One interpretation of the film has been that the loss of the Grail represents no less than the loss of hope and of certainties, matching the 1970s' loss of ideological systems and aspirations.

Is European cinema simply more political? This does not seem to be the answer to what makes it so fundamentally different from Hollywood. What European auteur films *do* have in common is that *they have no common 'message'*, or any other message than their directors' views on life. To that extent their common ground is not with one another but, sometimes, with the individual director's other films, which may have nothing to do with the Middle Ages. The premise of the auteur theory is that it is the specific personality, and skills, of the director which function as a criterion of value,[41] a director who alone gives the film its symbolic and aesthetic value and makes it into art. Valuing individual genius above all is thus set in direct contrast with the 'system' film, in which many people are involved in the production and it is the policy of the 'system', not the individual art of the director, which determines the subject and style, usually for specifically commercial purposes. Every European auteur film has its own, that is to say, a director's, 'agenda', and deals with issues and themes peculiar to him: mysticism (Dreyer, Bresson), the end of metaphysical certainties (Bresson), the sense of fatality in Lang's *Niebelungen*. This potential epic if there ever was one, although exalting German culture, national myths and heroes (in Part I) was nevertheless more interested in the visual, cinematographic, possibilities of the story, as well as turning it into a reflection on destiny (especially in Part II). Hence its failure with audiences and cold-shouldering by the Nazi authorities.[42]

European directors provided their own personal interpretations of major topics which are part of the common 'medieval' ground in Europe and elsewhere, for example Joan of Arc, Arthur and his knights, and the related issues pertaining to chivalry. However, many directors also used the Middle Ages as a vehicle for their reflection through a variety of other topics. Several themes were so used. A particularly popular one was that of the life of Francis of Assisi.[43] The Italians made about ten films about him, which showed him as everything from the sickly-sweet popular saint to a proto-pacifist, to a symbol of green politics and to a left-wing revolutionary. The first, 1911 version showed the traditional saint. Roberto Rossellini's neo-realist film of 1950 highlighted the humble, simple, human side of Francis's spirituality, so appropriate in post-1945 Italy. This also came through in Pier Paolo Pasolini's *Uccellacci e uccellini*, not a biography of Francis but rather a modern reinterpretation of his poetry. Liliana Cavani's film (1966) proposed a Marxist interpretation, in a straight biography interpreted by an actor then seen as a symbol of 1960s rebellious youth culture, though later, in 1989, she made another film on the same subject, this time less message-driven and focusing more on the inner life of the character, depicted in a series of flashbacks. Franco Zeffirelli in 1972 directed yet another film about Francis, shortly after his enormously successful *Romeo and Juliet*. Both films were aimed at young people in order to wean them off the booming materialistic consumer society of 1970s Italy, with its values of vulgarity and pornography, as the director saw them: the story of the sublimated love of Francis and Clare, together with the values of respect for nature, was meant to oppose these. By representing Francis as a reformer rather than a revolutionary bent on destroying the church and society, a man for whom the life of simplicity and poverty proposed a real if non-violent revolution against the powerful and wealthy, Zeffirelli returned to the spiritual motivation for Francis's life, and was far more in tune with the ecclesiastical authorities who received the film warmly.

Here is yet another example, as so many before in nineteenth- and twentieth-century medievalism, of the use of the same theme or character to imply or justify two different, even opposing, views. Interpretations of Joan of Arc and Robin Hood stories have provided examples of this phenomenon. Further afield, one encounters differing Russian views of the same aspects of Russian medieval history, by Sergei Eisenstein in *Nevski* and by Andrei Tarkovski in *Rublev*. For these two directors, the main enemy of the Russian people were, respectively, the Germans and the Tartars or Chinese – an obvious reflection of the different world politics of the 1930s and the 1960s. Another classic example of such contrasting views is that of Columbus, with some films following the modern anti-colonialist agenda, while others, such as Ridley Scott's *1492*, focusing on the utopian and adventure-seeking nature of the man.

While being different from Zeffirelli in almost every other way, a similar concern with opposing what he saw as the destruction of a specifically popular culture under the nefarious effect of a consumer-driven media-orientated society, spelling the end of the countryside and the rise of an urban proletariat stultified by the rising power of television, was the driving force behind Pier Paolo Pasolini's work. Pasolini reacted at first by making films, as well as painting and writing, about myths and the importance of the sacred, in the form of parables, like *Edipe re*, *Medea* and *Teorema*. In the 1970s he decided to fight for his ideals in a new way. This meant highlighting 'real life', which for him meant the popular spirit, through what was left of popular culture: a robust humour, sex, and the vitality of the body, of nature. Therein lies the emphasis in his two adaptations of Boccaccio and Chaucer.[44] These films are commentaries on, and interpretations of, the literary texts underpinning them (in the way that straight Shakespeare adaptations cannot be since the verse is fixed). The texts chosen underlined the director's own interest in particular aspects of medieval life, such as the mixture of religious feeling and earthy, sexual, direct nature of human relations, meant to express the instinct for life and the vitality of the human being.[45] Again like Zeffirelli but with very different means, Pasolini wished to fight against what he saw as the debasement of sex through pornography, in this case by making healthy eroticism rather than voyeuristic titillation the manifestation of this popular instinct for life. Such exaltation of the natural and healthy was to be by definition shocking to the Catholic middle classes, the defiance further accentuated by the characters' intense physicality (rough, lined, with bad teeth, speaking in dialect with strong accents and idiosyncratic idioms).

From the neo-realist period onwards Italian cinema, unlike Hollywood romantic glamour or Scandinavian and French concern with spiritual and metaphysical issues, acquired a strong realistic streak, in which nostalgia for the Middle Ages manifested itself in a return to the un-heroic, plebeian robustness of the late medieval Italian literature of picaresque novels, stories and farce. Using a similar technique to Pasolini's, that of highlighting the earthy, rough and rustic, humorous in a rather gravelly way, were Monicelli's films, notably his two about Brancaleone.[46] A parody of the medieval hero, leading a band of ill-assorted vagabonds through Italy, the derisive element of these popular epics, with their crude language, returns to a tradition of populism found in chronicles, sermons and, most famously, in Boccaccio. What surfaces in Monicelli's films, or in Dino Risi's *Dagobert* in the 1980s, showing another facet of the auteur culture, is what amounts to strong reservations about the Middle Ages, depicted as a period of oppression by the church, of superstition, witch-hunts, religious intolerance and absurd enterprises like the Crusades. If anyone, it is the Muslims who are closer to one's idea of knights, a view already put forward in medieval literature, which sometimes praised Saladin in this way, and one reprised by the only Egyptian film to take on the European Middle Ages in 1963. Such perceptions were not unusual, indeed were quite common within the traditions of Italian culture, at least prior to recent scholarly work and the impact of Umberto Eco's books. In a rather more sympathetic way, but also dealing above all with the issue of belief and its problems around the turn of the first millennium, we have the latest Italian auteur film about the period, Pupi Avati's *Magnificat* (1993).

Other European films had a variety of different agenda. While it has a political plot in the background, Henry II's reign and its vicissitudes, the accent in Anthony Harvey's *The Lion in Winter* (1968) is on the relationship of the Henry-Eleanor couple, a study of marital discord and dysfunctional family life. *Alfred the Great* (1969) deals not only with issues relating to power and its responsibilities, but also, in the pacifist 1960s, with the necessity of war to defend one's country when peace would be the king's favourite option. The director Clive Donner, said:

> I was attracted by the character of the man, especially by his affinity with young people today … Guthrum [the Viking leader] makes an interesting contrast with the tormented Alfred. Guthrum knows no inhibitions. He goes after, and gets, anything he sets his heart on. His character is not unlike that of some of today's outspoken, uninhibited young men. In many respects, Alfred the Great can be viewed in terms of current circumstances and events.[47]

Richard Lester, another 1970s 'rebel', concentrated on recreating the feel of the end of an era in his very personal reinterpretation of Robin Hood (*Robin and Marian*, 1976). The two heroes are old and tired, finding one another again after Robin's return from the Crusades twenty year later. Marian is living in a convent (a totally unglamorous location made up of a small house with a few mangy animals) – they both know this is their last time together, and their dialogue is ultimately a meditation on time and change. The screenplay had been written by James Goldman, who had previously been the screenwriter for *The Lion in Winter*, and, like *Alfred*, it too was made in the pacifist atmosphere of 70s, with its the anti-Vietnam War attitudes, suggesting a parallel between the atrocities witnessed by Robin during the Crusades and the then current Asian war.[48] Fabio Carpi's 1984 film *I cani di Gerusalemme* is even more unusual, in its story of a lord who has made a vow to go to Jerusalem on Crusade but, reluctant to leave his home, decides to fulfil his vow by covering the same distance and living through similar hardships by going round his own lands.[49] The mad premise leads the director on to a reflection about utopia, the heroic endeavour to pursue a cause and remain faithful to one's given word, but also about the way in which religion, like any other cause, can turn to fanaticism. Bertrand Tavernier's *La Passion Béatrice* is another film centred on a disturbed man, whose love for his daughter leads to incest, as part of a life of pain, loneliness and rage against himself and the world, a life which, for him, could be a paraphrase of Sartre's view that 'Hell is Others'.[50] The Swedish *Skärseld* uses the nervous breakdown of a contemporary writer who descends into Hell where he is led by Dante and Virgil to reconsider his life. The Dutch *Mariken van Nieumeghen* (director Jos Stelling, 1974) adapts a well-known miracle play. *L'oeuvre au noir* is a film about compromise, compassion and intolerance. *The Wanderer* (1991), using the title of an Anglo-Saxon poem, is made up of three stories about loneliness and rejection, the first in the Anglo-Saxon world, the second after the First World War and the last in the 1990s.

The most celebrated auteur film remains Ingmar Bergman's *The Seventh Seal*.[51] Like Dreyer, Bergman's main preoccupation too at that point in his life was the issue of spiritual aspirations, and he brought to the film his personal obsessions, inherited from a long Scandinavian tradition of metaphysical questioning from Kierkegaard to Ibsen and Strindberg, his secret nostalgia for what he saw as the certainties of medieval religion, and a fascination with the contemporary French existentialism of Jean Paul Sartre and Albert Camus.[52] It was not Bergman's only cinematic incursion into the Middle Ages. The following year he made *The Virgin Spring*, a harrowing story about the rape of a young peasant girl by her father's servants in a forest, and their subsequent concealment of it. Based on a

Swedish legend, as well as having the format of a morality play with traditional medieval themes like the forest and the journey, it had a great deal in common with other Bergman films made in that period, and carried a similar message of anguish and spiritual despair which, in this case, was at least offset by the ending, when purity is redeemed through the miraculous appearance of a spring flowing from the place where the girl's body had been murdered and buried. Bergman's choice of medieval settings was clearly dictated by his personal interest, not to say obsession, with Christian spiritual issues, redemption and salvation, religious freedom and toleration, the church's oppression, and personal religious devotion. He was fundamentally a 'religious' artist, whose films deal with the basic issues of human existence, notably the meaning of suffering and pain, existential loneliness, the acceptance of death and the attempt to find meaning in an apparently senseless universe. His choice of *the* period regarded as the 'Christian centuries' par excellence does not therefore come as a surprise. Neither does the accumulation of all the negative motifs associated with the Middle Ages in *The Seventh Seal*: the Crusades, the Black Death, the fanaticism of the Flagellants, and the burning of witches. The story was not entirely Bergman's invention: he used themes and motifs from several medieval texts, a poem written by a Cistercian monk in the twelfth century,[53] and the morality play *Everyman*, as well as the Book of Revelation, Faust, old Swedish legends and especially medieval wall paintings from Swedish churches, and Strindberg's *Dance of Death*. He was also clearly influenced by Johann Huizinga's *The Waning of the Middle Ages*. Huizinga's book had become a best seller and had greatly fashioned popular perceptions of the later medieval period, seen as one of decline and end of civilisation – but the book itself had been first published in 1919, in the immediate aftermath of the anger and pain of the First World War.

Bergman's hero character, Block, a knight returning from the Crusades in a Sweden devastated by the plague in 1350, has become an unbeliever against his will, and is thereby defined as a 'modern' character in the 1950s. He plays chess with Death, the master puppeteer behind all the above-mentioned calamities. As an intellectual, he eventually loses; the only winners, who escape Death, are a young couple with a new-born baby, the representatives of Life, who have the innocence of wandering players and live with very little, enjoying the simple pleasures of real love, plain food like milk and strawberries, and companionship. Just to make matters more complex, in true Bergmanian symbolic fashion, faith sneaks in through the back door, as the couple's names of Mary and Joseph suggest. Moreover, Christian symbols abound, for example, the milk and strawberries, both associated in Scandinavian lore with the Virgin Mary and with Sweden's national saint,

St Birgitta; and this very famous scene is often interpreted as both a kind of eucharistic communion, and a personal religious epiphany for Block. Bergman's love-hate relationship with Christianity is well-known and is especially obvious in this film. His expressed views at the time the film was made bear a striking similarity to those of artists as different as Ruskin, Pugin or Pasolini in their interest in the Middle Ages as a period of close-ness to the sacred: 'Regardless of my own beliefs and my own doubts, which are unimportant in this connection, it is my opinion that art lost its basic creative drive the moment it was separated from worship'.[54]

While the *Seventh Seal* is an earnest and meaningful parable, so is another film, possibly the most truly 'right' in terms of its understanding and use of medieval 'feel', spirit and atmosphere: *Monty Python and the Holy Grail*. The Monty Python team made another film set in the Middle Ages, *Time Bandits*, while Gilliam on his own then continued the medieval theme with *Jabberwocky* and more importantly *The Fisher King* in 1991. This was a modernised version of the quest for the Grail set in New York, transposing the quest in terms of the solidarity and complicity of a beggar and a DJ.[55] This stylistically innovative film did, in fact, return to the traditional 'prim-itivist' contrast between the myth of the Middle Ages as a period of wholeness with nature, of innocence, of faith and social cohesion, and the modern world, defined by homelessness, loneliness, alienation and social fragmentation. Terry Jones, incidentally a serious medieval scholar, also made a film set in the Middle Ages, *Erik the Viking*, confirming both the knowledge of the period by the Pythons, and its importance to them. None of these films though came anywhere near the brilliant 'take' of *The Holy Grail*. While many might only see it as an exceptionally funny piece of satire, the underlying erudition which enables the satire to function is staggering. Among numerous elements of this erudition are, for example, such appar-ently commonplace items as the Bridge of Death (an allusion to an old Welsh poem associated with Arthur)and the Trojan rabbit guarding the cave (another allusion, this time to the myth of the foundation of Britain by Bru-tus, who took refuge here from the Trojan War – a story recounted in 'Nennius' and Geoffrey of Monmouth).[56] At the same time, the burlesque takes on the 'great' themes of the medieval imaginary only function so well because they relate to the audience's own frame of cultural references: the quest, knighthood, the plague, kingship, virginity, purity and so on, for example in the famous Flagellants scene. This is further enriched with film history cultural references, in this case to Bergman's *Seventh Seal*, except that the Flagellants do not use flagellation, of course: instead, they bang their heads against wooden planks, creating humour out of the interplay of medieval chanting and the parody of modern despair. To the 'debunking' of modern academic interpretations of the Middle Ages, by Marxist historians for instance, is further added an ironical view of films such as Bresson's *Lancelot du Lac*, perceived by the Pythons as rather pretentious, in another wonderful parody of the 'duel' between Arthur and a knight, when the latter continues to fight even as his head, his arms, then his legs are cut off in turn, leaving only a leaping torso: presumably a reference to a similar, much weightier scene, in Bresson's film. *The Holy Grail* functions as a medieval play, a mixture of farce, morality play and sermon, with the slapstick, wit and profundity of these, in a way which Chaucer and later Shakespeare would have understood perfectly. That it should have been such a success with contemporary audiences, and one which would never be surpassed except by Monty Python's second and even better effort in *The Life of Brian*, bears testimony to the much greater subtlety of cinema-goers than the directors of historical pot-boilers could even dream of.

To these cinema films one could probably add a string of television adaptations set in the Middle Ages: *The Devil's Crown* in the 1970s, the 1994 Brother Cadfael stories in Britain, several purpose-written continental television series, such as the adventure children's series *Thierry-la-Fronde* (a French equivalent of Robin Hood) and *Quentin Durward*, the 1970s adaptation of Druon's *Les rois maudits*, the Italian-Franco-German biopic of Charlemagne, and the relatively recent French serialisation based on a famous episode from the *Histories* of Gregory of Tours, under the title *Wanda et les loups*. The latter presented an excellent portrayal of life in a sixth-century nunnery at Poitiers as depicted by one of our best medieval sources. The struggles involved in the fight with a harsh environment, slavery, disease, potential violence and the wolves literally at the door in the winter, may have been somewhat austere for a television audience taste. The choice of this particular, little known, medieval episode in the context of the 1990s and the emphasis set on the power and role of women in society may have also been a political and social one. At any rate, it was made with subtlety and the 'feel' of the time was very close to that gained from a reading of Gregory's text itself, written in the 590s. The most recent television film, the Franco-British *The Hour of the Pig*, was a wry and disillusioned story in which a Parisian lawyer decides to leave the equivalent of the fourteenth-century rat-race by going to practise in a small town in northern France. His naïve idealism leads him to try and teach the inhabitants to act more humanely than to put on trial a pig accused of murdering a child, without realising how deeply linked this weird practice happens to be to the murky underside of local power politics. Having failed to 'make a difference' and increasingly at risk himself, he decides that going back to the capital to make money as a lawyer in a corrupt world is his only way forward. A modern parable perhaps, but one showing some understanding of the subtleties of the medieval world, without either idealising or condemning it. Some might regard this as Middle Ages maturity.

Maturity could be seen as the complete opposite of the new genre of Hollywood pseudo-medieval productions known under the generic name of Heroic Fiction. This parallel to the literary genre of fantasy fiction, which began with Tolkien, has been fuelled by *Excalibur*, Japanese samurai films like *Kagemusha* and oriental martial arts films, and the plethora of 'Celtic'-style novels. The genre also has considerable affinities with science fiction.

The nineteenth-century code of Christian chivalry, still largely in use in Hollywood until the 1950s either in its traditional form with Arthurian films or in a disguised form through characters such as Zorro, the Scarlet Pimpernel, Beau Geste, Dick Tracy, Tarzan, Superman, Buck Rogers, Lew Archer and even RAF pilots, was heavily undermined during the 1960s.[57] Perceived as class-bound, patriarchal and inhibiting for personal freedom, this chivalrous role model lost its impact on young men, and a new image of masculinity came to the fore, that of the hero from Dark Age paganism. Directed at a young male audience which is supposed to feel attracted to it (unlike women who are catered for through the emphasis on sensitive, caring, New Man male figures), it includes large amounts of sex, violence, horror and a lack of any other religious element. Such are the characters portrayed by the likes of Charles Bronson, Sylvester Stallone in *Rambo*, and the *Mad Max* films. The main representative of the 'inarticulate Neanderthal thug'[58] is, of course, Arnold Schwarzenegger, and the best-known of these films are the *Conan* series, based on a character first set out in a popular book by R. E. Howard in 1932, *The Phoenix and the Sword*.[59]

Conan the Cimmerian, a 'dark hero in whose veins flowed the blood of Atlantis', was first used as the main character of John Milius's film *Conan the Barbarian* (1981), but became more of a Niebelung-type hero, partly to serve as a vehicle for Schwarzenegger, whose cinematic career it launched with great success. *Hawk the Slayer, Red Sonja, Army of Darkness, Dragonslayer, Galgameth, Sea Dragon* and numerous other such films made in the 1980s and 1990s are a composite of various themes: archaic (Prometheus and fire), Barbarian, Germanic, northern, Celtic, Oriental (ritual ceremonies, ritual fighting, yoga and zen, Buddhism, samurai), Arthurian (sacred sword), with the intention of producing a sort of model Viking warrior. The warrior does not usually fight for a cause, although sometimes he does so in order to exact revenge for a wrong done to him or his family, but mostly because he likes fighting for its own sake. Women too are warriors and love takes the form of affairs rather than undying romantic attachments. The basic ideology of these films appears to be one of 'freedom of the individual' rather than of a medieval hero who is part of a community (kingdom, fellowship) working for or against some authority, be it political or religious, or for a perceived greater goal or greater good. These films put forward an ideal based on a fundamental rejection of 'civilisation', regarded as decadent and corrupt, and the glorification of primitive violence and of fighting as the defining feature of masculine behaviour.[60]

A medieval theme remains present, however. In part this has to do with the time and place (some era in a pseudo-Barbarian or Viking age), in part with some debased ideas of chivalry (as something to do exclusively with brawn rather than brain). The story is basically one of initiation as an adult warrior into a fighting world, and a close link is forged between warrior and weapon, which harks back to the medieval association of knight and sword. The prominent position of the sword on the posters of the *Conan* films underlines this point visually. Such films have a link of sorts with the new Hollywood representations of medieval heroes such as Arthur and Robin Hood, who have themselves moved towards the green, eco-warrior, pagan model as in, for example, Boorman's *Excalibur* or Reynolds's *Robin Hood*.[61] In the Heroic Fiction mode, films like *Ladyhawke*, *Legend* or *Kull* all incorporate this green side, and the triumph of good over evil is ultimately dependent on the hero's understanding of, and respect for, nature. The ultimate example which closes the loop is the recent adaptation of Tolkien's *Lord of the Rings*, a much more complex version of such medieval fantasy fiction since it relies on a complex book, but visually belonging to a similar cinematic language.

This survey is by no means exhaustive. To make it so, one would have to add a whole range of films which do not fall easily into the above categories. Such examples would include *The Navigator: An Odyssey Across Time*, from New Zealand (director Vincent Ward, 1988), which sets out to show the parallel between the Black Death and AIDS, and to condemn the contemporary western world's loss of moral certainty in contrast with the richness of the medieval peoples' faith. More frivolous among antipodean productions is the Australian film from the musical *Grendel, Grendel, Grendel* (1981). Like it, *The Thirteenth Warrior* also used Beowulf as its basis, in Heroic Fiction mode, inserting such exotic touches as an Arab character travelling in the West, and elements akin to a Neolithic-style quest. The American film *The Midwife's Tale* (1996) retells Chaucer's tale in a feminist lesbian manner. *Laundamann Stauffacher*, a Swiss film about Wilhelm Tell made in 1941, could hardly have been a more open challenge to Nazi interests, and *El aliente del diablo* (1993) uses a medieval setting to put forward a message about current Spanish-Basque relations.[62]

Many films carried similar nationalistic messages by simply retelling the foundation myths of respective countries and exalting the role of their medieval rulers or saints and founders: Patrick (Ireland, 1920); Casimir the Great, Boleslaus II, the Teutonic Knights (Poland, 1975, 1971, 1960); Stephen the Great and Matthias Corvinus (Hungary, 1984, 1986); the saga of Olav (Norway, 1983 – this one a satirical spoof); and more sagas (Iceland, 1985, 1988).[63] Some of these films turned into aggressively patriotic propaganda, like the Serbian *Dorotej* (1980), while others, on the contrary, were seen as representing a militant but rebellious nationalism, as did Sergei Paradzhanov's *The Legend of Suram Fortress* (1984). One must assume that the Georgian director's international fame prevented him from having too much trouble with the Soviet authorities. One non-European example of the nationalistic use of the medieval period is Youssef Chahine's *Saladin*.[64] While following in the footsteps of western directors like Cecil B. de Mille who, inspired by Walter Scott's novel *The Talisman*, set during the Crusades, had made Saladin into a cultivated, pacifist Arab leader, Chahine used an Islamic slant to turn Saladin into a precursor of Nasser. The film was made in the year of the Suez crisis, and presented Nasser as the champion of Arab nationalism and unity, and the Arabs as peaceful victims of western aggression by the Crusaders. In fact, Nasser himself often used Saladin in his propaganda, comparing himself to him as a hero of unification; in more recent years, so did Saddam Hussein, for similar reasons, little realising that Saladin had been a Kurd.

It is not only possible, but taken for granted, that one can use the medieval period for a multitude of purposes, to make it say whatever one wishes to make it say because one can find in it whatever one wants to find in it. One last example, that of *El Cid*, provides an excellent illustration of the use of the Middle Ages for nationalist purposes, in this case in a way which began in the Middle Ages themselves. Though, of course, a Hollywood product, the film was made in Spain, and Charlton Heston in particular claimed to have taken great care with the historical details. These he checked with the film's historical adviser, a reputed Spanish literary specialist. This professor's association with the story focused on the text of the *Poema*, written well after the events it purports to relate, and already using the legend to turn the character of the Cid into the national hero of Spain. This went entirely against the grain of more contemporary texts, which described the Cid as a kind of mercenary *condottiere*, who fought mainly to defend his interests, and not rarely against his own king and against the

Christians, on the side of the Muslims. The latter slant on the myth was endorsed by Republican propaganda, which scholarship thus supported, and Franco himself liked to identify himself with the Cid. He notably commissioned a mural in which he had himself represented in the guise of the Cid, in medieval armour, holding a sword, and some of his speeches echo the opening of the poem very directly, with his comparison between his war and a crusade against the enemies of civilisation.[65]

Last but not least, mention must be made at least in passing of films either based on classic Gothic novels, for example, on Bram Stoker's *Dracula*, or on more modern ones, such as Anne Rice's *Interview with a Vampire*.[66] The lore of vampires, abandoned creaky houses, frightened heroines, the tradition of Gothic fear, monsters, phantoms and other such staple devices remain at the heart of these films, based on the original works of the same name, classics such as R. L. Stevenson's *Dr Jekyll and Mr Hyde*, Washington Irving's *Sleepy Hollow* and Daphne du Maurier's *Rebecca*, or modern classics such as Stephen King's *The Shining* and Angela Carter's *The Little Shop of Horrors*. The most famous may be Robert Bloch's story *Psycho*, on which Alfred Hitchcock's based one of his films. There is in these no overt medieval connection at all: directors, like their predecessors in print, use the Gothic as novels, stories and poetry did in the eighteenth, nineteenth and twentieth centuries, transforming it from a period into a mood. This was partly the attraction of horror films, the classic Hammer Studios offerings of the 1960s, the late 1960s ones by Hitchcock and Roman Polanski, the *Addams Family*, or the more recent, purely atmospheric films of David Lynch, for example his *Blue Velvet* (1986).

The treatment of the Middle Ages on film developed along two major lines. Hollywood cinema (which encompasses for this purpose the classic period pieces made in Italy and England in the 1950 and 1960s with a mixture of local and American input, artistic or financial) was interested in entertainment and escapism, with the general subliminal message of morality, political idealism and ultimately optimism and the final triumph of good over evil and of America over its enemies. Concealed behind the need to entertain the audience, and to provide them with a good yarn and plenty of local colour and special effects, this political and social message came from the studios and reflected their input. The 'message' of European films which, as auteur films, are more indifferent to the need to please and entertain the audience, reflects the directors' personal views. Both kinds of films are historically 'inaccurate', but for two totally different reasons: the American because it uses the period as a vehicle for a message through entertainment that has to be successful, the European because the films have no interest in matching the audience's views but rather in leading it to reflect on the director's preoccupations, expressed through his choice of themes. In both cases there was a deliberate choice on the studios' or the directors' part to set a film in this period. This was again done for different reasons: in Hollywood because of the potential for embroidering on adventures and local colour, in European films because directors like Bergman, Pasolini or Bresson matched their own preoccupations to themes which, rightly or wrongly, they saw as being particularly important to medieval people, such as mysticism or honour.

Poster for Vitraux 'Glacier', *c.* 1890. Recreating the Middle Ages at home in early advertising.

9

Selling the Middle Ages

It is a truth universally acknowledged that the Heritage Industry is big money; Jane Austen, who has become a major part of it, would have found this as much a source of wry amusement as Lizzie Bennett did when talking about the early nineteenth-century marriage industry. One can hardly doubt this fact when one watches the growing popularity of Heritage providers, from the main ones, such as the National Trust and English Heritage, to the smallest local charity. These have been set up in order to look after and run a variety of displays across Britain, from a piece of industrial archaeology such as a tin mine in Cornwall to a museum of everyday life. Just as significant are the extraordinary rise and impact of television programmes on history and archaeology, and the rising number of period dramas, and the increase of books and journals on history and archaeology on the market. Some magazines openly specialise in the field, for example, *Heritage: Britain's History and Countryside*. This book does not purport to examine the phenomenon as such. Others have examined the reasons for the success of the Heritage Industry,[1] while others again have discussed the issue from the providers' point of view.[2] My concern is to understand why it is that, both in the UK and in Continental Europe, and indeed in North America, the biggest attraction of the Heritage Industry remains the Middle Ages.

The Heritage Industry's use of Celtic Britain and of the Arthurian stories, books and films has already been examined.[3] What, might one ask, is there left? A great deal: for the perception of the medieval can hardly be expected to leave out such things as castles, cathedrals and abbeys, minstrels and medieval music, and generally the so-called 'everyday life' of people in the Middle Ages. Every issue of popular journals such as *History*, *History Today*, *Heritage* and others has at least one, more often two, major articles on medieval topics, 'in the footsteps of Chaucer's pilgrims', a 'journey through Celtic Britain', the history of a castle, a family and so on. In popular book club catalogues such as 'The History Book', where books are divided into broad categories such as the Ancient World, the Tudors, the Victorians, we find the two categories of the Medieval World and Celtic History, which together take by far the greatest amount of catalogue space. Another such book club divides its books into categories introduced by an overarching general sentence: 'Medieval Images of Faith and Piety' (books on the church and pilgrimages) and 'Champions and Chatelaines of the Middle Ages' (books on the crusades and knights). For a potentially different audience, one of teenagers and young people, which does not necessarily think in terms of books but of computer games, the same popularity accrues not only to the by now almost old-fashioned *Dungeons and Dragons*, but to CD-Rom games like 'The Guild', inviting one to

> step back in time to become the mayor of a miniature medieval town, bustling with authentic little tradesmen and townspeople. Starting as a landlord, shop keeper or other merchant, use your guile to get ahead in your chosen trade and gain favour and influence, while enjoying a real taste of the medieval life – from crowded taverns, to the glow of a blacksmith's forge. Zoom in to explore your city's streets and buildings at will, interacting with over 500 characters. Easy to play, hours of fun.

Heritage theme parks like the famous 'Shrewsbury Quest', based on Ellis Peters's Brother Cadfael novels, offer workshops in manuscript illumination or the cultivation of medicinal herbs, two activities eminently associated with Benedictine monks. The Jorvik Centre in York was regarded as a pioneering venture when it opened, enabling visitors to travel back through time to experience the 'sounds, sights and smells' of Viking York. The 'Towers of Eden' theme park, as advertised by the county of Cumbria, in a colourful 'illuminated manuscript' display, promises, in Gothic lettering and with coats of arms, 'five kingdoms, four castles, the treasure of Eden. A secret hidden for Three Thousand Year [sic]; a book, a treasure hunt, and a real life adventure – waiting for you in the North of England Today'. Medieval feasts and banquets are so popular, not only on the specialist circuit, that they have even become, on occasion, a part of corporate entertainment. A newspaper advert for The Medieval Banquet, London, with an email and website, invites the reader to 'come and join us in a medieval Pagaentry [sic] ... in this fulsome medieval feast amidst the light of flickering torches in the cellars ... Marvel at the battling knights and jesters [sic] antics and delight at the wenches [sic] caper. And after the merriment there is music and dance till late.' Does it matter to the people being entertained that knights did not battle at a feast, that the advertisers cannot spell, or that the costumes shown are mostly Tudor ones? Not a jot – what is this but a perfect opportunity to appear more cultivated than going clubbing, to titter at the 'wenches'' décolletage and to allow oneself to be transported to a period offering such hot-blooded fun?

Reproductions of medieval-style furniture, a fashion which began with the Gothic Revival in the nineteenth century and has continued ever since with

ever greater success, is currently matched by reproductions of medieval arte-
facts from museums and art collections, such as those from the British
Museum and British Library, the Victoria and Albert Museum and the Royal
Academy in London, the Ashmolean Museum in Oxford, the Louvre or
Cluny Museum in Paris, the Metropolitan and Cloisters Museum in New
York, and numerous others across Europe, typically of Virgin and Child
statuettes, pieces of jewellery, tapestries or ivories. Equally productive are
the 'medieval-style' objects sold by museums, especially at Christmas, or
firms like *Past Times*: table mats, ties, scarves, pendants, umbrellas, bags,
cushions, notelets and pads, calendars, bookends, with reproductions of
famous tapestries, stained glass and medieval themes or designs, fleur-de-
lys, mille-fleurs and tassels. This is in addition to the ubiquitous Christmas
cards, wrapping paper and other seasonal offerings, with reproductions of
medieval motifs. *Past Times* again, in its literature, covers the field. In its
medieval sections, 'a realm of fair maidens, troubadours and courtly love'
or 'the age of cathedrals', it sells objects such as carved caskets, wall sconces,
illuminated manuscript cushions, jackets and nightdresses, panels with
court or hunting scenes modelled on tapestries and, under the heading of
the 'medieval lady: the graceful maiden of Arthurian myth and legend',
objects supposedly associated with ladylike feminine occupations, rings,
writing paper, toiletries, gothic-shaped mirrors, cache-pots, lockets and
rings with exotic but (just) comprehensible French verse reminiscent of
courtly love. Even objects which signal a religious allegiance are more
acceptable under a medieval cover. Compilations of prayers, psalms, icons
and monastic offices are rendered palatable by being disguised as 'history'.
In an amusing 'medievalist' take on the Middle Ages, the same firm pro-
motes William Morris-inspired artefacts, themselves originally part of the
nineteenth-century medievalism of the Arts and Crafts movement. In a
recent development, the firm has extended its medieval range to cover
'Byzantine' objects – an added element of the exotic in this area.

As revealing as the objects themselves are the marketing techniques of
Past Times and other retailers when presenting their merchandise, for
example the changes in their catalogues over the years and the variations
at specific times of the year. When *Past Times* first arrived on the market,
it gave equal weight to objects under various headings: old catalogues
were divided into Roman, Anglo-Saxon, Viking, Celtic, Elizabethan or
Tudor, Georgian, Victorian, Other Lands (including Egypt, the East), and
Twentieth Century. Since then, various changes have taken place. The
medieval section now includes Anglo-Saxon, Viking, Later Medieval, and
even sometimes Celtic, all subsumed into the main selling point. This section is often placed at the beginning of the catalogue, especially at

Christmas, when the range expands to encompass seasonal objects, such as decorations, cards and wrapping paper. A whole range of products, notably Roman and Other Lands, has all but disappeared, or been remarketed as Indian, Byzantine, Eastern. The Twentieth Century, by now regarded as 'real' history, no longer has just one heading, but is separated into smaller sections: Edwardian, Art Nouveau, Art Deco, the War years, the Sixties. Another earlier category, Georgian, has also disappeared, in favour of a division between the Eighteenth Century, mostly understood as foreign (e.g. Sèvres, Capodimonte or Meissen porcelain, Aubusson tapestries), and Regency, the other great seller in the industry on account of the success of Jane Austen's novels in television serialisation or film. The commercial policies of the industry, going, as they do, with the flow of what sells, indicate very clearly that there are peak periods which attract customers for specific reasons, currently Regency and Twentieth Century being front runners. Then there is the Medieval and Celtic, which is a permanent fixture. It simply has ceased to be split into smaller, more 'scholarly' categories, to encompass within one mass Anglo-Saxon, Viking, Arthurian, monastic and chivalry objects, a formidable mixture in historical terms, but one which, one assumes, the retailer has been told by their advertising advisors, is all-powerful because the words *Medieval* and *Celtic* are the selling ones.

Another word of almost equal selling power is *Gothic*. We may have replaced the eighteenth- and nineteenth-century Gothic novel or Gothic Revival but the attraction of the word has been revived, once more signifying something to do with a Byronic Romantic fashion, against middle-class conventions and rules, with connotations of superiority through lack of conformity, exaggeration of emotion and flamboyance. The end of century Gothic is itself above all a manifestation of medievalism: but what it imitates or copies is not the medieval but nineteenth-century medievalism, even down to decorative styles. There is, appropriately enough, in an underground catacomb opening belonging to Camden Lock market in London, a workshop of furniture makers marketing its products as Gothic. Fantastic black wrought iron bedsteads, chairs and lamps with irregular and twisted shapes, using the Gothic arch as inspiration, are associated in their presentation with black or red fake fur and velvet furnishings and candles – the references are to both the imaginary world of Dracula or Frankenstein, and to William Morris. Even more evidently associated with the delicious thrills of the Frankenstein-style Gothic is the highly popular vampire look of the *Goth* image and subculture: young people dressed in black leather and velvet, wearing a profusion of chains and metallic jewellery including crosses as pendants and earrings, short spiky hair dyed black, with enamel-white face make-up complemented by deep-purple lipstick and nail varnish for girls.[4] The Goth culture may be simply one of surface and form, fuelled by heavy metal rock bands whose names have what is popularly perceived as medieval, Celtic or pagan associations: Avalon, Black Sabbath, Battle Axe, Mordred, Ostrogoth, Pestilence, Talisman. But it may also be a reflection of modern Romantic, anticonformist youth attitudes. That the 'look' of rebellion and difference should still be so strongly associated with the Gothic or 'medieval' is once again proof of the exceptional versatility and longevity of the concept.

The Heritage Industry is, above all, about marketing monuments and museums to visitors. A tour of the England and Wales to see what English Heritage and its Welsh equivalent prospectuses have to offer is most instructive.[5]

The area covered is divided, significantly, not into counties or administrative regions, but into historic regions with evocative names – Wessex, Northumbria, Cornwall. Castles of Devon is entitled *Mighty Fortresses and Romantic Ruins*, and offers 'Ghostly legends and medieval chivalry'. Wessex's *Ancient Peoples and Magical Settings* brochure offers 'Great castles and abbeys', Northumbria's *Historic Borderland of the North* 'battles for survival, saints preserved', and Cornwall's *Castles, Celts and Kings* 'mystery, myth and magic'. Other regions have been given half-modern names, mostly prefaced with 'Historic': East of England, East Midlands with 'Heroic tales, palaces of pleasure', West Midlands's *Royalty and Romance at England's Heart*, 'Ghosts and grandeur, atmospheric abbeys', and finally, Sussex, Surrey and Hampshire, which has *Castles, Battlefields and Abbeys*, 'Invasion, defence and daring deeds, medieval monarchs and monks'. These are only the titles. Inside the brochures descriptions follow of, for example, the site of the battle of Hastings and of Battle Abbey, the 'most famous date in English history', where the whole family is invited to 'let King Harold's mistress tell you what really happened – and stand on the very spot where Harold fell'. At Kenilworth Castle there follow, in this order, a Walter Scott quotation on 'this lordly place, where princes feasted and heroes fought', and the more naturalistic 'where Henry V rested after victory at Agincourt'. Okehampton Castle, 'medieval home of the Earls of Devon', and Ashby-de-la-Zouch Castle, where one is to stand 'in the footsteps of Ivanhoe', have both snob and romantic appeal. Churches too are taken on board: Lindisfarne Priory, 'cradle of Christianity, one of the holiest Anglo-Saxon sites in England'; Furness Abbey, where one can 'experience the grandeur of this 700-years old monastery', and, perhaps most revealing of all for the kind of ultimate experience sought by the visitor of the troubled present, Muchelney Abbey, 'where time has stood still'. Wales, whose equivalent body CADW is in charge of marketing Heritage, is similarly endowed with brochures describing, for example, 'the evocative ruins of Valle Crucis', a Cistercian abbey, including photographs of 'the nave looking West with white-robed Cistercian monk', presumably an extra hired to walk around dressed in costume to add verisimilitude to the site.

Descriptions are only the first point of contact. English Heritage, which offers interactive visiting, audiovisual displays and exhibitions also has, in each area, a whole range of events set up every year. Among the most frequent we have medieval entertainment, with jousting, displays of falconry, archery, music, 'meet a Viking', mumming, plays, story-telling, the arming of a knight and the dressing of a court lady, medieval tournaments, a 'strolling medieval minstrel', a medieval Christmas (or rather Yule Fayre), even a medieval murder mystery, and, naturally, re-enactments of battles such as Maldon, Hastings or Bosworth by local societies such as the Order of the Fighting Knights, who lovingly spend time and resources on recreating the right costumes, weapons, food and drink. English Heritage organises a whole range of such re-enactments of battles and tournaments throughout the year, for example at Hastings and Goodrich. But it also regards its brief as educational in terms of the daily life of the past. 'Come and see medieval knights fighting for their honour at the castle' and 'William versus Harold, who was the hero? Find out about the battle which changed England's history forever' are joined, in the 2003 Events brochure, by 'meet a Norman knight or Saxon warrior who will tell you their stories' and 'meet a Viking raider' as part of the Heroes and Villains of the Dark Ages. In another manifestation 'Brother Oswald and Sister Septima share with us their spooky tales'. Also available are a 'Birds of Prey Experience Day' with falconry displays, a portrayal of 'life during the reign of King Edwin of Northumberland, 627 AD', 'medieval games, authentic cures and folklore', 'the lavish social life of a royal court on tour as Richard III returns to his childhood home [with] entertainment staged for the monarch, such as drama, sport and music' and 'meet Ragnor Svensson the Viking and learn about Viking life'. Most of these activities are led by groups with evocative names such as The Lady and the Fool, The Vikings, Lammas, Early Medieval Alliance, Comitatus, War of the Roses Federation or the even more inventively named Crew of Patches, the latter inviting one to 'recreate the Arthurian legends on this magical day out. Become a knight of the round table and embark on the quest for the Holy Grail. Hear mythical tales of old about the great King Arthur and maybe learn a bit of magic!' These lines, with the combination of Arthur, knights, Grail, quest, tales of old, magic and myth, perfectly demonstrate what it is that maintains the prominence of the Middle Ages in the popular imagination.

While English Heritage is at the forefront of the medieval entertainment and leisure industry, with the largest means, publicity aids, and dissemination and educational programmes, they are by no means alone in their task. Local re-enactment societies and their extraordinary success have already been mentioned. Regional publicity exists in all areas, with pointers at places to visit and events to attend. Thus, for example, Essex County brochure suggests visits to anything from Mountfichet Castle and Norman village of 1066 to the fourteenth-century Thaxted Guildhall, twelfth-century churches, and fourteenth-century timber barns, as well as events such as jousting tournaments and medieval sieges. Individual museums and castles have followed the trend: the museum at Sutton Hoo, subtitled 'Warriors, Treasure, Kings' (a National Trust property), offers examples of 'how Anglo-Saxon nobles lived' as well as tours of the site and replicas of the treasure, which is itself, of course, in the British Museum, under heavy guard and protection. The separation of the original from the site, and the use of fakes on the site itself, is an interesting issue, linked to a whole range of problems of security as well as optimal conservation conditions. In 1986 in a revolutionary essay on fakes, entitled *Travels in Hyperreality*, the great Italian scholar and one of the leading intellectuals of the century Umberto Eco opened up a debate previously reserved to the elite of the conservation world.[6] He limited his discussion to the United States, analysing the demand, and indeed expectation, for more-real-than-real historical artefacts, meaning, to all intents and purposes, more or less total *reconstructions*, since there can only be, in the USA, bits and pieces of Old World history, imported and displayed at great expense. His analysis, extending as it did from the most outrageous manifestations of fake history, such as the bridal suites each decorated 'in' a historical period from prehistory to the Victorian via Louis XIV and Colonial Safari in the various Madonna Inns of California, to the 'tasteful' reconstructions of the missing links between parts of a cloister to make it 'feel more real' in the Getty Museum in Florida, has become a landmark in our questioning of our relationship with history and the fake. Now, twenty years later, in the age of computer archaeological reconstruction and interactive programmes and games, Eco must find even more cause for reflection.

The importance of the nostalgia element can be seen in other attempts at reviving medieval traditions, such as the annual Mystery Plays at York. An interesting analysis of the revival of a Mystery Play at Chester, in 1906–7 and again in 1951, has shown very clearly the evolution of popular perception and taste.[7] In the first instance a (bowdlerised) version was put on from a mixture of antiquarian interest and desire to educate the public and preserve a local tradition. In 1951 the same play, uncensored this time and thus preserving the original mix of the sacred and the bawdy, by then regarded as the only 'genuinely medieval' version acceptable, was partly revived as a public morale-booster during the austerity years, but also essentially as a nostalgia trip into a more innocent age.

Eco wrote about the American passion for recreating a 'real' past, and therefore one which could only be proportionately more 'fake' the more it tried to be perfectly 'realistic'. The United States has long been one of the most avid consumer and importer of the medieval European past, notably in the age of nineteenth-century millionaires travelling around Europe to buy columns from the cloisters of Moissac, illuminated manuscripts and a large range of artefacts to be found now in places such as the Cloisters Museum or the Pierpont Morgan in New York. But the fashion did not stop there, either chronologically or socially. It continued to be popular, indeed increasingly so, and broadened its spectrum and audience. In 1996 I found myself wandering, by chance, through a 'Mediaeval Day' in one of New York's parks; it had all the hallmarks of what we might call in Britain a New Age Festival, with a great deal of creative scope for improvisation in terms of 'medieval' clothes, beads, food, music, mead and general manifestations of 'alternative' culture. The very fact that the American spelling of the world, even in the field of scholarship, has often retained the old-style *mediaeval* rather than the European simplified *medieval* suggests the importance of the nostalgia factor for the evocative and the distant past. The fair could be regarded as the extreme manifestation of 'reinterpretation' of the period to fit the needs of an alternative lifestyle, if only for a day, in the kind of nostalgia trip which enables one to have access to what is perceived to have been a 'better', less stressful, more caring and nature-loving age.

Is the nostalgia limited to the English-speaking, 'driven', 'savagely capitalistic' world of the last twenty years? What of continental Europe? France, for example, has its share of medieval re-enactments, theme parks and spectacular *Son et Lumière* displays recounting the history of a place on stage, complete with costumes, text, music, fights and riding, at various castles, such as the well-known version of Le Lude in Anjou. The theme park of Puy du Fou in Vendée is, however, more in the nature of a 'day in the past' in general: while it offers a fortified castle complete with siege and battles, and a medieval city with old trades, jugglers and minstrels, hunting and falconry in the woods and so on, it is only a part of a history park, which also incorporates a Gallo-Roman amphitheatre with gladiatorial fights, a Renaissance castle and an eighteenth-century village; a kind of supermarket of history, meant to be a family day-out for entertainment but also for educational purposes. There are more specifically medieval events. In 2001 Provins had a 'Fête Médiévale'. More significant, however, are events repeated every year. At Sainte Suzanne in Normandy, there is an annual feast around the castle, in which the whole town takes part, in medieval dress, with events such as jousting, juggling and all the usual displays; it is a fairly recent development, and certainly profiting from the tourist market in the area. At Crèvecoeur, also in Normandy, a medieval site contains exhibitions around the 'lord's land' and the 'timbered buildings', with an annual festival called 'Les médié-vales', advertised thus: 'Come and discover the everyday life of a manor house with lords, knights, servants and craftsmen: they will give you a taste of their meals, their music and their pastimes – not forgetting the arts of war. The Middle Ages awaits you!' A few years ago, when staying at an old priory with a large park on the Normandy-Anjou border, I was somewhat startled to see preparations for a medieval banquet, and our hostess, like everyone else around, appearing in full medieval dress at tea-time: they were hosting a local wedding where the bride had decided to have the whole cer-emony as a medieval feast. It is interesting to note that most places mentioned so far, those best known for such events, are in fact situated in or near Normandy, and one may well ask oneself if there is some meaning in the historical and cultural proximity with England. One exception of some importance is associated with Burgundy, an area full of Romanesque churches but on the whole prouder of its ancient Gallic past (the battle of Alésia between Caesar and Astérix, as one of my students once put it to me). It is a project of rebuilding the thirteenth-century castle of Guédelon by local and other volunteers, helped by masons, carpenters, ropemakers, pot-ters and other craftsmen employed on the site full-time, using medieval tools and materials. The project, funded with public money, is scheduled to last twenty years, a sobering thought for twenty-first-century builders and those who commission them.

Italy has, so far, relatively little by way of medieval reconstructions. One might think that, here, popular perception would see the Roman period, or the Renaissance, as the highlights of the nation's past (even though, from a historian's point of view, the city republics of the late Middle Ages, Venice, Florence, Milan, Siena and others, with their trade and banking, artists like Giotto, Fra Angelico and Dante, or the papacy in Rome, belonged to equally glamorous as well as decisive periods in the history of Italy). We could thus expect the Heritage Industry to go at least for Ancient Rome or the Renais-sance. This is, however, not the case, and there are no Julius Caesar or Borgia festivals. Italy has been a conglomerate of small territorial units until the late nineteenth century and, many would claim, still is one, despite uni-fication. Almost every one of these areas or cities had its own major medieval traditions, mostly religious, which continued unabated over the centuries, known only to the local inhabitants and faithfully carried out by them every year: saints' days processions such as San Gennaro's in Naples, the Festa delle Cere in Gubbio, the Palio in Siena, and many others far too numerous to detail here. In the same way medieval festivals, Easter processions in Spain, the Binche Carnival in Belgium, the Pardons in Brittany are all still there, not as the result of the leisure and tourist industry, but as part of the past of the city, with a real medieval origin, and an unbroken tradition over the centuries. Certainly, there are 'medieval' manifestations in many parts of continental Europe. We find 'medieval markets' in some German towns like Aachen; a major celebration of the town's foundation 1000 years ago, in costume and with 'medieval entertainment' in even as small and relatively insignificant city as Bautzen (on the border of Germany, the Czech Republic and Poland); and medieval feast days when the whole town dresses up the part in the small town of Visby in Sweden. Even the Venice Carnival is a revival of an event that died out two hundred years ago, and the Oberammergau Passion Play in Bavaria was itself a medievalist seventeenth-century reinvention of a (probable) medieval event. But, on the whole, most parts of continental Europe do not actually need to recreate a medieval past; it has remained part of their landscape, especially in Catholic countries where there is continuity with medieval festivals for the local patron saint or a pilgrimage associated with a church feast. In some ways, this is the 'real Middle Ages', which many can even allow themselves to dismiss if they so wish, on the grounds of what they might regard as its negative side: oppressive, credulous, rigid and dangerous, but one which is not reinvented and continues to exist because a whole community sees it as part and parcel of its identity. Thus one can separate a local traditional festival with medieval origins, such as a Breton Pardon or an Italian patronal festival, from more general, sometimes negative connotations attached to the Middle Ages. This is still especially important in Germany, where the post-war trauma of Wagner's role, the Teutonic Knights or the exaltation of Frederick Barbarossa may still have an unpleasant ring to them, and where it is more acceptable to mediate the medieval through the spectrum of Romanticism, Heine's 'Lorelei', Ludwig II's Neuschwanstein or Kleist's plays. Other European countries too promote their medieval towns, castles, churches and monuments as tourist attractions, often with the by now required guides, postcards, CDs and websites: medieval cities in Switzerland and Austria, painted monasteries in Bulgaria and Romania, the Old Town in Prague, and innumerable others. They are there for one to visit and see, to attract visitors and money, but not actually to construct a 'new' medieval world attached to them, complete with accessories.

Back to Britain. Having just come across an advertisement in a national newspaper, which has apparently also run in some specialised magazines destined for theatre and literary people, I find that I am invited to apply, should I so wish, for the post of hermit on a National Trust property for two days. The Project Manager (how does one manage a hermit?) wishes to 'explore the nature of solitude and whether it has any resonance in the twenty-first century', and offers the chance to somebody to live in a tent near a cave, and thus provide the kind of resident pet hermit which an eighteenth-century landowner might have had living on his property, itself an eighteenth-century take on medievalism in the first place. This resident hermit, who is to be paid out of Staffordshire County Council funds, is there to provide a 'philosophical critique of the world in which we live ... an anti-dote to Big Brother reality television'. Apparently one hundred and fifty people have already applied; definitely more than would have been interested in doing so even at the height of the eremitic revival of the twelfth century – but if living in a forest was rather harder then, it is significant that the appeal to the bucolic and spiritual streak is once again regarded as the antidote to the stresses of living 'in the world'.

And this is, of course, what the appeal of the Middle Ages in general, and thus the impact of it within the Heritage Industry, is all about.

10

Which Middle Ages?

As soon as people started to see themselves as having left medieval times behind them, especially in England during the Tudor period and in sixteenth-century France, a nostalgia for what had been left behind emerged. The medieval past was used to lend authority to various changes, notably in politics. The new Tudor dynasty sought to legitimise itself through establishing its descent from King Arthur, and lawyers and philosophers in France attempted to find in medieval precedent a solution to the troubles generated by religious conflicts in their own time. In England, the risk to those interested in the Middle Ages that they might be suspected of Catholic sympathies was in fact minimal, since Anglican churchmen and apologists for the Reformation itself began seeking its roots in the history of the 'primitive' and 'pure' English church of the Venerable Bede. Medievalism was used to promote change by allegedly returning to the status quo of the medieval past.

From the seventeenth century onwards, the search for roots and vindication in the medieval period was used in the opposite way, too, justifying the revolutionary movements of the Civil War and the Commonwealth, and opposition to the established regime in constitutional, political and legal terms. A leading example of this was the 'Norman Yoke' theory which, through its exaltation of the alleged freedom of the Saxons before the Norman Conquest, supported the rise of Parliament and limitations on royal power in England. At the same time, the destruction wrought by the Civil War on churches, medieval monuments and artefacts allegedly tainted by 'popishness' gave rise to a fear of obliteration of the past among many in England. This led to a developing taste for examining the past and studying its remains, which in turn promoted the expansion of antiquarianism and the collection of medieval artefacts on a large scale in the seventeenth and eighteenth centuries. Gradually these remains themselves served to support the consolidation of national pride, contributing to the building up of a British national identity during the eighteenth century, at a time when Britain was constantly at war with various continental powers, notably France. As against France, England set itself up as the country of liberties inherited from its medieval founders led by King Alfred, justifying it in fighting French absolutism. It was in that context that the word 'Gothic' in English (and later in German) came to mean, in a medievalist sense, everything medieval. In contrast, in eighteenth- or nineteenth-century France *'Gothique'* continued to be used only for the art and architecture of the thirteenth century.

The creation of political and social myths, including the fight for the 'freedom of the ancestors' and the harmony of social relations, was the first form of medievalism. Another major political myth, of great importance in the nineteenth and twentieth centuries, and often associated with the medieval past, was nationalism. Scholars are still debating whether nationalism only really began in the late eighteenth century as a result of the American and French Revolutions, and of the Napoleonic Wars in Europe, or whether it actually began in the Middle Ages in western Europe, or in the sixteenth century with the Tudors in England. Even if one accepts that national feeling developed early in England, France or Spain, it certainly became much more visible and more widespread in the nineteenth century, when many European nation states either gained or regained their independence and unity.

Nationalism in relation to the medieval past usually took one of two forms. For some peoples, it was one of *peace with their past*: this past was accepted as *past* and the medieval period as *gone*, rather than as something continuously overshadowing the present and driving people to re-enact the battles of the past. This kind of nationalism, in countries such as England, France, but also in Italy and most of Scandinavia, could be defined as 'patriotism' or 'national pride'. It did not necessarily entail fighting against others and excluding them because they were regarded as inferiors. The length of time since historic unity and independence had been achieved was not usually a determining factor in the success or otherwise of achieving such acceptance. Although England had been unified and independent since at least the ninth century and Italy not before the nineteenth, but both succeeded in accepting their past *as past*. Neither was the success dependent on whether a country was Catholic or Protestant: Catholic France or Italy have had an easier relationship with their past than Protestant Germany. Two similarly Protestant-dominated countries, England and Germany, displayed contrasting attitudes in their relationships with the past: England made peace with it, while Germany provided the most extreme example of ultra 'exclusionist' attitudes in the first half of the twentieth century, with antisemitism ultimately leading to the Holocaust. Healthy 'national pride', through valuing one's history and culture, can also go hand in hand with the acceptance of political belonging to a greater political unit, in the tradition of the supranational medieval, as shown by the Habsburg Empire, which saw regional individuality prosper under the umbrella of a 'greater' unity. Such a goal is perhaps part of the agenda of the European Union, which sees itself in many respects as the heir to the medieval empire.

The second kind of relationship with the medieval presupposes a very different perception of the national past. This past is not perceived as being 'dead and buried', but is, on the contrary, constantly resurrected as a justification for present policies and insuperable enmities. This is particularly the case in south-eastern Europe and the Balkans, where it still informs inter-ethnic conflicts based on resentments about land, language and religion, and reinforces perennial hatreds. Such attitudes have been sometimes, though by no means exclusively, associated with Orthodox countries. Medieval history itself provides, in several of these cases, a possible explanation of this close interrelation of, and interdependence between, the Orthodox Church and nationalism, as the example of Serbia shows. In its early days within the Byzantine Empire, the church, which became the Orthodox Church in the eleventh century, was much more subservient to the emperors than was the Church of Rome towards western emperors. This led to a tradition of pliability by the ecclesiastical establishment towards political power, which lasted throughout the refounding of the new nation states of the nineteenth century, such as Serbia, Bulgaria and Greece, and often into their recent history as Communist or right-wing dictatorships.

Being allowed to live and function as a church often depended on accommodation with the state. When many of these Balkan kingdoms disappeared, losing their independence and identity in the fifteenth and sixteenth centuries after being incorporated into the Islamic Ottoman empire, the church was the only aspect of national identity allowed to survive. The alliance between national feeling and Orthodox Christianity became a lifeline and, by the same token, the two came to identify with one another. The post-1990 situation, to that extent, has only exacerbated nationalistic memories rather than bringing about *peace with the past*, all the more so in those areas where even Communism appeared to be less of an enemy than the subsequent rise of materialism and western, American-style culture. The division between countries where nationalism means 'national pride' and those where it means 'death to our enemies' increasingly corresponds, in recent years, to West versus East, old versus new states, more so than it ever did previously. While the nation state of nineteenth-century creation was not in itself an impediment to the development of healthy nationalism, many of the newer states seem to have taken on the more 'unhealthy' version. Such broad statements need qualification, with the well-known exceptions of Nazi Germany in the past, but also with the 'unhealthy' examples of today's Irish, Basque or Corsican nationalism in today's western

Europe. Things are constantly changing in this area, too, and English nation-alism, dormant for a long time, is now burgeoning again, alongside the weakening of the Union and the political rise of its 'Celtic fringes'. Sport has been often related to this phenomenon, in England as elsewhere.

Nostalgia for the Middle Ages, which began in the sixteenth century as mourning for the loss of an ideal world of freedom and for the age of chivalry and romance, continued for the next two centuries. By the late eigh-teenth, even the representatives of the Enlightenment such as Edmund Burke were expressing sadness at the passing of the great age of chivalry, and were putting forward the idea that English national identity (like any other in Europe) was rooted in its medieval past, arguing, against one of the most obtrusive of the Enlightenment's values, for the indispensability of this past. Escapism into a world of fantasy, through literature, poetry, art or music, continued this tradition. It often involved a search for an ideal perceived as being more *authentic* in a Romantic sense, notably a return to nature, the country, wholesome and pure ways, attitudes, products and spiritual efforts. From the mid eighteenth century medievalism was a permanent component of Romanticism.

The nostalgia did not stop there. The Gothic Revival in literature, art and architecture was paralleled by nostalgia for a perceived golden age of feu-dalism, for a patriarchal society in which the rich (especially the nobles and the church) looked after the poor, on the basis of *noblesse oblige*; an age in which social cohesion, founded on family and social obligations, was the fundamental bond for a mutually beneficial social order. This was the ulti-mate 'dream of order', the dream of nineteenth-century society to be part, once again, of an ordered universe, made of harmony, social cohesion, faith and creativity. These idealised Middle Ages were meant to be a corrective to the evils of the present. In the aftermath of the Agricultural and Industrial Revolutions, Victorians saw the yeoman class fast disappearing. In its place they witnessed the rise of industrialism and, with it, of an impoverished working class living in urban misery, exploited, diseased, hungry and totally alienated, once the traditional social structures of family and parish had broken down. Within the new social and economic framework, the rules were those of *laissez-faire* capitalism, belief in technological progress as the ultimate goal, and a competitive economic system based on the ideology of utilitarianism rather than on a communally regulated system of work.

Until the latter half of the nineteenth century the two major opponents to the new system, who both looked back to the medieval age as a model, were, on the one hand, the landed aristocracy and gentry, and on the other, the working class itself. The first felt a patriarchal responsibility for the poor, and attempted to reassert the feudal ideal of a social hierarchy with mutual responsibilities through an alliance of noblemen and the poor. Political representatives of this category in England hoped to achieve a reorganisation of society on the basis of small, closely-knit social structures, in which wealth would carry with it social responsibility, restoring a chain of mutual dependency of social groups. The working classes, rural and urban, who lamented the loss of the traditional rural backbone of English society, the free peasant, and with it the freedoms and structures which had kept this society alive, were the second category to use the Middle Ages as a way of criticising their own era and its faults. At a later stage, as extreme poverty was better managed and the worst of economic hardship was relieved through new national and local institutions which took the place of the traditional ones of parish, manor and church, medievalism also changed. The rising middle classes, which had until then only been interested in the Middle Ages as an aesthetic concept for their literature, paintings and houses, joined the fight, less in order to improve material conditions than to restore a better quality of life to the workers, whom they perceived as being enslaved by machines and alienated from the creative part of their work.

The need to bring society back in touch with nature and to harmony with the world, and to allow for the exercise of men's creative powers and joy in this creation, harked back to the traditional Romantic dreams of a return to nature, an exaltation of the 'primitive', the organic, the emotions, the supernatural, in opposition to the intellectual utilitarianism inherited from the so-called Age of Reason of the eighteenth century, as well as from the mechanisation of life. John Ruskin and William Morris are the best-known exponents of these themes, both highlighting the themes of joy in labour and creation of the medieval craftsman and artist. English (and later American) society was the first to experience the Agricultural and Industrial Revolutions and the rise of capitalism, and thus to be cut off from the country and land-based culture of pre-industrial Europe. In addition, Protestantism brought a discontinuity with the past in a way which Catholic countries did not experience to the same extent, since existing festivals, pilgrimages and almsgiving practices remained unbroken there. In part as a result of this, there was nostalgia for this order and for the idealised lifestyle and society of the Middle Ages, which identified it with a supposedly idyllic past.

Englishness as an identity has also often been associated with loss and nostalgia. It can be found, for example, in attachment to the monarchy, the Church of England and the language of the Authorised Version, but also in nostalgia for the village green and the church spire, old festivals and old houses in the country, and 'old ladies cycling away in the mist, village cricket and warm beer'. It is hardly surprising that John Major's speech at

Mansion House in 1993 may well be what he will be best remembered for. The Englishman's ideal of the countryside has been seen by Jeremy Paxman as one of the most fundamental traits of the modern English 'character', even when the English live in a country where less than 1 per cent of the population makes its livelihood from the land.[1] This harks back to a tradition of successful tradesmen, merchants, bankers and other professionals over several centuries, whereby having made enough money, they acquired an estate in the country with the land and status that belonged to it: only then could they begin to regard themselves as having 'arrived'.

From the moment that serious economic and social change came to be perceived as irreversible in the late eighteenth century, and the world which still linked with the Middle Ages was felt to be fast disappearing, the medieval became, on the one hand, properly 'dead' and, on the other, something to be cherished, studied and, more and more, 'resurrected', through fantasy and 'heritage' reconstructions. In the nineteenth century, when there was still much of the 'old world' around, attempts were made to remodel contemporary society by incorporating into it the best of medieval features, including chivalry as a model for behaviour and guilds as models for work places. By the twentieth century all of this world was definitely gone, and hence perceived as a 'museum piece'. As a result nostalgia through fantasy, books and films, and reconstructions, took on a new dimension.

The difference between pre twentieth-century escapism and the modern version is one of emphasis rather than of nature. The thirst for spiritual uplift has moved from the pursuit of an ideal reformed church to that of an attraction towards the alleged pre-Christian truths of paganism and esoteric practices. The backlash against artificial, high-tech medicine has led to the valuing of 'natural health' and organic produce. These trends have developed in recent decades, often based on the assumption that they reflect a world closer to the medieval period. Yet another form of medievalism, already at work during the Gothic Revival with fake medieval designs, objects and furnishings, has now reached unexpected heights in the so-called Heritage Industry, with its bonanza of imitation medieval artefacts and historical re-enactments, together with theme parks, a vast popular literature and history programmes on television. Lastly, where before 1900 medievalism was received either through the written word in literature, poetry or historical novels, or through fixed images in paintings and illustrations of all kinds, the twentieth century had, in addition, the vast resources of the new popular medium of film at its disposal. The same stories and myths could be reused and even more successfully disseminated to large audiences, becoming associated with the glamour of particular stars and the visual impact of this most powerful and versatile tool.

The wide variety of groups and individuals who looked back and appealed to the model of the Middle Ages often did so with reference to very different aspects of the period. They sometimes interpreted the same things in very different if not downright contradictory ways. Augustus Welby Pugin and John Ruskin both regarded medieval architecture as the ultimate in European art on account of its roots in Christianity, but they had very different views on how far they needed to go to put their theories into practice. Pugin converted to Roman Catholicism, which he saw as the soul of medieval life; Ruskin did not. Disraeli and his upper-class friends were fundamentally conservative in their nostalgia for the feudal world, which they saw as the epitome of medieval society. The middle classes in the north of England, while building grandiose civic buildings such as town halls, art galleries, schools, churches and railway stations in Gothic style, looked back on the medieval as the age of municipal freedom and of trade and manufacturing, with the tradesmen, merchants and craftsmen of Flanders and Italy being their predecessors. William Morris and his political friends insisted on the political revolution of a John Ball and the Peasants' Revolt as a model for contemporary socialist ideas, some of which later developed into the model of the Welfare State.

Already in the sixteenth and seventeenth centuries the Middle Ages were held as a model for both continuity and change, conservatism and challenges to authority. They have never ceased to be used in both ways, indeed in a multitude of ways, to support a variety of points of view, often opposing each other, and that is still very much the case today. This is hardly surprising since there was always a tendency to talk about the 'Middle Ages' as though the period did not, in fact, cover ten centuries. Most people do not find it difficult to accept that the world has changed radically between the year 1000 and today or, for that matter, between 1945 and today – but they rarely translate this into the awareness that, during the thousand years of medieval history, society, politics, culture, religion and art did not stand still. Hence the temptation, as well as the inclination, to choose particular aspects of the medieval period, to prove whatever one wants.

We also regularly encounter the intriguing phenomenon of a double-sided perception of the 'medieval' concept itself. There was, from the first, both fascination with the better, more Romantic, more authentic Middle Ages, and a rejection of the perceived barbaric, rough, alien, negative, oppressive, anti-modern Middle Ages. In some cultures like Italy, the latter perception had a much longer lifespan, and remained predominant until very recently, when widespread popularisation of scholarly research and the prestige of Umberto Eco has made the medieval period more fashionable. Even in France, where medievalism has a long history, the association of the medieval with the barbaric is far from dead. As recently as 1993, a well known French philosopher and historian, Alain Minc, wrote a book entitled *Le nouveau Moyen Age*, which made the headlines.[2] His basic argument was that, after the collapse of Communism, which was the last serious political world ideology, the modern word has made away with any overarching form of government principle, that it has seen the debasement of 'reason' and the discrediting of modernity with its attendant beliefs in order, progress and certainty. All these have been replaced by a diversity of styles of government, an end to shared common values, widespread immigration leading to strong xenophobia, a return to tribalism, the rise of religious fanaticism and political extremism, and the replacement of optimism, due to a belief in progress, by pessimism. The parallels between the end of the Roman world and the beginnings of what the author terms the 'Dark Ages' are illustrated by other political and social factors. These include the multiplication of civil wars, national break ups and separatist movements, the rise of a marginalised young unemployed population as a result of the breakdown of families, criminal armed bands and drug barons, outlaw states and generalised government corruption. All this in a world without any shared values, ideas and principles, where the only driving force is the law of the market. Whatever views one may have about Minc's philosophical and political approach, his essential argument remains that we are moving towards a 'new Middle Ages', epitomised for him by all these negative elements.

In the English-speaking world the derogatory use of 'Middle Ages' and 'medieval', and of words associated with the period, continues. Here are two examples picked up at random. A famous journalist, Fergal Keane, once said in a public lecture that he feared the popularity of the television series the *X-Files* threatened to replace serious reporting by the 'rumour-ridden gloom of the Middle Ages'; in an article in the *Independent* newspaper before the second Iraq War, another journalist used the following rhetoric to convince his audience of the awfulness of the Iraqi regime: 'It takes quite a lot of to evoke sympathy for the head-chopping, hand-severing, anti-feminist, misogynist, *feudal*, anti-democratic Saudis'. It is interesting to see such examples often come from the world of journalism, indicating that the audience is expected to think in the same way, since journalese is supposed to be a public-friendly language and to reflect popular opinion.

In the English-speaking world, however, a 'positive' perception of the Middle Ages has been competing with a negative one for a long time, and still does. Positive glimmers emerge every now and again. During a heated UN debate about the merits of engaging in war in Iraq, a French minister claimed to speak as the representative of 'an old country' (meaning one which, unlike America, knew the heavy price of war); when beginning his speech, the English Foreign Secretary countered this by claiming to speak as the representative of an 'old country founded in 1066', a formula which he obviously regarded as an example of one-upmanship. While his historical grasp may be debatable, he clearly thought this to be an unanswerable example of venerable antiquity and ethnic rootedness that would be immediately understood by his audience.

The nationalistic (or ethnic) element, which associates the period with the origins myth of a people, place or nation, is just one of the features associated with medievalism. It may seem a modern development, especially in the case of Celtic identity, but it was in fact already present in past centuries, for example in the rise of national consciousness and of Celtic studies in the eighteenth century. Ecological associations also go back at least to the eighteenth century, Romanticism and the return to nature. The stories used by cinema were equally popular before the twentieth century, though in different forms, notably the historical novel, poetry and art, while fantasy fiction and detective stories were preceded by the Gothic novel and the Fantastic literature of nineteenth- and early twentieth-century literature. The Middle Ages, which seem to epitomise in so many ways the pre-modern world through their values of spirituality and understanding of the sacred, community, and purity of nature as opposed to the industrial and the artificial, offer a refuge for those who would like to return to non-materialist and anti-capitalist values, to a comprehensible rather than global culture. They allow a rebellion against the perceived forces of the rational and masculine in favour of the feminine emotion and intuition. (Whether any of this actually applies to the medieval period is entirely irrelevant in this context.) Many seek their roots in this golden age and are able to cite at least some of the medieval legacies to the modern world, if only in the monarchy and the church.

Umberto Eco has argued that that there are numerous aspects of the modern world which reproduce medieval patterns, often for the same reasons.[3] Examples include the insecurity of travel and of urban life, which have led many to abandon the city centre for the suburbs (the nearest most can afford as a substitute countryside); the reassertion of a culture of the *visual*, rather than the written one of the 'Gutenberg Galaxy' (signs and images cater for a much more shakily literate majority than was the case in the recent past, and images and cathedral sculptures are replaced by road signs and moving pictures); an apocalyptic perception of the future of mankind; and the use of role-models on the basis of their personal charisma, with pop stars, footballers and Princess Diana as replacements for medieval saints.

The issue of popular culture is thereby brought to the fore. Throughout western Europe, including England, between the sixteenth and the early nineteenth centuries, history belonged to the arena of public debate for everyone who could claim to know enough to engage in it. This tradition has remained alive to a certain extent in countries like Italy and France (and in those countries whose educational system has been modelled on them, for example in Central Europe), where it is regarded as a legitimate part of public debate by the intellectual elites. Some attempts were made in England in the nineteenth century to preserve this tradition, through the availability of major medieval works published in translation in popular editions such as Bohn's Library or Everyman. After the mid eighteenth century, however, the 'non-scientific approach', which had previously prevailed in the works of antiquaries and collectors of ballads, who mixed medieval material and their own imitations thereof, was becoming no longer acceptable. (When Bishop Percy introduced his own poetry as part of a medieval collection in 1745, nobody saw this as a problem; when Chatterton's 'forgery' in his Rowley ballads was made public, he was disgraced, which is said to have contributed to his suicide.) The antiquary and historian were no longer associated with poetic fantasy: 'literature' was just that, whereas history had become a 'science'.

Gradually this science, in the form of academic history, became the prerogative of an elite, while popular medievalism, not interested in historical accuracy but in fantasy, found a refuge in romances, chapbooks, historical novels – the very audiences which make up so much of the readership of modern fantasy fiction, detective fiction and film. In the early nineteenth century already Jane Austen's Catherine Morland claimed not to be interested in history, which represented for her 'dry-as-dust tomes about kings and battles', but she avidly read Gothic novels set in the past. Nowadays, she might have also chosen popular history journals or television programmes, Hollywood blockbusters about Robin Hood or Braveheart – some of the very things that 'serious' medieval historians might complain about as misleading and inaccurate. Unless English historians, like their colleagues in some other European countries, also take to translating current academic research and views into a form suitable for a general, moderately cultivated audience, the gap between academic and popular history will remain, allowing people to talk about a set-up as 'positively feudal', whilst devouring the complete works of Ellis Peters.

The thirst for high-quality popular medieval history is only too evident from the success of specialist book clubs, the popularity of television programmes on medieval history and archaeology, and major international exhibitions, just as the thirst for the imagined Middle Ages leads people to visit sites and monuments and theme parks, and to watch or participate in historical reconstruction and re-enactments. The time may have come for the wheel to turn full circle, back to when the Middle Ages were not only part of the popular imagination but also part of popular knowledge and public debate. For this to happen, it would be necessary to teach the period in school to children as a component part of their general culture; to have Heritage bodies carry out research and use it to produce good popular history both on their sites and through their literature; and to disseminate good historical research from the world of academia to that of the reading public, through books or through those exceedingly efficient contemporary media: television, the Internet and CD-Roms, and history magazines. In the eighteenth century before the age of university-based research, the perception of the Middle Ages was, by today's standards, a fantasy equally open to all. Since then, the more specialised academic historical research has become and the more it has parted company with the perception of the general public, a lack of dialogue which often leads most people to have their Middle Ages stuck in a Walter Scott/Hollywood timewarp. Does this matter? Perhaps not, at least within the framework of the relatively unfettered 'liberal' societies, where a peaceful relationship with the past is generally accepted. It does matter very much in those times and places where the idea of the Middle Ages can be manipulated to suit a particular political agenda, as it has done in Germany, Russia or the Balkans, or when the medieval is equally misused for purposes such as the Holy Blood conspiracy theories. Above all, however, it seems a pity that the historic Middle Ages, which is every bit as fascinating as the imaginary one for our societies which seek their rootedness in the past and wish to understand the genesis and development of the world we live in, not to be allowed access to the historical material itself, and its good commentators. Good quality, accessible history, in the tradition of Umberto Eco or Carlo Ginzburg in Italy or Georges Duby and Emmanuel Le Roy Ladurie in France, is possible in England: the success of Roy Strong, Simon Schama, Michael Wood and others has proved it conclusively. The market for medievalism is out there, as it has been for the last five hundred years – which, among other things, is what this book has attempted to show.

Notes

Notes to Introduction

1. U. Eco, 'Dreaming the Middle Ages', in his *Travels in Hyperreality* (trans., London, 1986)
2. Thus, for example, the story of Faust, a characteristically sixteenth-century myth, is assumed to have been medieval.
3. A. Chandler, *A Dream of Order: The Medieval Ideal in Nineteenth-Century Literature* (Lincoln, Nebraska, 1970); C. A. Simmons, ed., *Medievalism and the Quest for the 'Real' Middle Ages* (London, 2001); C. Dellheim, 'Interpreting Victorian Medievalism', in F. Boos, ed., *History and Community: Essays in Victorian Medievalism* (New York and London, 1992); C. Pietropoli, ed., *Romanticismo, medievalismo* (Special issue of the journal *Questione Romantica*, 2, no. 7/3, 1999); L. Workman, 'Medievalism and Romanticism', *Poetica*, 39–40 (1994), pp. 1–40.

Notes to Acknowledgements

1. A. Chandler, *A Dream of Order: The Medieval Ideal in Nineteenth-Century Literature* (Lincoln, Nebraska, 1970).
2. M. Girouard, *The Return to Camelot: Chivalry and the English Gentleman* (New Haven and London, 1981).
3. C. Pietropoli, ed., *Romanticismo, medievalismo* (Special issue of the journal *Questione Romantica*, 2, no. 7/3, 1999); another major name in the field of medievalism in Italy is Piero Boitani.

Notes to Chapter 1: Survival and Revival

1. W. Farnham, *The Medieval Heritage of Elizabethan Tragedy* (Berkeley, 1936); J. P. McRoberts, *Shakespeare and the Medieval Tradition: An Annotated Bibliography* (New York, 1985); I. Ribner, *William Shakespeare* (Toronto, 1969); see especially the monumental study by G. Bullough, *Narrative and Dramatic Sources of Shakespeare* (8 vols, London, 1957–75).
2. C. Guilfoyle, *Shakespeare's Play within the Play: Medieval Imagery and Scenic*

Form in Hamlet, Othello and King Lear (Kalamazoo, Michigan, 1990), pp. 69–71; E. C. Pettet, *Shakespeare and the Romance Tradition* (London, 1949); V. Bourgeois Richmond, *Shakespeare, Catholicism and Romance* (London, 2000); D. J. O'Brien, 'Lord Berners' *Huon of Bordeaux*: The Survival of Medieval Ideals in the Reign of Henry VIII', *Studies in Medievalism*, 4 (1992), pp. 36–44; J. Simons, 'Christopher Middleton and Elizabethan Medievalism', in R. Utz and T. Shippey, eds, *Medievalism in the Modern World: Essays in Honour of Leslie Workman. Making the Middle Ages*, i (Turnhout, 1998), p. 49.

3. L. A. Cormican, 'Medieval Idiom in Shakespeare: Shakespeare and the Medieval Ethic', *Scrutiny*, 17 (1950), pp. 293–317; idem, 'Medieval Idiom in Shakespeare: Shakespeare and the Liturgy', ibid., pp. 186–202; S. J. Pyle, *Mirth and Morality of Shakespeare's Holy Fools* (Lampeter, 1998).

4. R. Weinmann, *Shakespeare and the Popular Tradition in the Theater* (Washington, 1978).

5. M. M. Bhattacharya, *Courtesy in Shakespeare* (Calcutta, 1940); H. Cooper, *Pastoral: Medieval into Renaissance* (Woodbridge, 1977).

6. F. Fergusson, *Trope and Allegory: Themes Common to Dante and Shakespeare* (Athens, Georgia, 1977).

7. W. G. Craven, *Giovanni Pico della Mirandola: Symbol of his Age: Modern Interpretations of a Renaissance Philosopher* (Geneva, 1981), pp. 131–54.

8. P. Saccio, *Shakespeare's English Kings: History, Chronicle and Drama* (New York, 1977); J. J. Norwich, *Shakespeare's Kings* (London, 2000).

9. G. Barraclough, 'Medium Aevum: Some Reflections on Mediaeval History and on the Term "The Middle Ages"', in *History in a Changing World* (Oxford, 1955), pp. 54–63.

10. J. Burckhardt, *The Civilisation of the Renaissance in Italy*, 2 vols, first published in 1860; B. Berenson, various works from the 1920 onwards, including, for example, *The Italian Painters of the Renaissance*. See also A. D. Culler, *The Victorian Mirror of History* (New Haven, Connecticut, 1985), pp. 249–53.

11. Barraclough, 'Medium Aevum', p. 55.

12. R. Krautheimer, *Rome: Profile of a City, 312–1308* (Princeton, New Jersey, 1980), pp. 27 and 233.

13. R. S. Crane, *The Vogue of Medieval Chivalric Romance during the English Renaissance* (Menasha, Wisconsin, 1919); E. McShane, *Tudor Opinions of the Chivalrous Romance: An Essay in Criticism* (Washington, 1950); A. Johnston, *Enchanted Ground: The Study of Medieval Romance in the Eighteenth Century* (London, 1964); Simons, 'Christopher Middleton', pp. 46–50, 54–60.

14. D. A. Summers, *Spenser's Arthur: The British Arthurian Tradition and 'The Faerie Queene'* (Lanham, Maryland, and Oxford, 1997); A. King, *'The Faerie Queene' and Middle English Romance* (Oxford, 2000); J. E. Hankins, *Source and Meaning in Spenser's Allegory: A Study of 'The Faerie Queene'* (Oxford, 1971);

C. B. Milligan, *Spenser and the Table Round: A Study in the Contemporaneous Background for Spenser's Use of the Arthurian Legend* (Cambridge, Massachusetts, 1932); M. Leslie, *Spenser's 'Fine Warres and Faithfull Loves': Martial and Chivalric Symbolism in 'The Faerie Queene'* (Woodbridge, 1983). For the Arthurian dimension, see also below, Chapter 6.

15. K. Duncan Jones, ed., *Sir Philip Sidney* (Oxford, 1989).

16. J. Briggs, '"New Times and Old Stories"': Middleton's *Hengist*, in D. Scragg and C. Weinberg, eds, *Literary Appropriations of the Anglo-Saxons: Thirteenth to the Twentieth Centuries* (Cambridge, 2000), pp. 107–21; J. Mulryan, *Milton and the Middle Ages* (East Brunswick, New Jersey, 1982); R. Simpson, '"Revisiting Cramalot": An Arthurian Theme in the Correspondence of William Taylor and Robert Southey', *Studies in Medievalism*, 4 (1992), p. 147.

17. P. Rogers, ed., *Alexander Pope* (Oxford, 1993): poems 'The Wife of Bath from Chaucer', pp. 66–76, and 'Eloisa to Abelard', pp. 137–46.

18. B. G. Keller, *The Middle Ages Reconsidered: Attitudes in France from the Eighteenth Century through the Romantic Movement* (New York, 1994), p. 5; W. Calin, 'Medievalism and *Ancien Régime* France: An Afterword', *Studies in Medievalism*, 3/1 (1987), pp. 99–106; R. Bonnel, 'Medieval Nostalgia in France, 1750–89: The Gothic Imagination at the End of the *Ancien Régime*', *Studies in Medievalism*, 5 (1993), pp. 139–63.

19. J. Pearson, 'Crushing the Convent and the Dread Bastille: The Anglo-Saxons, Revolution and Gender in Women's Plays in the 1790s', in Scragg, *Literary Appropriations*, pp. 122–35; see also below, Chapter 4.

20. Johnston, *Enchanted Ground*; Simons, 'Christopher Middleton', pp. 46–50, 54–60.

21. Simons, 'Christopher Middleton', p. 50.

22. Ibid., p. 47.

23. J. Simons, 'Medievalism as Cultural Process in Pre-Industrial Popular Literature', *Studies in Medievalism*, 6 (1994), pp. 5–21; idem, 'Romance in Eighteenth-Century Chapbooks', in his *From Medieval to Medievalism* (London, 1992), pp. 122–43.

24. Keller, *Middle Ages Reconsidered*, pp. 43–47.

25. C. Vasoli, *Profilo di un papa umanista: Tommaso Parentucelli* (Manduria, 1968); C. Bonfigli, *Niccolò V, papa della Rinascenza* (Rome, 1997), pp. 137–41; G. L. Coluccia, *Niccolò V umanista: papa e riformatore* (Venice, 1998), pp. 294–308. See also L. F. Boyle, 'Per la fondazione della Biblioteca Vaticana', in A. Manfredi, ed., *I codici latini di Niccolò V (edizione degli inventari e identificazione dei manoscritti* (Vatican City, 1994), pp. xiii–xvi.

26. G. Paparelli, *Enea Silvio Piccolomini: Pio II* (Bari, 1950).

27. C. K. Pullapilly, *Caesar Baronius: Counter Reformation Historian* (Notre Dame, Indiana, 1975), pp. 144–77.

28. Craven, *Giovanni Pico della Mirandola*; M. Fumagalli Beonio Broccheri, *Pico della Mirandola* (Casale Monferrato, 1999); A. Dulles, *Princeps Concordiae: Pico della Mirandola and the Scholastic Tradition* (Cambridge, Massachusetts, 1941); D. Hay, 'Flavio Biondo and the Middle Ages', *Proceedings of the British Academy*, 45 (1959), pp. 97–128.

29. D. Hay, *Polydore Vergil: Renaissance Historian and Man of Letters* (Oxford, 1952); Kenyon, *History Men*, pp. 3–4.

30. S. Lehmberg, 'Sir Thomas More's Life of Pico della Mirandola', *Studies in the Renaissance*, 3 (1956), pp. 61–74.

31. G. de Manteyer, 'Les manuscrits de la reine Christine aux archives du Vatican', *Mélanges d'Archéologie et d'Histoire*, 17 (1897), pp. 285–322; A. Wilmart, *Analecta reginensia: extraits des manuscrits latins de la reine Christine conservés au Vatican* (Vatican City, 1933).

32. J. G. A. Pocock, *The Ancient Constitution and the Feudal Law* (Cambridge, 1957), pp. 1–29.

33. Calin, 'Medievalism and Ancien Régime France', pp. 99–106; N. Edelman, *Attitudes of Seventeenth-Century France towards the Middle Ages* (New York, 1946); J. Zezula, 'Scholarly Medievalism in Renaissance France', *Studies in Medievalism*, 3/1 (1987), pp. 11–20; K. A. Campbell, 'The Renaissance Reader and Popular Medievalism in France', ibid., pp. 23–31; F. I. Triplett, 'Du Bellay's Ambivalent Defense of a Medieval Vernacular: *La Deffence et illustration de la langue françoise*', ibid., pp. 33–39; P. Burrell, 'Rabelais's Debts to the Medieval World', ibid., pp. 41–53.

34. J. Strype, *The Life and Times of Archbishop Parker* (3 vols, London, 1821); H. B. Walters, *The English Antiquaries of the Sixteenth, Seventeenth and Eighteenth Centuries* (London, 1934); M. McKisack, *Medieval History in the Tudor Age* (Oxford, 1971). By far the best overall summary of this whole subject is in D. R. Woolf, 'The Dawn of the Artifact: The Antiquarian Impulse in England, 1500–1730', *Studies in Medievalism*, 4 (1992), pp. 5–35, on which much of the material from the following pages relies.

35. R. G. Smith, *The Gothic Bequest: Medieval Institutions in British Thought, 1688–1863* (Cambridge, 1987), pp. 28–31.

36. R. Flower, 'Lawrence Nowell and the Discovery of England in Tudor Times', *Proceedings of the British Academy*, 21 (1935), pp. 47–74; R. M. Warnicke, *William Lambarde: Elizabethan Antiquary (1536–1601)* (London, 1973). Much of this section relies on Walters, *English Antiquaries*.

37. I. G. Philip, *The Bodleian Library in the Seventeenth and Eighteenth Centuries* (Oxford, 1983); W. D. Macray, *Annals of the Bodleian Library: With a Notice of the Earlier Library of the University* (1890; repr. 1997); C. G. C. Tite, *The Manuscript Library of Sir Robert Cotton* (London, 1994).

38. E. Edwards, *Libraries and Founders of Libraries* (London, 1865; repr. 1997);

A. G. Watson, *Medieval Manuscripts in Post-Medieval England* (Aldershot, 2004)

39. E. Edwards, *Lives of the Founders of the British Museum: With Notices of its Chief Augmentors and Other Benefactors, 1570–1870* (London, 1870; repr. 1997).

40. D. Brewer, 'Modernising the Medieval: Eighteenth-Century Translations of Chaucer', in M.-F. Alamichel and D. Brewer, eds, *The Middle Ages after the Middle Ages in the English-Speaking World* (Woodbridge, 1997), pp. 103–20.

41. Kenyon, *History Men*, p. 6.

42. Pocock, *Ancient Constitution*, pp. 30–55; J. Hostettler, *Sir Edward Coke: A Force for Freedom* (Chichester, 1997).

43. Kenyon, *History Men*, pp. 14–16; E. G. Stanley, 'Scholarly Recovery of the Significance of Anglo-Saxon Records', in his *Imagining the Anglo-Saxon Past* (Woodbridge, 2000), pp. 7–20.

44. Kenyon, *History Men*, pp. 5–18; Pocock, *Ancient Constitution*, p. 92; McKisack, *Medieval History*.

45. Woolf, 'Dawn of the Artifact', pp. 5–35.

46. Ibid., pp. 9–20.

47. J. Chifflet, *Anastasis Childerici I Francorum regis sive thesaurus sepulchralis Tornaci Neruiorum* (Antwerp, 1655).

48. Kenyon, *History Men*, pp. 8–10; M. McKisack, 'Samuel Daniel as Historian', *Review of English Studies*, 23 (1947), pp. 226–36.

49. Keller, *Middle Ages Reconsidered*, pp. 17–22.

50. L. Gossman, *Medievalism and the Ideologies of the Enlightenment: The World and Work of La Curne de Sainte-Palaye* (Baltimore, 1968).

51. Smith, *Gothic Bequest*, pp. 11–70; Pocock, *Ancient Constitution*, pp. 30–69, 148–228; Kenyon, *History Men*, pp. 23–40.

52. Cited in Pocock, *Ancient Constitution*, p. 49.

53. Pocock, *Ancient Constitution*, pp. 70–79.

54. Ibid., pp. 91–123.

55. C. Hill, 'The Norman Yoke', in his *Puritanism and Revolution: Studies in Interpretation of the English Revolution of the Seventeenth Century* (London, 1958), pp. 50–122 (quote on p. 57); D. Underdown, *A Freeborn People: Politics and the Nation in Seventeenth-Century England* (Oxford, 1996); M. Madoff, 'The Useful Myth of Gothic Ancestry', *Studies in Eighteenth-Century Culture*, 8 (1979), pp. 337–50; M. Wood, 'The Norman Yoke', in his *In Search of England: Journeys into the English Past* (Berkeley, California, 1999), pp. 3–22.

56. Pocock, *Ancient Constitution*, pp. 124–47; Hill, 'James Harrington and the People', in his *Puritanism and Revolution*, pp. 299–322, at 299–303.

57. Cited in Hill, 'Norman Yoke', p. 84.

58. Hill, 'Norman Yoke', pp. 87–99; Smith, *Gothic Bequest*, pp. 57–70.

59. Hill, 'Norman Yoke', pp. 101–9.

60. E. Burke, *Reflections on the Revolution in France* (London, 1790; repr. 1922), p. 29; on Burke's views of history, see for example S. Ayling, *Edmund Burke: His Life and Opinions* (London, 1988), and now F. P. Lock, *Edmund Burke (1730–1784)*, i (Oxford, 1998), pp. 154–64.

61. See below, Chapter 4.

62. C. A. Simmons, 'Absent Presence: The Romantic Era Magna Charta and the English Constitution', in Utz and Shippey, *Medievalism in the Modern World*, pp. 72–75.

63. Kenyon, *History Men*, pp. 8–10.

64. I. Berlin, *Vico and Herder* (London, 1976); C. Brooks, 'Historicism and the Nineteenth Century', in V. Brand, ed., *The Study of the Past in the Victorian Age* (Oxford, 1998), pp. 1–20; F. Meinecke, *Historicism: The Rise of a New Historical Outlook* (trans. London, 1972); see also below, Chapter 4.

65. G. Barraclough, 'The Mediaeval Empire: Idea and Reality', in his *History*, pp. 105–30.

66. L. Halphen, *Charlemagne and the Carolingian Empire* (trans. London, 1977); H. Fichtenau, *The Carolingian Empire* (trans. Oxford, 1968); R. Folz, *The Concept of Empire in Western Europe* (trans. London, 1969).

67. F. Heer, *The Holy Roman Empire* (trans. London, 1995); B. Arnold, *Medieval Germany, 500–1300* (Basingstoke, 1997), pp. 75–125.

68. J. Bérenger, *A History of the Habsburg Empire*, (2 vols, trans. London, 1994 and 1997).

69. H. G. Koenigsberger, *The Habsburgs and Europe, 1516–1660* (Ithaca, New York, and London, 1971).

70. M. Fernandez Alvarez, *Charles V* (trans. London, 1975); S. Macdonald, *Charles V: Ruler, Dynast and Defender of the Faith, 1500–58* (2nd edn, London, 2000); W. Blockmans, *Emperor Charles V* (London, 2001).

71. C. A. Macartney, *The Habsburg Empire, 1790–1918* (London, 1971); Bérenger, *History of the Habsburg Empire*.

72. J. B. Duroselle, *L'idée de l'Europe dans l'histoire* (Paris, 1965); D. Hay, *Europe: The Emergence of an Idea* (2nd edn, Edinburgh, 1968); M. Perrin, *L'idée de l'Europe au fil de deux millénaires* (Paris, 1994).

73. M. Lyons, *Napoleon Bonaparte and the Legacy of the French Revolution* (London, 1994), pp. 244–59.

Notes to Chapter 2: Gothic Thoughts

1. D. R. Woolf, 'The Dawn of the Artifact: The Antiquarian Impulse in England, 1500–1730', in *Studies in Medievalism*, 4 (1992), pp. 5–35; E. G. Stanley, *Imagining the Anglo-Saxon Past* (Woodbridge, 2000); H. Damico, ed., *Medieval Scholarship: Biographical Studies of the Foundation of a Discipline* (3 vols, New

York, 2000); C. T. Berkhout and M. McC.Gatch, eds, *Anglo-Saxon Scholarship: The First Three Centuries* (Boston, 1982); A. J. Frantzen, *A Desire for Origins: New Language, Old English and Teaching the Tradition* (New Brunswick and London, 1990); D. Matthews, '"Quaint Inglis": Walter Scott and the Rise of Middle English Studies', *Studies in Medievalism*, 6 (1994), pp. 33–48; C. A. Simmons, '"Iron-Worded Proof": Victorian Identity and the Old English Language',*Studies in Medievalism*, 4 (1992), pp. 202–14; eadem, 'Anglo-Saxonism, the Future and the Franco-Prussian War', *Studies in Medievalism*, 7 (1995), pp. 131–42.

2. M. Girouard, *The Return to Camelot: Chivalry and the English Gentleman* (London, 1981), p. 22; D. P. Varma, *The Gothic Flame* (London, 1957), p. 12; J. W. Hales and F. J. Furnivall, eds, *Bishop Percy's Folio Manuscript: Ballads and Romances* (3 vols, London, 1868), ii: 'The Revival of the Ballad Poetry in the Eighteenth Century', pp. x–xxxi; G. A. Morgan, 'Percy, the Antiquarians, the Ballad and the Middle Ages', *Studies in Medievalism*, 7 (1995), pp. 22–32; K. L. Haugen, 'Chivalry and Romance in the Eighteenth Century: Richard Hurd and the Disenchantment of *The Faerie Queene*', in C. A. Simmons, ed., *Medievalism and the Quest for the 'Real' Middle Ages* (London, 2001), pp. 45–60.

3. Hales and Furnivall, *Bishop Percy*, i: introduction by J. Pickford.

4. Hales and Furnivall, *Bishop Percy*, ii, p. xxi.

5. R. W. Ketton-Cremer, *Horace Walpole: A Biography* (London, 1940); T. Mowl, *Horace Walpole: The Great Outsider* (London, 1996).

6. *Monthly Review*, 32, May 1765, p. 394.

7. K. K. Mehrotra, *Horace Walpole and the English Novel: A Study of the Influence of 'The Castle of Otranto', 1764–1820* (Oxford, 1934).

8. The most general works on the Gothic novel are S. M. Gilbert and S. Gubar, *The Madwoman in the Attic: The Woman Writer and the Nineteenth-Century Literary Imagination* (2nd edn, London and New Haven, 2000); D. Punter, *The Literature of Terror: A History of Gothic Fictions from 1765 to the Present Day* (London, 1980); idem, ed., *Companion to the Gothic* (Oxford, 2000); R. Norton, ed., *Gothic Readings: The First Wave 1764–1840* (Leicester, 2000); M. Summers, *The Gothic Quest: A History of the Gothic Novel* (London, 1968); G. R. Thompson, ed., *The Gothic Imagination: Essays in Dark Romanticism* (Washington, 1974); Varma, *The Gothic Flame*; E. Birkhead, *The Tale of Terror* (London, 1921).

9. E. B. Gose Jr, *Imagination Indulged: The Irrational in the Nineteenth-Century Novel* (Montreal and London, 1972); E. J. Clery, *The Rise of Supernatural Fiction, 1762–1800* (Cambridge, 1995); Mehrotra, *Horace Walpole*, pp. 84, 100–1, 127–28 and 138.

10. C. A. Simmons, 'Bad Baronets and the Curse of Medievalism', *Studies in Medievalism*, 12 (2003), pp. 215–36.

11. A. Radcliffe, *The Mysteries of Udolpho*, ii, ch. 5.

12. W. Hutchison, *The Hermitage: A British Story* (York, 1772), p. 5.

13. C. Reeves, *The Old English Baron* (London, 1778), p. 56

14. H. Walpole, *The Castle of Otranto*, ch. 5.

15. C. A. Howells, *Love, Mystery and Misery: Feeling in Gothic Fiction* (London, 1978); Clery, *Rise of Supernatural Fiction*; Thompson, *Gothic Imagination*; E. Railo, *The Haunted Castle: A Study of the Elements of English Romanticism* (London, 1927).

16. J. Mee, *Romanticism, Enthusiasm and Regulation: Poetics and the Policing of Culture in the Romantic Period* (Oxford, 2003).

17. Varma, *Gothic Flame*; Summers, *Gothic Quest*.

18. J. Todd, *Sensibility: An Introduction* (London, 1986); P. Ilie, *The Age of Minerva: Counter-Rational Reason in the Eighteenth Century* (Philadelphia, Pennsylvania, 1995); J. Ellison, *Cato's Tears and the Making of Anglo-American Emotion* (Chicago and London, 1999); G. J. Barker-Benfield, *The Culture of Sensibility: Sex and Society in Eighteenth-Century Britain* (Chicago, 1992); J. McGann, *The Poetics of Sensibility: A Revolution in Literary Style* (Oxford, 1996).

19. H. Walpole, *The Castle of Otranto*, ch. 3.

20. R. Miles, *Gothic Writing 1750–1820: A Genealogy* (London, 1993).

21. On the whole issue of Romanticism and Catholicism, see below, Chapter 3, and K. L. Morris, *The Image of the Middle Ages in Romantic and Victorian Literature* (London, 1984), ch. 1. On Catholicism and the Gothic novel, see M. M. Tau, *Catholicism in Gothic Fiction: A Study of the Nature and Function of Catholic Materials in Gothic Fiction in England, 1762–1830* (Washington, 1946) and, on the Protestant side, V. Sage, *Horror Fiction in the Protestant Tradition* (Basingstoke, 1988).

22. J. Howard, *Introduction to 'The Mysteries of Udolpho'* (Harmondsworth, 2001), pp. x–xii and xxii.

23. R. Mighall, *A Geography of Victorian Gothic Fiction: Mapping History's Nightmares* (Oxford, 1996), pp. 9 and 21.

24. Howard, *Introduction to 'The Mysteries of Udolpho'*, p. xvii.

25. Among other well-known names were William Godwin, C. R. Maturin and Frederic Lathom.

26. R. Miles, *Ann Radcliffe: The Great Enchantress* (Manchester, 1995); R. Norton, *Mistress of Udolpho: The Life of Ann Radcliffe* (London, 1999).

27. The setting in southern European countries, and its association with the world of passion, was already commented on by near contemporaries. In the introduction to his edition of Radcliffe, Walter Scott claimed that she has 'uniformly selected the south of Europe for her place of action, whose passions, like the weeds of the climate, are supposed to attain portentous growth under

the fostering sun'; on this issue, see also C. Baldick, ed., *The Oxford Book of Gothic Tales* (Oxford, 1992), pp. xiii–xiv.

28. Other names include Charlotte Smith, Jane and Anna Maria Porter, Catherine Ward, Anne Fuller, Agnes Musgrove, and Mrs Bennett, Mrs Helme, Mrs Meeke, Mrs Parsons, Mrs Roche and Mrs Yorke.

29. S. Becker, *Forms of Feminine Fiction* (Manchester, 1999); W. P. Day, *In the Circles of Fear and Desire: A Study of Gothic Fantasy* (Chicago, 1985); K. F. Ellis, *The Contested Castle: Gothic Novels and the Subversion of Domestic Ideology* (Urbana and Chicago, Illinois, 1989); J. E. Fleenor, ed., *The Female Gothic* (Montreal, 1983); V. Jones, ed., *Women in the Eighteenth Century: Constructions of Femininity* (London, 1990); H. Devine Jump, ed., *Women's Writing of the Romantic Period, 1789–1836* (Edinburgh, 1997); M. Poovey, *The Proper Lady and the Woman Writer: Ideology as Style in the Works of Mary Wollstonecraft, Mary Shelley and Jane Austen* (Chicago, 1984); J. Spencer, *The Rise of the Woman Novelist* (Oxford, 1986).

30. Clery, *Rise of Supernatural Fiction*, quotes pp. 96 and 100, and see pp. 95–102.

31. W. W. Watt, *Shilling Shockers of the Gothic School: A Study of the Chapbook Gothic Romances* (Cambridge, Massachusetts, 1932); R. D. Mayo, 'Gothic Romance in the Magazines', *Proceedings of the Medieval Languages Academy*, 65 (1950), pp. 762–89; D. Richter, 'The Reception of the Gothic Novel', in R. W. Uphaus, ed., *The Idea of the Novel in the Eighteenth Century* (East Lansing, Michigan, 1988)

32. M. Praz, *The Romantic Agony* (2nd edn, London, 1970); M. Cranston, *The Romantic Movement* (London, 1994); R. T. Davies and R. G. Beaty, *Literature of the Romantic Period* (Liverpool, 1976); I. Durand-Le Guern, *Le Moyen Age des Romantiques* (Rennes, 2001); L. Workman, 'Medievalism and Romanticism', *Poetica*, 39–40 (1994), pp. 1–40.

33. Cranston, *Romantic Movement*, pp. 21–47; G. T. Hughes, *Romantic German Literature, 1760–1805* (New York, 1975); R. Pascal, *The German Sturm und Drang* (Manchester, 1953); S. Prawer, *The Romantic Period in Germany* (New York, 1970).

34. F. Barnard, *Herder's Social and Political Thought: From Enlightenment to Nationalism* (Oxford, 1965); see also below, Chapter 4.

35. E. Höltenschmidt, *Die Mittelalterrezeption der Brüder Schlegel* (Paderborn, 2000); G. G. Iggers, *The German Conception of History: The National Tradition of Historical Thought from Herter to the Present* (Middletown, Connecticut, 1983).

36. A. Schmit, *Fouqué und einige seiner Zeitgenossen* (Karlsruhe, 1958); C. E. Seibicke, *Friedrich Baron de la Motte Fouqué: Krise und Verfall der Spätromantik im Spiegel seiner historisierenden Ritterromane* (Munich, 1985), pp. 117–23, 124–36.

37. A. Wawn, *The Vikings and the Victorians: Inventing the Old North in Nineteenth-Century Britain* (Woodbridge, 2002), pp. 325–26.

38. Novalis, cited in Morris, *Image of the Middle Ages*, p. 11.

39. Novalis and Heine, cited in Morris, *Image of the Middle Ages*, p. 13.

40. See below, Chapter 3.

41. The political impact of Romanticism as nationalism is examined in Chapter 4, below.

42. Cranston, *Romantic Movement*, pp. 99–119; E. H. Wilkins, *A History of Italian Literature* (Cambridge, Massachusetts, 1974).

43. See above, Chapter 1.

44. D. Beales, ed., *The Risorgimento and the Unification of Italy* (London, 1971).

45. J. Zipes, *The Brothers Grimm* (London, 1988); idem, *The Brothers Grimm: From Enchanted Forests to the Modern World* (2nd edn, New York, 2000); E. H. Antonsen et al., eds, *The Grimm Brothers and the Germanic Past* (Amsterdam and Philadelphia, 1990); Iggers, *German Conception of History*.

46. Trans. by Gumbrecht and Schnapp, in R. H. Bloch and S. G. Nichols, eds, *Medievalism and the Modernist Temper* (Baltimore, Maryland, and London, 1996), p. 483.

47. M. Warner, ed., *Wonder Tales: Six Stories of Enchantment* (London, 1996).

48. Cranston, *Romantic Movement*, pp. 77–98; B. G. Keller, *The Middle Ages Reconsidered: Attitudes in France from the Eighteenth Century through the Romantic Movement* (New York, 1994); D. C. Charlton, ed., *The French Romantics*, 2 vols (Cambridge, 1984); Norris J. Lacy, 'The French Romantics and Medieval French Literature: A Bibliography', *Studies in Medievalism*, 3/1 (1987), pp. 87–97; C. Amalvi, *Le goût du Moyen Age* (2nd edn, Paris, 2002), pp. 19–60.

49. J. F. de Chateaubriand, *Le génie du Christianisme*, pt 2, bk 3, ch. 9.

50. N. Havely, 'Losing Paradise: Dante, Boccaccio and Mary Shelley's *Valperga*', in C. Pietropoli, ed., *Romanticismo, medievalismo* (special issue of the journal *Questione Romantica*, 2, no. 7/3, 1999), pp. 29–35.

51. Amalvi, *Goût*, p. 25; P. Antoine, 'Une imagination puissante, mais déréglée: les représentations du Moyen Age dans les *Mémoires d'Outre-Tombe*', in Pietropoli, *Romaticismo*, pp. 75–86.

52. Keller, *Middle Ages Reconsidered*, p. 54.

53. Idem, pp. 127–39; Amalvi, *Goût*, pp. 31–58.

54. P. Ward, *The Medievalism of Victor Hugo* (Philadelphia, Pennsylvania, 1975); P. Berret, *Le Moyen Age dans la Légende des Siècles et les sources de Victor Hugo* (Paris, 1911); Amalvi, *Goût*, pp. 25–31 and pp. 46–52 on the serialisation of novels by the likes of Eugène Sue and Michel Zevaco.

55. Cranston, *Romantic Movement*, pp. 48–76; M. Butler, *Romantics, Rebels and Reactionaries: English Literature and its Background, 1760–1830* (Oxford, 1981); J. Clubbe and E. J. Lovell, *English Romanticism: The Grounds of Belief* (London,

1983); M. Gaull, *English Romanticism* (New York, 1983); J. Kiely, *The Romantic Novel in England* (Cambridge, Massachusetts, 1972); A. Hull, *English Romanticism* (London, 2000); Workman, 'Medievalism and Romanticism'; Morris, *Image of the Middle Ages*.

56. C. Brinton, *The Political Ideas of the English Romantics* (Ann Arbor, Michigan, 1962); E. Nower Schamber, *The Artist as Politician: The Art and Politics of the French Romantics* (New York, 1984); A. Zamoyski, *Holy Madness: Romantics, Patriots and Revolutionaries, 1776–1871* (London, 1999).

57. E. Fay, *Romantic Medievalism: History and the Romantic Literary Ideal* (Basingstoke, 2002), pp. 64–108.

58. Morris, *Image of the Middle Ages*, pp. 49–52.

59. Fay, *Romantic Medievalism*, pp. 109–96.

60. See below, Chapter 6.

61. G. Lucacs, *The Historical Novel* (1937; trans. 1962; repr. London, 1976), remains the classic theoretical introduction to the subject.

62. H. Orel, *The Historical Novel from Scott to Sabatini: Changing Attitudes towards a Literary Genre, 1814–1920* (New York, 1995), p. 10.

63. N. Rance, *The Historical Novel and Popular Politics in Nineteenth-Century England* (London, 1975), p. 25.

64. A. Chandler, *A Dream of Order: The Medieval Ideal in Nineteenth-Century Literature* (Lincoln, Nebraska, 1970), pp. 12–51; eadem, 'Sir Walter Scott and the Medieval Revival', *Nineteenth-Century Fiction*, 19 (1964), pp. 315–32; Girouard, *Return to Camelot*, pp. 30–38.

65. I. Mitchell, *Scott, Chaucer and Medieval Romance: A Study of Sir Walter Scott's Indebtedness to the Literature of the Middle Ages* (Lexington, Kentucky, 1987).

66. T. A. Shippey, 'The Undeveloped Image: Anglo-Saxon in Popular Consciousness from Turner to Tolkien', in D. Scragg and C. Weinberg, eds, *Literary Appropriations of the Anglo-Saxons, Thirteenth to the Twentieth Centuries* (Cambridge, 2000), pp. 215–36.

67. Wawn, *Vikings and the Victorians*, pp. 5–8, 65–83, 315–19.

68. Girouard, *Return to Camelot*, pp. 72–76; A. Sanders, '"Utter Indifference"? The Anglo-Saxons in the Nineteenth-Century Novel', in Scragg and Weinberg, *Literary Appropriations*, pp. 157–73.

69. Orel, *Historical Novel*, pp. 22–25.

70. A. Sanders, *The Victorian Historical Novel, 1840–1880* (New York, 1979).

71. Wawn, *Vikings and the Victorians*, pp. 312–15, 331–35; J. Hammer, '*Eric Brighteyes*: Rider Haggard Rewrites the Saga', *Studies in Medievalism*, 12 (2003), pp. 137–70.

72. See below, Chapter 6.

Notes to Chapter 3: Romantic Visions

1. N. Pevsner, *The Englishness of English Art* (London, 1956), ch. 4.
2. C. Brooks, *The Gothic Revival* (London, 1999); C. L. Eastlake, *A History of the Gothic Revival*, introduction by J. Mordaunt Crook (1872; repr. Leicester, 1970), pp. 13–57.
3. D. Watkin, *The English Vision: The Picturesque in Architecture, Landscape and Garden Design* (London, 1982).
4. Much of the architectural section relies on M. Aldrich, *The Gothic Revival* (London, 1994); Brooks, *Gothic Revival*; and M. Girouard, *The Return to Camelot: Chivalry and the English Gentleman* (New Haven and London, 1981).
5. S. Bending, 'The True Rust of the Barons' War: Gardens, Ruins and the National Landscape', in M. Myrone and L. Peltz, eds, *Producing the Past* (Aldershot, 1999), p. 87.
6. All cited in K. K. Mehrotra, *Horace Walpole and the English Novel: A Study of the Influence of the 'The Castle of Otranto', 1764–1820* (Oxford, 1934), p. 8.
7. Letter from Walpole, 9 September 1758, cited in R. W. Ketton-Cremer, *Horace Walpole: A Biography* (London, 1940), p.
8. J. Mordaunt Crook, *John Carter and the Mind of the Gothic Revival* (London, 1995).
9. Idem, 'John Britton and the Genesis of the Gothic Revival', in J. Summerson, ed., *Essays on Architectural Writers and Writing Presented to Nikolaus Pevsner* (London, 1968), pp. 98–119.
10. S. Bradley, 'The Englishness of Gothic: Theories and Interpretations from William Gilpin to J. H. Parker', *Architectural History*, 45 (2002), pp. 325–46.
11. Girouard, *Return to Camelot*, pp. 40–41.
12. Ibid., p. 53.
13. Cited in Aldrich, *Gothic Revival*, p. 137.
14. Ibid., p. 103.
15. H. M. Colvin, 'Aubrey's *Chronologia Architectonica*', in Summerson, *Essays*, pp. 1–12.
16. P. Atterbury and C. Wainwright, *Pugin: A Gothic Passion* (London, 1994); B. Bergdoll, *A. W. N. Pugin: Master of the Gothic Revival* (New Haven, 1996).
17. Aldrich, *Gothic Revival*, p. 145.
18. J. A. Auerbach, *The Great Exhibition of 1851: A Nation on Display* (New Haven, 1999).
19. C. Dellheim, 'Interpreting Victorian Medievalism', in F. Boos, ed., *History and Community: Essays in Victorian Medievalism* (New York and London, 1992), pp. 39–58, at p. 52.
20. J. J. Parkinson-Bailey, *Manchester: An Architectural History* (Manchester, 2000).

21. C. W. London, *Bombay Gothic* (London, 2003).

22. P. B. Stanton, *The Gothic Revival and American Church Architecture: An Episode in Taste 1840–56* (Baltimore, 1968); W. Anders, *American Gothic* (New York, 1975).

23. D. M. Cassidy, 'The Collegiate Designs of Maginnis and Walsh', *Studies in Medievalism*, 3/2 (1990), pp. 153–85.

24. J. Mordaunt Crook, *The Strange Genius of William Burges 'Art-Architect', 1827–81* (Cardiff, 1981).

25. B. G. Keller, *The Middle Ages Reconsidered: Attitudes in France from the Eighteenth Century through the Romantic Movement* (New York, 1994), pp. 105–12.

26. P. Auzas, *Viollet-le-Duc* (Paris, 1979); J. P. Midant, *Viollet-le-Duc: The French Gothic Revival* (Paris, 2002).

27. Dict. VIII, cited in N. Pevsner, *Ruskin and Viollet-le-Duc: Englishness and Frenchness in the Appreciation of Architecture* (London, 1969), p. 38.

28. *Actes du Colloque International Viollet-le-Duc* (Paris, 1982), which has several papers addressing this issue; see also P. Greenhalgh, ed., *Art Nouveau: 1890–1914* (Washington, DC, 2000).

29. G. Germann, *Gothic Revival in Europe and Britain: Sources, Influences and Ideas* (trans. London, 1972); O. Boucher-Rivalain, 'Attitudes to Gothic Revival in French Architectural Writings of the 1840s', *Architectural History*, 41 (1998), pp. 145–52; P. Hunter-Stiebel, *Of Knights and Spires: Gothic Revival in France and Germany* (New York, 1989).

30. E. Emery and L. Morowitz, *Consuming the Past: The Medieval Revival in Fin de Siècle France* (Aldershot, 2003), p. 91.

31. E. Emery, *Romancing the Cathedral: Gothic Architecture in Fin de Siècle French Culture* (Albany, New York, 2001), and Emery and Morowitz, *Consuming the Past*, pp. 85–110, for the following.

32. Cited and trans. in ibid., n. 50 and p. 103; on Emile Mâle, see Emery, *Romancing the Cathedral*, pp. 34–35 and 41–43.

33. Ibid., pp. 32–42 and 89–128; eadem, 'J.-K. Huysmans and the Middle Ages', *Modern Languages Studies*, 29/3 (2002); R. Baldick, *The Life of J.-K. Huysmans* (Oxford, 1955).

34. Cited and trans. in Emery and Morowitz, *Consuming the Past*, p. 85; see also Emery, *Romancing the Cathedral*, pp. 129–60; L. Fraisse, *L'oeuvre cathédrale: Proust et l'architecture médiévale* (Paris, 1990), and R. Bales, *Proust and the Middle Ages* (Geneva, 1975), pp. 33–77.

35. Emery and Morowitz, *Consuming the Past*, pp. 61–84, 111–41 and 171–208.

36. Ibid., pp. 111–41; for a history of the cabaret, see A. Fields, *Le Chat Noir: A Montmartre Cabaret and its Artists in Turn-of-the-Century Paris* (Santa Barbara, California, 1993).

37. Emery and Morowitz, *Consuming the Past*, pp. 171–208.

38. Germann, *Gothic Revival.*

39. D. E. Barclay, 'Medievalism and Nationalism in Nineteenth-Century Germany', *Studies in Medievalism*, 5 (1993), p. 13.

40. K. David-Sirocko, 'Anglo-German Interconnexions during the Gothic Revival: A Case Study from the Work of Georg Gottlob Ungewitter (1820–64)', *Architectural History*, 41 (1998), pp. 153–78.

41. N. Pevsner, *Pioneers of Modern Design from William Morris to Walter Gropius* (rev. edn, London, 1991).

42. C. Frèches-Thory and A. Terrasse, *The Nabis: Bonnard, Vuillard and their Circle* (New York, 1991).

43. M. Frank, 'The Nazarene "Gemeinschaft": Overbeck and Cornelius', in L. Horowitz and W. Waughan, eds, *Artistic Brotherhoods in the Nineteenth Century* (Aldershot, 2000), pp. 48–66; R. P. Gray, 'Questions of Identity at Abramtsevo', in ibid., pp. 105–21; L. Horowitz, 'Art Brotherhoods and the Art Market in the Fin de Siècle', in ibid., pp. 185–96; A. Faxon, 'The Pre-Raphaelite Brotherhood as Knights of the Round Table', in L. de Girolami Cheney, ed., *Pre-Raphaelitism and Medievalism in the Arts* (Lampeter, 1992), pp. 53–74.

44. W. Hofmann, *Caspar David Friedrich* (London, 2000); W. Vaughan, *Friedrich* (London, 2004); J. L. Koerner, *Caspar David Friedrich and the Subject of Landscape* (London, 1990); K. Hartley et al., *The Romantic Spirit in German Art, 1790–1990* (London, 1994).

45. K. Andrews, *The Nazarenes* (Oxford, 1964); Frank, 'The Nazarene "Gemeinschaft"', pp. 48–66.

46. D. E. Barclay, 'Representing the Middle Ages: Court Festivals in Nineteenth-Century Prussia', in R. Utz and T. Shippey, eds, *Medievalism in the Modern World: Essays in Honour of Leslie Workman: Making the Middle Ages*, i (Turnhout, 1998), pp. 105–16.

47. Frank, 'The Nazarene "Gemeinschaft"', p. 54.

48. W. Vaughan, *German Romanticism and English Art* (London, 1980).

49. On this vast topic see, among others, L. Lambourne, *Victorian Painting* (London, 1999); J. Thomas, *Victorian Narrative Painting* (London, 2000); J. Treuherz, *Victorian Painting* (London, 1993); M. Warner, *The Victorians: British Painting, 1837–1901* (London, 1996); C. Wood, *Victorian Painting* (London, 1999); R. Strong, *And When Did You Last See Your Father? The Victorian Painter and British History* (London, 1978); M. Bills, ed., *Art in the Age of Queen Victoria* (London, 2001).

50. R. Jeffrey Easby, 'The Myth of Merrie England in Victorian Painting', in Boos, *History and Community*, pp. 59–80.

51. The literature on the Pre-Raphaelites is considerable. These are a few examples of recent work: C. Wood, *The Pre-Raphaelites* (London, 1981); R. Barnes, *The*

Pre-Raphaelites and their World (London, 1998); T. Barringer, *Reading the Pre-Raphaelites* (New Haven, 1998); S. P. Casteras and A. Craig Faxon, *Pre-Raphaelite Art in its European Context* (Madison, New Jersey, and London, 1995); L. Des Cars, *Pre-Raphaelitism: Romance and Realism* (London, 2000); E. Prettejohn, *The Art of the Pre-Raphaelites* (London, 2000).

52. J. Marsh, *Dante Gabriel Rossetti, Painter and Poet* (London, 1999); E. Prettejohn, *Rossetti and his Circle* (London, 1997); Barringer, *Reading the Pre-Raphaelites*, pp. 146–49.

53. A. D. Culler, *The Victorian Mirror of History* (New Haven, 1985), p. 224; see also H. Roberts, 'The Medieval Spirit of Pre-Raphaelitism', in de Girolami Cheney, *Pre-Raphaelitism and Medievalism in the Arts*, pp. 15–28.

54. L. de Girolami Cheney, 'Locks, Tresses and Manes in Pre-Raphaelite Paintings', in de Girolami Cheney, *Pre-Raphaelitism and Medievalism in the Arts*, pp. 159–92; B. Miliaras, 'Womanly Noblesse: The Influence of the Courtly Love Tradition on Edward Burne-Jones', in ibid., pp. 193–220; K. Powell, 'Burne-Jones, Swinburne and the *Laus Veneris*', in ibid., pp. 221–40.

55. A. Wilton and R. Upstone, eds, *The Age of Rossetti, Burne-Jones and Watts: Symbolism in Britain, 1860–1910* (London, 1997); see also E. Prettejohn, *After the Pré-Raphaelites: Art and Aestheticism in Victorian England* (Manchester, 1999); L. Brogniez, *Préraphaélisme et Symbolisme: peinture littéraire et image poétique* (Paris, 2003); and Casteras and Craig Faxon, *Pre-Raphaelite Art in its European Context*.

56. Emery and Morowitz, *Consuming the Past*, p. 254 n. 536.

57. de Girolami Cheney, 'Locks, Tresses and Manes in Pre-Raphaelite Paintings', pp. 159–92.

58. In the prose writings of, for example, Huysmans, Gérard de Nerval and Villiers de l'Isle Adam in France. Major poets were the 'Parnassian' poets, notably Lecomte de Lisle, José Maria de Hérédia, then Paul Verlaine, Stéphane Mallarmé and Guillaume Apollinaire in France, Emile Verhaeren and Maurice Maeterlinck in Belgium, Rainer Maria Rilke and Hugo von Hoffmansthal in the Habsburg world, Gabriele d'Annunzio in Italy. See also H. Dorra, *Symbolist Art Theories: A Critical Anthology* (Berkeley, California, 1995).

59. P. Jullian, *Dreamers of Decadence: The Symbolist Painters of the 1890s* (trans. London, 1971); E. Lucie-Smith, *Symbolist Art* (London, 1972); R. Delevoy, *Symbolists and Symbolism* (Geneva, 1982).

60. J. R. Dakyns, *The Middle Ages in French Literature, 1851–1900* (London, 1973), p. 206.

61. E. Aslin, *The Aesthetic Movement: Prelude to Art Nouveau* (London, 1969); L. Lambourne, *The Aesthetic Movement* (London, 1996)

62. On another rich bibliographical topic, see, for example, A. Compton-Rickett, *William Morris: A Study in Personality* (London, 1913); E. P. Thompson,

William Morris: Romantic to Revolutionary (rev. edn, London, 1977); F. Mac-Carthy, *William Morris: A Life for Our Times* (London, 1994); G. Naylor, ed., *William Morris by Himself* (London and Boston, 2000).

63. A. Bingaman, 'The Business of Brotherhood: Morris, Marshall, Faulkner and Co. and the Pre-Raphaelite Culture of Youth', in Horowitz and Vaughan, *Artistic Brotherhoods*, pp. 82–104; E. Cumming and W. Kaplan, *The Arts and Crafts Movement* (London, 1991); A. Anscombe, *Arts and Crafts Style* (London, 1996).

64. J. Harris, 'William Morris and the Middle Ages', in J. Banham and J. Harris, eds, *William Morris and the Middle Ages* (Manchester, 1984), pp. 1–17.

65. W. Morris, article on 'Art' in the *New Review* series on the socialist ideal, cited in MacCarthy, *William Morris*, p. 599.

66. Ibid., pp. 602–4.

67. Wawn, *Vikings and the Victorians*, pp. 278–79.

68. Letter to Andreas Scheu, 5 September 1883, printed in Naylor, *William Morris by Himself.*

69. MacCarthy, *William Morris*, pp. 65–68.

70. Barringer, *Reading the Pre-Raphaelites*, pp. 114–15.

71. Classic studies of the Oxford Movement, such as O. Chadwick, *The Mind of the Oxford Movement* (London, 1960) and I. Faber, *Oxford Apostles: A Character Study of the Oxford Movement* (London, 1974), are now usefully supplemented by K. L. Morris, *The Image of the Middle Ages in Romantic and Victorian Literature* (London, 1984) and J. C. Livingston, *Modern Christian Thought: The Enlightenment and the Nineteenth Century*, i (2nd edn, Upper Saddle, New Jersey, 1992), pp. 162–84; see also R. Chapman, 'Last Enchantments: Medievalism and the Early Anglo-Catholic Movement', *Studies in Medievalism*, 4 (1992), pp. 170–85.

72. Warton, cited in Morris, *Image of the Middle Ages*, p. 41.

73. Morris, *Image of the Middle Ages*, pp. 35–49, and quotes at p. 47.

74. Cited in Chapman, 'Last Enchantments', p. 184.

75. P. Brendon, *Hurrell Froude and the Oxford Movement* (London, 1974).

76. Chadwick, *Mind of the Oxford Movement*, p. 55.

77. Ibid., pp. 40–58; P. Butler, ed., *Pusey Rediscovered* (London, 1985).

78. Chapman, 'Last Enchantments', p. 172.

79. Morris, *Image of the Middle Ages*, pp. 140–58.

80. K. Bergeron, *Decadent Enchantments: The Revival of Gregorian Chant at Solesmes* (Berkeley, California, and London, 1988).

81. N. Smart et al., *Nineteenth-Century Religious Thought in the West*, ii (2nd edn, Cambridge, 1985), p. 85.

82. For the interest for historical themes in nineteenth-century opera, see G. Jellinek, *History Through the Opera Glass* (White Plains, New York, 1994)

83. C. White, *An Introduction to the Life and Works of Richard Wagner* (Englewood Cliffs, New Jersey, 1967); D. Aberbach, *The Ideas of Richard Wagner: An Examination and Analysis of his Major Aesthetic, Political, Economic, Social and Religious Thoughts* (Lanham and London, 1984); V. Mertens, 'Wagner's Middle Ages', in U. Müller and P. Wapnewsky, eds, *Wagner Handbook* (trans. London, 1992);

84. Letter from Wagner to S. Lehrs, 12 June 1842, cited in Aberbach, *Ideas of Richard Wagner*, p. 92.

85. Ibid., pp. 91–92, 141–4 and 373; see also E. R. Haymes, 'Two-Storied Medievalism in Wagner's *Die Meistersinger von Nürnberg*', *Studies in Medievalism*, 3/4 (1991), pp. 505–13.

86. Aberbach, *Ideas of Richard Wagner*, p. 142.

87. Letter from Wagner to Mathilde Wesendonck, 29 October 1859, cited in ibid., p. 70.

88. A. Leighton Cleather and B. Crump, *Parsifal, Lohengrin and the Legend of the Holy Grail, Described and Interpreted in Accordance with Wagner's Own Writings* (London, 1904).

89. See below, Chapter 4.

Notes to Chapter 4: From Aachen to Maastricht

1. B. R. Anderson, *Imagined Communities: Reflections on the Origin and Spread of Nationalism* (London, rev. 1991); E. J. Hobsbawm, *Nations and Nationalism since 1780* (Cambridge, 1990); idem and T. Ranger, eds, *The Invention of Tradition* (Cambridge, 1983); E. Gellner, *Nationalism* (London, 1997); L. Greenfeld, *Nationalism: Five Roads to Modernity* (Cambridge, Massachusetts, 1992).

2. A. Hastings, *The Construction of Nationhood: Ethnicity, Religion and Nationalism* (Cambridge, 1997); L. Colley, *Britons: Forging the Nation, 1707–1837* (New Haven, 1992); A. M. Thiesse, *La création des identités nationales: Europe, XVIIe-XXe siècles* (Paris, 1999).

3. A. D. Smith, *Nationalism and Modernism* (London, 1998); the best recent summary of nineteenth-century nationalism in Europe is P. J. Geary, *The Myth of Nations: The Medieval Origins of Europe* (Princeton and Oxford, 2002), ch. 1.

4. W. Wunderlich, 'Medieval Images: Joseph Viktor von Scheffel's Novel *Ekkehard* and St Gall', in R. Utz and T. Shippey, eds, *Medievalism in the Modern World: Essays in Honour of Leslie Workman. Making the Middle Ages*, i (Turnhout, 1998), pp. 193–225.

5. C. A. Simmons, '"Iron-Worded Proof": Victorian Identity and the Old English Language', *Studies in Medievalism*, 4 (1992), pp. 202–14; D. J. Palmer, *The Rise*

of English Studies (London, 1965), chs 6 and 7; A. J. Frantzen, *The Desire for Origins: New Language, Old English and Teaching the Tradition* (New Brunswick, New Jersey, and London, 1990); H. Damico, ed., *Medieval Scholarship: Biographical Studies of the Foundation of a Discipline* (3 vols, New York, 2000).

6. Hastings, *Construction of Nationhood*, pp. 130–38.

7. Cited in B. Anzulovic, *Heavenly Serbia: From Myth to Genocide* (New York, 1999), p. 90.

8. Ibid., p. 124; on contemporary issues, see also L. J. Cohen, *Serpent in the Bosom: The Rise and Fall of Slobodan Milosevic* (Boulder, Colorado, and Oxford, 2001), pp. 3–42.

9. Hastings, *Construction of Nationhood*, p. 133.

10. D. E. Barclay, 'Medievalism and Nationalism in Nineteenth Century Germany', *Studies in Medievalism*, 5 (1993), pp. 5–6ff., on which much of this is based.

11. Literature on this topic is considerable; see, for example, J. Whaley, 'German Lands before 1815', in M. Fulbrook, ed., *Germany Since 1800* (London, 1997), pp. 15–37; S. Berger, 'The German Tradition of Historiography', in ibid., pp. 478–80; J. R. Liobera, *The God of Modernity: The Development of Nationalism in Western Europe* (Oxford, 1996), pp. 164–70; F. C. Beiser, *Enlightenment, Revolution and Romanticism: The Genesis of Modern German Political Thought, 1790–1800* (Cambridge, Massachusetts, 1992); M. Hughes, *Early Modern Germany* (London, 1992); eadem, *Nationalism and Society: Germany, 1800–1945* (London, 1988); L. Kerssen, *Das Interesse am Mittelalter im deutschen Nationaldenkmal* (Berlin and New York, 1975); F. Barnard, *Herder's Social and Political Thought: From Enlightenment to Nationalism* (Oxford, 1965); E. Höltenschmidt, *Die Mittelalterrezeption der Brüder Schlegel* (Paderborn, 2000); G. G. Iggers, *The German Conception of History: The National Tradition of Historical Thought from Herter to the Present* (Middletown, Connecticut, 1983).

12. Berger, 'The German Tradition', p. 480.

13. M. Lyons, *Napoleon Bonaparte and the Legacy of the French Revolution* (Basingstoke, 1994), p. 244.

14. Barclay, 'Medievalism and Nationalism', p. 10, notably citing de la Motte-Fouqué.

15. Idem, 'Representing the Middle Ages: Court Festivals in Nineteenth-Century Prussia', in Utz and Shippey, *Medievalism in the Modern World*, pp. 105–16.

16. Cited in Barclay, 'Medievalism and Nationalism', p. 11.

17. S. A. Crane, 'Story, History and the Passionate Collector', in M. Myrone and L. Peltz, eds, *Producing the Past* (Aldershot, 1999), pp. 196–97.

18. Barclay, 'Medievalism and Nationalism', pp. 5–22; K. David-Sirocko, 'Anglo-German Interconnexions during the Gothic Revival: A Case Study from the Work of Georg Gottlob Ungewitter (1820–64)', *Architectural History*, 41 (1998), pp. 153–78.

19. G. L. Mosse, *The Crisis of German Ideology: Intellectual Origins of the Third Reich* (London, 1964), pp. 16–21, 34–35, 54–73, 92–93.

20. Cited in Mosse, *Crisis of German Ideology*, p. 35.

21. F. Spotts, *Bayreuth: A History of the Wagner Festival* (New Haven and London, 1994), pp. 112–14, 130–43, 164–88.

22. L. Barzini, *The Italians* (trans. London, 1983), p. 187.

23. J. Kenyon, *The History Men: The Historical Profession in England since the Renaissance* (2nd edn, London, 1993), pp. 54–56, 61-; Damico, *Medieval Scholarship*; C. T. Berkhout and M. McC.Gatch, eds, *Anglo-Saxon Scholarship: The First Three Centuries* (Boston, 1982); J. W. Burrow, *A Liberal Descent: Victorian Historians of the English Past* (Cambridge, 1981); P. Levine, *The Amateur and the Professional: Antiquarians, Historians and Archaeologists in Victorian England, 1838–1886* (Cambridge, 1986); S. G. Barczewski, *Myth and National Identity in Nineteenth-Century Britain: The Legends of King Arthur and Robin Hood* (Oxford, 2000), pp. 82–89; A. Briggs, *Saxons, Normans and Victorians* (Historical Association, Hastings and Bexhill Branch, 1966); Geary, *Myth of Nations*, pp. 25–30.

24. R. J. Smith, *The Gothic Bequest: Medieval Institutions in British Thought, 1688–1863* (1987), pp. 171–200; Kenyon, *The History Men*, pp. 154–61.

25. On the debate, see S. Reynolds, *Fiefs and Vassals* (1994).

26. A. Chandler, 'Carlyle and the Medievalism of the North', in Utz and Shippey, *Medievalism in the Modern World*, p. 173.

27. A. Chandler, *A Dream of Order: The Medieval Ideal in Nineteenth-Century Literature* (Lincoln, Nebraska, 1970), pp. 79 and 52–81; R. J. Smith, 'Cobbett, Catholic History and the Middle Ages', *Studies in Medievalism*, 4 (1992), pp. 113–42; K. L. Morris, *The Image of the Middle Ages in Romantic and Victorian Literature* (London, 1984), pp. 52–54.

28. Chandler, *Dream of Order*, pp. 152–83; Morris, *Image of the Middle Ages*, pp. 119–26.

29. Chandler, *Dream of Order*, pp. 122–51; eadem, 'Carlyle and the Medievalism of the North', pp. 173–91; A. D. Culler, *The Victorian Mirror of History* (New Haven, 1985), pp. 68–69; R. Jann, 'The Condition of England Past and Present: Thomas Carlyle and the Middle Ages', *Studies in Medievalism*, 1/1 (1979), pp. 15–31.

30. Must of the following relies on E. Emery and L. Morowitz, *Consuming the Past: The Medieval Revival in Fin De Siècle France* (Aldershot, 2003), especially pp. 1–35 and 143–69; quote by C. Morice, *Les Cathédrales de France*, p. 1.

31. H. Redman, *The Roland Legend in Nineteenth-Century French Literature* (Lexington, Kenctucky, 1991); E. Emery, 'The "Truth" About the Middle Ages: *La Revue des Deux Mondes* and Later Nineteenth-Century French Medievalism', in C. A. Simmons, ed., *Medievalism and the Quest for the 'Real' Middle Ages* (London, 2001), pp. 105–8; S. Hibberd, 'Marianne: Mystic or Madwoman?:

Representations of Jeanne d'Arc on the Parisian Stage in the 1820s', in ibid., pp. 87–98; C. Beaune, *Naissance de la nation France* (Paris, 1985); J. R. Dakyns, *The Middle Ages in French Literature, 1851–1900* (Oxford, 1973); C. Amalvi, *Le goût du Moyen Age* (2nd edn, Paris, 2002), pp. 96–114, 231–38.

32. Ibid., pp. 99–115.

33. D. Nelson, 'Gaston Paris in Context: His Predecessors and his Legacy', *Studies in Medievalism*, 2/2 (1982), pp. 53–66.

34. Emery, 'The "Truth" About the Middle Ages', p. 107.

35. Emery and Morowitz, *Consuming the Past*, quote p. 15.

36. H. B. Walters, *The English Antiquaries of the Sixteenth, Seventeenth and Eighteenth Centuries* (London, 1934); Hastings, *Construction of Nationhood*, pp. 58–59; M. McKisack, *Medieval History in the Tudor Age* (Oxford, 1971).

37. Hastings, *Construction of Nationhood*, pp. 82–84.

38. R. Simpson, 'Revisiting Cramalot: An Arthurian Theme in the Correspondence of William Taylor and Robert Southey', *Studies in Medievalism*, 4 (1992), pp. 143–60.

39. E. G. Stanley, *Imagining the Anglo-Saxon Past* (Woodbridge, 2000).

40. A. Wawn, *The Vikings and the Victorians: Inventing the Old North in Nineteenth-Century Britain* (Woodbridge, 2000), pp. 41–59 and 92–116.

41. E. H. Antonsen et al., eds, *The Grimm Brothers and the Germanic Past* (Amsterdam and Philadelphia, 1990); F. R. Jacoby, 'Historical Method and Romantic Vision in Jacob Grimm's Writings', *Studies in Medievalism*, 3/4 (1991), pp. 489–504; E. Höltenschmidt, *Die Mittelalterrezeption der Brüder Schlegel* (Paderborn, 2000); Frantzen, *Desire for Origins*.

42. J. Pearson, 'Crushing the Convent and the Dread Bastille: The Anglo-Saxons, Revolution and Gender in Women's Plays of the 1790s', in D. Scragg and C. Weinberg, eds, *Literary Appropriations of the Anglo-Saxons, Thirteenth to the Twentieth Centuries* (Cambridge, 2000), pp. 122–35.

43. Wawn, *Vikings and the Victorians*, pp. 215–44.

44. Ibid., pp. 142–208 and 283–311.

45. E. Stanley, 'The Glorification of King Alfred of Wessex', in his *Imagining the Anglo-Saxon Past*, pp. 410–38; S. Keynes, 'The Cult of King Alfred', *Anglo-Saxon England*, 28 (1999), pp. 225–356.

46. L. Pratt, 'Anglo-Saxon Attitudes? Alfred the Great and the Romantic National Epic', in Scragg and Weinberg, *Literary Appropriations of the Anglo-Saxons*, pp. 138–56.

47. Cited by J. Mordaunt Crook in C. L. Eastlake, *A History of the Gothic Revival*, introduced by J. Mordaunt Crook (1872; repr. Leicester, 1970) p. 40.

48. J. Parker, 'The Day of a Thousand Years: Winchester's 1901 Commemoration of Alfred the Great', *Studies in Medievalism*, 12 (2003), pp. 113–36.

49. Simmons, '"Iron-Worded Proof"', pp. 202–14.

50. Antonsen, *Grimm Brothers*, passim.

51. Cited in T. A. Shippey, 'The Undeveloped Image: Anglo-Saxon in Popular Consciousness from Turner to Tolkien', in Scragg and Weinberg, *Literary Appropriations of the Anglo-Saxons*, pp. 226–27.

52. L. Kendrick, 'The American Middle Ages: Eighteenth-Century Saxonist Myth-Making', in M.-F. Alamichel and D. Brewer, eds, *The Middle Ages after the Middle Ages in the English-Speaking World* (Woodbridge, 1997), pp. 121–36.

53. C. Brooks, *The Gothic Revival* (London, 1999), p. 55.

54. Shippey, 'The Undeveloped Image', pp. 215–36.

55. Wawn, *Vikings and the Victorians*, pp. 112–15.

56. Cited in D. Cannadine, 'The Context, Performance and Meaning of Ritual: The British Monarchy and the "Invention of Tradition", *c.* 1820–1979', in E. J. Hobsbawm and T. Ranger, *The Invention of Tradition*, pp. 145–46.

57. J. B. Duroselle, *L'idée de l'Europe dans l'histoire* (Paris, 1965); D. Hay, *Europe: The Emergence of an Idea* (2nd edn, Edinburgh, 1968); M. Perrin, *L'idée de l'Europe au fil de deux millénaires* (Paris, 1994); see also above, Chapter 1.

58. D. Heater, *The Idea of European Unity* (Leicester, 1992); P. M. R. Stirk and D. Weigall, eds, *The Origins and Development of European Integration* (London, 1999).

59. Barzini, *The Italians*, p. 199.

60. *Oxford University Gazette*, 2 May 2002, p. 1102.

61. G. Gandino, 'Le Moyen Age dans le cinéma fasciste, un territoire évité', in *Cahiers de la Cinémathèque*, 42/43 (1985), pp. 133–42.

62. R. Taylor, *Film Propaganda: Soviet Russia and Nazi Germany* (London, 1979).

63. Cited in Taylor, *Film Propaganda*, p. 58.

64. J. Aberth, *A Knight at the Movies: Medieval History on Film* (London, 2003), at p. 110.

65. Goebbels, cited in A. Welch, *Nazi Propaganda: The Power and the Limitations* (London, 1983), p. 97.

66. Taylor, *Film Propaganda*, p. 33.

67. M. Wood, *Hitler's Search for the Holy Grail* (Mayavision International, 1999), shown on Channel 4 TV.

68. Welch, *Nazi Propaganda*, p. 310.

69. D. Welch, *Propaganda and the German Cinema, 1933–1945* (Oxford, 1983), pp. 100–7.

70. P. Kenez, *Cinema and Soviet Society, 1917–1953* (Cambridge, 1992); M. Seton, *Sergei M. Eisenstein* (London, 1978).

71. Aberth, *Knight at the Movies*, at p. 108.

72. Ibid., pp. 78, 107–20.

73. J. Richards, *Films and British National Identity: From Dickens to 'Dad's Army'* (Manchester, 1997), pp. 60–75.

74. Cited in ibid., p. 71.

75. Geary, *Myth of Nations*, pp. 1–14.

76. Hobsbawm, *Nations and Nationalism since 1780*, pp. 103–41; D. Conversi, *The Basques, the Catalans and Spain: Alternative Routes to Nationalist Mobilisation* (London, 1997).

77. On these individual cases, see M. Teich and R. Porter, eds, *The National Question in Europe in Historical Context* (Cambridge, 1993).

Notes to Chapter 5: The Celtic Bandwagon

1. M. Chapman, *The Celts: The Construction of a Myth* (Basingstoke, 1992); S. James, *The Atlantic Celts: Ancient People or Modern Invention?* (London, 1999). Currently, even this concept is hotly contested by archaeologists like Simon James, for whom there never was a 'Celtic culture,' or Celtic migrations, in Britain.

2. The best recent discussion is in O. Davies, 'Celtic Christianity: Texts and Representations', in M. Atherton, ed., *Celts and Christians: New Approaches to the Religious Traditions of Britain and Ireland* (Cardiff, 2002), pp. 23–38.

3. Davies, 'Celtic Christianity', p. 28.

4. R. Hutton, 'Introduction: Who Possesses the Past', in P. Carr-Gomm, ed., *The Druid Renaissance: The Voice of Druidry Today* (London, 1996), pp. 28–29.

5. Particularly good examples of this trend are the key 'textbooks' on the subject until about twenty years ago, such as L. Gougaud, *Christianity in Celtic Lands* (trans. London, 1932); J. Ryan, *Irish Monasticism: Origins and Early Development* (1931; repr. Shannon, 1972); N. K. Chadwick, *The Age of the Saints in the Early Celtic Church* (London, 1961); J. Godfrey, *The Church in Anglo-Saxon England* (Cambridge, 1962); L. Bieler, *Ireland: Harbinger of the Middle Ages* (Dublin, 1963); F. Henry, *Irish Art in the Early Christian Period (to AD 800)* (London, 1965).

6. K. Hughes, 'The Celtic Church: Is This a Valid Concept?', *Cambridge Medieval Celtic Studies*, 1 (1981), pp. 1–20; W. Davies, 'The Myth of the Celtic Church', in N. Edwards and A. Lane, eds, *The Early Church in Wales and the West* (Oxford, 1992), pp. 12–21.

7. H. Trevor-Roper, 'The Invention of Tradition: The Highland Tradition of Scotland', in E. J. Hobsbawm and T. Ranger, eds, *The Invention of Tradition* (Cambridge, 1983), pp. 15–41.

8. On the Welsh issue, see P. Morgan, 'From a Death to a View: The Hunt for the Welsh Past in the Romantic Period', in Hobsbawm and Ranger, *Invention of Tradition*, pp. 43–100, at p. 63.

9. Ibid., p. 66.

10. Chapman, *The Celts*; James, *Atlantic Celts*.

11. P. B. Ellis, *The Celtic Dawn: A History of Pan Celticism* (London, 1993).

12. D. B. Haycock, *William Stukeley: Science, Religion and Archaeology in Eighteenth-Century England* (Woodbridge, 2002); R. Hutton, *The Pagan Religions of the Ancient British Isles: Their Nature and Legacy* (Oxford, 1991); S. Piggott, *The Druids* (London, 1975); P. B. Ellis, *A Brief History of the Druids* (London, 2002); Carr-Gomm, *The Druid Renaissance*; L. E. Jones, *Druid, Shaman, Priest: Metaphors of Celtic Paganism* (Thorsons, 1998).

13. Cited by Carr-Gomm, *Druid Renaissance*, p. 11.

14. R. Hutton et al., *Witchcraft and Magic in Europe*, vi: *The Twentieth Century* (London, 1999) and G. Harvey and C. Harman, eds, *Paganism Today* (London, 1995). On the new witchcraft movements, see also D. Purkiss, *The Witch in History: Early, Modern and Twentieth-Century Representations* (London, 1996) and N. Drury, *Magic and Witchcraft* (London, 2004).

15. Cited by Hutton in *Witchcraft and Magic*, pp. 41–42.

16. Ibid., p. 61.

17. I. Adler, *Drawing Down the Moon* (Boston, 1984), p. 178.

18. Cited by Hutton, *Witchcraft and Magic*, p. 62.

19. Ibid., p. 72.

20. Ibid., p. 74.

21. Adler, *Drawing Down the Moon*, p. 93.

22. Hutton, *Witchcraft and Magic*, p. 76.

23. Ibid., pp. 75–77.

24. Carr-Gomm, 'Foreword: The Door', in Carr-Gomm, *The Druid Renaissance*, pp. 1–16.

25. I. Bonewitz, 'The Druid Revival in Modern America', in ibid., p. 85.

26. M. Freeman, 'The Connection Thread: Deep Ecology and the Celtic Vision', in ibid., p. 283.

27. F. MacEwen Owen, 'Nemeton: Healing the Common Wound and the Re-Enchantment of Everyday Life', in ibid., pp. 127–28.

28. Idem, pp. 129–30.

29. C. Matthews, 'Following the Awen: Celtic Shamanism and the Druid Path in the Modern World', in ibid., pp. 133, 138.

30. Cited in Hutton, *Witchcraft and Magic*, pp. 53–54.

31. R. Lowe and W. Shaw, eds, *Travellers: Voices of the New Age* (London, 1993); P. Heelas, *The New Age Movement: The Celebration of the Self and the Sacralization of Modernity* (Oxford, 1996); J. Davis, 'New Age Travellers in the Countryside: Incomers with Attitude', in P. Milbourne, ed., *Revealing Rural 'Others': Representation, Power and Identity in the British Countryside* (London, 1997), pp. 117–34; K. Hetherington, *New Age Travellers: Vans of Uproarious Humanity* (London, 2000).

32. J. J. Jusserand, *English Wayfaring Life in the Middle Ages* (1889; trans. London, 4th edn, 1950; repr. 1960).

33. Heelas, *New Age Movement*, passim. See also N. Drury, *The New Age: Searching for the Spiritual Self* (London, 2004).
34. Hetherington, *New Age Travellers*, p. 12.
35. Idem, p. 119.
36. See above, Chapter 4.
37. See below, Chapter 7.
38. See below, Chapter 8.
39. Even then it was not altogether acceptable: I distinctly recall my tutor at Oxford in the early 1980s pulling me up sharply when I was in the process of waxing lyrical about the learning of the Glastonbury monks, with a crisp: 'get a grip on these romantic fantasies'

Notes to Chapter 6: King Arthur

1. The most accessible editions are J. Morris, ed., *Nennius: British History and the Welsh Annals* (London and Chichester, 1980), pp. 35 and 45; and Geoffrey of Monmouth, *The History of the Kings of Britain* (Harmondsworth, 1966), pp. 211–61.
2. S. G. Barczewski, *Myth and National Identity in Nineteenth-Century Britain: The Legends of King Arthur and Robin Hood* (Oxford, 2000), pp. 16–17.
3. M. Biddle, *King Arthur's Round Table* (Woodbridge, 2000).
4. Barczewski, *Myth and National Identity*, pp. 17–18; A. Davis, *Chivalry and Romance in the English Renaissance* (Woodbridge, 2003), pp. 73–98.
5. M. Girouard, *The Return to Camelot: Chivalry and the English Gentleman* (New Haven and London, 1981), p. 17.
6. D. A. Summers, *Spenser's Arthur: The British Arthurian Tradition and The Faerie Queene* (Lanham, Maryland, and Oxford, 1997); C. B. Milligan, *Spenser and the Table Round: A Study in the Contemporaneous Background for Spenser's Use of the Arthurian Legend* (Cambridge, Massachusetts, 1932); M. Leslie, *Spenser's 'Fine Warres and Faithfull Loves': Martial and Chivalric Symbolism in 'The Faerie Queene'* (Woodbridge, 1983); J. D. Merriman, *The Flower of Kings: A Study of the Arthurian Legend in England between 1485 and 1835* (Lawrence, Kansas, 1973), pp. 38–43.
7. See above, Chapter 4.
8. Fulke Greville, *The Life of the Renowned Sir Philip Sidney* (1652), ed. W. W. Wooden (New York, 1984).
9. Davis, *Chivalry and Romance*.
10. Barczewski, *Myth and National Identity*, pp. 17–18; R. L. Entzminger, 'Jonson, the Myth of Sidney and Nostalgia for Elizabeth', in W. Gentrup, ed., *Reinventing the Middle Ages and the Renaissance: Constructions of the Medieval and Early Modern Period* (Turnhout, 1998), pp. 89–96;

R. F. Brinkley, *Arthurian Legend in the Seventeenth Century* (Baltimore and London, 1932).

11. R. Shay, 'Dryden and Purcell's *King Arthur*: Legend and Politics on the Restoration Stage', in R. Barber, ed., *King Arthur in Music* (Woodbridge, 2002), pp. 9–22; Merriman, *Flower of Kings*, pp. 49–63.

12. Ibid., pp. 64–70; Barczewski, *Myth and National Identity*, pp. 30–35.

13. Ibid., pp. 28–35 and 38–43.

14. Ibid., pp. 38–40; D. N. Mancoff, *The Return to Camelot of King Arthur: The Legend through Victorian Eyes* (London, 1995), p. 22.

15. Sir Ambrose Hardinge Giffard, *Verses* (London, 1824), p. 30, cited in Barczewski, *Myth and National Identity*, pp. 38–39.

16. Girouard, *Return to Camelot*, pp. 22–28.

17. J. Richards, 'From Christianity to Paganism: The New Middle Ages and the Values of "Medieval" Masculinity', *Cultural Values* 3/2 (1999), p. 217.

18. Girouard, *Return to Camelot*, pp. 19–23.

19. E. Burke, *Reflections on the Revolution in France* (1790; London, 1912), p. 73.

20. A. Chandler, 'The Quarrel of the Ancients and Moderns: Peacock and the Medieval Revival', *Bucknell Review*, 13 (1965), pp. 39–50.

21. On Walter Scott, see Girouard, *Return to Camelot*, pp. 30–54; A. Chandler, *A Dream of Order: The Medieval Ideal in Nineteenth Century Literature* (Lincoln, Nebraska, 1970), pp. 12–51; eadem, 'Sir W. Scott and the Medieval Revival', *Nineteenth-Century Fiction*, 19 (1964), pp. 315–32; I. Mitchell, *Scott, Chaucer and Medieval Romance: A Study of Sir Walter Scott's Indebtedness to the Literature of the Middle Ages* (Lexington, Kentucky, 1987); H. Orel, *The Historical Novel from Scott to Sabatini: Changing Attitudes towards a Literary Genre, 1814–1920* (New York, 1995).

22. Merriman, *Flower of Kings*, pp. 117–21, 149–58 and 149–57; on Scott and the Arthurian material see also E. Fay, *Romantic Medievalism: History and the Romantic Literary Ideal* (Basingstoke, 2002), pp. 71–78.

23. Barczewski, *Myth and National Identity*, pp. 106–8; R. Jeffrey Easby, 'The Myth of Merrie England in Victorian Painting', in F. Boos, ed., *History and Community: Essays in Victorian Medievalism* (New York and London, 1992), pp. 59–80.

24. R. Bales, *Proust and the Middle Ages* (Geneva, 1975), pp. 90–103.

25. Girouard, *Return to Camelot*, pp. 56–65; K. L. Morris, *The Image of the Middle Ages in Romantic and Victorian Literature* (London, 1984), pp. 103–19.

26. Girouard, *Return to Camelot*, pp. 69–86; Chandler, *Dream of Order*, pp. 152–83; Barczewski, *Myth and National Identity*, pp. 64–68; Morris, *Image of the Middle Ages*, pp. 119–26.

27. Cited in A. D. Culler, *The Victorian Mirror of History* (New Haven, 1985), p. 159; see also pp. 159–60.

28. B. Disraeli, *Sybil*, bk 3, ch. 5.

29. Girouard, *Return to Camelot*, pp. 88–110.

30. Ibid., pp. 112–15.

31. Ibid., pp. 116–28.

32. D. Barclay, 'Representing the Middle Ages: Court Festivals in Nineteenth- Century Prussia', in R. Utz and T. Shippey, eds, *Medievalism in the Modern World: Essays in Honour of Leslie Workman. Making the Middle Ages*, i (Turnhout, 1998), pp. 105–16.

33. B. Taylor and E. Brewer, eds, *The Return to Camelot of King Arthur: British and American Arthurian Literature since 1800* (Cambridge, 1983); A. Lupack and B. Tepa Lupack, *King Arthur in America* (Woodbridge, 2002); A. Lupack, 'The Figure of King Arthur in America', in Mancoff, *Return to Camelot of King Arthur*, pp. 121–36; K. I. Moreland, *The Medievalist Impulse in American Literature: Twain, Adams, Fitzgerald and Hemingway* (Charlottesville, Virginia, and London, 1996), pp. 3–4.

34. E. D. Genovese, 'The Southern Slaveholders' View of the Middle Ages', in B. Rosenthal and P. E. Szarmach, eds, *Medievalism in American Culture: Special Studies* (*Studies in Medievalism*, special issue, New York 1987), pp. 31–52.

35. K. Verduin, 'Medievalism and the Mind of Emerson', ibid., pp. 128–50.

36. G. Barnes, 'The Fireside Vikings and the "Boy's Own" Vinland: Vinland in Popular English and American Literature (1841–1926)', in Gentrup, *Reinventing the Middle Ages*, pp. 149–52.

37. W. Calin, 'What *Tales of a Wayside Inn* Tells us about Longfellow and about Chaucer', *Studies in Medievalism*, 12 (2003), pp. 197–214.

38. See below, Chapter 4.

39. See below, Chapter 8.

40. L. White, 'The Legacy of the Middle Ages in the American Wild West', *Speculum*, 40 (1965), p. 191; M. W. Bloomfield, 'Reflections of a Medievalist: America, Medievalism and the Middle Ages', in Rosenthal and Szarmach, *Medievalism in American Culture*, pp. 13–29; L. Kendrick, 'The American Middle Ages: Eighteenth-Century Saxonist Myth-Making', in M.-F. Alamichel and D. Brewer, eds, *The Middle Ages after the Middle Ages in the English-Speaking World* (Woodbridge, 1997), pp. 121–24.

41. Girouard, *Return to Camelot*, pp. 132–44, 164–76; Barczewski, *Myth and National Identity*, pp. 68–70.

42. Girouard, *Return to Camelot*, p. 222.

43. Ibid., pp. 220–29.

44. Ibid., pp., 253–58, 260–63; Barczewski, *Myth and National Identity*, passim; R. Simpson, 'St George and the Pendragon', in Utz and Shippey, *Medievalism in the Modern World*, pp. 134–39; R. Hutton, *The Stations of the Sun: A History of the Ritual Year in Britain* (Oxford, 1996; repr. 2001), pp. 216–17.

45. Sir Robert Baden Powell, cited by J. A. Kestner, 'The Return of St George, 1850–1915', in D. N. Mancoff, ed., *King Arthur's Modern Return to Camelot* (New York, 1998), p. 95.

46. Kestner, 'Return of St George', pp. 85–93.

47. Seen in Northam churchyard (Devon); with thanks to P. Glare.

48. Girouard, *Return to Camelot*, pp. 276–93; A. J. Frantzen, *Bloody God: Chivalry, Sacrifice and the Great War* (Chicago, 2004) has appeared too late for me to consult it: I have been able to read a review of it, and many issues mentioned are clearly of relevance to this section.

49. C. Ricks, *Tennyson* (2nd edn, Berkeley, California, 1989); N. U. Haghofer, *The Fall of Arthur's Kingdom: A Study of Tennyson's 'The Holy Grail'* (Salzburg, 1997); A. H. Harrison, *Victorian Poets and the Politics of Culture: Discourse and Ideology* (Charlottesville, Virginia, and London, 1998); idem, 'Medievalism and the Ideologies of Victorian Poetry', *Studies in Medievalism*, 4 (1992), pp. 219–34; R. Simpson, *Camelot Regained: The Arthurian Revival and Tennyson, 1800–1849* (Woodbridge, 1990); Mancoff, *Return to Camelot of King Arthur*, passim; Barczewski, *Myth and National Identity*, pp. 173–89.

50. Girouard, *Return to Camelot*, pp. 178–85; Harrison, 'Medievalism and the Ideologies of Victorian Poetry', pp. 223–33.

51. Girouard, *Return to Camelot*, pp. 198–216; Barczewski, *Myth and National Identity*, pp. 165–81.

52. A. H. Harrison, *Swinburne's Medievalism: A Study in Victorian Love Poetry* (Baton Rouge, Louisiana, and London, 1988); idem, *Victorian Poets*, pp. 23–43; L. C. and R. T. Lambdin, *Camelot in the Nineteenth Century: Arthurian Characters in the Poems of Tennyson, Arnold, Morris and Swinburne* (Westport, Connecticut, and London, 2000); V. A. Countryman, *Swinburne's Medievalism in Context* (Oxford, 2002); K. Powell, 'Burne-Jones, Swinburne, and "Laus Veneris"', in L. de Girolami Cheney, ed., *Pre-Raphaelitism and Medievalism in the Arts* (Lampeter, 1992), pp. 221–40.

53. L. de Girolami Cheney, 'The Fair Lady and the Virgin in Pre-Raphaelite Art: The Evolution of a Societal Myth', in her *Pre-Raphaelitism*, pp. 241–80, and eadem, 'Locks, Tresses and Manes in Pre-Raphaelite Paintings', pp. 159–92; Barczewski, *Myth and National Identity*, pp. 177–89; R. Cochran, 'Tennyson's Hierarchy of Women in "*Idylls of the Kings*"', in Boos, *History and Community*, pp. 81–108.

54. D. de Rougemont, *Love and the Western World* (1939; trans. Princeton, 1983) and *The Myths of Love* (trans. London, 1963).

55. D. Watson, 'Wagner: *Tristan und Isolde* and *Parsifal*', in Barber, *King Arthur in Music*, pp. 23–34.

56. Harrison, *Victorian Poets*, p. 39.

57. Cheney, 'Fair Lady', pp. 241–80.

58. N. J. Woodall, '"Women Are Knights-Errant to the Last": Nineteenth-Century Women Writers Reinvent the Medieval Literary Damsel', in Gentrup, *Reinventing the Middle Ages*, pp. 201–21.

59. Barczewski, *Myth and National Identity*, pp. 187–9; B. Taylor, 'Re-Vamping Vivien: Reinventing Myth in Victorian Iconography', in Mancoff, *King Arthur's Modern Return to Camelot*, pp. 65–82; L. K. Hughes, '"Come Again and Thrice as Fair": Reading Tennyson's Beginning', in ibid., pp. 56–75.

60. Barczewski, *Myth and National Identity*, pp. 190–200.

61. Ibid., pp. 82–89, 94–95, 108–45.

62. Ibid., pp. 202–24.

63. V. M. Lagorio, 'King Arthur and Camelot, USA, in the Twentieth Century', in Rosenthal and Szarmach, *Medievalism in American Culture*, pp. 152–55.

64. A. E. Mathis, *The King Arthur Myth in Modern American Literature* (Jefferson, North Carolina, and London, 2002), p. 25; Moreland, *Medievalist Impulse in American Literature*, pp. 28–71; R. B. Salomon, *Twain and the Image of History* (New Haven, 1961), pp. 95–128; H. Nash Smith, *Mark Twain's Fable of Progress: Political and Economic Ideas in 'A Connecticut Yankee at King Arthur's Court'* (New Brunswick, 1964), pp. 47–99.

65. This is the title of a recent book by W. Schivelbusch (London, 2003), which discusses, among others, the consequences of the Civil War defeat on the Deep South, notably by examining the prevalent mood of an imagined romantic society which both allowed it to happen and maintained the nostalgia for that society in the post-war years. The book clearly reuses Twain's perception of the problems besetting the South.

66. Cited in Moreland, *Medievalist Impulse in American Literature*, p. 34.

67. Moreland, *Medievalist Impulse in American Literature*, p. 22; Lupack, 'Figure of King Arthur in America', pp. 133–35; T. Hayashi, ed., *Steinbeck and the Arthurian Theme*, Steinbeck Monograph Series, 5 (1975).

68. Steinbeck, cited by Lupack in Mancoff, *King Arthur's Modern Return*, p. 133.

69. Lagorio, 'King Arthur and Camelot', pp. 151–69; Mathis, *King Arthur Myth*, pp. 95–105.

70. The musicologist William Everett, cited in Mathis, *King Arthur Myth*, p. 100.

71. Thomas Brown, cited in ibid., p. 104.

72. C. Lindahl, 'Three Ways of Coming Back: Folklore Perspectives on Arthur's Return', in Mancoff, *King Arthur's Modern Return to Camelot*, p. 24.

73. Moreland, *Medievalist Impulse in American Literature*, pp. 118–60 (for Scott Fitzgerald), pp. 23–24 (for Faulkner); Mathis, *King Arthur Myth*, pp. 43–60 for Chandler.

74. A. C. Lupack, 'Modern Arthurian Novelists on the Arthurian Legend', *Studies in Medievalism*, 2/4 (1983), pp. 79–88; Lupack, 'Figure of King Arthur in America', pp. 125–26.

75. Idem, 'Visions of Courageous Achievement: Arthurian Youth Groups in America', *Studies in Medievalism*, 6 (1994), pp. 50–68.

76. J. Fox-Friedman, 'The Chivalric Order for Children: Arthur's Return in Late Nineteenth- and Early Twentieth-Century America', in Mancoff, *King Arthur's Modern Return to Camelot*, p. 149, and also pp. 137–58.

77. Mathis, *King Arthur Myth*, pp. 18–20.

78. Cited in ibid., p. 20.

79. Mathis, *King Arthur Myth*, pp. 2, 60–64.

80. Taylor and Brewer, *Return to Camelot of King Arthur*, passim.

81. Ibid.

82. Ibid.; Barczewski, *Myth and National Identity*, pp. 231–35.

83. Norris J. Lacy, 'King Arthur Goes to War', in Mancoff, *King Arthur's Modern Return to Camelot*, pp. 121–67; Mathis, *King Arthur Myth*, pp. 122–38.

84. J. O. Fichte, 'The End of Utopia and the Treatment of Arthur and his Court in Contemporary German Drama', in P. Boitani and A. Torti, eds, *Medievalitas: Reading the Middle Ages* (Woodbridge, 1996), pp. 153–69.

85. K. Filmer-Davies, *Fantasy Fiction and Welsh Myth: Tales of Belonging* (Basingstoke, 1996); Lagorio, 'King Arthur and Camelot', pp. 155–63.

86. Most representative among the books on this subject is the famous or infamous *Holy Blood, Holy Grail*, by M. Baigent et al., with its large accompanying literature of refutation; see M. Baine Campbell, 'Finding the Grail: Fascist Aesthetics and Mysterious Objects', in Mancoff, *King Arthur's Modern Return to Camelot*, pp. 213–26.

Notes to Chapter 7: Medieval Inspirations

1. On the Victorian Gothic and the ghost story genre, see, for example, K. Hurley, 'British Gothic Fiction, 1885–1930', in J. E. Hogle, ed., *The Cambridge Companion to Gothic Fiction* (Cambridge, 2004), pp. 189–207; A. Millbank, 'The Victorian Gothic in English Novels and Stories', in ibid., pp. 145–65; J. Briggs, *Night Visitors: The Rise and Fall of the English Ghost Story* (London, 1977); R. Robbins and J. Wolfreys, eds, *Victorian Gothic: Literary and Cultural Manifestations in the Nineteenth Century* (Houndmills, 2000); J. Wolfreys, *Victorian Hauntings: Spectrality, Gothic, the Uncanny and Literature* (Basingstoke, 2002); C. Schmitt, 'The Gothic Romance in the Victorian Period', in P. Brantlinger and W. B. Thesig, eds, *A Companion to the Victorian Novel* (Oxford, 2002), pp. 302–17; D. Punter, *The Literature of Terror: A History of Gothic Fictions from 1765 to the Present Day* (2nd edn, 2 vols, London, 1996); and ibid. and G. Byron, eds, *The Gothic* (Oxford, 2004), pp. 21–31.

2. On Fantastic literature, see, among others, R. Caillois, *Au coeur du Fantastique* (Paris, 1965); C. N. Manlove, *Modern Fantasy: Five Studies* (Cambridge, 1975);

idem, *The Impulse of Fantasy Literature* (London, 1983); P. Penzoldt, *The Supernatural in Fiction* (London, 1952); E. S. Rabkin, *The Fantastic in Literature* (Princeton, 1976); D. Scarborough, *The Supernatural in Modern English Fiction* (London, 1952); T. Siebers, *The Romantic Fantastic* (Ithaca, New York, 1984); T. Todorov, *The Fantastic* (trans. New York, 1973); L. Vax, *L'art et la littérature fantastiques* (Paris, 1974); D. Jasper, 'The Fantastic', in J. Raimond and J. R. Watson, eds, *A Handbook of English Romanticism* (Houndmills, 1992), pp. 103–5.

3. L. Hüning, *Geschichte und Fiktion bei Jeanne Bourin and Jean Markale* (Bonn, 1991).

4. Cited in ibid., p. 27.

5. N. Havely, ed., *Dante's Modern Afterlife: Reception and Response from Blake to Heaney* (Basingstoke, 1998): see especially B. O'Donoghue, 'Dante's Versatility and Seamus Heaney's Modernism', pp. 242–57, on Heaney's translation and the direct structural influence of Dante, especially in *Station Island.*

6. G. M. Gugelberger, *Ezra Pound's Medievalism* (Frankfurt, 1978), pp. 45–72 and 95–144; see also S. Y. McDongal, *Ezra Pound and the Troubadour Tradition* (Princeton, New Jersey, 1972), and D. Anderson, 'A Language to Translate into: The Pre-Elizabethan Idiom of Pound's Later Cavalcanti Translations', *Studies in Medievalism*, 2/1 (1982), pp. 9–18.

7. L. Tarte-Holley, 'Chaucer, T. S. Eliot and the Regenerative Pilgrimage', ibid., pp. 19–33.

8. G. Ralph, 'Medievalism and Twentieth-Century Religious Drama', ibid., pp. 35–57.

9. E. C. Dunn, T. Fotitch and B. Feebles, eds, *The Medieval Drama and its Claudelian Revival* (Washington, DC, 1970).

10. I. Boyd, 'Chesterton's Medievalism', *Studies in Medievalism*, 3/3 (1991), pp. 243–55; C. Heady, 'Heraldry and Red Hats: Linguistic Skepticism and Chesterton's Revision of Ruskinian Medievalism', in C. A. Simmons, ed., *Medievalism and the Quest for the 'Real' Middle Ages* (London, 2001), pp. 131–43.

11. M. Alexander, *Catholicism Romantically Revived: Hopkins and Medievalism* (Hopkins Society Annual Lecture, 2001).

12. F. Marucci, *'The Fine Delight that Fathers Thought': Rhetoric and Medievalism in Gerard Manley Hopkins* (trans. Washington, DC, 1994).

13. E. Emery and L. Morowitz, *Consuming the Past: The Medieval Revival in Fin de Siècle France* (Aldershot, 2003), ch. 1; E. Emery, 'The "Truth" about the Middle Ages: *La Revue des Deux Mondes* and Later Nineteenth-Century French Medievalism', in Simmons, *Medievalism and the Quest for the 'Real' Middle Ages*, pp. 99–115; J. R. Dakyns, *The Middle Ages in French Literature, 1851–1900* (Oxford, 1973); C. Beaune, *Naissance de la nation France* (Paris, 1985);

M. Warner, *Joan of Arc: The Image of Female Heroism* (Berkeley, California, 2000); B. G. Keller, *The Middle Ages Reconsidered: Attitudes in France from the Eighteenth Century through the Romantic Movement* (New York, 1994).

14. K. I. Moreland, *The Medievalist Impulse in American literature: Twain, Adams, Fitzgerald and Hemingway* (Charlottesville, Virginia, 1996), pp. 35–36.

15. J. L. Singman, *Robin Hood: The Shaping of a Legend* (Westport, Connecticut, and London, 1998); S. G. Barczewski, *Myth and National Identity in Nineteenth-Century Britain: The Legends of King Arthur and Robin Hood* (Oxford, 2000), pp. 30–31 and 39–43.

16. J. V. McMahon, 'Spruchdichter und Liedermacher: Songs Then and Now', in A. Classen, ed., *Medieval German Voices in the Twenty-First Century* (Atlanta, Amsterdam, 2000), pp. 61–79.

17. D. F. Finsley, 'Medieval German Religious Literature as a Paradigm for Gender Studies', in ibid., pp. 123–44; on Hildegard's impact on music, see A. Kreutziger-Herr and D. Radepenning, eds, *Mittelalter-Sehnsucht? Texte des interdisziplinären Symposiums zur musikalischen Mittelalterrezeption an der Universität Heidelberg, April 1998*, pp. 187–261.

18. E. Little, *The Fantasts: Studies in J. R. R. Tolkien, Lewis Carroll, Mervyn Peake, Nikolay Gogol and Kenneth Grahame* (Amersham, 1984), pp. 1–12.

19. M. R. Hillegas, ed., *Shadows of Imagination* (Carbondale, Illinois, 1969), pp. 68–69.

20. Ibid., pp. 100–6; Little, *Fantasts*, pp. 31–38.

21. J. Chance, *Tolkien's Art: A Mythology for England* (Lexington, Kentucky, 2001), pp. 42–43, 77–79 and 162–83.

22. T. Shippey, *The Road to Middle Earth* (London, 1982), p. 189.

23. H. Carpenter, *Tolkien* (London, 1977), pp. 77, 101–2, 136–40.

24. Ancient and Medieval History Book Club catalogue, May 2003.

25. Letter cited in J. Chance, ed., *Tolkien the Medievalist* (London, 2003), p. 2.

26. Carpenter, *Tolkien*, pp. 192 and quote p. 89.

27. M. Yorke, *Mervyn Peake: My Eyes Mint Gold. A Life* (London, 2000), p. 344.

28. Little, *Fantasts*, p. 84.

29. Ibid., pp. 54–73; T. J. Gardiner-Scott, *Mervyn Peake: The Evolution of a Dark Romantic* (New York, 1989), pp. 3–4, 9, 22–23, 373–74.

30. Yorke, *Mervyn Peake*, pp. 341–44.

31. M. Peake, *Titus Groan* (Harmondsworth, 1968; repr. 1979), p. 196.

32. Art. in the *Daily Mail*, 19 March 2004, p. 3.

33. D. Leech-Wilkinson, 'Yearning for the Sound of Medieval Music', in Kreutziger-Herr and Radepenning, *Mittelalter-Sehnsucht?*, pp. 295–317.

34. E. E. Christian and B. Lindsay, 'The Habit of Detection: The Medieval Monk as Detective in the Novels of Ellis Peters', *Studies in Medievalism*, 4 (1992), pp. 276–89.

Notes to Chapter 8: Camelot Goes Celluloid

1. P. Sorlin, *The Film in History: Restaging the Past* (Oxford, 1980).
2. See above, Chapter 4.
3. See above, Chapter 1.
4. K. J. Harty, *The Reel Middle Ages: American, Western and Eastern European, Middle Eastern and Asian Films about Medieval Europe* (Jefferson, North Carolina, 1999).
5. The following discussion and statistics rely on Harty, *Reel Middle Ages*; V. Attolini, *Immagini del Medioevo nell'cinema* (Bari, 1993); J. Aberth, *A Knight at the Movies: Medieval History on Film* (London, 2003); G. A. Smith, *Epic Films: Cast, Credits and Commentaries on over 250 Historical Spectacle Movies* (Jefferson, North Carolina, and London, 1991); D. Elley, *The Epic Film: Myth and History* (London, 1984), ch. 11.
6. P. Lucanio, *With Fire and Sword: Italian Spectacle on American Screens, 1958–1968* (Metuchen, New Jersey, 1994).
7. K. D. Jones and A. F. McClure, *Hollywood at War: The American Motion Picture and World War Two* (New York, 1974).
8. Elley, *The Epic Film*, p. 154.
9. Aberth, *Knight at the Movies*, who includes every kind of 'moving image' form, counts about 242 versions of King Arthur and over 41 of Joan of Arc.
10. S. Harper, *Picturing the Past: The Rise and Fall of British Costume Film* (London, 1994).
11. They include new versions of the Pia de' Tolomei story as well as that of Paolo and Francesca (also from Dante), Cola di Rienzo, Joan of Naples, Giulia Colonna, Lucrece Borgia, the *Gerusalemme Liberata*, the life of Boccaccio, Lohengrin, Catherine of Siena, Anthony of Padua, Wilhelm Tell, Ugolino, the Sicilian Vespers, the Empress Theodora, Joan of Arc, Siegfried, the Mongols, Genghis Khan, the Thief of Baghdad, Marco Polo, Aladdin, Sinbad, the Normans in Sicily, Ivanhoe, the Moors in Spain, the Crusades, Roland and the Paladins, Dagobert, Ivanhoe, Don Giovanni, and several versions of Robin Hood, the last in date seeing the hero use his karate and martial arts skills taught him by an eastern master.
12. D. Lorenzen and U. Weinitschke, '"Les Niebelungen", de Fritz Land à Harald Reinl', in *Cahiers de la Cinémathèque*, 42/43 (1985), pp. 106–12.
13. A comparison made independently by one of my students, also noticed by Aberth, *Knight at the Movies*, p. 17.
14. Attolini, *Immagini del Medioevo*, p. 20, author's trans.
15. See for example, S. Knight, 'A Garland of Robin Hood Films', *Film and History*, 29 (1999), pp. 34–44.

16. J. Richards, 'Robin Hood on Film and Television Since 1945', in *Visual Culture in Britain*, ii (Aldershot, 2001), pp. 67–77, 79–80.

17. L. Blunk, 'Red Robin: The Radical Politics of Richard Carpenter's *Robin of Sherwood*', in T. Hahn, ed., *Robin Hood in Popular Culture* (Cambridge, 2000), pp. 29–40.

18. R. Hutton, *The Triumph of the Moon* (Oxford, 1999), pp. 369–88.

19. K. Biddick, *The Shock of Medievalism* (Durham and London, 1998), pp. 71–80.

20. Aberth, *Knight at the Movies*, pp. 170–73.

21. Elley, *The Epic Film*, p. 142.

22. R. Pernoud, 'Jeanne d'Arc à l'écran', *Cahiers de la Cinémathèque*, 42/43 (1985), pp. 40–42; K. Harty, 'Jeanne au cinema', in B. Wheeler and C. T. Wood, eds, *Fresh Verdicts on Joan of Arc* (New York, 1996); G. Lerner, 'Joan of Arc: Three Films', in T. Mico et al., *Past Imperfect: History According to the Movies* (New York, 1995); C. Yervasi, 'The Faces of Joan: Cinematic Representations of Joan of Arc', *Film and History*, 29 (1999), pp. 8–19; see also N. Margolis, *Joan of Arc in History, Literature and Film* (New York, 1990).

23. M. Oms, 'De Lavisse à Michelet ou Jeanne d'Arc entre les deux guerres', *Cahiers de la Cinémathèque*, 42/43 (1985), pp. 43–44.

24. Aberth, *Knight at the Movies*, p. 278.

25. R. Python, 'Joan of Arc de Victor Fleming: de la résistance à la nuée', *Cahiers de la Cinémathèque*, 42/43 (1985), pp. 50–58.

26. H. Agel, 'La Jeanne d'Arc de Dreyer', ibid., pp. 45–49.

27. Carl Dreyer, cited in Aberth, *Knight at the Movies*, p. 281.

28. G. Morgan, 'Modern Mystics, Medieval Saints', *Studies in Medievalism*, 12 (2003), pp. 39–54.

29. Harty, *Reel Middle Ages*, p. 5.

30. Literature on this subject is vast. In addition to the general books like Harty, *Reel Middle Ages* and Attolini, *Immagini del Medioevo*, see K. J. Harty, ed., *Cinema Arthuriana: Essays on Arthurian Film* (New York, 1991); B. Olson, *Arthurian Legends on Film and Television* (Jefferson, North Carolina, 2000); 'La chevalerie à l'écran', *Avant-Scène du Cinema*, 221, February 1979, pp. 29–40; R. A. and S. J. Umland, *The Use of Arthurian Legend in Hollywood Film from Connecticut Yankees to Fisher Kings* (Westport, Connecticut, 1996); S. Gorgievski, 'The Arthurian Legend in the Cinema: Myth or History?', in R. Utz and T. Shippey, eds, *Medievalism in the Modern World: Essays in Honour of Leslie Workman. Making the Middle Ages*, i (Turnhout, 1998), pp. 153–66; F. de la Bretèque, 'La Table Ronde au Far West: les Chevaliers de la Table Ronde de Richard Thorpe (1953)', *Cahiers de la Cinémathèque*, 42/43 (1985), pp. 97–102.

31. F. de la Bretèque, 'Une "figure obligée" du film de chevalerie: le Tournoi', *Cahiers de la Cinémathèque*, 42/43 (1985), pp. 21–26, esp. 21–24.

32. J. Jenkins, 'The Aging of the King: Arthur and America in *First Knight*', in D. N. Mancoff, ed., *King Arthur's Modern Return* (New York, 1998), pp. 204–10.

33. M. Plas, '"Merlin l'enchanteur" de Walt Disney: du roman médiéval au conte de fées', *Cahiers de la Cinémathèque*, 42/43 (1985), pp. 103–4.

34. N. Haydock, 'Arthurian Melodrama, Chaucerian Spectacle and the Waywardness of Cinematic Pastiche in *First Knight* and *A Knight's Tale*', *Studies in Medievalism*, 12 (2003), pp. 20–38.

35. Aberth, *Knight at the Movies*, pp. 111–16.

36. Haydock, 'Arthurian Melodrama', pp. 20–24; Biddick, *The Shock of Medievalism*, pp. 71–80.

37. R. Hein and C. Saisset, 'La chevalerie dans les étoiles: les thèmes chevaleresques dans la trilogie de George Lucas', *Cahiers de la Cinémathèque*, 42/43 (1985), pp. 167–69.

38. F. de la Bretèque, 'L'épée dans le lac: *Excalibur* de John Boorman ou les aléas de la puissance', ibid., pp. 91–96; Gorgievski, 'Arthurian Legend in the Cinema', pp. 157–61, 163–65.

39. Attolini, *Immagini del Medioevo*, pp. 139–56; J. Marty, '*Perceval le Gallois* d'Eric Rohmer: un itinéraire roman', *Cahiers de la Cinémathèque*, 42/43 (1985), pp. 125–32.

40. A. Cugier, '*Lancelot du Lac* de Robert Bresson: le Moyen Age revisité ou la dimension tragique du XXe siècle', ibid., pp. 119–24.

41. R. Maltby and I. Craven, *Hollywood Cinema: An Introduction* (Oxford, 1995), pp. 30–31.

42. Elley, *The Epic Film*, pp. 145–46.

43. Attolini, *Immagini del Medioevo*, pp. 97–117; J.-F. Six, 'François d'Assise', *Cahiers de la Cinémathèque*, 42/43 (1985), pp. 29–35.

44. One could add to the corpus his *Arabian Tales* made the following year, in the same vein.

45. Attolini, *Immagini del Medioevo*, pp. 55–62; G. Freixe, 'Approche du *Décameron* de Pier Paolo Pasolini', *Cahiers de la Cinémathèque*, 42/43 (1985), pp. 143–51; C. L. Robinson, 'Celluloid Criticism: Pasolini's Contribution to a Chaucerian Debate', *Studies in Medievalism*, 5 (1993), pp. 115–26.

46. P. A. Sigal, 'Brancaleone s'en va-t-aux croisades: satire d'un Moyen Age conventionnel', *Cahiers de la Cinémathèque*, 42/43 (1985), pp. 152–54; Attolini, *Immagini del Medioevo*, pp. 43–52.

47. Elley, *The Epic Film*, pp. 154–55, quotation on p. 155.

48. Aberth, *Knight at the Movies*, pp. 182, 184.

49. Attolini, *Immagini del Medioevo*, pp. 70–73.

50. L. de Looze, 'Modern Approaches and the"Real" Middle Ages: Bertrand Tavernier's La *Passion Béatrice*', *Studies in Medievalism*, 5, pp. 183–99.

51. There is a vast literature on Bergman and on this film in particular. See especially I. Bergman, *The Seventh Seal* (trans. London, 1968) and M. Bragg, ed., *The Seventh Seal* (BFI Film Classics, London, 1968); B. Steene, *Focus on the Seventh Seal* (Englewood Cliffs, New Jersey, 1972); P. Cowie, 'Milieu and Texture in the Seventh Seal', in S. J. Solomon, ed., *The Classic Cinema: Essays in Criticism* (New York, 1973); S. Björkman et al., *Bergman on Bergman* (trans. London, 1973); P. Cowie, *Ingmar Bergman: A Critical Biography* (London, 1982); J. Donner, *The Films of Ingmar Bergman* (New York, 1972); F. Gado, *The Passion of Ingmar Bergman* (Durham and London, 1986); R. E. Long, *Ingmar Bergman: Film and Stage* (New York, 1994); Ingmar Bergman, *Images: My Life in Film* (trans. New York, 1994); R. G. Oliver, ed., *Ingmar Bergman: An Artist's Journey* (New York, 1995).

52. R. E. Lauder, *God, Death, Art and Love: The Philosophical Vision of Ingmar Bergman* (New York, 1989).

53. W. D. Paden, 'Reconstructing the Middle Ages: The Monk's Sermon in *The Seventh Seal*', in Utz and Shippey, *Medievalism in the Modern World*, pp. 287–305.

54. Bergman, preface to the screenplay for *The Seventh Seal*, p. 8

55. R. H. Osberg, 'Pages Torn from the Book: Narrative Disintegration in Gilliam's *The Fisher King*', *Studies in Medievalism*, 7, pp. 194–224.

56. Aberth, *Knight at the Movies*, pp. 24–28.

57. J. Fraser, *America and the Pattern of Chivalry* (Cambridge, 1982), pp. 12 and 16; J. Richards, 'From Christianity to Paganism: The New Middle Ages and the Values of "Medieval" Masculinity', *Cultural Values*, 3/2 (1999), pp. 216–20.

58. Ibid., p. 223.

59. Attolini, *Immagini del Medioevo*, pp. 94–96; P. Bordes, 'Moyen Age ou Heroic Fantasy?', *Cahiers de la Cinémathèque*, 42/43 (1985), pp. 171–82.

60. Richards, 'From Christianity to Paganism', p. 226.

61. Ibid., pp. 227–30.

62. Harty, *Reel Middle Ages*, pp. 5 and 7.

63. Ibid., p. 6.

64. Aberth, *Knight at the Movies*, pp. 86–107. I have been unable to see this film, and am therefore relying on Aberth's analysis of it.

65. Ibid., pp. 79–86 and 127–457.

66. D. Punter and G. Byron, eds, *The Gothic* (Oxford, 2004).

Notes to Chapter 9: Selling the Middle Ages

1. Among many, it is worth mentioning at least the now classic R. Hewison, *The Heritage Industry: Britain in a Climate of Decline* (London, 1987); J. Carman,

Archaeology and Heritage: An Introduction (London, 2002); M. Hunter, ed., *Preserving the Past: The Rise of Heritage in Modern Britain* (Stroud, 1996) and P. Wright, *On Living in an Old Country* (London, 1985).

2. English Heritage, *Health, Safety and Security: Managing and Presenting Heritage Sites* (London, 2001); S. Macdonald, *The Politics of Display: Museums, Sciences, Culture* (London, 1998); P. M. McManus, *Archaeological Displays and the Public: Museology and Interpretation* (London, 1996); N. Merriman, *Beyond the Glass Case: The Public, Museums and Heritage in Britain* (Leicester, 1991).

3. See above, Chapters 5 and 6.

4. G. Baddeley, *Goth Chic: A Connoisseur's Guide to Dark Culture* (London, 2002); P. Hodkinson, *Goth: Identity, Style and Subculture* (Oxford, 2002); S. Martin, 'Gothic Scholars Don't Wear Black: Gothic Studies and Gothic Subcultures', *Gothic Studies*, 4/1, pp. 28–43.

5. The following titles and quotes are all taken from English Heritage and CADW prospectuses, mostly from 2003.

6. U. Eco, *Travels in Hyperreality* (trans. London, 1986), pp. 3–57.

7. D. Mills, 'Replaying the Medieval Past: Revival of Chester's Mystery Plays', *Studies in Medievalism*, 7 (1995), pp. 181–93.

Notes to Chapter 10: Which Middle Ages?

1. J. Paxman, *The English* (London, 2000); see also other similar views on this, such as R. Scruton's in *England: An Elegy* (London, 2001).

2. A. Minc, *Le nouveau Moyen Age* (2nd edn, Paris, 2002).

3. U. Eco, *Travels in Hyperreality* (trans. London, 1986), pp. 77–85.

Bibliography

Aberbach, D., *The Ideas of Richard Wagner: An Examination and Analysis of his Major Aesthetic, Political, Economic, Social and Religious Thoughts* (Lanham and London, 1984).

Aberth, J., *A Knight at the Movies: Medieval History on Film* (London, 2003).

Ackroyd, P., *Albion: The Origins of the English Imagination* (London, 2002).

Adler, I., *Drawing Down the Moon* (Boston, 1984).

Agel, H., 'La Jeanne d'Arc de Dreyer', *Cahiers de la Cinémathèque*, 42/43 (1985), pp. 45–49.

Agrawal, R. R., *The Medieval Revival and its Influence on the Romantic Movement* (New Delhi, 1990).

Alamichel, M.-F. and Brewer, D., eds, *The Middle Ages after the Middle Ages in the English-Speaking World* (Woodbridge, 1997).

Alcock, L., *Arthur's Britain* (London, 1971).

Aldrich, M., *The Gothic Revival* (London, 1994).

Alexander, M., *Catholicism Romantically Revived: Hopkins and Medievalism* (Hopkins Society Annual Lecture, 2001).

Allaire, G., *Andrea da Barberino and the Language of Chivalry* (Florida, 1997).

Amalvi, C., *Le goût du Moyen Age* (2nd edn, Paris, 2002).

Anders, W., *American Gothic* (New York, 1975).

Anderson, B. R., *Imagined Communities: Reflections on the Origin and Spread of Nationalism* (London, rev. 1991).

Anderson, D., 'A Language to Translate Into: The Pre-Elizabethan Idiom of Pound's Later Cavalcanti Translations', *Studies in Medievalism*, 2/1 (1982), pp. 9–18.

Andrews, K., *The Nazarenes* (Oxford, 1964).

Anscombe, A., *Arts and Crafts Style* (London, 1996).

Antoine, P., 'Une imagination puissante mais déréglée: les représentations du Moyen Age dans les *Mémoires d'Outre-Tombe*", in Pietropoli, *Romanticismo*, pp. 75–86.

Antonsen, E. H., et al., eds, *The Grimm Brothers and the Germanic Past* (Amsterdam and Philadelphia, 1990).

Anzulovic, B., *Heavenly Serbia: From Myth to Genocide* (New York, 1999).

Arblaster, A., *Viva la Libertà: Politics in Opera* (London, 1997).

Arnold, B., *Medieval Germany, 500–1300* (Basingstoke, 1997).

Ashe, G., *King Arthur: The Dream of a Golden Age* (London, 1990).

Ashe, G., and Lacy, Norris J., *The Arthurian Handbook* (New York, 1988).

Aslin, E., *The Aesthetic Movement: Prelude to Art Nouveau* (London, 1969).

Atherton, M., ed., *Celts and Christians: New Approaches to the Religious Traditions of Britain and Ireland* (Cardiff, 2002).

Atterbury, P., and Wainwright, C., *Pugin: A Gothic Passion* (London, 1994).

Attolini, V., *Immagini del Medioevo nell'cinema* (Bari, 1993).

Auerbach, J. A., *The Great Exhibition of 1851: A Nation on Display* (New Haven, Connecticut, 1999).

Auzas, P., *Viollet-le-Duc* (Paris, 1979).

Ayling, S., *Edmund Burke: His Life and Opinions* (London, 1988).

Baddeley, G., *Goth Chic: A Connoisseur's Guide to Dark Culture* (London, 2002).

Baer, M., 'The Memory of the Middle Ages: From History of Culture to Cultural History', *Studies in Medievalism*, 4 (1992), pp. 290–308.

Baine Campbell, M., 'Finding the Grail: Fascist Aesthetics and Mysterious Objects', in Mancoff, *King Arthur's Modern Return*, pp. 213–26.

Baldick, R., *The Life of J.-K. Huysmans* (Oxford, 1955).

Baldick, C., ed., *The Oxford Book of Gothic Tales* (Oxford, 1992).

Bales, R., *Proust and the Middle Ages* (Genève, 1975).

Banham, J., and Fell, P., *William Morris* (1999).

Banham, J., and Harris, J., eds, *William Morris and the Middle Ages* (Manchester, 1984).

Barber, R., ed., *King Arthur in Music* (Woodbridge, 2002).

Barclay, D. E., 'Medievalism and Nationalism in Nineteenth-Century Germany', *Studies in Medievalism*, 5 (1993), pp. 5–22.

—, 'Representing the Middle Ages: Court Festivals in Nineteenth-Century Prussia', in Utz and Shippey, *Medievalism in the Modern World*, pp. 105–16.

Barczewski, S. G., *Myth and National Identity in Nineteenth-Century Britain: The Legends of King Arthur and Robin Hood* (Oxford, 2000).

Barker-Benfield, G. J., *The Culture of Sensibility: Sex and Society in Eighteenth-Century Britain* (Chicago, 1992).

Barnard, F., *Herder's Social and Political Thought: From Enlightenment to Nationalism* (Oxford, 1965).

Barnes, G., 'The Fireside Vikings and the "Boy's Own" Vinland: Vinland in Popular

English and American Literature (1841–1926)', in Gentrup, *Reinventing the Middle Ages*, pp. 149–52.

Barnes, R., *The Pre-Raphaelites and their World* (London, 1998).

Barraclough, G., *History in a Changing World* (Oxford, 1955).

Barrell, J., *The Idea of Landscape and the Sense of Place, 1730–1840* (Cambridge, 1972).

Barringer, T., *Reading the Pre-Raphaelites* (New Haven, Connecticut, 1998).

Barta, T., ed., *Screening the Past: Film and the Representation of History* (Westport, Connecticut, 1998).

Barzini, L., *The Italians* (trans. London, 1983).

Batchelor, J., *Mervyn Peake: A Biography and Critical Exploration* (London, 1974).

Baumann, Z., 'Soil, Blood and Identity', *Sociological Review*, 40 (1992), pp. 675–701.

Beales, D., ed., *The Risorgimento and the Unification of Italy* (London, 1971).

Beaune, C., *Naissance de la nation France* (Paris, 1985).

Becker, S., *Forms of Feminine Fiction* (Manchester, 1999).

Behlmer, R., 'Robin Hood on the Screen', *Films in Review*, June-July 1965, pp. 91–102

—, 'Swordplay on Screen', ibid., pp. 362–75.

Beiser, F. C., *Enlightenment, Revolution and Romanticism: The Genesis of Modern Political Thought, 1790–1800* (Cambridge, Massachusetts, 1992).

Bending, S., 'The True Rust of the Barons' War: Gardens, Ruins and the National Landscape', in Myrone and Peltz, *Producing the Past*, pp. 83–93.

Berenger, J., *A History of the Habsburg Empire* (2 vols, trans. London, 1994 and 1997).

Bergdoll, B., *A. W. N. Pugin: Master of the Gothic Revival* (New Haven, Connecticut, 1996).

Bergeron, K., *Decadent Enchantments: The Revival of Gregorian Chant at Solesmes* (Berkeley, California, and London, 1988).

Bergman, I., *The Seventh Seal* (trans. London, 1968).

—, *Images: My Life in Film* (trans. New York, 1994).

Berkhout, C. T., and McC. Gatch, M., eds, *Anglo-Saxon Scholarship: The First Three Centuries* (Boston, 1982).

Berlin, I., *Vico and Herder* (London, 1976).

Berret, P., *Le Moyen Age dans la 'Légende des Siècles' et les sources de Victor Hugo* (Paris, 1911).

Berthelot, A., *King Arthur: Chivalry and Legend* (Thames and Hudson, 2001).

Bhattacharya, M. M., *Courtesy in Shakespeare* (Calcutta, 1940).

Biddick, K., *The Shock of Medievalism* (Durham and London, 1998).

Biddle, M., *King Arthur's Round Table* (Woodbridge, 2000).

Bills, M., ed., *Art in the Age of Queen Victoria* (London, 2001).

Bingaman, A., 'The Business of Brotherhood: Morris, Marshall, Faulkner and Co. and the Pre-Raphaelite Culture of Youth', in Horowitz and Vaughan, *Artistic Brotherhoods*, pp. 82–104.

Birkhead, E., *The Tale of Terror* (London, 1921).

Bjorkman, S., *Bergman on Bergman* (trans. London, 1973).

Blaney-Brown, D., *Romanticism* (London, 2001).

Bloch, R. H., and Nichols, S. G., eds, *Medievalism and the Modernist Temper* (Baltimore and London, 1996), art. Gumbrecht and Schnapp, eds of Grimm's Preface.

Blockmans, W., *Emperor Charles V* (London, 2001).

Bluestone, G., *Novels into Films* (Berkeley, California, 1968).

Bloomfield, M. W., 'Reflections of a Medievalist: America, Medievalism and the Middle Ages', in Rosenthal and Szarmach, *Medievalism in American Culture*, pp. 13–29.

Blunk, L., 'Red Robin: The Radical Politics of Richard Carpenter's '*Robin of Sherwood*'', in Hahn, *Robin Hood in Popular Culture*, pp. 29–40.

Boitani, P., and Torti, A., eds, *Medievalitas: Reading the Middle Ages* (Woodbridge, 1996).

Boldrini, L., ed., *Medieval Joyce* (Amsterdam, New York, 2002).

Bond, G. C., and Gilliam, A., eds, *The Social Construction of the Past: Representation as Power* (London, 1994).

Bonfigli, C., *Niccolò V, papa della Rinascenza* (Rome, 1997).

Bonnel, R., 'Medieval Nostalgia in France, 1750–89: The Gothic Imagination at the End of the Ancien Regime', *Studies in Medievalism*, 5 (1993), pp. 139–63.

F. Boos, ed., *History and Community: Essays in Victorian Medievalism* (New York and London, 1992.

Bordes, P., 'Moyen Age ou Heroic Fantasy?', *Cahiers de la Cinémathèque*, 42/43 (1985), pp. 171–82.

Boucher-Rivalain, O., 'Attitudes to Gothic Revival in French Architectural Writings of the 1840s', *Architectural History*, 41 (1998), pp. 145–52.

Bourgeois Richmond, V., *Shakespeare, Catholicism and Romance* (London, 2000).

Bouwsma, W. J., *The Culture of Renaissance Humanism*, American Historical Association Pamphlets, 401 (Washington, DC, 1973).

Boyd, I., 'Chesterton's Medievalism', *Studies in Medievalism*, 3/3 (1991), pp. 243–55.

Boyle, L. F., 'Per la fondazione della Biblioteca Vaticana', in Manfredi, A., ed., *I codici latini di Niccolò V (edizione degli inventari e identificazione dei manoscritti* (Vatican City, 1994), pp. xiii–xvi.

Bradley, S., 'The Englishness of Gothic: Theories and Interpretations from William Gilpin to J. H. Parker', *Architectural History*, (45) 2002, pp. 325–46.

Bragg, M., *The Seventh Seal*, BFI Film Classics (London, 1968).

Brand, V., ed., *The Study of the Past in the Victorian Age* (Oxford, 1998).

Braysmuth, H., 'Medievalism in German Romantic Art: Reading the Political Text in the Gothic Style', *Studies in Medievalism*, 5 (1993), pp. 38–47.

Brendon, P., *Hurrell Froude and the Oxford Movement* (London, 1974).

Brétèque, F., de la, 'Le Moyen Age au cinéma français', 1940–87, in M. Perrin, ed., *Dire le Moyen Age hier et aujourd'hui* (Laon, 1987).

—, 'La Table Ronde au Far West: les *Chevaliers de la Table Ronde* de Richard Thorpe (1953)', *Cahiers de la Cinémathèque*, 42/43 (1985), pp. 97–102.

—, 'Une "figure obligée" du film de chevalerie: le tournoi', ibid., pp. 21–26.

—, 'L'épée dans le lac: *Excalibur* de John Boorman ou les aléas de la puissance', ibid., pp. 91–96.

Brewer, D., 'Modernising the Medieval: Eighteenth-Century Translations of Chaucer', in Alamichel and Brewer, *Middle Ages after the Middle Ages*, pp. 103–20.

Brewer, E., T. H. White's 'The Once and Future King', *Arthurian Studies*, 30 (1993).

Briggs, A., *Saxons, Normans and Victorians* (Historical Association, Hastings and Bexhill Branch, 1966).

Briggs, J., *Night Visitors: The Rise and Fall of the English Ghost Story* (London, 1977).

—, '"New Times and Old Stories": Middleton's "Hengist"', in Scragg and Weinberg, *Literary Appropriations*, pp. 107–21.

Brinkley, R. F., *Arthurian Legend in the Seventeenth Century* (Baltimore and London, 1932).

Brinton, C., *The Political Ideas of the English Romantics* (Ann Arbor, Michigan, 1962).

Brogniez, L., *Preraphaélisme et Symbolisme: peinture littéraire et image poétique* (Paris, 2003).

Brook, V. J. K., *A Life of Archbishop Parker* (Oxford, 1962).

Brooks, C., *The Gothic Revival* (London, 1999).

—, 'Historicism and the Nineteenth Century', in Brand, *Study of the Past*, pp. 1–20.

Brownlee, M. S. K. and Nichols, S. G., *The New Medievalism* (Baltimore and London, 1991).

Brubaker, R., *Nationalism Reframed: Nationhood and the National Question in the New Europe* (Cambridge, 1996).

Bryant, A., *Spirit of England* (London, 1982).

Bullough, G., *Narrative and Dramatic Sources of Shakespeare* (8 vols, London, 1957–75).

Burell, P., 'Rabelais's Debt to the Medieval World', *Studies in Medievalism*, 3/1 (1987), pp. 41–53.

Burke, P., *Culture and Society in Renaissance Italy, 1420–1540* (London, 1972).

Burrow, J. W., *A Liberal Descent: Victorian Historians of the English Past* (Cambridge, 1981).

Butler, M., *Romantics, Rebels and Reactionaries: English Literature and its Background 1760–1830* (Oxford, 1981).

Butler, P., ed., *Pusey Rediscovered* (London, 1985).

Caillois, R., *Au coeur du Fantastique* (Paris, 1965).

Calhoun, B., *The Pastoral Vision of William Morris: The 'Earthly Paradise'* (Athens, Georgia, 1975).

Calin, W., 'Medievalism and Ancien Régime France: An Afterword', *Studies in Medievalism*, 3/1 (1987), pp. 99–106.

—, 'What "Tales of a Wayside Inn" Tells us about Longfellow and about Chaucer', *Studies in Medievalism*, 12 (2003), pp. 197–214.

Campbell, K. A., 'The Renaissance Reader and Popular Medievalism in France', *Studies in Medievalism*, 3/1 (1987), pp. 23–31.

Cannadine, D., 'The Context, Performance and Meaning of Ritual: The British Monarchy and the "Invention of Tradition", *c.* 1820–1979', in Hobsbawm and Ranger, *Invention of Tradition*, pp. 101–64.

Cantor, N., *Inventing the Middle Ages: Lives, Works and Ideas of Great Medievalists of the Twentieth Century* (Cambridge and New York, 1991).

Carman, J., *Archaeology and Heritage: An Introduction* (London, 2002).

Carpenter, H., *Tolkien: A Biography* (London, 1977).

Carr-Gomm, P., ed., *The Druid Renaissance: The Voice of Druidry Today* (London, 1996).

Cassidy, D. M., 'The Collegiate Designs of Maginnis and Walsh', *Studies in Medievalism*, 3/2 (1990), pp. 153–85.

Casteras, S. P., *English Pre-Raphaelitism and its Reception in America in the Nineteenth Century* (Washington, DC, 1990).

Casteras, S. P. and Craig-Faxon, A., *Pre-Raphaelite Art in its European Context* (Madison, New Jersey, and London, 1995).

Chadwick, O., *The Mind of the Oxford Movement* (London, 1960).

Chance, J., ed., *Tolkien the Medievalist* (London, 2003).

—, *Tolkien's Art: A Mythology for England* (Lexington, Kentucky, 2001).

—, and Day, D. D., 'Medievalism in Tolkien: Two Decades of Criticism in Review', *Studies in Medievalism*, 3/3 (1991), pp. 375–87.

Chandler, A., *A Dream of Order: The Medieval Idea in Nineteenth-Century Literature* (Lincoln, Nebraska, 1970).

—, 'Carlyle and the Medievalism of the North', in Utz and Shippey, *Medievalism in the Modern World*, pp. 173–91.

—, 'Sir Walter Scott and the Medieval Revival', *Nineteenth-Century Fiction*, 19 (1964), pp. 315–32.

—, 'The Quarrel of the Ancients and the Moderns: Peacock and the Medieval Revival', *Bucknell Review*, 13 (1965), pp. 39–50.

Chapman, H., *The Celts: The Construction of a Myth* (Basingstoke, 1992).

Chapman, R., 'Last Enchantments: Medievalism and the Early Anglo-Catholic Movement', *Studies in Medievalism*, 4 (1992), pp. 170–85.

Charlton, D. C., ed., *The French Romantics* (2 vols, Cambridge, 1984).

'Chevalerie l'écran, La', *Avant-Scène du Cinéma*, 221 (February 1979), pp. 29–40.

Choay, F., *The Invention of the Historic Monument* (trans. Cambridge, 2001).

Christian, E. E., and Lindsay, B., 'The Habit of Detection: The Medieval Monk as Detective in the Novels of Ellis Peters', *Studies in Medievalism*, 4 (1992), pp. 276–89

Clark, K., *The Gothic Revival* (Phaidon, 1928).

Clarkson, P., *Chivalry and Medievalism in Cheltenham's Victorian Public Schools, 1841–1918* (Bath, 2002).

Classen, A., ed., *Medieval German Voices in the Twenty-First Century* (Atlanta, Georgia, and Amsterdam, 2000).

Clery, E. J., *The Rise of Supernatural Fiction, 1762–1800* (Cambridge, 1995).

Clubbe, J. and Lovell, E. J., *English Romanticism: The Grounds of Belief* (London, 1983).

Cochran, R., 'Tennyson's Hierarchy of Women in "Idylls of the Kings"', in Boos, *History and Community*, pp. 81–108.

Colley, L., *Britons: Forging the Nation, 1707–1837* (New Haven, Connecticut, 1992).

Coluccia, G. L., *Niccolò V umanista: papa e riformatore* (Venice, 1998).

Colvin, H., *A Biographical Dictionary of British Architects, 1600–1840* (3rd edn, London, 1995).

—, 'Aubrey's Chronologia Arcitectonica', in [Pevsner] Summerson, *Essays*, pp. 1–12

Compton-Rickett, A., *William Morris: A Study in Personality* (London, 1913).

Conversi, D., *The Basques, the Catalans and Spain: Alternative Routes to Nationalist Mobilisation* (London, 1997).

Cook, D. A., *A History of Narrative Film* (2nd edn, New York, 1990).

Cooper, H., *Pastoral: Medieval into Renaissance* (Woodbridge, 1977).

Cooper, J., *Victorian and Edwardian Furniture Interiors: From the Gothic Revival to Art Nouveau* (London, 1987).

Copley, S., ed., *Literature and the Social Order in Eighteenth-Century England* (London, 1984).

Cormican, L. A., 'Medieval Idiom in Shakespeare: Shakespeare and the Liturgy', *Scrutiny*, 17 (1950), pp. 186–202.

—, 'Medieval Idiom in Shakespeare: Shakespeare and the Medieval Ethic', ibid., pp. 293–317.

Cottom, D., *The Civilized Imagination: A Study of Ann Radcliffe, Jane Austen and Sir Walter Scott* (Cambridge, 1985).

Countryman, V. A., *Swinburne's Medievalism in Context* (Oxford, 2002).

Cowie, P., 'Milieu and Texture in the Seventh Seal', in Solomon, S. J., ed., *The Classic Cinema: Essays in Criticism* (New York, 1973).

Crane, R. S., *The Vogue of Medieval Chivalric Romance during the English Renaissance* (Menasha, Wisconsin, 1919).

Crane, S. A., 'Story, History and the Passionate Collector', in Myrone and Peltz, *Producing the Past*, pp. 187–203.

Cranston, M., *The Romantic Movement* (London, 1994).

Craven, W. G., *Giovanni Pico della Mirandola: Symbol of his Age. Modern Interpretations of a Renaissance Philosopher* (Geneva, 1981).

Crick, B., ed., *National Identities: The Constitution of the United Kingdom* (Oxford, 1991).

Crow, C. L., ed., *American Gothic: An Anthology, 1787–1916* (Oxford, 1999).

Crowley, V., *A Woman's Guide to the Earth Traditions: Exploring Wicca, Shamanism, Paganism, Native American and Celtic Spirituality* (London, 2001).

Cubbitt, G., ed., *Imagining Nations* (Manchester, 1998).

Cugier, A., '"Lancelot du Lac" de Robert Bresson: Le Moyen Âge revisité ou la dimension tragique du XXe siècle', *Cahiers de la Cinémathèque*, 42/43 (1985), pp. 119–24.

Culler, A. Dwight, *The Victorian Mirror of History* (New Haven, Connecticut, 1985).

Cumming, E. and Kaplan, W., *The Arts and Crafts Movement* (London, 1991).

Curtis, T., *Wales: The Imagined Nation* (Bridgend, 1986).

D'Amico, J. F., *Renaissance Humanism in Papal Rome: Humanists and Churchmen on the Eve of the Reformation* (Baltimore and London, 1983).

Dakyns, J. R., *The Middle Ages in French Literature, 1851–1900* (Oxford, 1973).

Damico, H., ed., *Medieval Scholarship: Biographical Studies of the Foundation of a Discipline*, (3 vols, New York, 2000).

Daniel, E., *The Art of Gormenghast: The Making of a TV Fantasy* (London, 2000).

David-Sirocko, K., 'Anglo-German Interconnexions during the Gothic Revival: A Case Study from the Work of Georg Gottlob Ungewitter (1820–64)', *Architectural History*, 41 (1998), pp. 153–78.

Davies, H., *Worship and Theology in England*, ii, *From Watts and Wesley to Martineau, 1690–1900* (Grand Rapids, Michigan, and Cambridge, repr. 1996).

Davies, O., 'Celtic Christianity: Texts and Representations', in Atherton, *Celts and Christians*, pp. 23–38.

Davies, R. T., and Beaty, R. G., *Literature of the Romantic Period* (Liverpool, 1976).

Davies, W., 'The Myth of the Celtic Church', in Edwards, N., and Lane, A., eds, *The Early Church in Wales and the West* (Oxford, 1992), pp. 12–21.

Davis, A., *Chivalry and Romance in the English Renaissance* (Woodbridge, 2003).

Davis, J., 'New Age Travellers in the Countryside: Incomers with Attitude', in Milbourne, P., ed., *Revealing Rural 'Others': Representation, Power and Identity in the British Countryside*, Rural Studies Series (London, 1997), pp. 117–34.

Day, M. and Lagorio, V., *King Arthur Through the Ages* (New York, 1990).

Day, W. P., *In the Circles of Fear and Desire: A Study of Gothic Fantasy* (Chicago, 1985).

Dean, C., *A Study of Merlin in English Literature from the Middle Ages to the Present Day* (New York, 1992).

Delevoy, R., *Symbolists and Symbolism* (Geneva, 1982).

Dellheim, C., 'Interpreting Victorian medievalism', in Boos, *History and Community*, pp. 39–58

Des Cars, L., *Pre-Raphaelitism: Romance and Realism* (London, 2000).

Devine Jump, H., ed., *Women's Writing of the Romantic Period, 1789–1836* (Edinburgh, 1997).

Diaz Andreu, M., and Champion, T., eds, *Nationalism and Archaeology in Europe* (London, 1996).

Dixon, R., and Muthesius, S., *Victorian Architecture* (London, 1985).

Doel, F. and Lloyd, G. T., *Worlds of Arthur: King Arthur in History, Legend and Culture* (Stroud, 1998).

Donner, J., *The Films of Ingmar Bergman* (New York, 1972).

Donoghue, D., 'Lady Godiva', in Scragg and Weinberg, *Literary Appropriations*, pp. 194–214.

Dorra, H., *Symbolist Art Theories: A Critical Anthology* (Berkeley, California, 1995).

Drury, N., *The New Age: Searching for the Spiritual Self* (London, 2004).

Dulles, A., *Princeps Concordia: Pico della Mirandola and the Scholastic Tradition* (Cambridge, Massachusetts, 1941).

Duncan-Jones, K., ed., *Sir Philip Sidney* (Oxford, 1989).

Dunn, E. C., Fotich, T., and Feebles, B., eds, *The Medieval Drama and its Claudelian Revival* (Washington, DC, 1970).

Durand Le-Guern, I., *Le Moyen Age des Romantiques* (Rennes, 2001).

Duroselle, J. B., *L'idée de l'Europe dans l'Histoire* (Paris, 1965).

Dwyer, P. G., ed., *Napoleon and Europe* (London, 2001).

Eastlake, L., *A History of the Gothic Revival* (intro. by J. Mordaunt Crook) (1872; repr. Leicester, 1970).

Eco, U., *Travels in Hyperreality* (trans. London, 1986).

Edelman, N., *Attitudes of Seventeenth-Century France towards the Middle Ages* (New York, 1946).

Edwards, E., *Libraries and Founders of Libraries* (London, 1865: repr. 1997).

—, *Lives of the Founders of the British Museum* (London, 1870; repr. 1997).

Ehrmann, J., ed., *Literature and Revolution* (Boston, 1970).

Elley, D., *The Epic Film: Myth and History* (London, 1984).

Ellis, K. F., *The Contested Castle: Gothic Novels and the Subversion of Domestic Ideology* (Urbana and Chicago, Illinois, 1989).

Ellis, P. Beresford, *A Brief History of the Druids* (London, 2002).

—, *The Celtic Dawn: A History of Pan-Celticism* (London, 1993).

Ellison, J., *Cato's Tears and the Making of Anglo-American Emotion* (Chicago and London, 1999).

Emery, E., *Romancing the Cathedral: Gothic Architecture in Fin de Siècle French Culture* (Albany, New York, 2001).

—, 'J.-K. Huysmans and the Middle Ages', *Modern Language Studies*, 29/3 (2002).

—, 'The "Truth" about the Middle Ages: *La Revue des Deux Mondes* and Later Nineteenth-Century French Medievalism', in Simmons, *Medievalism and the Quest*, pp. 99–115.

—, and Morowitz, L., *Consuming the Past: The Medieval Revival in Fin de Siècle France* (Aldershot, 2003).

English Heritage, *Health, Safety and Security: Managing and Presenting Heritage Sites* (London, 2001).

Essl, M., *Die Rezeption des Artusstoffes in der englischen und amerikanisches Literatur des 20. Jahrhunderts bei Thomas Berger, Marion Zimmer Bradley, E. A. Robinson, Mary Stewart und T. H. White* (Lewinston, New York, and Lampeter, 1995).

Etzminger, R. L., 'Jonson, the Myth of Sydney and Nostalgia for Elizabeth', in Gentrup, *Reinventing the Past*, pp. 89–96.

Faber, I., *Oxford Apostles: A Character Study of the Oxford Movement* (London, 1974).

Farnham, W., *The Medieval Heritage of Elizabethan Tragedy* (Berkeley, 1936).

Faxon, A., 'The Pre-Raphaelite Brotherhood as Knights of the Round Table', in de Girolami Cheney, *Pre-Raphaelitism*, pp. 53–74.

Fay, E., *Romantic Medievalism: History and the Romantic Literary Ideal* (Basingstoke, 2002).

Ferguson, A. B., *The Chivalric Tradition in Renaissance England* (Washington, DC, and London, 1986).

Fergusson, F., *Trope and Allegory: Themes Common to Dante and Shakespeare* (Athens, Georgia, 1977).

Fernandez-Alvarez, M., *Charles V* (trans. London, 1975).

Ferro, M., *Cinéma et histoire* (Paris, 1977).

Fichte, J. O., 'The End of Utopia and the Treatment of Arthur and his Court in Contemporary German Drama', in Boitani and Torti, *Medievalitas*, pp. 153–69.

Fichtenau, H., *The Carolingian Empire* (trans. Oxford, 1968).

Fields, A., *Le Chat Noir: A Montmartre Cabaret and its Artists in Turn of the Century Paris* (Santa Barbara, California, 1993).

Filmer-Davies, K., *Fantasy-Fiction and Welsh Myth: Tales of Belonging* (Basingstoke, 1996).

Finsley, D. F., 'Medieval German Religious Literature as a Paradigm for Gender Studies', in Classen, *Medieval German Voices*, pp, 123–44.

Fleenor, J. E., ed., *The Female Gothic* (Montreal and London, 1983).

Flower, R., 'Lawrence Nowell and the Discovery of England in Tudor Times', *Proceedings of the British Academy*, 21 (1935), pp. 47–74.

Folz, R., *The Concept of Empire in Western Europe* (trans. London, 1969).

Fowler, P. J., *The Past in Contemporary Society: Then, Now* (London, 1992).

Fox-Friedman, J., 'The Chivalric Order for Children: Arthur's Return in Late Nineteenth- and Early Twentieth-Century America', in Mancoff, *King Arthur's Modern Return*, pp. 137–58.

Fraisse, L., *L'oeuvre cathedrale: Proust et l'architecture medievale* (Paris, 1990).

Frank, M., 'The Nazarene *Gemeinschaft*: Overbeck and Cornelius', in Horowitz and Vaughan, *Artistic Brotherhoods*, pp. 48–66.

Frankl, P., *The Gothic: Literary Sources and Interpretations through Eight Centuries* (Princeton, 1960).

Frantzen, A. J., *A Desire for Origins: New Language, Old English and Teaching the Tradition* (New Brunswick and London, 1990).

Frantzen, J., and Niles, J. D., eds, *Anglo-Saxonism and the Construction of Social Identity* (Gainesville, Florida. 1997).

Fraser, J., *America and Patterns of Chivalry* (New York and Cambridge, 1982).

Frèches-Thory, C., and Terrasse, A., *The Nabis: Bonnard, Vuillard and Their Circle* (New York, 1991).

Freixe, G., 'Approche du "Décameron" de Pier Paolo Pasolini', *Cahiers de la Cinémathèque*, 42/43 (1985), pp. 143–51.

Frye, N., *The Secular Scripture: A Study of the Structure of Romance* (Cambridge, Massachusetts, 1976).

Fuhrhammer, L., and Isaksson, F., *Politics and Film* (trans. London, 1971).

Fulbrook, M., ed., *Germany Since 1800* (London, 1997).

Fumagalli Beonio Broccheri, M., *Pico della Mirandola* (Casale Monferrato, 1999).

Furst, L. R., *The Contours of European Romanticism* (London, 1979).

Gado, F., *The Passion of Ingmar Bergman* (Durham and London, 1986).

Gandino, G., 'Le Moyen Age dans le cinéma fasciste, un térritoire évité', *Cahiers de la Cinémathèque*, 42/43 (1985), pp. 133–42.

Gardiner-Scott, T. J., *Mervyn Peake: The Evolution of a Dark Romantic* (New York, 1989)

Gaull, M., *English Romanticism* (New York, 1983).

Geary, P. J., *The Myth of Nations: The Medieval Origins of Europe* (Princeton and Oxford, 2002).

Gellner, E., *Nationalism* (London, 1997).

Gellner, E., and Ionescu, G., eds, *Populism: Its Meanings and National Characteristics* (London, 1970).

Genovese, E. D., 'The Southern Slaveholders' View of the Middle Ages', in Rosenthal and Szarmach, *Medievalism in American Culture*, pp. 31–52.

Gentrup, W., ed., *Reinventing the Middle Ages and the Renaissance: Constructions of the Medieval and Early Modern Period* (Turnhout, 1998).

Gentry, F., 'The Politicization of the Middle Ages: Nationalism and Festivals in Nineteenth-Century Germany', *Studies in Medievalism*, 3/4 (1991), pp. 467–88.

Gentry, F. G. and Muller, V., 'The Reception of the Middle Ages in Germany: An Overview', ibid., pp. 399–422.

Germann, G., *Gothic Revival in Europe and Britain: Sources, Influences and Ideas* (trans. London, 1972).

Gerrard, C., *Medieval Archaeology: Understanding Traditions and Contemporary Approaches* (London, 2003), pt I.

Gilbert, S. M. and Gubar, S., *The Madwoman in the Attic: the Woman Writer and the Nineteenth-Century Literary Imagination* (2nd edn, New Haven, Connecticut and London, 2000).

Gilmore, M. P., *The World of Humanism, 1453–1517* (New York, 1952).

Girolami-Cheney, L., ed., *Pre-Raphaelitism and Medievalism in the Arts* (Lampeter, 1992).

—, 'Locks, Tresses and Manes in Pre-Raphaelite Painting', in de Girolami Cheney, ibid., pp. 159–92.

—, 'The Fair Lady and the Virgin in Pre-Raphaelite Art: The Evolution of a Societal Myth', ibid., pp. 241–80.

Girouard, M., *The Return to Camelot: Chivalry and the English Gentleman* (New Haven, Connecticut, and London, 1981).

Glencross, M., *Reconstructing Camelot: French Romantic Medievalism and the Arthurian Tradition* (Woodbridge, 1995).

Gorgievski, S., 'The Arthurian Legend in the Cinema: Myth or History?', in Utz and Shippey, *Medievalism in the Modern* World, pp. 153–66.

Gose, Jnr, E. B., *Imagination Indulged: The Irrational in the Nineteenth Century Novel* (Montreal and London, 1972).

Gossman, L., *Medievalism and the Ideologies of the Enlightenment: The World and Work of la Curne de Sainte-Palaye* (Baltimore, 1968).

Grahame, K. W., ed., *Gothic Fictions: Prohibition/Transgression* (New York, 1989).

Gray, R. P., 'Questions of Identity at Abramtsevo', in Horowitz and Vaughan, *Artistic Brotherhoods*, pp. 105–21.

Greenfeld, L., *Nationalism: Five Roads to Modernity* (Cambridge, Massachusetts, 1992).

Greenhalgh, P., ed., *Art Nouveau, 1890–1914* (Washington, 2000).

Gugelberger, G. M., *Ezra Pound's Medievalism* (Frankfurt, 1978).

Guilfoyle, C., *Shakespeare's Play within the Play: Medieval Imagery and Scenic Form in Hamlet, Othello and King Lear* (Kalamazoo, Michigan, 1990).

Haghofer, N. U., *The Fall of Arthur's Kingdom: A Study of Tennyson's 'The Holy Grail'* (Portland, Oregon, 1997).

Hahn, T., ed., *Robin Hood in Popular Culture* (Cambridge, 2000).

Hales, J. W., and Furnivall, F. J., eds, *Bishop Percy's Folio Manuscript: Ballads and Romances* (3 vols, London, 1868).

Halphen, L., *Charlemagne and the Carolingian Empire* (trans. London, 1977).

Hammer, J., '*Eric Brighteyes*: Rider Haggard Rewrites the Saga', *Studies in Medieval-ism*, 12 (2003), pp. 137–70.

Hankins, J. E., *Source and Meaning in Spenser's Allegory: A Study of the* 'Faerie Queene' (Oxford, 1971).

Hares-Stryker, C., ed., *An Anthology of Pre-Raphaelite Writings* (Sheffield, 1997).

Harper, S., *Picturing the Past: The Rise and Fall of British Costume Film* (London, 1994).

Harrison, A. H., 'Medievalism and the Ideologies of Victorian Poetry', *Studies in Medievalism*, 4 (1992), pp. 219–34.

—, *Swinburne's Medievalism: A Study in Victorian Love Poetry* (Baton Rouge, Louisiana, 1988).

—, *Victorian Poets and the Poetry of Culture: Discourse and Ideology* (Charlottesville, Virginia, 1998).

Hartley, K., *The Romantic Spirit in German Art, 1790–1990* (London, 1994).

Harty, K. J., ed., *Cinema Arthuriana: Essays on Arthurian Film* (New York, 1991).

—, 'Jeanne au cinéma', in Wheeler, B., and Wood, C. T., eds, *Fresh Verdicts on Joan of Arc* (New York, 1996).

—, *The Reel Middle Ages: American, Western and Eastern European, Middle Eastern and Asian Films About Medieval Europe* (Jefferson, North Carolina, 1999).

Harvey, G., and Hardman, C., eds, *Paganism Today* (London, 1995).

Haskell, F., 'The Manufacture of the Past in Nineteenth-Century Painting', *Past and Present*, 55 (1972), pp. 109–20.

Hastings, A., *The Construction of Nationhood: Ethnicity, Religion and Nationalism* (Cambridge, 1997).

Haugen, K. L., 'Chivalry and Romance in the Eighteenth Century: Richard Hurd and the Disenchantment of *The Faerie Queene*' in Simmons, *Medievalism and the Quest*, pp. 45–60.

Havely, N. R., *Dante's Modern Afterlife: Reception and Response from Blake to Heaney* (Basingstoke, 1998).

—, 'Losing Paradise: Dante, Boccaccio and Mary Shelley's *Valperga*', in Pietropoli, *Romanticismo*, pp. 29–35.

Hay, D., 'Flavio Biondo and the Middle Ages', *Proceedings of the British Academy*, 45 (1959), pp. 97–128.

—, *Europe: The Emergence of an Idea* (2nd edn, Edinburgh, 1968).

—, *Polydore Vergil: Renaissance Historian and Man of Letters* (London, 1952).

Hayashi, T., ed., *Steinbeck and the Arthurian Theme*, Steinbeck Monograph 5 (1975).

Haycock, D. B., *William Stukeley: Science, Religion and Archaeology in Eighteenth-Century England* (Woodbridge, 2002).

Haydock N., 'Arthurian Melodrama, Chaucerian Spectacle, and the Waywardness of Cinematic Pastiche in "First Knight" and "A Knight's Tale"', *Studies in Medievalism*, 12 (2003), pp. 5–38.

Haymes, E. R., 'Two-Storied Medievalism in Wagner's *Die Meistersinger von Nürnberg*', *Studies in Medievalism*, 3/4 (1991), pp. 505–13.

Heady, C., 'Heraldry and Red Hats: Linguistic Skepticism and Chesterton's Revision of Ruskinian Medievalism', in Simmons, *Medievalism and the* Quest, pp. 131–43.

Heater, D., *The Idea of European Unity* (Leicester, 1992).

Hechter. M., *Internal Colonialism: The Celtic Fringe in British National Development, 1536–1966* (London, 1975).

Heelas, P., *The New Age Movement: The Celebration of the Self and the Sacralization of Modernity* (Oxford, 1996).

Heer, F., *The Holy Roman Empire* (trans. London, 1995).

Hein, R. and Saisset, C., 'La chevalerie dans les étoiles: les thèmes chevaleresques dans la trilogie de George Lucas', *Cahiers de la Cinémathèque*, 42/43 (1985), pp. 167–69.

Henson, E., *The Fictions of Romantick Chivalry: Samuel Johnson and Romance* (Rutherford, New Jersey and London, 1992).

Hetherington, K., *New Age Travellers: Vans of Uproarious Humanity* (London, 2000).

Hewison, R., *The Heritage Industry: Britain in a Climate of Decline* (London, 1987).

Hibberd, S., 'Marianne: Mystic or Madwoman?: Representations of Jeanne d'Arc on the Parisian stage in the 1820s', in Simmons, *Medievalism and the Quest*, pp. 87–98.

Hibbert, C., *The English: A Sociological History, 1066–1945* (London, 1987).

Higham, N. J., *King Arthur: Myth Making and History* (London, 2002).

Hill, C., 'The Norman Yoke', in his *Puritanism and Revolution: Studies in Interpretation of the English Revolution of the Seventeenth Century* (London, 1958), pp. 50–122.

Hillegas, M. R., ed., *Shadows of Imagination* (Carbondale, Illinois, 1969).

Hilton, T., *The Pre-Raphaelites* (London, 1970).

Hobsbawm, E. J., *Nations and Nationalism since 1780* (Cambridge, 1990).

Hobsbawm, E., and Ranger, T., eds, *The Invention of Tradition* (Cambridge, 1983).

Hodkinson, P., *Goth: Identity, Style and Subculture* (Oxford, 2002).

Höltenschmidt, E., *Die Mittelalterrezeption der Brüder Schlegel* (Paderborn, 2000).

Hofmann, W., *Caspar David Friedrich* (London, 2000).

Hogle, J. E., ed., *The Cambridge Companion to Gothic Fiction* (Cambridge, 2004).

Horowitz, L. and Vaughan, W., *Artistic Brotherhoods in the Nineteenth Century* (Aldershot, 2000).

Hostettler, J., *Sir Edward Coke: A Force for Freedom* (Chichester, 1997).

Howells, C. A., *Love, Mystery and Misery: Feeling in Gothic Fiction* (London, 1978).

Hughes, G. T., *Romantic German Literature, 1760–1805* (New York, 1975).

Hughes, K., 'The Celtic Church: Is this a Valid Concept?', *Cambridge Medieval Celtic Studies*, 1 (1981), pp. 1–20.

Hughes, L. K., '"Come Again and Thrice as Fair": Reading Tennyson's Beginning', in Mancoff, *King Arthur's Modern Return*, pp. 56–75.

Hughes, M., *Early Modern Germany* (London, 1992).

—, *Nationalism and Society: Germany, 1800–1945* (London, 1988).

Hull, A., *English Romanticism* (London, 2000).

Hull, D. S., *Film in the Third Reich* (London, 1969).

Hume, R. D., 'Gothic Versus Romantic: A Revaluation of the Gothic Novel', *Publications of the Modern Language Association*, 84 (1969), pp. 282–90.

Hüning, L., *Geschichte und Fiktion bei Jeanne Bourin and Jean Markale* (Bonn, 1991)

Hunt, W. H., *Pre-Raphaelitism and the Pre-Raphaelite Brotherhood* (2 vols, 2nd edn, London, 1913).

Hunter, M., ed., *Preserving the Past: The Rise of Heritage in Modern Britain* (Stroud, 1996).

Hunter Stiebel, P., *Of Knights and Spires: Gothic Revival in France and Germany* (New York, 1989).

Hurley, K., 'British Gothic Fiction, 1885–1930', in Hogle, *Cambridge Companion to Gothic Fiction*, pp. 189–207.

Hutton, R., *The Pagan Religions of the Ancient British Isles: Their Nature and Legacy* (Oxford, 1991).

—, *The Stations of the Sun: A History of the Ritual Year in Britain* (Oxford, 1996 repr. 2001).

—, *The Triumph of the Moon* (Oxford, 1999).

—, *Witchcraft and Magic in Europe*, vi: *The Twentieth Century* (London, 1999).

Iggers, G. G., *The German Conception of History: The National Tradition of Historical Thought from Herter to the Present* (Middletown, Connecticut, 1983).

Ilie, P., *The Age of Minerva: Counter-Rational Reason in the Eighteenth Century* (Philadelphia, 1995).

Jackson, R., *Fantasy: The Literature of Subversion* (London, 1981).

Jacoby, F. R., 'Historical Method and Romantic Vision in Jacob Grimm's Writings', *Studies in Medievalism*, 3/4 (1991), pp. 489–504.

James, S., *The Atlantic Celts: Ancient People or Modern Invention?* (London, 1999).

Jann, R., 'The Condition of England Past and Present: Thomas Carlyle and the Middle Ages', *Studies in Medievalism*, 1/1 (1979), pp. 15–31.

Jasper, D., 'The Fantastic', in Raimond, J. and Watson, J. R., eds, *A Handbook of English Romanticism* (Houndmills, 1992), pp. 103–5.

Jeffrey Easby, R., 'The Myth of Merrie England in Victorian Painting', in Boos, *History and Community*, pp. 59–80.

Jellinek, G., *History through the Opera Glass* (White Plains, New York, 1994).

Jenkins, J., 'The Aging of the King: Arthur and America in "First Knight"', in Mancoff, *King Arthur's Modern Return*, pp. 199–212.

Johnston, A., *Enchanted Ground: The Study of Medieval Romance in the Eighteenth Century* (London, 1964).

Jones, K. D., and McClure, A. F., *Hollywood at War: The American Motion Picture and World War Two* (New York, 1974).

Jones, L. E., *Druid, Shaman, Priest: Metaphors of Celtic Paganism* (Hisarlik, 1998).

Jones, P., and Matthews, C., *Voices from the Circle* (Wellingborough, 1990).

Jones, S., *The Archaeology of Ethnicity: Constructing Identities in the Past and Present* (London, 1997).

Jones, V., ed., *Women in the Eighteenth Century: Constructions of Femininity* (London, 1990).

Jullian, P., *Dreamers of Decadence: The Symbolist Painters of the 1890s* (trans. London, 1971).

Jurzig, K., *Mittelalterrezeption in Wackenroders 'Herzensergiessungen'* (Driesen, 2000).

Kaufman, E., and Irish, S., eds, *Medievalism: An Annotated Bibliography of Recent Research in the Architecture and Art of Britain and North America* (New York and London, 1988).

Keller, B. G., *The Middle Ages Reconsidered: Attitudes in France from the Eighteenth Century through the Romantic Movement* (New York, 1994).

Kellman, M., *T. H. White and the Matter of Britain: A Literary Overview* (Lewinston, New York and Lampeter, 1988).

Kelso, R., *The Doctrine of the English Gentleman in the Sixteenth Century* (Urbana, Illinois, 1929).

Kendrick, L., 'The American Middle Ages: Eighteenth-Century Saxonist Myth-Making', in Alamichel and Brewer, *Middle Ages after the Middle Ages*, pp. 121–36.

Kenez, P., *Cinema and Soviet Society, 1917–1953* (Cambridge, 1992).

Kenyon, P., *The History Men: The History Profession in England since the Renaissance* (London, 1983).

Kerssen, L., *Das Interesse am Mittelalter im deutschen Nationaldenkmal* (Berlin and New York, 1975).

Kestner, J. A., 'The Return of St George, 1850–1915', in Mancoff, *King Arthur's Modern Return*, pp. 83–98.

Ketton-Cremer, R. W., *Horace Walpole: A Biography* (London, 1940).

Keynes, S., 'The Cult of King Alfred', *Anglo-Saxon England*, 28 (2000), pp. 225–356.

Kiely, J., *The Romantic Novel in England* (Cambridge, Massachusetts, 1972).

King, A., *The 'Faerie Queene' and Middle English Romance* (Oxford, 2000).

Kitromilides. P., ' "Imagined Communities" and the Origins of the National Question in the Balkans', *European History Quarterly*, 19 (1989), pp. 149–92.

Kliger, S., *The Goths in England: A Study in Seventeenth- and Eighteenth-Century Thought* (Cambridge, Massachusetts, 1952).

Knight, S., 'A Garland of Robin Hood Films', *Film and History*, 29 (1999), pp. 33–44.

—, *Robin Hood: A Complete Study of the English Outlaw* (Oxford, 1994).

—, ed., *Robin Hood: An Anthology of Scholarship and Criticism* (Cambridge, 1999).

Knowles, D., *Great Historical Enterprises: Problems in Monastic History* (London, 1963).

Koenigsberger, H. G., *The Habsburgs and Europe, 1516–1660* (Ithaca, New York, and London, 1971).

Koerner, J. L., *Caspar David Friedrich and the Subject of Landscape* (London, 1990).

Koerner, L., 'Nazi Medieval Art and the Politics of Memory', *Studies in Medievalism*, 5 (1993), pp. 48–75.

Kohn, H., *Pan-Slavism* (2nd edn, New York, 1960).

Kreutziger-Herr, A., and Radepenning, D., eds, *Mittelalter-Sehnsucht? Texte des interdisziplinären Symposiums zur musikalischen Mittelalterrezeption an der Universität Heidelberg, April 1998*, pp. 187–261.

Lacy, J. Norris, 'King Arthur Goes to War', in Mancoff, *King Arthur's Modern Return*, pp. 159–70.

—, 'The French Romantics and Medieval French Literature: A Bibliography', *Studies in Medievalism*, 3/1 (1987), pp. 87–97.

Lagorio, V. M., 'King Arthur and Camelot, USA, in the Twentieth Century', in Rosenthal and Szarmach, *Medievalism in American Culture*, pp. 151–69.

Lambdin, L. C. and R. T., *Camelot in the Nineteenth Century: Arthurian Characters in the Poems of Tennyson, Arnold, Morris and Swinburne* (Westport, Connecticut, and London, 2000).

Lambourne, L., *The Aesthetic Movement* (London, 1996).

—, *Victorian Painting* (London, 1999).

Lascelles, M., *The Story-Letter Retrieves the Past: Historical Fiction and Fictitious History in the Art of Scott, Stevenson, Kipling and Some Others* (Oxford, 1980).

Lauder, R. E., *God, Death, Art and Love: The Philosophical Vision of Ingmar Bergman* (New York, 1989).

Leighton-Cleather, A. and Crump, B., *Parsifal, Lohengrin and the Legend of the Holy Grail, Described and Interpreted in Accordance with Wagner's Own Writings* (London, 1904).

Lerner, G., 'Joan of Arc: Three Films', in Mico, T., et al., eds, *Past Imperfect: History According to the Movies* (New York, 1995).

Lesier, E., *Nazi Cinema* (trans. London, 1974).

Leslie, M., *Spenser's 'Fine Warres and Faithfull Loves': Martial and Chivalric Symbolism in 'The Faerie Queene'* (Woodbridge, 1983).

Levine, P., *The Amateur and the Professional. Antiquarians, Historians and Archaeologists in Victorian England, 1838–1886* (Cambridge, 1986).

Lewis, M., *Edith Pargeter: Ellis Peters* (Bridgend, 1994).

Lewis, M. J., *The Gothic Revival* (London, 1985).

Leyda, J., *Kino: A History of the Russian and Soviet Film* (3rd edn, Princeton, 1983).

Lindahl, C., 'Three Ways of Coming Back: Folklore Perspectives on Arthur's Return', in Mancoff, *King Arthur's Modern Return*, pp. 13–30.

Linton, R. C., 'The Glory of Gothic: International Decoration and the Gothic Revival', in Rosenthal and Szarmach, *Medievalism in American Culture*, pp. 65–87.

Liobera, J. R., *The God of Modernity: The Development of Nationalism in Western Europe* (Oxford, 1996).

Little, E., *The Fantasts: Studies in J. R. R. Tolkien, Lewis Carroll, Mervyn Peake, Nikolay Gogol and Kenneth Grahame* (Amersham, 1984).

Livingston, J. C., *Modern Christian Thought*, i, *The Enlightenment and the Nineteenth Century* (2nd edn, Upper Saddle, New Jersey, 1992), pp. 162–84.

Lloyd-Smith, A., and Sage, V., eds, *Gothick: Origins and Innovations* (Amsterdam, 1994), pp. 23–33.

Lock, F. P., *Edmund Burke*, i, 1730–1784 (Oxford, 1998).

London, C. W., *Bombay Gothic* (London, 2003).

Long, R. E., *Ingmar Bergman: Film and Stage* (New York, 1994).

Looze, L., 'Modern Approaches and the 'Real' Middle Ages: Bertrand Tavernier's "La Passion Béatrice"', *Studies in Medievalism*, 5 (1993), pp. 183–99.

Lorenzen, D., and Weinitschke, U., '"Les Niebelungen", de Fritz Lang à Harald Reinl', *Cahiers de la Cinémathèque*, 42/43 (1985), pp. 106–12.

Low, M., 'The Natural World in Early Irish Christianity: An Ecological Footnote', in Atherton, *Celts and Christians*, pp. 169–203.

Lowe, R., and Shaw, W., *Travellers: Voices of the New Age* (London, 1993).

Lowenthal, D., *The Heritage Crusade and the Spoils of History* (London, 1996).

Lucacs, G., *The Historical Novel* (1937; trans. 1962; repr. London, 1976).

Lucanio, P., *With Fire and Sword: Italian Spectacle on American Screens, 1958–1968* (Metuchen, New Jersey, 1994).

Lucie-Smith, E., *Symbolist Art* (London, 1972).

Lupack, A. C., 'Modern Arthurian Novelists on the Arthurian Legend', *Studies in Medievalism*, 2/4 (1983), pp. 79–88.

—, 'The Figure of King Arthur in America', in Mancoff, *King Arthur's Modern Return*, pp. 121–36.

—, 'Visions of Courageous Achievement: Arthurian Youth Groups in America', ibid., 6 (1994), pp. 50–68.

—, *King Arthur in America* (Woodbridge, 2002).

—, and Tepa Lupack, B., *Arthurian Literature by Women* (New York, 1999).

Lyons, M., *Napoleon Bonaparte and the Legacy of the French Revolution* (London, 1994).

MacAndrew, E., *The Gothic Tradition in Fiction* (New York, 1979).

MacCarthy, F., *William Morris: A Life for Our Times* (London, 1994).

MacDougall, H., *Racial Myth in English History: Trojans, Teutons and Anglo-Saxons* (Montreal, 1982).

Macartney, C. A., *The Habsburg Empire, 1790–1918* (London, 1971).

Macaulay, J., *The Gothic Revival, 1745–1845* (Glasgow, 1975).

Macdonald, S., *The Politics of Display: Museums, Sciences, Culture* (London, 1998).

Macdonald, S., *Charles V: Ruler, Dynast and Defender of the Faith, 1500–1558* (2nd edn, London, 2000).

Macray, W. D., *Annals of the Bodleian Library, Oxford: With a Notice of the Earlier Library of the University* (1890; repr. London, 1997).

Madoff, M., 'The Useful Myth of Gothic Ancestry', *Studies in Eighteenth-Century Culture*, 8 (1979), pp. 337–50.

Magee, B., *Aspects of Wagner* (Oxford, 1970).

Magill, F. N., ed., *Survey of Modern Fantasy Literature* (Englewood Cliffs, New Jersey, 1983).

Mahoney, E. P., *Medieval Aspects of the Renaissance* (Durham, 1974).

Maigron, L., *Le roman historique à l'époque romantique: essai sur l'influence de Walter Scott* (Paris, 1898).

Maltby, R. and Craven, I., *Hollywood Cinema: An Introduction* (Oxford, 1995).

Mancoff, D. N., ed., *King Arthur's Modern Return* (New York, 1998).

—, *The Return to Camelot: The Legend Through Victorian Eyes* (London, 1993).

Mangan, J. A., 'Noble Specimen of Manhood: Schoolboy Literature and the Creation of a Colonial Chivalric Code', in Richards, J., ed., *Imperialism and Juvenile Literature* (Manchester, 1989), pp. 173–94.

Manlove, C. N., *Modern Fantasy: Five Studies* (Cambridge, 1975).

—, *The Impulse of Fantasy Literature* (Kent, 1983).

Manteyer, G., 'Les manuscrits de la reine Christine aux archives du Vatican', *Mélanges d'Archéologie et d'Histoire*, 17 (1897), pp. 285–322.

Margolis, N., *Joan of Arc in History, Literature and Film* (New York, 1990).

Marsh, J., *Dante Gabriel Rossetti: Painter and Poet* (London, 1999).

Martin, S., 'Gothic Scholars Don't Wear Black: Gothic Studies and Gothic Subcultures', *Gothic Studies*, 4/1 (2002), pp. 28–43.

Marty, J., '"Perceval le Gallois" d'Eric Rohmer: un itinéraire roman', *Cahiers de la Cinémathèque*, 42/43 (1985), pp. 125–32.

Marucci, F., *'The Fine Delight that Fathers Thought': Rhetoric and Medievalism in Gerard Manley Hopkins* (trans. Washington, DC, 1994).

Mast, G., ed., *Film Theory and Criticism* (New York, 1985).

Mathis, A. E., *The King Arthur Myth in Modern American Literature* (Jefferson, North Carolina, and London, 2002).

Matthews, D., '"Quaint Inglis": Walter Scott and the Rise of Middle English Studies', *Studies in Medievalism*, 6 (1994), pp. 33–48.

—, *The Making of Middle English, 1765–1910* (Minneapolis, Minnesota, and London, 1999).

Mayo, R. D., 'Gothic Romance in the Magazines', *Proceedings of the Medieval Languages Academy*, 65 (1950), pp. 762–89.

McCarthy, M., *The Origins of the Gothic Revival* (New Haven, Connecticut, 1987).

McDongal, S. Y., *Ezra Pound and the Troubadour Tradition* (Princeton, 1972).

McGann, J., *The Poetics of Sensibility: A Revolution in Literary Style* (Oxford, 1996).

McKisack, M., *Medieval History in the Tudor Age* (London, 1971).

—, 'Samuel Daniel as Historian', *Revue of English Studies*, 23 (1947), pp. 226–36.

McMahon, J. V., 'Spruchdichter und Liedermacher: Songs Then and Now', in Classen, *Medieval German Voices*, pp. 61–79.

McManus, P. M., *Archaeological Displays and the Public: Museology and Interpretation* (London, 1996).

McRoberts, J. P., *Shakespeare and the Medieval Tradition: An Annotated Bibliography* (New York, 1985).

McShane, E., *Tudor Opinions of the Chivalrous Romance: An Essay in Criticism* (Washington, DC, 1950).

Mee, J., *Romanticism, Enthusiasm and Regulation: Poetics and the Policing of Culture in the Romantic Period* (Oxford, 2003).

Mehrotra, K. K., *Horace Walpole and the English Novel: A Study of the Influence of The Castle of Otranto, 1764–1820* (Oxford, 1934).

Meinecke. F., *Historicism: The Rise of a New Historical Outlook* (trans. London, 1972).

Mellor, A. K., *Romanticism and Gender* (London, 1993).

Merriman, J. D, *The Flower of Kings: A Study of the Arthurian Legend in England between 1485 and 1835* (Lawrence, Kansas, 1973).

Merriman, N., *Beyond the Glass Case: The Public, Museums and Heritage in Britain* (Leicester, 1991).

Mertens, V., 'Wagner's Middle Ages', in Müller, U., and Wapnewsky, P., eds, *Wagner Handbook* (trans. London, 1992).

Midant, J. P., *Viollet-le-Duc: The French Gothic Revival* (Paris, 2002).

Mighal, R., *A Geography of Victorian Gothic Fiction: Mapping History's Nightmares* (Oxford, 1996).

Miles, R., *Ann Radcliff: The Great Enchantress* (Manchester, 1995).

—, *Gothic Writing, 1750–1820: A Genealogy* (London, 1993).

Miliaras, B., 'Womanly Noblesse; The Influence of the Courtly Love Tradition on Edward Burne-Jones', in de Girolami Cheney, *Pre-Raphaelitism*, pp. 193–220.

Millbank, A., 'The Victorian Gothic in English Novels and Stories', in Hogle, *Cambridge Companion*, pp. 145–65.

Milligan, C. B., *Spenser and the Table Round: A Study in the Contemporaneous Background for Spenser's Use of the Arthurian Legend* (Cambridge, Massachusetts, 1932).

Mills, D., 'Replaying the Medieval Past: Revivals of Chester's Mystery Plays', *Studies in Medievalism*, 7 (1995), pp. 181–93.

Milward, P., *The Mediaeval Dimension in Shakespeare's Plays* (Lewinston, New Jersey, and Lampeter, 1990).

Minc, A., *Le Nouveau Moyen Age* (2nd edn Paris, 2002).

Mitchell, I., *Scott, Chaucer and Medieval Romance: A Study of Sir Walter Scott's Indebtedness to the Literature of the Middle Ages* (Lexington, Kentucky, 1987).

Moore, D., ed., *Ossian and Ossianism* (London, 2004).

Mordaunt Crook, J., 'John Britton and the Genesis of the Gothic Revival', in [Pevsner] Summerson, *Essays*, pp. 98–119.

—, *John Carter and the Mind of the Gothic Revival* (London, 1995).

—, ed., *The Strange Genius of William Burges 'Art-Architect', 1827–81* (Cardiff, 1981).

Moreland, K. I., *The Medievalist Impulse in American Literature: Twain, Adams, Fitzgerald and Hemingway* (Charlottesville, Virginia, and London, 1996).

Morgan, C., *Don Carlos and Company* (Oxford, 1996).

Morgan, G., 'Modern Mystics, Medieval Saints', *Studies in Medievalism*, 12 (2003), pp. 39–54.

Morgan, G. A., 'Percy, the Antiquarians, the Ballad and the Middle Ages', *Studies in Medievalism*, 7 (1995), pp. 22–32.

Morgan, P., 'From a Death to a View: The Hunt for the Welsh Past in the Romantic Period', in Hobsbawm and Ranger, *Invention of Tradition*, pp. 43–100.

Morris, K. L., *The Image of the Middle Ages in Romantic and Victorian Literature* (London, 1984).

Mosse, G. L., ed., *Nazi Culture: Intellectual, Cultural and Social Life in the Third Reich* (London, 1966).

—, *The Crisis of German Ideology: Intellectual Origins of the Third Reich* (London, 1964).

Mowl, T., *Horace Walpole: The Great Outsider* (London, 1996).

Mulryan, J., *Milton and the Middle Ages* (East Brunswick, New Jersey, 1982).

Muthesius, S., *The High Victorian Movement in Architecture, 1850–70* (London, 1972).

Myrone, M., and Peltz, L., eds, *Producing the Past* (Aldershot, 1999).

Nash Smith, H., *Mark Twain's Fable of Progress: Political and Economic Ideas in 'A Connecticut Yankee at King Arthur's Court'* (New Brunswick, 1964).

Naylor, G., ed., *William Morris by Himself* (London and Boston, 2000).

Nelson, D., 'Gastron Paris in Contexts: His Predecessors and his Legacy', *Studies in Medievalism*, 2/2 (1982), pp. 53–66.

Newman, G., *The Rise of English Nationalism, 1740–1830* (London, 1987).

Norton, R., ed., *Gothic Readings: The First Wave 1764–1840* (Leicester, 2000).

—, *Mistress of Udolpho: The Life of Ann Radcliffe* (London, 1999).

Norwich, J. J., *Shakespeare's Kings* (London, 2000).

Nower-Schamber, E., *The Artist as Politician: The Art and Politics of the French Romantics* (New York, 1984).

O'Brien, D. J., 'Lord Berners's *Huon de Bordeaux*': The Survival of Medieval Ideas in the Reign of Henry VIII', *Studies in Medievalism*, 4 (1992), pp. 36–44.

O'Donoghue, B., 'Dante's Versatility and Seamus Heaney's Modernism', in Havely, *Dante's Modern Afterlife*, pp. 242–57.

Oergel, M., *The Return of King Arthur and the Nibelungen: National Myth in Nineteenth-Century English and German Literature* (Berlin, 1998).

Oliver, R. G., ed., *Ingmar Bergman: An Artist's Journey* (New York, 1995).

Olson, B., *Arthurian Legends on Film and Television* (Jefferson, North Carolina, 2000).

Oms, M., 'De Lavisse à Michelet ou Jeanne d'Arc entre les deux guerres', *Cahiers de la Cinémathèque*, 42/43 (1985), pp. 43–44.

Orel, H., *The Historical Novel from Scott to Sabatini: Changing Attitudes towards a Literary Genre, 1814–1920* (New York, 1995).

Osberg, R. H., 'Pages Torn from the Book: Narrative Disintegration in Gilliam's *The Fisher King*', *Studies in Medievalism*, 7 (1995), pp. 194–224.

Paden, W. D., 'Reconstruction the Middle Ages; The Monk's Sermon in *The Seventh Seal*', in Utz and Shippey, *Medievalism in the Modern World*, pp. 287–305.

Palmer, D. J., *The Rise of English Studies* (London, 1965).

Paparelli, G., *Enea Silvio Piccolomini (Pio II)* (Bari, 1950).

Parker, J., 'The Day of a Thousand Years: Winchester's 1901 Commemoration of Alfred the Great', *Studies in Medievalism*, 12 (2003), pp. 113–36.

Parkinson-Bailey, J. J., *Manchester: An Architectural History* (Manchester, 2000).

Pascal, R., *The German Sturm und Drang* (Manchester, 1953).

Pauphilet, A., *Le legs du Moyen Age: études de littérature médiévale* (Melun, 1950).

Paxman, J., *The English* (London, 2000).

Peardon, T. P., *The Transition in English Historical Writing, 1760–1880* (New York, 1933).

Pearson, J., 'Crushing the Convent and the Dread Bastille: The Anglo-Saxons, Revolution and Gender in Women's Plays in the 1790s', in Scragg and Weinberg, *Literary Appropriations*, pp. 122–35.

Pearson, R., 'Fact, Fantasy, Fraud: Perceptions and Projections of National Revival', *Ethnic Groups*, 10/1–3 (1993), pp. 43–64.

Peck, L. F., *A Life of Matthew Lewis* (Cambridge, Massachusetts, 1961).

Penzoldt, P., *The Supernatural in Modern English Fiction* (London, 1952).

Pernoud, R., 'Jeanne d'Arc à l'écran', *Cahiers de la Cinémathèque*, 42/43 (1985), pp. 40–42.

Perrin, M., *L'idée de l'Europe au fil de deux millénaires* (Paris, 1994).

Pettet, E. C., *Shakespeare and the Romance Tradition* (London, 1949).

Pevsner, N., *Pioneers of Modern Design from William Morris to Walter Gropius* (rev. edn, London, 1991).

—, *Ruskin and Viollet-le-Duc: Englishness and Frenchness in the Appreciation of Architecture* (London, 1969).

—, *The Englishness of English Art* (London, 1956).

Pfaff, R., *M. R. James* (London, 1980).

Philip, I. G., *The Bodleian Library in the Seventeenth and Eighteenth Centuries* (Oxford, 1983).

Pietrapaolo, D., 'Eco on Medievalism', *Studies in Medievalism*, 5 (1993), pp. 127–38.

Pietropoli, C., ed., *Romanticismo, medievalismo* (special issue of the journal *Questione Romantica*, ii, no. 7/3, 1999).

Piggott, S., *The Druids* (London, 1975).

Pittock, M. G. H., *Celtic Identity and the British Image* (Manchester, 1999).

Plas, M., '"Merlin l'enchanteur" de Walt Disney: du roman médiéval au conte de fées', *Cahiers de la Cinémathèque*, 42/43 (1985), pp. 103–4.

Pocock, J. G. A., *The Ancient Constitution and the Feudal Law* (Cambridge, repr. 1957).

Poovey, M., *The Proper Lady and the Woman Writer: Ideology as Style in the Works of Mary Wollstonecraft, Mary Shelley and Jane Austen* (Chicago, 1984).

Poulson, C., 'Arthurian Legend in Fine and Applied Art of the Nineteenth and Early Twentieth Centuries: A Catalogue of Artists', *Arthurian Literature*, 9 (1989), pp. 81–142.

Powell, K., 'Burne-Jones, Swinburne, and *Laus Veneris*', in de Girolami Cheney, *Pre-Raphaelitism*, pp. 221–40.

Pratt, L., 'Anglo-Saxon attitudes?: Alfred the Great and the Romantic National Epic', in Scragg and Weinberg, *Literary Appropriations*, pp. 138–56.

Prawer, S., *The Romantic Period in Germany* (New York, 1970).

Praz, M., *The Romantic Agony* (2nd edn, London, 1970).

Prettejohn, E., *Rossetti and his Circle* (London, 1997).

—, *After the Pre-Raphaelites: Art and Aestheticism in Victorian England* (London, 1999).

—, *The Art of the Pre-Raphaelites* (London, 2000).

Pullapilly, C. K., *Caesar Baronius: Counter Reformation Historian* (Notre Dame, Indiana, 1975).

Punter, D., *The Literature of Terror: A History of Gothic Fictions from 1765 to the Present Day* (London, 1980).

—, ed., *Companion to the Gothic* (Oxford, 2000).

Punter, D. and Byron, G., eds, *The Gothic* (Oxford, 2004).

Purkiss, D., *The Witch in History: Early Modern and Twentieth-Century Representations* (London, 1999).

Pyle, S. J., *Mirth and Morality of Shakespeare's Holy Fools* (Lampeter, 1998).

Python, R., 'Joan of Arc de Victor Fleming: de la résistance à la nuée', *Cahiers de la Cinémathèque*, 42/43 (1985), pp. 50–58.

Rabkin, E. S., *The Fantastic in Literature* (Princeton, 1976).

Railo, E., *The Haunted Castle: A Study of the Elements of English Romanticism* (London, 1927).

Ralph, G., 'Medievalism and Twentieth-Century Religious Drama', *Studies in Medievalism*, 2/1 (1982), pp. 35–57.

Rance, N., *The Historical Novel and Popular Politics in Nineteenth-Century England* (London, 1975).

Redman, H., *The Roland Legend in Nineteenth-Century French Literature* (Lexington, Kenctucky, 1991).

Reiss, H., ed., *The Political Thought of the German Romantics* (Oxford, 1955).

Rentschler, E., *The Ministry of Illusion: Nazi Cinema and its Afterlife* (Cambridge, Massachustts, and London, 1996).

Reusch, J., 'Caspar David Friedrich and National Antiquarianism in Northern Germany', in Myrone and Peltz, *Producing the Past*, pp. 95–114.

Reynolds, W. D., 'Arthuriana: A Bibliography of Published Treatments of the Arthurian Legend, 1951–83', *Studies in Medievalism*, 2/4 (1983), pp. 89–112.

Ribner, I., *William Shakespeare* (Toronto, 1969).

Richards, J., *Films and British National Identity: From Dickens to 'Dad's Army'* (Manchester, 1997).

—, 'From Christianity to Paganism: The New Middle Ages and the Values of "Medieval" Masculinity', *Cultural Values*, 3/2 (1999), pp. 216–20.

—, 'Robin Hood on Film and Television Since 1945', in *Visual Culture in Britain*, ii, (Aldershot, 2001), pp. 66–80.

—, and Aldgate , A., eds, *Best of British: Cinema and Society from 1930 to the Present* (London, 1999).

Richter, D., 'The Reception of the Gothic Novel', in Uphaus, R. W., ed., *The Idea of the Novel in the Eighteenth Century* (East Lansing, Michigan, 1988).

Richter, D. H., 'From Medievalism to Historicism: Representations of History in the Gothic Novel and Historical Romance', *Studies in Medievalism*, 4 (1992), pp. 79–104.

Ricks, C., *Tennyson* (2nd edn, Berkeley, 1989).

Riding, C., and J., *The Houses of Parliament: History, Art, Architecture* (London, 2000).

Righetti, A., 'Browning's Medievalism', in Boitani and Torti, *Medievalistas*, pp. 129–37.

Robbins, R. and Wolfreys, J., eds, *Victorian Gothic: Literary and Cultural Manifestations in the Nineteenth Century* (Houndmills, 2000).

Roberts, H., 'The Medieval Spirit of Pre-Raphaelitism', in de Girolami Cheney, *Pre-Raphaelitism*, pp. 15–28.

Roberts, M., *Gothic Immortals: The Fiction of the Brotherhood of the Rosy Cross* (London, 1990).

Robinson, C. L., 'Celluloid Criticism: Pasolini's Contribution to a Chaucerian Debate', *Studies in Medievalism*, 5 (1993), pp. 115–26.

Rogers, P., ed., *Alexander Pope* (Oxford, 1993).

Roquemore, J., *History Goes to the Movies* (New York, 1999).

Rosenstone, A., ed., *Revisioning History: Film and the Construction of a New Past* (Princeton, New Jersey, 1995).

Rosenthal, B., and Szarmach, P. E., eds, *Medievalism in American Culture: Special Studies, Studies in Medievalism* issue, (New York, 1987).

Rossetti, W. M., *Pre-Raphaelite Diaries and Letters* (London, 1900; repr. 1976).

Rougement, D. de, *Love and the Western World* (1939; trans. London, 1983).

—, *The Myths of Love* (trans. London, 1963).

Rovang, P. R., *Refashioning 'Knights and Ladies Gentle Deeds': The Intertextuality of Spenser's 'Faerie Queene' and Malory's 'Morte Darthur'* (London, 1996).

Saccio, P., *Shakespeare's English Kings: History, Chronicle and Drama* (New York, 1977).

Sage, V., *Horror Fiction in the Protestant Tradition* (Basingstoke, 1988).

Salmon, N., ed., *William Morris on History* (Sheffield, 1995).

Salomon, R. B., *Twain and the Image of History* (New Haven, Connecticut, 1961).

Samuel, R., ed., *Patriotism: The Making and Unmaking of British National Identity* (3 vols, London, 1989).

Sanders, A., *The Victorian Historical Novel, 1840–1880* (New York, 1979).

—, '"Utter indifference"?: The Anglo-Saxons in the Nineteenth-Century Novel', in Scragg and Weinberg, *Literary Appropriations*, pp. 157–73.

Sarris, A., *The American Cinema: Directors and Directions* (New York, 1968).

Scarborough, D., *The Supernatural in Modern English Fiction* (London, 1952).

Schmit, A., *Fouqué und einige seiner Zeitgenossen* (Karlsruhe, 1958).

Schmitt, C., 'The Gothic Romance in the Victorian Period', in Brantlinger, P., and Thesig, W. B., eds, *A Companion to the Victorian Novel* (Oxford, 2002), pp. 302–17.

Scragg, D. and Weinberg, C., eds, *Literary Appropriations of the Anglo-Saxons: Thirteenth to the Twentieth Centuries* (Cambridge, 2000).

Scruton, R., *England: An Elegy* (London, 2001).

Seibicke, C. E., *Friedrich Baron de la Motte Fouqué: Krise und Verfall der Spatromantick im Spiegel seiner historisierenden Ritterromane* (Munich, 1985).

Seton, M., *Sergei M. Eisenstein* (London, 1978).

Seton-Watson, H., *Nations and States: An Enquiry into the Origins of Nations and the Politics of Nationalism* (London, 1977).

Sharp, W., *Dante Gabriel Rossetti: A Record* (London, 1882; repr. 1970).

Shippey, T. A., *J. R. R. Tolkien: Author of the Century* (London, 2001).

—, *The Road to Middle Earth* (London, 1982).

—, 'The Undeveloped Image: Anglo-Saxon in Popular Consciousness from Turner to Tolkien', in Scragg and Weinberg, *Literary Appropriations*, pp. 215–36.

Siebers, T., *The Romantic Fantastic* (Ithaca, New York, 1984).

Sigal, P. A., 'Brancaleone s'en va-t-aux croisades: satire d'un moyen âge conventionnel', *Cahiers de la Cinémathèque*, 42/43 (1985), pp. 152–54.

Silverstein, T., *Medieval Latin Scientific Writings in the Barberini Collection: A Provisional Catalogue* (Chicago, 1957).

Simmons, C. A., '"Absent Presence": The Romantic Era Magna Charta and the English Constitution', in Utz and Shippey, *Medievalism in the Modern World*, pp. 69–84.

—, 'Anglo-Saxonism, the Future and the Franco-Prussian War', *Studies in Medievalism*, 7 (1995), pp. 131–42.

—, 'Bad Baronets and the Curse of Medievalism', *Studies in Medievalism*, 12 (2003), pp. 215–36.

—, '"Iron-Worded Proof": Victorian Identity and the Old English Language', *Studies in Medievalism*, 4 (1992), pp. 202–14.

—, ed., *Medievalism and the Quest for the 'Real' Middle Ages* (London, 2001).

Simons, J., 'Christopher Middleton and Elizabethan Medievalism', in Utz and Shippey, *Medievalism in the Modern World*, pp. 43–60.

Simpson, R., *Camelot Regained: The Arthurian Revival and Tennyson, 1800–1849* (Woodbridge, 1990).

—, *From Medieval to Medievalism* (London, 1992).

—, 'Medievalism as Cultural Process in Pre-Industrial Literature', *Studies in Medievalism*, 6 (1994), pp. 5–21.

—, '"Revisiting Cramalot": An Arthurian Theme in the Correspondence of William Taylor and Robert Southey', *Studies in Medievalism*, 4 (1992), pp. 143–60.

—, 'St George and the Pendragon', in Utz and Shippey, *Medievalism in the Modern World*, pp. 134–39.

Singman, J. L., *Robin Hood: The Shaping of a Legend* (Westport, Connecticut, and London, 1998).

Sir Thomas Bodley: His Library (Exhibition Catalogue, Oxford, 2002).

Six, J. F., 'François d'Assise', *Cahiers de la Cinémathèque*, 42/43 (1985), pp. 29–35.

Sklar, E. S., and Hoffman, D. L., *King Arthur in Popular Culture* (Jefferson, North Carolina, 2002).

Smart, N., *Nineteenth-Century Religious Thought in the West*, ii (2nd edn, Cambridge, 1985).

Smith, A. D., *Nationalism and Modernism* (London, 1998).

—, *Nationalism: Theory, Ideology, History* (Cambridge, 2001).

Smith, G. A., *Epic Films: Cast, Credits and Commentaries on over 250 Historical Spectacle Movies* (London, 1984).

Smith, P., ed., *The Historian and Film* (Cambridge, 1976).

Smith, R. G., *The Gothic Bequest: Medieval Institutions in British Thought, 1688–1863* (Cambridge, 1987).

Smith, R. J., 'Cobbett, Catholic History and the Middle Ages', *Studies in Medievalism*, 4 (1992), pp. 113–42.

Snowdon, Lord, and Headley, G., *London: Sight Unseen* (London, 1999).

Sorlin, P., *The Film in History: Restaging the Past* (Oxford, 1980).

Spencer, J., *The Rise of the Woman Novelist* (Oxford, 1986).

Spotts, F., *Bayreuth: A History of the Wagner Festival* (New Haven, Connecticut and London, 1994).

Stanley, E. G., *Imagining the Anglo-Saxon Past* (Woodbridge, 2000).

—, 'The Early Middle Ages = The Dark Ages = The Heroic Age of England and the English', in Alamichel and Brewer, *Middle Ages after the Middle Ages*, pp. 43–77.

Stanton, P. B., *The Gothic Revival and American Church Architecture: An Episode in Taste 1840–56* (Baltimore, 1968).

Starr, N. C., *King Arthur Today: The Arthurian Legend in English and American Literature* (Gainesville, Florida, 1954).

Steene, *Focus on 'The Seventh Seal'* (Englewood Cliffs, New Jersey, 1972).

Stirk, P. M. R., and Weigall, D., eds, *The Origins and Development of European Integration* (London, 1999).

Stokoe, F. W., *German Influence on the English Romantic Period, 1788–1818* (Cambridge, 1926).

Strong, R., *And When Did You Last See Your Father? The Victorian Painter and British History* (London, 1978).

Strype, J., *The Life and Times of Archbishop Parker* (3 vols, London, 1821).

Sugar, P., ed., *Ethnic Diversity and Conflict in Eastern Europe* (Santa Barbara, California, 1980).

Summers, D. A., *Spenser's Arthur: The British Arthurian Tradition and 'The Faerie Queene'* (Lanham, Maryland and Oxford, 1997).

Summers, M., *The Gothic Quest: A History of the Gothic Novel* (London, 1968).

Summerson J., ed., *Essays on Architectural Writers and Writing Presented to N. Pevsner* (London, 1968).

Sweet, R., *Antiquaries: The Discovery of the Past in Eighteenth-Century Britain* (London, 2004).

Szarmach, P. E., and Rosenthal, J. T., eds, *The Preservation and Transmission of Anglo-Saxon Culture* (Kalamazoo, Michigan, 1997).

Tagil, S., ed., *Ethnicity and Nation Building in the Nordic World* (London, 1995).

Tarte-Holley, L., 'Chaucer, T. S. Eliot and the Regenerative Pilgrimage', *Studies in Medievalism*, 2/1 (1982), pp. 19–33.

Tau, M. M., *Catholicism in Gothic Fiction: A Study of the Nature and Function of Catholic Materials in Gothic Fiction in England, 1762–1830* (Washington, DC, 1946).

Taylor, B., 'Re-Vamping Vivien: Reinventing Myth in Victorian Iconography', in Mancoff, *King Arthur's Modern Return*, pp. 65–82.

—, and Brewer, E., eds, *The Return of King Arthur: British and American Arthurian Literature since 1800* (Cambridge, 1983).

Taylor, R., *Film Propaganda: Soviet Russia and Nazi Germany* (London, 1979).

Teich, M., and Porter, R., eds, *The National Question in Europe in Historical Context* (Cambridge, 1993).

Thiesse, A. M., *La création des identités nationales: Europe, XVIIe-XXe siècles* (Paris, 1999).

Thomas, J., *Victorian Narrative Painting* (London, 2000).

Thompson, E. P., *The Work of William Morris* (Oxford, 1993).

—, *William Morris: Romantic to Revolutionary* (rev. edn, London, 1977).

Thompson, G. R., ed., *The Gothic Imagination: Essays in Dark Romanticism* (Washington, 1974).

Thompson, R. H., 'Arthurian Legend and Modern Fantasy', in Magill, F. N., ed., *Survey of Modern Fantasy Literature* (Englewood Cliffs, New Jersey, 1983), pp. 2299–315.

Tite, C. G. C., *The Manuscript Library of Sir Robert Cotton* (London, 1994).

Todd, J., *Sensibility: An Introduction* (London, 1986).

Todorov, T., *The Fantastic* (trans. New York, 1973).

Tompkins, J. M. S., *The Popular Novel in England, 1770–1800* (London, 1932).

Triplett, F. I., 'Du Bellay's Ambivalent Defense of a Medieval Vernacular: *La Deffence et illustration de la langue françoise*', *Studies in Medievalism*, 3/1 (1987), pp. 33–39.

Treuherz, J, *Victorian Painting* (London, 1993).

Trevor-Roper, H., 'The Invention of Tradition: The Highland Tradition of Scotland', in Hobsbawm and Ranger, *Invention of Tradition*, pp. 15–41.

Umland, R. A. and S. J., *The Use of Arthurian Legend in Hollywood Film from Connecticut Yankees to Fisher Kings* (Westport, Connecticut, 1996).

Underdown, D., *A Freeborn People: Politics and the Nation in Seventeenth-Century England* (Oxford, 1996).

Utz, R., and Shippey, T., eds, *Medievalism in the Modern World: Essays in Honour of Leslie Workman: Making the Middle Ages*, i (Turnhout, 1998).

Varma, D. P., *The Gothic Flame* (London, 1957).

Vasoli, C., *Profilo di un papa umanista: Tommaso Parentucelli* (Manduria, 1968).

Vaughan, W., *Friedrich* (London, 2004).

—, *German Romanticism and English Art* (London, 1980).

—, *German Romantic Painting* (New Haven, Connecticut, 1980).

Vax, L., *L'Art et la Littérature Fantastiques* (Paris, 1974).

Verduin, K., 'Medievalism and the Mind of Emerson', in Rosenthal and Szarmach, pp. 128–50.

Viollet-le-Duc: *Actes du Colloque International* (Paris, 1982).

Walsh, K., *The Representation of the Past: Museums and Heritage in the Post-Modern World* (London, 1992).

Walters, H. B., *The English Antiquaries of the Sixteenth, Seventeenth and Eighteenth Centuries* (London, 1934).

Ward, P., *The Medievalism of Victor Hugo* (Philadelphia, 1975).

Warner, M., *Joan of Arc: The Image of Female Heroism* (Berkeley, California, 2000).

—, ed., *Wonder Tales: Six Stories of Enchantment* (London, 1996).

Warner, M., *The Victorian: British Painting, 1837–1901* (London, 1996).

Warnicke, R. M., *William Lambarde: Elizabethan Antiquary (1536–1601)* (London, 1973).

Watkin, D., *The English Vision: The Picturesque in Architecture, Landscape and Garden Design* (London, 1982).

Watkinson, R., *Pre-Raphaelite Art and Design* (London, 1970).

Watson, A. G., *Medieval Manuscripts in Post Medieval England* (Aldershot, 2004).

Watt, J., *Contesting the Gothic: Fiction, Genre and Cultural Conflict, 1764–1832* (Cambridge, 1999).

Watt, W. W., *Shilling Shockers of the Gothic School: A Study of the Chapbook Gothic Romances* (Cambridge, Massachusetts, 1932).

Wawn, A., *The Vikings and the Victorians: Inventing the Old North in Nineteenth-Century Britain* (Woodbridge, 2000).

Weinmann, R., *Shakespeare and the Popular Tradition in the Theater* (Washington, 1978).

Weisl, A. J., *The Persistence of Medievalism: Narrative Adventures in Contemporay Culture* (Basingstoke, 2002).

Weiss, T., *Fairy Tale and Romance in Works of Ford Madox Brown* (Lanham and London, 1984).

Welch, A., *Nazi Propaganda: The Power and the Limitations* (London, 1983).

—, *Propaganda and the German Cinema, 1933–1945* (London, 1983).

Weston, N., *Daniel Maclise: An Irish artist in Victorian London* (2001).

White, C., *An Introduction to the Life and Works of Richard Wagner* (Englewood Cliffs, New Jersey, 1967).

White, H., *Tolkien: A Biography* (London, 2001).

White, L., 'The Legacy of the Middle Ages in the American Wild West', *Speculum*, 40 (1965), pp. 191–202.

White, R., ed., *King Arthur in Legend and History* (London, 1997).

Whiteman, R., *The Cadfael Companion* (London, 1991).

Whittaker, H., *The Arthurian Revival in Victorian Art* (New York, 1990).

Whittaker, M., 'The Legends of King Arthur in Art', *Arthurian Studies*, 22 (1990).

Wiehe, R., 'Sir Gawain, Sir Lancelot, the Pre-Raphaelite Brotherhood and Tennyson', in de Girolami Cheney, *Pre-Raphaelitism*, pp. 75–92.

Wildman, M., 'Twentieth-Century Arthurian Literature: An Annotated Bibliography', *Arthurian Literature*, 1 (1982).

Wilkins, E. H., *A History of Italian Literature* (Cambridge, Massachusetts, 1974).

Wilmart, A., *Analecta reginensia: extraits des manuscrits latins de la reine Christine conservés au Vatican* (Vatican City, 1933).

Wilton, A. and Upstone, R., eds, *The Age of Rossetti, Burne Jones and Watts: Symbolism in Britain, 1860–1910* (London, 1997).

Witcomb, A., *Re-Imagining the Museum: Beyond the Mausoleum* (London, 2003).

Wolfreys, J., *Victorian Hauntings: Spectrality, Gothic, the Uncanny and Literature* (Basingstoke, 2002).

Womack, P., *Improvement and Romance: Inventing the Myth of the Highlands* (Basingstoke, 1989).

Wood, C., *The Pre-Raphaelites* (London, 1981).

—, *Victorian Painting* (London, 1999).

Wood, M., *In Search of the Dark Ages* (London, 1981).

—, *Hitler's Search for the Holy Grail* (Mayavision International, 1999).

—, *In Search of England: Journeys into the English Past* (Berkeley, California, 1999).

Woodall, N. J., '"Women are Knights-Errant to the Last": Nineteenth-Century Women Writers Reinvent the Medieval Literary Damsel', in Gentrup, *Reinventing the Middle Ages*, pp. 201–21.

Wooding, J., 'The Idea of the Celt', in Atherton, *Celts and Christians*, pp. 39–59.

Woolf, D. R., 'The Dawn of the Artifact: The Antiquarian Impulse in England, 1500–1730', *Studies in Medievalism*, 4 (1992), pp. 5–35.

Workman, L., 'Medievalism and Romanticism', *Poetica*, 39–40 (1994), pp. 1–40.

Wright, P., *On Living in an Old Country* (London, 1985).

Wunderlich, W., 'Medieval Images: Joseph Viktor von Scheffel's Novel *Ekkehard* and St Gall', in Utz and Shippey, *Medievalism in the Modern World*, pp. 193–225.

—, 'The Arthurian Legend in German Literature in the 1980s', *Studies in Medievalism*, 3/4 (1991), pp. 423–42.

Yervasi, C., 'The Faces of Joan: Cinematic Representations of Joan of Arc', *Film and History*, 29 (1999), pp. 8–19.

Yorke, M., *Mervyn Peake: My Eyes Mint Gold. A Life* (London, 2000).

Zahorski, K. J. and Boyer, R. H., *Fantasy Literature: A Core Collection and Reference Guide* (London, 1979).

Zamoyski, A., *Holy Madness: Romantics, Patriots and Revolutionaries, 1776–1871* (London, 1999).

Zeman, Z. A. B., *Propaganda and the German Cinema, 1933–1945* (Oxford, 1983).

Zezula, J., 'Scholarly Medievalism in Renaissance France', *Studies in Medievalism*, 3/1 (1987), pp. 11–20.

Zipes, J., *The Brothers Grimm* (London, 1998).

—, *The Brothers Grimm: From Enchanted Forests to the Modern World* (2nd edn, New York, 2000).

Zuchold, G. H., 'The Prussian Royal House and Pictorial Representations in the Nibelung Saga', *Studies in Medievalism*, 5 (1993), pp. 23–37.

Index